Dynamics of Speech

Dynamics of Speech

Toward Effective Communication

Virginia Myers
Speech Communication Instructor
Lubbock Independent School District
Lubbock, Texas

Rosanna T. Herndon
Professor and Chair
Department of Communication
Hardin-Simmons University
Abilene, Texas

Consulting Editor
Maridell Fryar
Director of Secondary Education and
Coordinator of Secondary Language Arts
Midland Independent School District
Midland, Texas

NATIONAL TEXTBOOK COMPANY • Lincolnwood, Illinois U.S.A.

To our students,
past, present, and future,
who inspired the writing of this book
and to our families
whose love and support
made the writing possible.

Contents

Part 5

Toward Effective Public Speaking   249

Preface

Dynamics of Speech is an introduction to the exciting and important study of speech communication. It is based on the idea that communication is a *dynamic* force in our lives—basic to personal effectiveness and productive relationships at home, at school, at work, and in the community. An understanding of the communication process provides a base from which students can make effective and responsible communication choices. The goals of this text are to help students understand the communication process and then build the skills necessary for a lifetime of effective communication.

Dynamics of Speech is divided into five Parts. Each Part focuses on skill development in an area of speech communication: intrapersonal communication, interpersonal communication, communication in groups, and communication in the public setting. Special features of *Dynamics of Speech* include:

Learner Outcomes at the beginning of each chapter to sharpen readers' expectations and provide guidance to learning.

Key Terms for each chapter. These important vocabulary words are listed at the beginning of each chapter and they appear in bold type when they are defined in the chapters.

Checkpoints at the ends of critical text sections to offer students a variety of opportunities to stop and think about the text. Some are experiential activities; some are short writing assignments.

Marginal notes that are printed in color to offer extra guidance to reading.

Eight Communication Essays to generate reader interest in topics related to the chapter material.

At the ends of the chapters:

Check Your Knowledge: a list of questions that give students a chance to test their memories.

Check Your Understanding: a list of questions and activities designed to assess comprehension.

Check Your Skills: activities and exercises that give students opportunities to use the chapter lessons to build communication skills.

Appendix A. This Appendix contains seven model speeches to illustrate the speech forms discussed in the text. Two of the speeches are annotated to focus on organization and development.

Appendix B. This is an Appendix of Applications. The first section is a Guide to Competitive Speaking Events; the second section is a Guide to Being Interviewed. This Appendix will help students apply the ideas discussed in *Dynamics of Speech* to communication choices and situations in the real world.

Glossary: a complete list of the important vocabulary words found in the text with their definitions.

A thorough Index for convenient reference.

Acknowledgements

The authors thank the following people for their encouragement, support, and contributions during the development of *Dynamics of Speech*.

A special thanks to Marcia Myers Swanson, speech communication instructor at Central City Business Institute, Syracuse, New York, for her valuable contributions during the writing of both the student text and the teacher's resource book.

Bill Meadors, librarian at Lubbock (Texas) High School, for his help in writing the research chapter.

Wayne Dickey, Instructional Program Administrator for Language Arts, Lubbock Independent School District, Lubbock, Texas.

Pam Ehret, Hardin-Simmons University student and future teacher of communication, who worked far beyond word processing and provided answer keys, proofreading, advice, and enthusiasm.

Charlene Strickland, Hardin-Simmons University faculty member, former high school teacher, and consultant to the Texas Interscholastic League, who provided advice and valuable assistance in the development of the teacher's resource book and the Guide to Competitive Speaking Events.

Maridell Fryar, Director of Secondary Education and Coordinator of Secondary Language Arts; Midland Independent School District, Midland, Texas.

Helen Shafer, Angelo State University; Vera Simpson, formerly of Texas Tech University; Jean Clough, Ball High School, Galveston, Texas.

Doyle Herndon, CPA, and controller and communications consultant at Hardin-Simmons University and Don Myers, Texas public school administrator, for patient encouragement and general support.

Thanks to Judith A. Clayton, patient editor at National Textbook Company, and to Rebecca Strehlow, cheerful and efficient copy editor.

TOWARD UNDERSTANDING
Communication

Communication is the vitally important, dynamic, and exciting process of sending and receiving messages. The process continues throughout life, in every moment and every interaction between people.

Effective communication is the result of understanding and applying communication skills. In this Part, you will discover the basic skills and variables that are involved in effective speech communication. An understanding of these elements and how they work together in the communication process will provide a basis for your growth as an effective and responsible communicator. Also, as you learn what teachers and researchers think about communication as a process, you can begin to develop your own theory about communication. Your ideas and perspective will help you set goals and assess your progress in developing effective communication skills.

CHAPTER 1

Understanding the Communication Process

After reading this chapter, you should be able to:

1

Explain the importance of communication.

2

List the variables of the communication process.

3

Define each variable of the process.

4

Explain how each variable functions within the process.

5

Explain the two levels or dimensions of message.

6

Describe how barriers and noise influence the communication process.

Key Terms

Communication

Process

Variable

Sender/Receivers

Receiver/Senders

Context

Channel

Stimuli

Sensory perception

Encoding

Decoding

Transmitting

Nonverbal messages

Verbal messages

Receiving

Message

Response

Feedback

Barriers

Noise

Human history is a chronicle of physical quests to conquer new frontiers. Those frontiers have been varied: unknown oceans, unexplored continents, and uncharted space. Courage and determination were the keys to conquering the unknown. Along with our quest to conquer physical frontiers, records of the past and the present are filled with our continuing efforts to explore and conquer the frontier of our relationships with one another. Human communication, the dynamic means by which we share ideas and forge common goals, is central to those efforts.

You are beginning your own personal quest to conquer the frontier of communication skill. You will be working toward communication *competence* (what you know about communication) and *performance* (how you apply and use that knowledge). You will be moving toward more effective communication. As you do so, it is important for you to realize that what you will study in speech communication is *you!* The focus of a study of speech communication is you—your behaviors and attitudes—as you establish and maintain personal, professional, and public relationships through communication.

Whether you are a fourteenth-century explorer or a twentieth-century student, success comes from understanding an area, assessing a need, setting a goal, analyzing the task, and initiating the process. Those steps will be used throughout this study as you move toward more effective communication.

Understanding Communication

Since long before your conscious memory began, you were communicating with those around you. You already have a set of communication behaviors and some ideas about your own and others' communication. However, what you will do now is increase your knowledge of communication, heighten your awareness and understanding, acquire a basis for making effective communication choices, and develop a wide variety of communication skills.

Broadly defined, **communication** is the process of exchanging messages. We will be trying to master human speech communication, a process in which individuals send and receive messages in order to reach common understanding. A

Communication is a dynamic process that involves ongoing interaction.

casual conversation between friends, a committee meeting, a political debate, a trial, a telephone call—all are among the varied ways in which humans engage in speech communication. All represent ways in which we strive to reach common understandings in our personal, professional, and public lives. All involve the skills we will focus on in this book.

Speech communication provides a way for us to form personal and professional relationships. The quality of those relationships helps us to determine our own personal communication effectiveness. Successful, positive relationships are important to successful and productive living.

Our effectiveness as citizens in a democracy also depends on our communication skills. Through communication, we seek out information, consider and articulate alternatives, and formulate our opinions. In 1978, the United States Congress passed the Elementary and Secondary Act in which five basic skills, essential for all citizens, were identified as: speaking, listening, reading, writing, and computation. Thus, the process of speech communication you will study in this course is basic and essential in every aspect of our lives.

Understanding Process

The first step in our study is to realize that communication is a process, not an act. In order to make the distinction, think about an *act* as something that begins and ends within a specific time frame, and of a **process** as something that is ongoing, cyclical and fluid.

You may have studied the water cycle in a science class. In the cycle, water in the atmosphere comes to earth as rain or snow. Plants, animals, and soil absorb the water. Eventually, soil water enters streams, rivers, and oceans. From these bodies of water, the moisture gradually evaporates into the atmosphere. The cycle is ongoing, and it would be difficult to find a starting or stopping point in the process. Also, energy is transferred or lost all through the cycle, making it dynamic.

When we think of the process of speech communication with a goal of building our communication skills, we must see the process as a dynamic force. Human communication is energetic, involves movement, and is fluid. It is a series of interrelated elements and processes. Communication is interaction; it is a process involving the exchange of ideas and feelings.

The process of human communication creates a product: the relationship among people. When the communication process is weak, relationships can also be weak. Understanding the process nature of communication helps you to analyze what is strong and what is weak about communication in which you are involved. It can give you the ability to change the parts of the process that are weak. Only when you truly grasp that communication is process can you begin to make intelligent and informed decisions about communication.

Each variable in the communication process is essential to effective communication.

Understanding the Process of Speech Communication

The first step in understanding the communication process is to examine the parts or variables in it. A **variable** is an element or component *within* a process that has the potential to change (or vary) *during* the process. It is this potential for change that gives the process its dynamic or interactive nature. The effectiveness of the communication process depends on the variables involved. The variables in the communication process are the sender, the receiver, context, channel, message, feedback, and barriers. We will also discuss the processes of sensory perception, encoding, decoding, transmitting (or sending), and receiving.

Senders and Receivers

The first two variables in the communication process are those of the sender and the receiver. The desire or intent to communicate, or to exchange messages, is held by an individual who initiates the communication and is, initially, the *sender.* The target of the communication is, initially, the *receiver.*

In truth, we should call ourselves **sender/receivers** and **receiver/senders,** because each individual in the process is constantly processing incoming and outgoing messages simultaneously. The role of sender/receivers is to constantly interact with themselves, the environment, and with other sender/receivers.

sender/receiver   receiver/sender

Context

Communication takes place within a context. The immediate **context** (or environment) includes the obvious aspects of *time* and *place,* but cannot be defined that simply. Think, for example, of all the elements that combine in one time and place.

We know that lighting, color, temperature, ventilation, and space have an impact on the quality of communication that takes place within an environment. Time may also be an important influence. Since childhood we have all known to choose the right time and the right place to ask for something we wanted, somehow sensing that the environ-

ment in which an interaction takes place has an impact on the quality of that interaction.

Context includes other influences or levels. We may talk about an emotional context for communication, an intellectual context, and an attitudinal context. All of them should be considered because of their impact or importance to the process in any given situation.

Each person who enters your speech communication class brings different experiences, attitudes, understandings, and feelings into the environment. Everything you are, everything you know, or think and feel, enters with you to become an important part of your own frame of reference or context of communication. Context can thus be thought of as a kind of "situational" component of the communication process.

The next time you enter a classroom, pause a moment to consider what attitudes, ideas, and feelings you are taking in with you. Observe the situation, time, and place. Ask yourself how the communication is affected by the quality of the environment. What intellectual and emotional atmosphere exists? How do you feel? How do your feelings affect your behavior?

Channel

Messages are passed from one participant to another through a channel. The **channel** for communication is the means for interaction. It can be thought of as a kind of pipeline, through which communication passes from one person to another. The channel can consist of vibrations in air, telephone lines, or electronic impulses. Whatever the *kind* of channel, it means space through which messages must pass to be sent from one person to another.

Stimuli within the channel motivate interaction. An unlimited amount of data exist within a channel, all competing for attention. Sights, sounds, and smells are always there. Your skin picks up stimuli from the temperature, a gentle breeze, or the hardness of your chair. You may think about what you did yesterday or what you're going to do tomorrow. All of these things are stimuli you may select from the channel at any given moment. What claims your attention are stimuli or data that can motivate *intrapersonal* (within you) or *interpersonal* (with another person) interaction.

Context, channel, and stimuli can be compared to a fishbowl. The transparent bowl provides a framework or context; the water in the bowl represents the channel; and the plants, rocks, and decorations represent stimuli claiming the attention of the fish as they glide through the water.

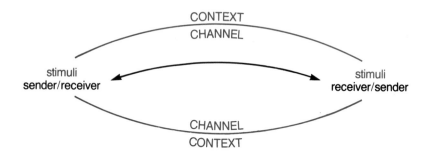

Sensory Perception

You may be surprised to learn that everything you know is acquired through the physical process of **sensory perception.** Your senses (seeing, hearing, smelling, tasting, and touching) bring you the world. The things you perceive through your senses—a fly on the windowsill, the sounds of your favorite music, the article you read—are stimuli, and all exist as raw and meaningless data until, through sensory perception, images are relayed by nerve impulses to the brain.

Encoding and Decoding

Impulses are received by the brain as electrical energy, and are then processed by the brain in a complex and instantaneous process of assigning meaning. This complicated intellectual process is done through classifying, organizing, and naming—assigning a code or language to the abstractions were perceived through the senses. Because the conversion to meaning involves a language or coding process, the components are called **encoding** (assigning a code) and **decoding** (personalizing a code).

In encoding, we choose a name for a concept and assign meaning. In decoding, we filter and interpret things we perceive, and thus personalize the meanings we assign through our interpretations. For example, if you feel the stimulus of a breeze, you may encode _breeze_ and decode _too cool._

When people want to share such meanings and interpretations, it is necessary that those involved in the communication share codes. No matter how eloquently I might express myself to you, if I were speaking French and you did not know that language (or code), I could not share my meaning with you verbally.

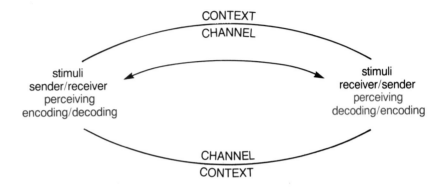

By the same token, my experiences, biases, prejudices, feelings, or attitudes may have led me to build up some meanings for "dentist" that you do not share because you have not shared those experiences. I might therefore encode my message in such a way that you could not accurately decode it. So, meaning as encoded and decoded by the sender and receiver in communication is a product of more than just a common language. It is also a product of common perceptions.

One of the many ways by which we can assign meanings is illustrated in Mark Twain's *Diary of Adam and Eve*. Eve, awed by her new world, places creatures into categories based on her observation of their function. She tells Adam of the "swimmers" and the "flyers" she has discovered, classifying the creatures we call *fish* and *birds* by the function they perform. She could have chosen other classifications. If she had classified the creatures by touch, she might have called them "slickies" and "downies." Had she decided to classify her new friends by appearance, she might have named them "scalies" and "featheries." The point is that Eve had received stimuli through her sensory perceptions and had processed the stimuli, classified them, and assigned a code, or a name, to what she perceived. Eve had encoded a message. When she told Adam of her discoveries, he had to interpret her code, to decode her message.

Transmitting

Transmitting (or sending) is an important element of the communication process. You may frown, smile, point, slouch, shrug, turn away, avoid eye contact, or wave. You laugh, cry, or utter sounds of surprise, disgust, or anger. All of these actions and vocalizations involve the transmission of **nonverbal messages. Verbal messages** are transmitted through the use of speech or language. You can transmit a message by making a statement, asking a question, or verbalizing an exclamation in order to communicate your needs verbally. The transmitting of _any_ message involves giving cues or sending signals that are received and assigned meaning or decoded by others.

Receiving

Receiver/senders acquire messages as stimuli, through the process of sensory perception. Seeing and hearing, as well as other senses in some cases, are involved in the physical process of **receiving.** Whether the message is nonverbal or verbal, it must be decoded by the receiver/sender. The process is usually unconscious, but some decoding may require extra applications of energy, as when the receiver/sender is listening for information that must be remembered. The receiver/sender may then encode a response to the message that has been decoded. Ultimately, then, the receiver determines the actual meaning of the message acquired.

Message

The concept of _message_ is difficult to define, but a functional definition might be that a **message** is any idea, concept, or feeling that is transmitted by a sender/receiver and is acquired and assigned meaning by a receiver/sender. Message has two components or levels of meaning. One level is the _intellectual component_—that which is usually transmitted verbally to the best of the speaker's ability. The second level is the _emotional_ or _relationship component_—that which is transmitted by nonverbal behavior. Message consists of what you say, how you feel about what you say, and what you feel about the person with whom you are interacting. There can be a marked difference between the message intended by the sender/receiver and the actual message interpreted by the receiver/sender.

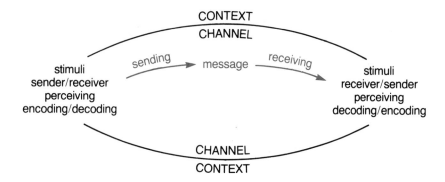

Feedback

We all respond to the stimuli we receive. **Response,** in the general sense, is any voluntary or involuntary physical or mental reaction to a stimulus. In the context of the communication process, response is more purposeful and is called *feedback*.

The receiver of the message provides **feedback,** which is a verbal or nonverbal response to the message. This completes the circular nature of the communication process. Feedback is possibly one of the most important variables in the process because it indicates whether or not the message is received, how accurately the message is interpreted, and the response of the receiver in the form of a new message. It also reflects on the quality of an interaction and, to a large extent, defines relationships.

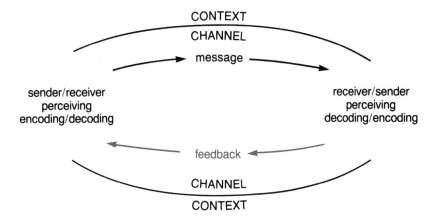

Barriers

Barriers are obstructions to communication, and may intrude at any point in the process, even within the sender or receiver. The speaker who cannot speak clearly and distinctly inserts a barrier into the process. Barriers may exist in the channel. Confusion over meaning, prejudice, lack of interest, and closed-mindedness can all be identified as barriers.

Noise a temporary, static-like condition that inhibits communication. When a classroom is too warm, the heat may compete with the teacher for attention, providing distraction or noise. During your next class, you may be thinking about a test or about meeting your friends after school. This is intellectual noise. Perhaps you are upset about a conversation with a friend. This is emotional noise. You may be sleepy—that is physical noise.

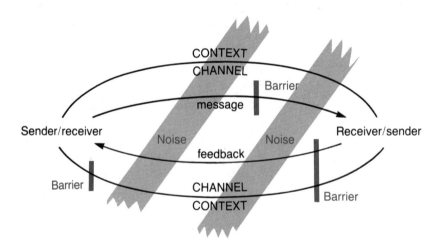

Checkpoint

Analyze the communication in your classroom. What is the context? What is the channel? What are the stimuli? What are the verbal and nonverbal messages? Do any barriers exist? What feedback is given?

Summary

Communication is a process, which means that it is ongoing, cyclical, and dynamic. Variables within the process include the sender/receiver, the receiver/sender, context, channel, message, feedback, and barriers.

The process also involves the active steps of sensory perception, encoding, decoding, sending, and receiving. The better we understand the dynamics of the communication process, the more effective we will be as communicators.

Check Your Knowledge

1. What is communication competence?

2. What are the variables in the communication process? How do they function? How do they relate to each other?

3. What are the two levels of message? Explain each.

4. What are barriers to communication?

Check Your Understanding

1. What is communication?

2. What is the communication process?

3. What is the importance of effective communication in the world today, on the community, state, regional, national, and/or international level?

4. What is the importance of effective communication in your own day-to-day interactions and relationships with adults and with your peers?

Check Your Skills

1. Construct an original model of the communication process emphasizing the aspect of communication you think is the most important.

2. Observe a communication interaction and analyze the components.

3. Keep a log of your own interactions for one day. Analyze the components of the communication process of which you are aware.

CHAPTER 2

Understanding Communication Theory

After reading this chapter, you should be able to:

1

Explain why it is important to study communication theory.

2

Explain several truths and myths about communication.

3

Describe the forms of communication.

4

List and explain the characteristics of effective communication.

5

Describe some barriers to effective communication.

6

Develop your own theory of communication.

7

Evaluate your communication effectiveness.

8

Begin to build communication skills.

Key Terms

Effective communication

Openness

Supportiveness

Positiveness

Equality

Empathy

Competitiveness

Defensiveness

Stereotyping

Prejudice

Choice

Appropriateness

Responsibility

A theory is a way of explaining how something operates, and often offers a hypothesis to be tested and tried. Theories grow out of the experiences, knowledge, and beliefs a person has, and are constantly influenced by the observations a person makes. Theories are tested and refined, and often spawn new theories. They are the basis of all scientific, social, and artistic discovery.

Galileo had a theory about gravity, which he tested and formalized. Einstein had a theory about relativity. Thomas Jefferson had a theory about how a government should operate, which formed the basis for our own system of government and which continues to be tested, refined, and changed. In each of these instances, ideas grew from observations that were examined and thoughtfully evaluated. Each theory resulted in contributions from which we all benefit.

In the same way, a clear and consistent theory of communication is being developed. Scholars and researchers have been examining communication for centuries. Out of the body of literature they have produced, we have many ideas about the way human speech communication operates.

As you examine the knowledge you gain and the experiences you have, you will begin to formulate your own ideas about communication. You will then have a theory of communication you can test and refine as you continue to communicate with those around you. This chapter will assist you by presenting some of the theories that already exist and by giving you some direction as you begin to develop your own theory of communication.

Throughout your study of communication, keep in mind that the communication process is critically important to the development of personal and professional relationships. Essentially, the process of effective communication results in effective relationships at a number of levels.

Levels of Communication Processes

One of the ways to explain how communication works is the classification of the "levels" of that process. If we remember that communication is the sending (encoding and transmitting) and receiving (decoding) of messages between

This television studio is a part of the message sending process at the mass communication level.

and among individuals (sender/receivers and receiver/senders), we can see that a classification of speech-communication levels would focus on the nature and number of individuals involved in the process.

Generally, five levels of the communication process have been identified and studied. *Intrapersonal communication* is the sending and receiving of messages within yourself. *Interpersonal communication* is the sending and receiving of messages in direct interaction between a few persons, usually two or three. *Group communication* is the term used when direct interaction takes place among a number of individuals. *Public communication* describes communication that occurs when a single speaker sends messages to an audience of receivers in a public-speaking context. *Mass communication* occurs when the sending and receiving processes occur electronically, through radio and television, or through mass print media.

In addition to the number and nature of senders and receivers, the kinds of *feedback* differ in each of these levels. In intrapersonal communication, feedback is instantaneous— as you tell yourself something, you respond simultaneously. The process is so immediate, you may rarely realize it is occurring. As individuals engage in interpersonal communication, feedback is also swift, direct, and continuous. Each message triggers feedback, which is then a new message, and the process ebbs and flows as messages are exchanged.

Much the same kind of feedback pattern can occur in group communication, but it may also be slower and more formalized in that situation. In public communication, feedback may be temporarily withheld or may be very indirect. In mass communication, feedback will always be delayed. Even in radio talk shows, where telephone feedback may occur, there is a time-lag between sending the original message and the reception by the sender of the receivers' reactions.

Communication Dynamics

In Chapter 1, we said that each variable in the communication process has the potential to change during the process. We also said that this potential for change gives communication its dynamic, interactive quality. At every level of communication, individuals engage in meaningful interactions with other individuals. When people interact, they use energy. They adjust their messages, try harder to listen and decode carefully, or work to overcome barriers and noise. Communication dynamics reflect ongoing activity and patterns of growth within and between individuals. Each time we use energy to communicate, we change and grow.

Communication can also be thought of as negotiation. We are constantly bargaining or trading with one another so that our needs may be met. In one sense, the words and gestures we use in communication are mediums of exchange, and we trade messages to reach agreement or understanding. Even when understanding is reached in communication, it remains dynamic, since interaction is ongoing and variables are constantly changing.

Checkpoint

In the past week, have you been aware of examples of each of the communication levels? What were they?

Testing Beliefs about Communication

It is important for artists to know about their craft and to have personal theories or philosophies about it in order for them to develop personal styles. It is important for athletes to know about their sports and develop personal beliefs about the game and sportsmanship in order to become effective players. In the same way, it is important for you to know about communication and develop a personal belief system concerning communication so that you can become as effective as possible. In your quest to formulate a theory of communication, you need to examine, consider, and test for yourself some of the generally accepted beliefs about communication.

Communication is Complex

Because communication is a dynamic, constantly changing process made up of many variables, it is highly complex. Additionally, each participant added to an exchange makes interaction even more complex. Since we have always communicated, we may take communication for granted, and may tend to view interaction simplistically. One young professor of communication was known for waving his arms and exclaiming, "Complicate! Complicate!" when advising students on the nature of communication. You can appreciate this when you remember how the model of communication evolved in Chapter 1. Your insights about the complexity of communication and the need for care in communication will grow as you observe interactions and keep track of your awareness and responses.

Communication is Irreversible

Another important aspect of communication is that we cannot take it back. Once a message is sent, it can't be erased. We can say something to someone (or not say something) and can return later to apologize or explain, but we can't replace the original interaction. The irreversibility of communication can suggest changing the axiom, "Look before you leap!" to "Think before you speak—or don't speak!"

Communication is Unrepeatable

Because communication is a process made up of variables that alter within and between interactions, what might have been effective in one instance may not be effective in another.

Sometimes we attempt to recapture an experience we enjoyed—an evening out with friends or a quiet interlude at home—only to discover that the next time it is not quite the same. Communication, too, cannot be exactly duplicated. Knowing this will help us form more realistic expectations and avoid disillusionment and disappointment.

Communication is Reciprocal

One part of academic communication theory deals with the merits of "one-way" versus "two-way" communication and emphasizes the idea that communication is sometimes one-way: "I tell you what to do. You do it!" However, we already know that effective communication is circular. Feedback, which contributes to the circular nature of communication, plays a vital role in any successful interaction.

If there is a single moment at which communication occurs, it is the moment of interaction when energy is exchanged. When eyes meet, hands clasp, or a smile answers a greeting, messages are exchanged. Reciprocal interaction forms a circular bond and makes each participant both a sender and a receiver.

Feedback is a very important part of successful learning situations.

**Communication
is Effect
Producing**

Communication always has some kind of effect. Some kind of meaning or energy is exchanged, and we are affected by the interaction. We respond to the intellectual and emotional components of message and are affected by the responses of others. Responses initiate other responses, relationships are affected, and interaction continues. Just as ripples spread into ripples when we throw a pebble into water, interactions extend into our continuing relationships and have impact.

**Testing Myths
about
Communication**

There are many myths about communication. As you work to develop a theory of communication, you will want to examine some of those myths and test them against your own knowledge and experiences.

**You Can Choose
Not to
Communicate**

One prevailing myth about communication is that you can _not_ communicate. In fact, one of the most unrealistic things someone can say is, ''You're not communicating with me!'' Averted eyes, unacknowledged greetings, and walking away are all messages - and their meaning is loud and clear. In other words, in communication, even a lack of a response is a response.

Although you may choose to hide or mask your response and not to furnish overt feedback, you are still responding. Each visible response is a kind of feedback and elicits a response (a new message) from the other person. The truth is that as living, breathing human beings, there is no way for us to avoid giving cues or messages to other human beings in the same environment. And now that we know those people will assign meaning to (decode) those responses, we know that it is not possible _not_ to communicate.

**You Can Have a
Communication
Breakdown**

Another myth to explore is that of the ''communication breakdown.'' Knowing the process nature of communication, we know that a communication interaction always continues. The communication may become negative; it may take a different direction from the one intended by the communicators; but it does not break down. The individuals involved are affected by the lack of effectiveness, and new messages and altered relationships continue the communication process.

Communication is Audible

Each of the above myths is probably an outgrowth of the notion that the only way we communicate is through the audible use of words. The child who sits sullenly in the principal's office is communicating. The elderly woman who smiles quietly amid the chorus of a family reunion is communicating. The poet Edgar Lee Masters' work, "Silence" and the popular song entitled, "The Sound of Silence," both express artistically what we know academically to be true. Messages are communicated both verbally and nonverbally—with equal intensity.

Assessing Characteristics of Effective Communication

As we look at some beliefs and myths about communication, we need to focus on the concept of effective communication. We can define **effective communication** as an interaction in which the message in the mind of the sender is accurately recreated in the mind of the receiver. However, this definition expresses an ideal that, because of the dynamic variables in the process, is rarely realized. The effective communication toward which we strive will be realized as we move closer and closer to that ideal. In order to make that possible, we need to begin to develop an awareness of characteristics that lead to positive results in communication. We must also learn to avoid the barriers that can be present in the process.

Effective communication results in a thorough discussion of issues and successful problem solving.

Effective Communication Is Open Communication   Try to think about **openness** from three perspectives. First, when people usually think of openness, they think of being willing to share feelings and ideas with others. Words such as *sincerity, honesty,* and *truthfulness* can be associated with this kind of openness, as well as words such as self-discipline and assertiveness.

A second kind of openness is characterized by a willingness to listen. "I am interested" and "I want to know about you" and "I want to hear what you have to say" are typical statements of openness to others. In addition, a willingness to listen without making judgement is characteristic of open communication.

A third kind of open communication involves being open to experience. A willingness to experiment, to learn, and to benefit from experience indicates open communication.

Supportiveness Characterizes Effective Communication   People involved in productive relationships are supportive of each other. This does not always mean that those involved *approve* of each other's behavior. People can disapprove and still be supportive. Each person can recognize and respect the worth and dignity of others. A teacher indicates **supportiveness** by telling a student "I want you to try to do better work. Let's try to solve your problem." We may show supportiveness for a friend when we say "I am concerned about you. Can I help?" or "I am glad you were nominated for class president. Can I help you with your campaign?"

Positiveness Is Vital to Effective Communication   We can understand **positiveness** by thinking of the kind and amount of energy we invest in an interaction or relationship. To the extent that we expend energy to move an interaction or relationship forward, we indicate positiveness. When we suppress energy or use energy for self-defeating purposes, our actions are negative. Positiveness is characterized by good feelings toward self and others as well as toward the interaction and relationship involved.

Equality Is Important In Effective Communication   Since each of us is unique, with many differences in abilities, talents, goals, and intelligence, it might seem that people are generally unequal. In many important aspects, however, people *are* equal. **Equality** means each of us has equal rights and each of us should be accorded equal dignity. Each of us should have equal opportunities to make choices and to participate in interaction. Despite our differences, we all have equal worth as human beings.

A healthy, long-term relationship cannot succeed when one person consistently communicates superiority to another, or seeks to dominate the total interaction and relationship. When one person assumes a role of superiority, equality is shattered, and a relationship eventually suffers.

Empathy Is A Key to Sensitive Interaction   **Empathy** involves putting one's self in another person's place. Like supportiveness, empathy does not necessarily indicate agreement. It is quite possible, in fact, to empathize with another's point of view and still disagree. Empathy means "I can understand where you're coming from," and implies the ability to "feel with" someone else. The essence of empathy is to understand with appreciation. "I know exactly what you mean and I understand" reflects empathy and does not need to indicate agreement or disagreement. Instead, such a statement implies understanding and appreciation—which are far more important.

The extent to which all five of these characteristics are present in an interaction influences the effectiveness of the communication and, consequently, the effectiveness of the relationship as well. A relationship will suffer when any one of these characteristics is not an active force in communication.

Testing Barriers to Communication

Just as it is important to know the characteristics of effective, productive communication, it is important to understand barriers to effective communication. When barriers are present in interactions, communication is blocked or becomes negative.

Competitiveness   In our society, competitiveness is not only valued, it is rewarded. The enormous financial gains available to professional athletes are testimony to that fact. However, in communication, **competitiveness** often presents a barrier because it diminishes trust. When we are competing, we may find it difficult to be open, supportive, or positive. Individuals who adopt a "win at all costs" attitude in an interaction may even be secretive and untruthful if it serves their purpose. This behavior is the opposite of effective communication.

Defensiveness   Both language and attitudes can foster **defensiveness** in communication. When either party becomes defensive, the effectiveness of the communication is diminished. If we think that others are seeking to gain from our mistakes, or if we become afraid or jealous, we may exhibit defensive communication behaviors. If we use negative responses, argumentative statements, insults, or put-downs, we are communicating defensively. When that occurs, productive and positive interactions become unlikely.

Stereotyping   Stereotyping, or judging everyone in a group to have common characteristics, is not only a negative and inappropriate social behavior, it is a major barrier to effective communication. Frequently, we do not openly stereotype, but we act on a stereotype and behave in communication as if it were true.

One of the most serious results of stereotyping is prejudice. **Prejudice** is judging without personal knowledge. In communication, it prohibits interaction with an individual on a personal level and causes us to relate, instead, as if the person possesses only those characteristics which have been preassigned on the basis of such factors as gender, race, age, or physical appearance.

Communication Apprehension   If we have a need to initiate some kind of interaction but cannot because of fear, we suffer from *communication apprehension*. This personal barrier to communication can evidence itself in any of the forms of communication processes. You are probably already aware of this behavior and refer to it by various names: shyness, fear, stage fright, reticence, anxiety. The key is that these behaviors are barriers to communication. They can be replaced by a sense of self-confidence, and by assertiveness, which can facilitate communication.

Checkpoint *Observe the interaction and environment in one of your classes. How many of the characteristics of effective communication can you identify? Are any barriers present? If so, how can they be overcome? How does the communication in the classroom affect the total attitude of the class?*

Developing Communication Skills

If you are convinced that positive, effective communication is essential to developing relationships and to achieving your own personal goals, you are probably wondering how and where to begin your quest for communication competence and improved performance. As a beginning to that process, we will look at the ways you can assess your communication effectiveness, some steps in building communication skills, and some principles that will furnish direction for your work.

Speech communication, including public speaking, depends on following some established rules and procedures.

Testing Communication Effectiveness

In order to set goals and to build competencies and skills, you need a system for evaluating important aspects of communication. This system will allow you to determine standards and set goals for performance and skill building.

Assessing The Role Of Self   Assessing the role and behavior of self in interaction is the first step in skill development. Self-awareness begins with questions like "What do I want? What are my choices or alternatives? What communication strategies are most appropriate in this particular instance? What are my responsibilities? Am I pleased with the results of my communication behaviors?"

Assessing The Role Of Others   We must also assess the roles and behaviors of others who are communicating with us. The purpose of this would *not* be to control or judge the choices and behaviors of others. Rather, it would be to increase your awareness and sensitivity to the behavior of others, in order to alter your own behavior when necessary and to choose appropriate responses whenever possible. Your communication effectiveness will increase as you grow in your skills of understanding, accepting, and adjusting to the communication behaviors of others.

Assessing Feedback   Evaluating feedback is an important factor in assessing your effectiveness in encoding and transmitting messages. Do most people seem to respond to your messages as you had hoped? Do their reactions indicate understanding? Are the responses you get to requests, questions, directions, or suggestions the ones you expected? If they are not, can you identify whether the problem lies in your message or in some other variable in the communication process?

Assessing Perception Of Messages   An important criterion for evaluating the effectiveness of your communication is to assess, to the best of your ability, the accuracy of your decoding of messages. How can you check your reception? Just as you monitor the responses of others to your messages, you can begin to monitor the appropriateness of your own responses. Do you answer most questions appropriately? Do you find it easy to follow instructions most of the time? Is your own feedback behavior usually accepted and understood by others? Are you pleased with most of your communication interactions? Do you feel that clear, precise messages have been exchanged?

Assessing Interaction   As you reflect on the total interaction in a communication context, some assessment of the overall quality will help you assess your effectiveness. At any given time, a particular interaction can be unsatisfactory for a variety of reasons. However, if you generally feel dissatisfied with interactions with a variety of individuals, a look at your own communication behaviors may help you analyze the problem. If you have generally positive and productive interactions, your communication effectiveness has been affirmed. When we remember that relationships are the products of communication interactions, the quality of our relationships becomes important in measuring our communication effectiveness.

Assessing Responsibilities   Perhaps the most important test of your communication effectiveness is the extent to which you are willing to own the responsibility for your behavior and its results. Those who seek to blame or to give credit to others sacrifice such ownership, and also hinder their ability to alter behaviors and become more effective. When you are able to articulate, "I want people to understand what I am saying," and, "I want to understand what others are saying," you are also able to add, "I will work to make those results possible!"

Assessing Ethical And Artistic Standards Effective communicators assess ethical and artistic standards of communication. *Ethics* involve the requirements of good character, sound qualifications, credibility, and good will or intent involved in communication. Not all communicators meets those ethical standards, but communicators whose effectiveness is respected over time *do* meet the standards.

By the same token, artistic standards, which reflect specific expectations of quality, impact communication effectiveness. Every field has artistic standards: music, art, athletics, dance. The style, the form, and the execution of skills in each of those areas carries certain quality expectations. The same is true for communication. Artistic standards may change over time, but they serve as a measurement for performance while they are in place.

Assessing Results A final consideration for measuring communication effectiveness is testing the results. You will find in this final step the prescription for your own growth. When results are what you desire, you can determine what you did to bring about those results, and you can maintain those behaviors. When results are not what you desire, you can identify behaviors that need to be altered in order to achieve the desired results.

Building Communication Effectiveness

The development of communication skills is a never-ending, ongoing process. As you grow as a communicator, you will set new goals to replace those you have already attained. You will develop new skills to meet your needs as your lifestyle changes. For effective communication, your communication skills change as your needs change.

Throughout your study of speech communication, you are going to monitor your communication behaviors, measure

Our communication styles change to fit the activity situation.

or assess your effectiveness, set communication goals, and master appropriate communication competencies and performance skills to meet your needs. In order to accomplish this, you need to become aware of the skill-building process for communication.

Steps For Skill Building

A first step in improving your communication is to develop a knowledge of communication in order to master its various concepts. How can you want to improve your verbal communication skills if you don't know what verbal skills are?

How can you want to improve your listening skills if you don't know about the listening process? This step is a knowledge and awareness step that provides an information base for skill development.

The second step is to identify areas where improvement is needed. The assessment process we have just described is the basis for that identification. In addition to your own assessment, you will receive specific feedback for improvement from your instructor and your classmates. An attitude of critical analysis is essential to knowing what skills you are going to have to build.

Once you have identified areas for growth, you can establish some communication goals for yourself. Build an image of the communicator you want to be, and then pursue that goal with dedication. In this third step, you can set goals that will help you communicate as you want to.

Having set your goals, you will need to observe others as models. Listen to others as they communicate. Observe the verbal and nonverbal behaviors that seem to add to their effectiveness. In step four, evaluate the effectiveness of others; adopt and use positive behaviors; avoid and change negative behaviors. Build a bank of knowledge from which you can draw for increased effectiveness.

The fifth, and sometimes the most difficult, step is to monitor your own behavior. Self-awareness can become the key to building skills. If you don't know how you use a behavior, how can you correct it? You may have noticed that many people interviewed on television overuse the phrases, ''Ya know'' or ''OK.'' You realize that these phrases clutter their speech and detract from their effectiveness. But unless you also become aware that *you* use these or other phrases, you cannot begin to correct your behavior.

Sixth, you will need to develop a system of replacing undesirable behaviors with more appropriate and effective behaviors. Your goals should be clear and specific so that you can begin to experiment with behaviors to accomplish those goals. It helps to have a system and a schedule, and then to stick to it. The seventh and final step is to evaluate your progress. You may find you wish to establish new goals.

While you are involved in this course, the skill-building system will be largely designed by your instructor, and the assignments in class will give you specific opportunities to

Steps in Skill Building	
Step 1	Develop communication knowledge
Step 2	Identify areas for improvement
Step 3	Establish communication goals
Step 4	Observe others as models
Step 5	Monitor personal communication behavior
Step 6	Develop a system for change
Step 7	Evaluate progress

experiment with your communication. But this class is a beginning, not an end. Throughout your life, you can follow these steps for building communication effectiveness in order to move toward greater levels of satisfaction with the interactions in which you engage.

Principles For Skill Building

Several principles will guide your skill-building process and will contribute to the development of your own communication theory. You will find these underlying principles throughout this text.

Choice   People always have choices. We choose the things we pay attention to. We choose to listen or not to listen. We choose to be interested or bored. We choose to initiate communication or not to. We choose to respond or not to. In every situation, as communicators, we exercise **choice.**

Appropriateness   In communication, we speak of the appropriateness of behavior. We measure the choices made in terms of their appropriateness for the sender, the receiver, the occasion, and the task. **Appropriateness,** when applied in this manner, usually relates to whether a communication choice reflects good judgment and represents the ethical and artistic standards expected in the particular instance.

Responsibility   A very important factor to remember in developing communication competency and performance skills is the principle of **responsibility.** Just as we have choices, we ultimately must assume responsibility for the choices we make. When responsibility is assumed, it provides the basis for productive growth in the skills of communication.

Checkpoint *Think about your communication behavior in your classes today. What choices did you make? Were they effective for you? Are you willing to take the responsibility for their outcome? What could you do to improve the effectiveness of your communication?*

Summary

Understanding the communication process and the relationship of each of the variables is the first step on the path to communication competency. This understanding is also necessary for you to have a basis for your performance choices. Studying and testing communication theories—both true and mythical—provides a second step, so that you can begin to be aware of your own communication behaviors. Then you can begin to build your own communication skills, to help you make effective, appropriate, and responsible choices.

Check Your Knowledge

1. What are the characteristics of effective communication?

2. What are some of the barriers to effective communication?

3. What are some generally accepted beliefs about communication?

4. What are some myths about communication?

5. What steps are involved in building communication skills?

Check Your Understanding

1. Explain the importance of studying communication theory.

2. Explain the concept of communication effectiveness.

3. What role does feedback play in the communication process?

4. Why can't you avoid communicating with someone?

5. Why is responsibility an important factor in communication?

Check Your Skills

1. Observe the communication behavior of one of your acquaintances. What does he or she do that is effective? What behaviors did not please you? What does the other person's behavior tell you about your own communication competencies?

2. Monitor your own communication behavior for one day. Try to objectively observe your interactions and then evaluate their effectiveness. What worked for you and what didn't? How could you improve those interactions that didn't please you?

Communication in History

History books of every nation are filled, not only with wars and treaties and explorations, but with a record of human events set in motion by the power and process of communication. Great communicators throughout world history include Aristotle, Pericles, Cicero, Quintillian, St. Augustine, Martin Luther, John Calvin, Edmund Burke, Benjamin Disraeli, Mohandas Gandhi, and Winston Churchill.

The development of our own nation is a record of the power of communication. Patrick Henry, Benjamin Franklin, and Thomas Jefferson forged rebellion and designed peace for our nation because they communicated with skill and effectiveness. Abraham Lincoln gave new meaning to the concept of the "common man" as a communicator. Susan B. Anthony applied the persuasive powers of skillful communication to obtaining voting rights for women. Woodrow Wilson planted the seeds of international cooperation as an alternative to war. Theodore Roosevelt imprinted forever in our collective consciousness the idea that we can communicate from a position of strength. Franklin D. Roosevelt provided not only exhilarating moments of public address, but also a series of "fireside chats" in which he demonstrated the power of a leader in personal communication with his constituents. John F. Kennedy helped us know what our collective power could do when he asked us to make a personal commitment to our country.

Orators such as Daniel Webster, William Jennings Bryan, Charles Lindburgh, Barbara Jordan, Jeane Kirkpatrick, and Dr. Martin Luther King have shared their divergent drama with the world.

The study of communication is the study of human tradition. It is the study of humans reaching out to one another. To be effective in communication is the highest form of human interaction, and history gives us countless examples by which we can model our own growth.

TOWARD UNDERSTANDING

Self as a Communicator

Part

2

Each receiver and sender in the communication process is a unique individual whose messages are influenced by self-concept, perception, and choices. An individual's self-concept is continually influenced by intrapersonal communication, or "self-talk." Perceptions affect self-talk as well as interpersonal communication. When people receive messages through their senses—including through communication—they select, organize, and interpret those messages through the process of perception. When people communicate with one another, they often are checking their perceptions against those of others.

Effective communication depends on making appropriate choices in intrapersonal, interpersonal, group, and public communication situations. These choices influence every aspect of the messages we send and receive.

CHAPTER 3

Exploring Self-Concept and Communication

After reading this chapter you should be able to:

1

Define self-concept.

2

Describe the process by which self-concept develops.

3

List some ways to alter self-concept.

4

Explain the general effect of self-concept on communication with others.

Key Terms

Self-concept

Intrapersonal communication

Physical self

Intellectual self

Emotional self

Repression

Intention

Self-acceptance

Grace Leonardi, a 75-year-old great-grandmother, is an identical twin. When she was a child, she says, the look-alikes were distinguished with a statement she came to resent, but never protested aloud. Pointing to Gloria they said, "She's the talking twin," and then indicating Grace they added, "She's the quiet one." Grace remembers that often when she was asked, "Which twin are you?" she answered, "I'm the quiet one," instead of telling her name. Even now, she says, "Once in a while at a party or a club meeting when I feel like speaking out about something, I think, 'No, I'm the *quiet* one,' and remain silent."

The whole notion each of us has of who we are affects the way we communicate with each other. **Self-concept** is your total attitude and definition of yourself, which develops out of communication with others throughout life. Self-concept is generally considered to be the most important influence on the way we communicate.

The sender's combined mental, physical, and emotional condition may be the reason for sending a message. The internal communication the sender has with and about him or herself certainly influences the content and style of the message that is sent. The same is true for receivers. Learning about yourself as a sender and receiver of messages is a worthwhile effort.

The Concept of Self

If you were asked to write a short essay to answer the question, "Who are you?" you would perhaps include your name, age, grade level, club memberships, sports interests, and other similar information you consider important to your identity. There is far more, however.

Your self-concept is never "completed." It continues to be altered by contact with people and events as long as you live. Many factors are involved. Self-concept includes all of the following things and more:

Everything you have learned about being a part of your particular family.

All the roles you know how to carry out (pedestrian, motorist, student, cousin, employee, ball player, friend, etc.)

All of your feelings of self-worth, pride, confidence, and esteem.

All of your attitudes, beliefs, values, priorities, and opinions.

The standards of behavior you have set for yourself.

Your feelings about the people, possessions, and causes you cherish.

Every group membership that is important to you.

Your overall idea about your place in the world as you know it.

Your past experiences, your present needs or concerns, and your dreams or ambitions for the future.

As you can see, people are very complex, and there is no single answer to the question, "Who are you?" The way you feel about yourself in any specific situation affects the way you communicate.

You have probably observed that when you are ill, your voice has less energy, your face is less animated, your gestures are somewhat limp, your posture is less erect, and your language usage may be less precise. In general, you may not communicate very well. The way you are feeling physically changes what you can do intellectually and emotionally. We could say that your physical self, your intellectual self, and your emotional self are out of balance. When you feel mentally, physically, and emotionally *well,* your communication style will change. No part of you operates independently, and all three areas of self-concept influence the way you communicate.

Checkpoint

If you were asked for a short statement about the topic, "Who are you?" where would you begin? What are the most important things to include in your self-description?

The Development of Self-Concept

From birth on, other people influence the way we think about ourselves, and, often, the way we behave. The toddler hears, "What a good boy to pick up your toys," or "Stupid, can't you do anything right?" or "Mom, she's being a pest."

Adults influence children's self-concepts through many kinds of communication.

*Communication
with others*

Labels like "good boy," "stupid," or "pest," are not easily set aside, and like all experiences, they leave their marks on the way we see ourselves.

We all begin our discovery of ourselves through communication with other people, and we define ourselves as they seem to define us. We actually learn who we are from the people around us. We learn as children to respect ourselves as worthwhile individuals when other people respect us. We learn to think of ourselves as unacceptable when others reject us.

In numerous ways, people communicate their expectations of us. We discover early in life that some behaviors are acceptable and some are not. Little by little, we learn what kinds of people we are expected to be. Both authors of this book are redheads and can remember as children hearing comments like, "Look at that red hair. I'll bet she has a temper." Both remember that after a time they responded with, "I'm supposed to have a temper, so let me show you." The expectations of others had helped bring about a portion of their self-concepts that later took great effort to replace with a more acceptable behavior.

When children hear themselves defined as *timid, dumb, cute, lazy, smart, healthy, talented,* or *troublsome,* they begin to behave in similar ways. So powerful is the concept that we see ourselves mirrored in others' views of us, that one author has used the phrase, "The Looking-Glass Self."

Checkpoint *Can you recall some labels from childhood that you still identify with yourself?*

Maintaining Self-Concept Through Communication

Even when we no longer consciously remember that we first heard a label from someone else, we may privately keep the label and apply it to ourselves. We can often discover labels we have accepted by listening to the way we talk to ourselves. Do you occasionally scold or congratulate yourself? If you make an embarrassing mistake, what do you say to yourself? Do you say something like, "Clumsy, you always spill something when you should be making a good impression," or "Well, stupid, you've done it again." When we want to give ourselves a verbal pat on the back, we may use phrases like, "Good job, Ace," or "You're great," or "You're a whiz."

In addition to the labels we attach to ourselves, every new role we learn (such as student, brother, cashier, or musician) becomes a part of our self-concepts. As we learn things about ourselves, develop new skills, and meet people who respond to us in different ways, our awareness of ourselves and our attitudes toward ourselves become more and more complex, until we gradually get to know ourselves in a way no other person ever can.

Intrapersonal Communication

We all talk to ourselves. The internal dialogue we have with ourselves is called **intrapersonal communication** or *self-talk,* and is the means by which we keep alive the elements of self-concept we first acquired from other people. We each know some things about ourselves that no one else knows. We know some things we like about ourselves, and some things we dislike. We are also aware that some people perceive us differently than we see ourselves.

Slowly, through *inter*personal and *intra*personal communication (communication with others and communication

Self-talk occurs constantly, as we think about who we are and what we would like to be.

with ourselves), self-concept develops into three parts: 1) the way we see ourselves to really be, 2) the way we ideally want to be, and 3) the way we think others perceive us and expect us to be. The three parts will always differ, but in a healthy self-concept the differences are not extreme. Each part affects the physical, intellectual, and emotional aspects of self-concept.

Physical Aspects of Self

Many elements of your self-concept are related to the physical person you perceive yourself to be. Aspects of your **physical self** include: 1) an awareness of the space your body fills and requires in order to do things like sit, stand or move about; 2) an evaluation of your appearance; 3) your general feeling of health or well-being; 4) appraisal of your coordination and agility in movement; and 5) an awareness of your ability to see, hear, taste, touch, and smell.

These awareness factors are kept alive by self-talk. They are kept alive by our communication. They are kept alive by our behaviors. For example, if you think of yourself as well coordinated, you may decide to try out for an athletic team. If you think of yourself as a poor student, you may not attempt to succeed in school. The way we think of ourselves generally determines the way we behave and interact.

Body Image

The physical image of yourself that you carry in your mind is called your *body image.* Body image is a way that we first become aware of our "self." If you are standing in front of a full-length mirror observing yourself, what do you see? Look first at your whole form and shape. What labels come to mind? What image do you have of your overall shape? Which part of your body do you like best? Which part do you like least? Which part of your appearance would you change if you could? Now remember, this is the way you appear to yourself, not necessarily the way you appear to others.

We may not always see ourselves the way others do.

Changing Physical Self

Once your body image is formed, it takes time and conscious effort for you to change it. It is appropriate, however, to alter your perceptions of yourself as you change and grow. It would be self-defeating for a grown woman to continue to think of herself as "Daddy's cute little girl," or for a robust man to think of himself as "Little Jimmy." Minor changes occur in your description of yourself from situation to situation and from day to day, but major changes take place slowly. They usually appear over a long period of time.

Anything that changes health or physical states modifies self-concept. Illness can change your appraisal of who you are, what you can and should do, and what you are willing to attempt. Fatigue or other physical conditions can impair your ability to think clearly or to communicate effectively. Two changes in physical state that you have probably experienced are your reactions to hunger and thirst. As those needs progress, they crowd out other concerns and choices. Any teacher can tell you how difficult it is to keep students' attention during the period just before lunch!

When you are ill, you see a doctor or take medication to rebalance the way you feel. When you feel a physical need, you react to reestablish balance. Some young people, however, see alcohol or drugs as ways to improve self-concept. Actually, such substances distort the senses and often bring about dangerous physical and psychological situations. Drugs distort perceptions of self and the environment by creating a chemical imbalance. Some destroy incentive to try to meet appropriate goals, and others create false confidence to do the impossible. Chemical alteration of "self" is dangerous and may have permanent, adverse physical effects. But any effect those chemicals have on self-concept is temporary and is often ultimately negative.

Intellectual Aspects of Self

We decide who we are intellectually in much the same way as we develop a body image and physical awareness. Your **intellectual self** involves: 1) an appraisal of your intellectual ability (how smart you think you are); 2) an assessment of your own intelligence in relation to other people (how smart you think you are compared to your friends, parents, teachers, etc.); 3) your general feeling of being capable of thinking clearly and productively (how well you think you comprehend information and solve problems); 4) your expectations of intellectual accomplishment (how well you expect to do at tasks like mental puzzles, thought problems, and academic subject mastery); and 5) your willingness to attempt intellectual tasks (what you are willing to try to learn or solve).

Perception of self

In both physical and intellectual aspects of self we have discussed our *perception* of physical and mental ability. To be sure, thinking you can master some subject does not necessarily mean it will be easy (or even possible) for you. No amount of thinking you are the world's brightest man or woman will make that so, unless there are other factors besides your perception to make it true. Thinking you are a mastermind will not cause you to be one, any more than thinking you can leap over the Grand Canyon will make that physically possible.

You do, however, want to have a positive feeling about your own ability to think and to have the courage to try basic tasks. Most of all, you will want to allow every intellectual success to add to your positive appraisal of your intellectual self.

Changing Intellectual Self

Some students "discover" their own intellectual ability because of positive feedback from teachers and other students. Often when that happens, the students' grades rise. Why? Because their feelings of capability, their expectations of themselves, and their willingness to attempt academic achievement have changed. Intellectually, we try what we think we are capable of doing.

One student was convinced of her mediocre intellect, but a teacher kept treating her like a bright student and insisting that she behave and perform like a scholar. Years later, the student wrote a letter to the teacher saying, "Yesterday I received my PhD. That was possible because you never gave up on me, even when I tried to prove I was dumb. You forced me to believe in my own intellect and demanded that I be a scholar. Thank you for helping me find a new self-concept."

Checkpoint

Have you ever used an inappropriate view of your own intelligence as an excuse for not doing well on an exam or in a course? ("I'm not smart enough to learn or understand this," can frequently seem to relieve us of an obligation to try.)

Choose an intellectual task and try replacing the "I'm not smart enough" view with, "I think I can. Let's see."

Emotional Aspects of Self

We cannot completely separate emotion from the physical and intellectual parts of ourselves, but at least two emotional factors should be considered. The aspects of **emotional self** are 1) awareness of feelings and 2) appropriate communication of emotions. Emotional awareness develops first, and the ability to communicate emotions in acceptable ways comes later.

It is natural for people to be concerned about the impressions they are making on others.

Feelings are our internal reactions to our experiences. Surprisingly enough, many people "tune out" what they feel, and find it very difficult to acknowledge their own emotions. They deny they are feeling angry, sad, lonely, bored, or proud. They see emotions as signs of weakness instead of the natural reactions they are. Hiding feelings inside does not mean controlling them; it simply causes them to be expressed in another way or at another time.

Control of feelings comes by being aware of them, accepting them, taking at least a moment to decide on an appropriate means of expression, and then expressing them. It takes great energy to hide fear or any other emotion and pretend it does not exist. The denial of feelings is called **repression.** Sometimes repression of feelings like anger results in physical symptoms like ulcers. Repression always results in a form of deceit or dishonesty in communication. A healthy self-concept includes owning and expressing the emotions we feel.

Changing Emotional Self

Tears, laughter, shouting, trembling and other similar external behaviors tell others *about* our feelings. But, in order to share feelings verbally, we must first be aware of what we are feeling and must then be willing to let others hear evidence of our feelings.

Acknowledging a feeling to yourself but hiding it from others is a choice that you make. However, as communicators, we need to be aware that a decision to hide emotions and fail to communicate about them can result in internal resentment toward yourself or toward another person. If internal resentment is carried unexpressed for a long time, it may burst forth in an exaggerated form in an inappropriate situation.

When feelings are communicated in some inappropriate way, it may be in the form of unfair verbal accusations such as, "You don't think about anyone but yourself!" Inappropriate expressions of emotions can destroy relationships. Your **intention** guides your choice of a means for expressing a feeling. *To understand, to defend, to protest,* or *to avoid* are examples of intentions.

By taking a moment to consider your intention, you can decide how to communicate your feeling. The communication may be a smile, a frown, or a few words of explanation. When we discuss listening and responding, we will suggest some ways of expressing feelings and asking for change that can help rather than harm relationships.

Checkpoint

Have you ever held back the expression of some mild annoyance and later surprised yourself and another person by exploding in an inappropriate angry outburst? If such a situation existed now, could you apply the suggestions above to express the annoyance before it became an outburst?

Modifying Self-Concept

Because self-concept strongly influences our communication, a constant assessment and appropriate modification of self-concept is important. Once self-concept becomes established, it is not easily changed, but replacing a negative self-concept with a positive, healthy one is a goal worth pursuing. Since we influence ourselves through self-talk, we can change our self-concepts if we choose by 1) listening to others give

Feedback is exchanged freely between friends who are comfortable with one another.

feedback that tells us how they perceive us, 2) carefully selecting the labels we need to keep and repeat to ourselves, and 3) recognizing attitudes and habits that are self-defeating and then working to change them.

Because we are able to make choices, we can, with persistence, determine how we let our experiences influence us. We cannot change our past experiences, but we can change our feelings about those experiences. It is self-defeating to blame others for any lack of self-acceptance we may feel. The responsibility for maintaining a positive self-concept is our own.

Self-Acceptance

When we have healthy self-concepts, we value ourselves and feel generally good about ourselves. We acknowledge our strengths, but we are also aware of our weaknesses. We are not overpowered by our negative traits, because we know we are capable of changing many of the things we dislike about ourselves. With such feelings of **self-acceptance** (or positive self-concept) we can be comfortable in our communication with others, because we feel no great need to conceal the sort of people we think we are. Not only do we feel free to share portions of those people we *really are,* but we are likely to discover that it is easier to accept other people as well.

Improving self-concept

To improve your self-concept, you can choose to congratulate yourself on your successes. When people compliment you on a job well done, don't argue with their perception of you. Simply say "thank you," and later remind yourself that someone thought you did a good job. When you hear a criticism, review your behavior to see if you need to make a change, and then avoid repeating the critical view to yourself. Change the things you can, and put the rest of the criticism aside. The choice is yours regarding what to do with feedback from others. Hold on to as many positives as possible, or supply your own to counteract the negatives that come your way.

Checkpoint *Can you recall the three steps to use in changing your self-concept if you choose?*

The Effect of Self-Concept on Communication

Communication styles should be appropriate to our changing views of self. The appropriate communication style of a "cute little girl" or a "little Jimmy" is very different from that of an adult woman or man. The woman must put into the background the "cute little girl" portion of her self-concept to make way for "woman," "executive," "responsible wife," or some other equally mature concept of herself. She must make communication choices to accompany her new self-view. Not only will "little Jimmy's" own communication style change, but the way other people communicate with him will change. The way people relate to someone who thinks and acts like a little boy is quite different from the way they behave toward an athlete, a husband, or a businessman who views himself in appropriate ways and communicates in a manner that fits his role.

How we present ourselves

We seldom share the people we think we really are with anyone. We try instead to show ourselves to others in an improved form. We use cosmetics or wear clothes we think will make a particular impression. We attempt to show others we are smarter, kinder, or wiser than we see ourselves to be in those private moments when we confront who we really are.

It is natural to want to "put the best foot forward." It is only when the impressions we try to make differ strongly from our images of ourselves that we should be concerned. Of course, the less we like the people we think we really are (that is, the more negative our self-concept), the more likely we are to pretend in order to convince others we are different.

Negative feelings

Negative self-feelings can produce shyness, or boastful displays of pretending to be important. Shy people have usually learned through negative feedback (harsh criticism or ridicule) that being quiet is a way to avoid pain. Communication apprehension (or fear of communicating) commonly results from a self-concept that is less than positive at the moment. The most common form of communication apprehension is stage fright—a fear of public speaking situations.

Self-acceptance

The need for self-acceptance is basically a need for an accurate, workable image of one's self that is positive and comfortable. Self-acceptance leaves individuals free to com-

Self-acceptance encourages positive and confident communication.

municate with others without trying to impress them. It allows them to act with assertiveness and confidence. Self-accepting individuals will not feel threatened by meeting new people. They will be free to explore and reevaluate themselves through the responses of each new acquaintance.

Checkpoint *What are some common characteristics of people with negative self-concepts? What are some communication characteristics of self-accepting people?*

Presenting Self in Communication

We have discussed the aspects of self-concept that influence our communication. Now, let's look more closely at how we choose to share our self-concepts with others. Making these choices is an essential skill in building meaningful interpersonal relationships. We must know how, when, where, and most important, with whom we can share information about the person we feel we really are.

*Self-concept
and role*

First Impressions Influence Our Choice to Share   When we meet new people, our first impressions are important. Most of us make some initial decisions about the kind of person we are meeting. The way we communicate with the new acquaintance depends upon three questions and how we answer them. The first question is about how we define ourselves. "Who am I?" Second, we define the situation we are in and our role in it. "Who am I in this situation? What role behaviors are expected of me?" For example, if you are clerking in a store and a customer enters, you are expected to act in your role as clerk. You greet the customer, and ask if you can help him or her. Failure to do so means you have not met the customer's expectations of you in the role of clerk.

*Defining
others*

The third question concerns the other person and how we define her or him in the situation with us. "Who is this person and what is his or her role in this situation?" Based on these first three assumptions, we strive to create a particular image of ourselves with others, just as other people try to create a particular image of themselves with us.

The Purpose of Sharing Self   Until we begin to share with a friend some emotion, experience, belief, or other self-information that has been hidden, our relationship with a new person remains distant and superficial. When we make disclosures to each other, and each of us responds to the other's disclosures in a supportive manner, we feel closer to each other and a friendship can begin.

Sharing self-concept
can be an important
part of developing
relationships.

Over a long period of time we may share enough information about ourselves to know each other very well, but we seldom share *all* of the person we think we really are with anyone. We try instead to show ourselves to others in a form we think is better, and while we are trying, the people we attempt to impress develop images of us that are different from our concept of our "real selves," *and* different from "the selves we want them to see."

Self-Concept is Shared Verbally and Nonverbally   We communicate things about ourselves to each other through our words, voices, facial expressions, physical posture and movement, the way we dress, and many other aspects of our communication. The information we share is usually private, emotional information. It may be a feeling, an attitude, or a past experience that we have chosen not to tell everyone. Whether we feel the need to reserve a particular item of information, and later share it, depends on our self-concept. Because each of us is unique, our decision to share is also unique.

Feelings, attitudes, experiences

When *I* meet *you,* each of us brings to our meeting the three-part self-concept we discussed earlier. The resulting conversation is not really a dialogue between two people—you and me. It may best be seen as an encounter of *six* imaginary people. A diagram of the "persons" who are participating is shown in the figure below.

Person A

(A3) The person B sees .... A to be

(A2) The person A wants .... to be (and wants B to see

(A1) The person A sees herself .... to be

Person B

.... (B3) The person A sees B to be

.... (B2) The person B wants to be (and wants A to see)

.... (B1) The person B sees himself to be

If A sees herself in a positive, self-accepting way (A1), she will not feel it necessary to hide her "real self" from B by trying to make him see a different or ideal self (A2). The result will be that (A3), the person B sees and gets to know, is much the same as (A1) and (A2).

The reverse is also true. We can state a communication rule about one-to-one meetings like this: When (A1) and (A2) are similiar, (A3) will also be similiar; and when (A1) is very different from (A2), (A3) will be very different from either (A1) or (A2).

Let's look at an example. Jeff has had some problems that have left him feeling he is not a worthwhile person, and although he is lonely and wants friends, he thinks his teacher and classmates will not like him if they ever see him as he sees himself. Jeff tries to protect himself from having them know "the Jeff he thinks he really is" and from rejection by pretending he doesn't want to have anything to do with the other students. He may even say critical things that sound as if he thinks his classmates are childish and immature.

The class's impression of Jeff is not of the same "unworthwhile Jeff" that Jeff sees, and not the "more grown up Jeff" he tries to make them see. Instead, the class may think Jeff is conceited, someone who thinks he is better than they are. What a sad outcome. Jeff needs friends and good experiences with people who accept him, but his negative self-concept makes sharing seem too risky, and friendships are impossible. His classmates would accept Jeff if they only knew he wants to be friends, and that he does not really feel superior.

Checkpoint _List the six imaginary people present in one-to-one encounters._

Summary

Self-concept affects communication in several important ways. Our physical, intellectual, and emotional selves should be in balance for us to make effective communication choices. Our self-concepts develop and change through communication with other people.

Self-talk and our interactions with others are important in maintaining self-concept. Self-concept is made up of three parts: 1) the way we see ourselves to really be; 2) the way we ideally want to be; and 3) the way we think others perceive us and expect us to be. Healthy self-concepts lead to self-acceptance, which helps us to be comfortable in communicating with others.

The sharing of self-concept is important in interpersonal relationships. First impressions influence our choice to share self-concepts verbally and nonverbally. Because our self-concepts are unique, our choices to share are also unique.

Check Your Knowledge

1. Define self-concept.

2. List some nonverbal means by which we share information about ourselves.

3. What is the process by which self-concept develops?

Check Your Understanding

1. How many ways can you think of to modify self-concept?

2. What impact does a positive self-concept have on communication?

3. Why are first impressions important in communication?

4. Explain the role of sharing self-concept in developing meaningful relationships.

Check Your Skills

1. Describe some self-defeating attitudes and their results.

2. Discuss some ways you can help those around you develop more positive self-concepts.

3. See if you can think of some additional guidelines for knowing when, where, or with whom it is appropriate to share self-concept.

4. Compile a list of verbal and nonverbal messages from other people that help you feel good about yourself.

5. Make a list of phrases you use to scold yourself when you make mistakes. Now think of some ways to compliment yourself when you have done something well.

CHAPTER 4

Understanding Perception in Communication

After reading this chapter you should be able to:

1

Explain the influence of the perceiver, the person perceived, and the situation on the process of perception.

2

Name aspects of the object perceived that affect perception.

3

Name aspects inside the perceiver that can influence perception.

4

Describe the use of categories in organizing perceptions.

5

Explain how clarifying perceptions can solve communication problems.

Key Terms

Perception

Selection

Perceptual readiness

Organization

Interpretation

Consensual perception

Consensual reality

Perception check

Perception is the process of noticing and developing mental impressions of persons or things. The process is very complex, and its importance in our communication with others is enormous, because all communication is essentially an effort at creating matched perceptions. No matter what we say or what our immediate purpose is, we communicate with each other to share the world as we know it, or as we *perceive* it. Some understanding of the perception process will help you improve your communication skills.

The process occurs in three parts or stages: 1) we limit or *select* what we will notice; 2) we *organize* what we have selected so that it makes sense to us; and 3) we *interpret* what we perceive by identifying or evaluating it. The three stages are not distinctly separate. They blend together, but we will discuss them separately.

Checkpoint *Quickly (before you forget), review the three stages of perception. What are they?*

We Select What We Notice

The first stage of perception, selecting what we will notice, is necessary because at any given moment our senses are being bombarded by many things, all making bids for our attention. We must focus on some of them and exclude others from our attention. We cope with a world filled with millions of things to see, hear, taste, touch, and smell by paying attention to some things and ignoring others.

It can take a lot of energy to pay attention to one thing among so many.

Selection is based on three kinds of influence. They are conditions inside the perceiver, conditions related to the situation, and characteristics of the object perceived. Some influences are related to the self-concept of the perceiver—his or her interests, needs, past experiences, and expectations for the future. Some influencing factors are products of the situation at the time, since our needs and interests change moment by moment. The last group of influences relate to characteristics of the person or thing being perceived.

Aspects of The Object Perceived

The very nature of the things we discover through our senses determines whether we select them for real notice. We ''see'' things without noticing. We hear without listening. We taste, touch, and smell many objects without choosing them for special consideration. What is there about some objects that causes us to notice them?

Intensity   The _intensity_ of the object perceived can be readily understood when you think of the attention-getting capability of the loudest voice in the room, the most vividly colored object on your desk, or the brightest neon sign on the street. _Size_ and _contrast_ factors are equally obvious, because you already know that large lettering, large pictures, and huge newspaper advertisements are likely to catch your eye before the small items do. Factors inside you can change the impact of size. For example, if you are searching for one particular tiny advertisement, you may not even see the large ones.

Size

Contrast

Contrast is a factor when you consider some objects. Generally, you will notice a large bus more quickly than a small car. That may not be true if you see a loading area filled with buses and only one small car. Often it is a contrast to its surroundings that causes you to select and focus on one object.

Repetition   _Repetition_ is another aspect of the thing perceived that affects selection. If a radio commercial is somewhat ordinary you may not really listen to it the first time you hear it, but if you hear it several times in one day, the repetition will cause your selection. Later, however, you may ignore the same commercial and notice a contrasting one instead.

If you drive along the highway at night and see a bright light marking a hazardous intersection, you may notice it. But if the light blinks or appears to move like the point of an arrow, you are far more likely to heed it. *Motion* affects perceptual selection. You may have already noticed that an animated public speaker is easier to listen to than a motionless one.

Familiarity *Familiarity* or *novelty* works in two ways. If you place a strange object among your familiar household belongings, the unusual item will be noticed. Familiar people or things in an unfamiliar place will command your attention as well. It is the *novelty* of the strange object that captures attention. If you walk down a London street and pass dozens of ordinary-looking people, you may not notice any one of them in a special way. However, a girl with hair dyed green, blue, and red will probably be noticed. The ordinary appearance of some escapes notice and the novelty of the girl is seen. Farther down the street filled with "ordinary" strangers, you may meet a neighbor from your hometown. You notice the neighbor because of a *familiar* appearance among the ordinary, unfamiliar faces. In some ways, familiarity and novelty are influenced by contrast—the contrast between familiar and novel persons or things.

Novelty

It is the *novelty* of the strange object that captures your attention.

Proximity　*Proximity* refers to how near something is to you. Distance distorts, but so does nearness. Things that are physically close to you seem larger and draw your attention. Things and people that are psychologically close seem more important and more like us. Psychological closeness can also cause physically distant people or things to be noticed.

Situations and Conditions Inside the Perceiver

In the examples above you can see that while the characteristics of the thing perceived are important in selection, the situations in which they occur are also important. There are perhaps even more determining factors inside the person who does the perceiving than there are in the object selected and the situation or context. What we select to notice is largely based on our definitions of ourselves, our interests, needs, and past experiences.

Many of M. C. Escher's drawings challenge our perceptions.

Needs　*Needs* affect your selection of objects to notice. For example, you may drive down the same street day after day without ever noticing a telephone booth in front of a store. If some rainy day you have an accident and need a telephone in a hurry, however, you will "discover" the pay phone that has always been there. In the same way, because of our needs and interests, we hear and recognize the familiar footsteps of people we love, and when we are hungry we notice in an exaggerated manner the aroma of bread baking nearby.

Perceptual Readiness　**Perceptual readiness** involves the internal state of the perceiver and is a major factor in perception. It is a condition of expecting to find, or being "ready" to notice, some things. Experiences, knowledge, and expectations at the moment create perceptual readiness, an anticipation of what will be perceived. We notice what we know about and expect to encounter. You may walk over a clump of wildflowers daily without really being aware of their presence until after you have a few lessons in botany (the study of plant life). Suddenly you are "seeing" the wildflowers for the first time.

Checkpoint *Have you ever noticed for the first time something you had been "seeing" every day, but never really stopped to look at?*

We Organize What We Have Selected

Because we receive information around us in a random manner, we must make some sense of it—we must give it **organization**. Organization is possible only because the world is a rather stable place. Things and people keep their general forms from one day to the next, and once we have identified some classes or types of objects like *books, dogs,* or *children,* we see similarities in new observations. We group things as a way of organizing the world around us.

We Assume Likenesses

Dog

Dachshund

Hamlet

As we notice likenesses in pets, we may sort a newly noticed animal first into the category *dog.* Later, we may sort that dog into the subcategory *dachshund.* Still later, if we become acquainted with that particular dog, we create a new category named *Hamlet,* like the dog.

Sorting   Have you ever watched a postal worker sort mail into Post Office boxes? We organize things and people we perceive by a similar process. We search for patterns or categories (like addresses on envelopes) to help us sort what we perceive into some meaningful order. We identify or label things or people by associating them with some larger group. For example, when we see a four-footed animal on the sidewalk we do some rapid mental sorting to put it into a known animal category. The sorting sometimes occurs by elimination (*not* Hamlet, *not* dachshund, but *a strange dog of unknown breed*). Like the progression from *dog,* to *dachshund,* to *Hamlet,* our sorting of people into categories (boxes) advances to a special one-person category for an intimate friend.

Stereotyping   What if the postal worker decided to sort mail by the color of the envelopes? If he or she decided all brown envelopes should oe placed in the same box, we would say he or she was sorting by the wrong identifying factor. We sometimes make a similar error when we sort people into ''boxes.'' When we categorize individuals we may assume that they are like other people or groups we have observed, on the basis of real or imagined similarities. We oversimplify when we decide that because a person resembles the members of a group in one way, he or she is like group members in other ways.

We call this *stereotyping,* and it can keep us from considering each individual as a unique human being. The better you get to know a person, the less you will be able to stereotype him or her.

We Develop Categories

Every category we develop has identifying characteristics we use in determining whether new things encountered fit the category. Suppose, for instance, that you had developed a category *Teacher*. It would not be unusual for such a category to include the following characteristics:

1. intelligent but boring

2. reads for recreation

3. is unathletic

4. dresses conservatively

5. likes only classical music

Upon first impression, the uniqueness of each individual is often not apparent.

If one day you see Miss West, your math teacher, playing an outstanding game of tennis, and later you discover her favorite recreation is playing saxaphone with an informal jazz group, how do you fit her into the *Teacher* category? Your options are 1) to define Miss West as *not Teacher,* 2) to alter or expand the *Teacher* category to include some previously unconsidered characteristics, or 3) to create an entirely new category for the amazing Miss West alone. Either of the last two options would be appropriate.

We Enlarge and Seek Closure

Enlarging is one way of making sense of our perception. We try to determine the meaning of an act observed or a message received in its larger context. We watch bodily movements and facial expressions, and we listen to vocal characteristics to find out what is meant by all the verbal and nonverbal messages combined.

Creating closure is another part of organizing. We create closure or finish a perception when we take part of an impression and complete it to create the whole thing as we expect it to be. We see parts of familiar forms and finish them in our imaginations; we hear a phrase of a tune and in our minds we hear its completion.

Checkpoint

What characteristics do you expect in the following:
all police officers?
all television commercials?
all school buildings?
Are your assumptions logical? Are they stereotypes?

We Interpret Information

If one day you saw a boy running down a sidewalk carrying a woman's handbag, and at the same time you heard a woman shouting for help, you would probably assume a robbery had occurred. As a witness in a courtroom, however, you may tell only what you actually *saw* and *heard.* Your **interpretation** of the boy running and the woman shouting as *robbery* is your imaginary completion of the event. Interpretation cannot be used in an eyewitness account.

To interpret perceptions, we attach meanings to the information received through our senses, and the result may be inaccurate. The steps in noticing, organizing, and interpreting may occur as follows.

Selection of Sensory Messages:

1. You _saw_ a boy running.
2. You _saw_ a woman's purse in his hand.
3. You _heard_ a woman shouting, "Help."

Organization:

1. You _sort_ the women's shouting into a category of unusual events.
2. You _enlarge_ to connect the runner with the shouter into an overall meaning.
3. You _seek closure_ by creating a whole from the parts known.

Interpretation:

1. You _imagine_ the boy has grabbed the purse away from the shouting woman.
2. You _assume_ she shouts "Help" because she has been robbed.
3. You _decide_ that a robbery has occurred.
4. You _decide_ that the running boy is the thief.

The interpretation of sensory messages (what is _seen_ and _heard_) is influenced by factors inside the perceiver. Let's assume that the perceiver is a woman. The internal factors could be a great fear of being robbed, her certainty about what she has "seen," and her past experiences. Her interpretation is also influenced by her definition of the situation she is observing ("This is a robbery").

A third area of influence is centered on characteristics of the thing or person perceived. If the boy appears to be frightened, if he looks over his shoulder occasionally, and if he is someone she recognizes as part of a neighborhood gang of troublemakers, she uses those observations to support her interpretation.

Checkpoint

Look at the photograph on this page and try separating the three stages of your perception.

What did you see?

What categories did you use to create meaning?

What did you imagine, assume, and infer?

Did your three-stage process follow the description you have just read?

Perception is Limited by Physical Senses

Everything we encounter in the world around us, we discover or become aware of through our senses. Because our information about the world comes to us through our senses, it may be limited by our physical ability to taste, touch, see, smell, or hear. People who cannot see or hear from birth must develop perceptions with their other senses, and their ability to know the world is limited to what they can discover through those remaining senses. If you could not see, how would that change your perception of the room you are in? If you had no sense of smell, how would that change your perception of food?

Some people who have adequate use of all five senses grow accustomed to using some of their senses more than others. They may develop clearer images from reading about an event or a place than from hearing a description of it, for example. Most of us use all our senses to learn about the world, although in different situations we may rely more on one sense than on others.

Checkpoint *How aware are you of your senses and their use? Think of the following sensory cues. Which of your senses do you use in your perception of each?*

The texture of a fabric	*The tartness of a lemon*
The color of a house	*The shape of a sculptured form*
The pitch of a voice	*The fragrance of roses*
The saltiness of popcorn	*The volume of music*
The heat from a radiator	*The brightness of a light*

Perception is Altered by Time

Our awareness of objects about us is limited by our knowledge and past experiences, our needs and interests at the moment, and our dreams and expectations for the future. We tend to assume that the things and people around us are alike to everyone, and that our perception of them is the way they "really are." However, each of us forms perceptions through a creative mental process that results in impressions unique to us. Through self-talk we "make sense" of our past, our present, and our future, and it is what we *tell ourselves* about events that causes us to treat them as important or unimportant.

Past Experiences

Our past experiences have a great impact on the way we perceive situations. Sometimes an experience changes our perception of an object without our being aware of what caused the change. For instance, a perfume associated with someone we did not like may cause us to find that perfume unpleasant long after the person is forgotten. Having lived near the ocean, the sound of the surf may be beautiful to the ear, and by association, the sound may mean "home." We perceive things as we do partly because of what we have known or learned in the past.

Consider the influence of memories for a moment. We select what we notice, and we select what we will remember. We build fantasy into our memories. That does not make a memory less important; it makes it more personal. Memory is what we have *chosen* to keep from the past. It is our selected perception of what was, which we keep alive and alter in self-talk. We may distort or fantasize a memory into something very unlike the event as viewed or remembered by others. It is sometimes very difficult to match perceptions of the past.

These are three common optical illusions.

Which line appears longer?

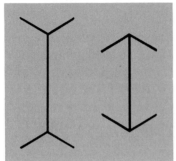

Which line appears longer?

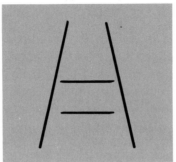

What do you see first?

Future Expectations

Now consider the impact of future expectations on our perceptions. We daydream about what will be, and some fantasies of the future become goals and plans. We "try on" roles, relationships, or lifestyles in our minds. As a child, did you ever try on clothes belonging to a parent or an older brother or sister? Most of us wanted to see how it would feel to be a military officer, an actor, a business executive, a college student, a sales clerk, or a chef. When we have found a role or an occupation that seems right for us, we plan and predict our own future in the role. We can even rehearse or practice the role in fantasy.

Our fantasies, ambitions, and prophecies about the future color the way we perceive the present. In self-talk we carry on a dialogue about things such as what we need to learn, how we should behave, what kind of friends to make, and what the events of the present mean to us and our future. We have chosen the way we perceive the past (and we alone can change that perception), we choose and shape our perceptions of the future, and those past and future perceptions help us choose what we will focus on, organize, and make meaningful in the present.

Present Needs

Past experience is always with us, and the future stretches out in our imaginations, but we must continually cope with the here and now. We must focus on the present, and our self-talk enables us to weigh past experience and future consequences in developing perceptions and making present communication choices.

We must avoid dwelling in the past or focusing completely on future ambitions in order to develop and appreciate present relationships. Blaming the present on some past event, keeping alive the memory of a misfortune, or talking constantly of "the way things were" is self-defeating.

On the other hand, a constant obsession with getting a date, making more money, getting some future award, or getting elected to school office will rob us of the present as well. Many relationships have suffered because the future became more important than the present. The present is a precious, disappearing commodity to be kept clearly in mind. It should balance with the past and future in the way we perceive the world around us.

Sometimes we forget to heed lessons learned in the past and our goals for the future, when our present interests and needs override them. If on your way to school you are involved in a collision, your goal of making an A on a first-period exam might be set aside completely. The present has taken precedence over the future.

The past, the present, and future situations influence our perceptions.

When we each come from such different worlds of experience, and have such different needs from moment to moment, how do we find enough similarities to allow for communication? We carry on a continuous searching or checking for common perceptions with the people around us. When our impressions are at least *similar,* we communicate well; when our perceptions differ drastically, we encounter problems.

Checkpoint

Examine this book. Which senses did you use most? Least? If you closed your eyes, how could you examine it? Are you making assumptions about this book because of its similarity to or difference from some other book you have used in the past? Are your assumptions based on expectations or goals? Are they based on present needs?

Verifying Perceptions Through Communication

Even if the impressions of a whole group of people are in general agreement, the perceptions of the individuals involved are still different in many ways, and we never have an absolute match among group members. We may, however, find enough similarities to verify perceptions and form friendships and compatible interpersonal relationships. Even then, the general perception of one group may be quite different from the general perception of some other group.

Consensual Perception

When an entire group agrees about something, we say they have reached a *consensus.* If that agreement is a perception, we say they have a **consensual perception.** The larger the group of people with whom we have found a similar perception, the more convinced we are of the perception's accuracy.

We seek agreement in our perceptions. Long ago people living on a coastline watched ships go out to sea and "drop" over the horizon. Many people saw ships disappear, and based on their individual observations and similar observations by others, they arrived at a general agreement or consensual perception about the shape of the world. They

were certain the world was flat, and that ships venturing too far out to sea dropped over the edge. Now, since little was known about the nature of the oceans or of navigation, and even less was known about building ships to withstand the rigors of a journey on the high seas, many ships were lost at sea, and the lack of returning ships seemed to reinforce the general perception.

If you had lived in the twelfth century you would perhaps have arrived at the same conclusion through these perceptual steps.

Selection of Sensory Messages:

1. You _look_ at the ocean and the ocean _appears_ flat.
2. You _look_ at the ship and the ship appears to "go down" in the distance.
3. You _hear_ your friends say, "The earth is flat."

Organization:

1. You _enlarge to connect_ the ship's disappearance, the sea's appearance, and information about a "flat earth" into a whole meaning.
2. You sort information to _seek a reasoned explanation_ for a ship's disappearance.

Interpretation:

1. You _wish_ to "prove" your _belief,_ that the earth is flat.
2. You _imagine_ the ship dropping over the edge.
3. You _decide_ the earth is flat.

Perception is not always reality

Your conclusion would have matched the perceptions of people around you fairly well. The consensual perception did not reflect _reality,_ however. It offered a perceived reality, and the explorers who doubted the general perception of a flat world and set sail to test that conclusion were considered quite mad. Today, if we observe the same visual phenomenon of a ship's disappearing over the horizon, our past experiences with globes, maps, history, and the comings and goings of ships cause us to create an entirely different perceptual interpretation of the occurrence.

Consensual Reality

We tend to think of our worlds as being made up of objects that we all see and know alike. Each of us assumes his or her knowledge of things is accurate, and that the way we see and know those things is the way they "really are." But how can you know the room that seems uncomfortably cold to you *really is* colder than usual?

You make comparisons that can be called *reality checks*. You communicate your perception of cold to others, either verbally or nonverbally, and listen for feedback from them to know whether they, too, consider the room cold. If they do, you have what is called **consensual reality.** We "know" the room is cold because we all agree that it "really is." If we disagree, we persuade, instruct, research, compare, and contrast in search of agreement about the condition of the room.

Matching Perceptions

Developing compatible perceptions is a major purpose of interpersonal communication. Sometimes that purpose takes the form of *social communication,* an effort at matching perceptions about each other and our situations in order to establish human relationships. Sometimes the purpose becomes *instruction* or informative speaking—to give the listener a view of some part of the world as the instructor perceives it. Often the form is *persuasion*. In convincing or persuading another person of the rightness, the workability, or the appropriateness of a proposed change, we are attempting to alter that person's general three-staged perception to match our own.

We could even say that all the messages you send are about your perceptions of things, and that regardless of your subject, the underlying messages are always, "This is the way the world (or some small portion of the world) seems to me," and the literal or implied question, "How does the world (or some part of it) seem to you?" Even if a researcher is reading her scientific findings to other research scientists, she reports her perception of one tiny part of the world, as she has come to know it through the three-staged perceptual process of selection, organization, and interpretation.

**_Perception
Checks Improve
Communication_**

We have said that our perceptions of self, our current situations, and the other person or persons in those situations influence our communication. Your individual perception of the world around you is unique. It is your view of reality. If it is extremely different from the way other people perceive reality, your perception may become a communication barrier. While no two people have precisely the same perception of things and others, some matching should be possible.

The differences in our perceptions of situations or events, and our beliefs in the possibility of matching or unifying different perceptions, are the factors that motivate us to inform and persuade each other. We try over and over to convince our companions that things really _are_ as we perceive them, and they in turn try to convince us of the accuracy of their perceptions. Basically, different perceptions underlie political debates, family arguments, and friendly discussions. When mismatched perceptions go uncorrected, misunderstandings grow bigger, and sometimes embarrassing situations arise. Consequently, as we work to be more effective communicators, we should become skillful in checking our perceptions.

Steps in Matching Perceptions. Let's look at some steps we can follow. We have already suggested sharing personal perceptions as a step toward building meaningful relationships. Sharing views is also the first step in matching perceptions. If we never risk disclosing our views, we will probably never know whether or not they are held by others.

Pause often to clarify meanings, just to be sure both participants have similar perceptions. We call those pauses **perceptions checks.** Without them, we may not discover mismatched perceptions until problems occur. Sometimes it is helpful to use phrases such as, "What I hear you saying is . . . ," or "Do you mean . . . ," followed by a clarifying paraphrase of the other person's view.

Avoid jumping to conclusions. Instead of assuming that you and your friends have the same views of a situation, check with them. Try not to assume that you know why people behave as they do until you know more about the way _they_ view the situation. Also, avoid making judgments of others' motives and actions until you have time to know

Matching perceptions involves thoughtful, open communication.

more about their perceptions. Gathering more information about a situation often dispels conflict before it arises. Finally, in the process of matching perceptions, remember that *you* may need to adjust. Be willing to listen openly to the views of others and adjust as needed. Realize that none of us has totally accurate perception.

Checkpoint *What is a perception check? How can a perception check be used to avoid conflict?*

Summary

Perception is the process of noticing, organizing, and interpreting parts of the world around us. We base our selection of people and things we will notice on factors inside us, aspects of the situation we are in, and attributes of the person or object perceived. We give structure to what we have noticed by assuming some similarities among things perceived and by sorting them into categories. Perceptions are then interpreted and assigned meanings.

Our perception is limited by our five senses, and by psychological factors inside us. We assume others perceive as we do, and we compare our perceptions in an effort to bring our views of the world into agreement. When our perceptions match, we establish a consensual reality. Wh   our perceptions do not match, we inform and persuade each other to develop agreement.

Check Your Knowledge

1. List and describe the three stages of perception.
2. What factors cause an object to be noticed? Give examples.
3. Define stereotyping.
4. What is consensual perception?
5. What is a perception check?

Check Your Understanding

1. Most people rely more on some senses than on others. Do you? If so, which ones do you use most?
2. What do you notice first about a new person you meet?
3. What first causes you to decide you are going to like or dislike a new person?
4. How does stereotyping effect communication? Think of some common stereotypical descriptions of (a) cheerleaders (b) debaters (c) football players (d) computer experts.
5. Which senses do *you* use most when you are studying? Do you learn best by reading or hearing?
6. Can you recall a time when you had a conflict with someone because the two of you had different perceptions of a situation? How did you correct the problem?

7. How can you develop sensory perceptions of the following items? How many require the use of more than one sense?

an echo	a fish	a tree
an apple	a carpet	a stream
a passing train	a smoldering log	an elevator
a candle	a pizza	a towel

Check Your Skills

1. a) Have you ever been surprised to hear someone's perception of *you?* Did it match the way you perceive yourself? b) Describe yourself briefly to someone near you. Make a perception check by asking your partner to describe you as she or he perceives you. Compare your perceptions.

2. How do your ambitions and expectations of the future effect your present perception of a) school, b) leisure-time activities, c) relationships with your friends, and d) relationships with your family?

3. Do you remember meeting a new person you were "sure" you weren't going to like, and then changing your mind completely? Write a description of what happened. a) What were you using as the basis for your first judgment? Were you stereotyping? b) Why did you categorize the person as you did? c) What made you change your perception of the person?

4. Choose an object that interests you. a) Give a detailed description of the object. Include only sensory information. b) Now describe the psychological factors you think are influencing your perception of the object. c) Add to your description the perceptions from your past, present, and future expectations.

CHAPTER 5

Making Communication Choices

After reading this chapter, you should be able to:

1

Explain intrapersonal choice as the basis of all communication behavior.

2

Identify the basic needs represented in Maslow's hierarchy and relate them to communication.

3

Identify four basic categories of values and explain their role in advertising, public issues, and conflict.

4

Explain the concept of ethics.

5

Describe characteristics of ethical and unethical behavior.

Needs

Hierarchy of needs

Value

Priorities

Experience

Attitudes

Ethics

Dilemma

The characteristics of effective communication (openness, equality, empathy, supportiveness, and positiveness) apply directly to the process of making choices for interaction. Such processes include the intrapersonal communication processes of sensory perception, decoding and encoding messages, and filtering and interpreting messages. Self-concept and perception are also vital to processing and making effective choices. ''Self-talk'' has a direct influence on making choices.

Additional factors that influence communication choices are our interpersonal needs, our values and priorities, and our ethical considerations. *Needs* refer to innate human drives that are often satisfied through interaction with others. *Values* are acquired through experiences and reflect our basic beliefs and priorities. *Ethics* refers to our code or system for making choices relating to intrapersonal, interpersonal, and public communication. Our ethics reflect our standards for interaction with ourselves and with others.

Choosing becomes the basis for all communication interaction on every level, from intrapersonal to interpersonal to public communication. When we become more aware of our choices, apply criteria for measuring the appropriateness of our choices, and assume the responsibility for our choices, we can improve our skills in sending and receiving messages.

Understanding Needs

''No man is an island, entire of itself; every man is a piece of the continent, a part of the main; . . .'' (John Donne, *Devotions* XII)

One of the most difficult things to say is ''I need . . .'' ''I need you!'' ''I need help!'' ''I need to get away!'' ''I need a break!'' Yet all of us have needs. **Needs** are innate human drives. It is natural to reach out to interact with others to meet those needs because, in many instances, we are incapable of meeting needs by ourselves. The first step to formulating appropriate choices based on needs is to recognize needs as needs.

We already understand that communication is practical: We communicate when we need to communicate. Interpersonal needs can only be met through interaction with others.

We speak when we need to speak and we listen when we need to listen. We bargain or negotiate with others to ensure that our needs are met.

Identifying Needs

One popular source for identifying needs is Abraham Maslow's **hierarchy of needs.** You may have studied these needs in a social studies class, but you may not have focused on using these needs as a means to determine your personal communication choices.

When we try to identify our needs and their various levels, it sometimes helps to picture them as a pyramid, just as Maslow did when he developed his hierarchy. Each type of need combines to form the whole, with survival needs at the base of the pyramid. When your needs are met at the basic level, you are free to consider your higher needs such as security and esteem. Finally, when all of the more essential needs are met (even to the point of being sure we have the respect of others) we are free to pursue self-actualization. At this level, we can discuss philosophical ideas or engage in creative activities. We can share our interests and thoughts with friends without having other needs dictate what we should say to make us sound clever, gain prestige, or bring us social, financial, and academic rewards.

Maslow's Hierarchy of
Needs

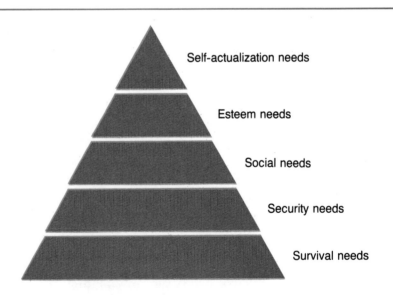

*Survival
needs*

The basic need is survival. Ultimately, this is the strongest of all needs. We can understand that if we were faced with a life-or-death situation, we would have little time or energy for other needs. Primitive people battled the elements and wild beasts merely to survive. Today, however, when our survival is threatened, we may call a police officer, firefighter, or paramedic to help us meet this need.

*Security
and social
needs*

Security needs replace survival needs as we cease to feel the anxiety of life-threatening events. Adequate food (more than just enough to survive), shelter, clothing, transportation, and other "necessities" help us to feel more comfortable and secure. Once these needs are met, we begin to feel a need for belonging or for meaningful relationships. Friends and family meet our important social needs.

*Esteem
needs*

The fourth level in Maslow's hierarchy is the need for esteem. We all would like to be recognized and respected. We may choose to run for a school or class office. We may become involved in committee or group functions and enjoy leadership roles. Sometimes in meeting esteem needs, we must sacrifice security and social ties.

*Self-
actualization
needs*

The fifth level of need is self-actualization. The self-actualized, free state can be a kind of goal for communication students. Actualization, however, results from experience, maturity, insight, and from intensified effort to know ourselves and become aware of the consequences of our choices. Self-actualization comes when we know who we are, what our goals are (in every sense), and when we are willing to accept the responsibility for our choices.

We must be aware of our needs at any given moment so that we can make effective communication choices. When we choose one thing, we eliminate others, and we must accept the responsibility for our choices. If we need security, our relationships may suffer. If our social needs are important to us, material concerns may be diminished.

**Applying
Needs to
Communication**

Once we have identified our needs, we have to determine how they relate to communication. At any given time, our responses to our needs shift and change, depending on our perceptions of the strength of those needs.

We respond to needs in making communication choices. When we seek friends or communicate love to our families,

Public speaking experiences may meet esteem needs.

we do so partly in response to our social needs. When we give speeches or run for school offices, we respond to our esteem needs. When we communicate to resolve conflict, we may be responding to social or self-actualization needs.

When we become aware of our needs and how they influence our communication, we can make choices to improve our effectiveness in communicating to meet our needs. Our responses to our needs are important motivators in our communication.

Some questions that can help you become aware of the role needs play in your communication include:

1. Where am I on Maslow's hierarchy right now?

2. What do I really need? What conditions account for these needs?

3. Do I need assistance in meeting my needs? Who can assist me? What communication choices can I make to get assistance?

4. In asking for assistance, what do I have to gain? What do I have to lose?

5. If my needs cannot be met, what are my alternatives?

6. If my needs are met, what happens next?

Checkpoint

Alan is meeting with his boss, Teresa. Teresa asks him for his honest opinion about a new policy she has designed. Alan personally disagrees with the policy, but must make a communication choice based on his own needs and an awareness of what Teresa's needs might be. What needs may be present in this situation? How might Alan phrase his response to Teresa to satisfy his own needs? Can he satisfy Teresa's needs as well?

Understanding Values and Priorities

Communication choices are frequently based on values and priorities. Even though the word **value** represents a complex concept, it can be defined as a personal evaluation of various beliefs according to their importance or worth. **Priorities** reflect the degree of importance that individuals attach to a particular value.

For example, you may "value" making good grades in school and work hard to achieve them. On the other hand, you may attach more importance to spending time with a hobby or job you also value. The hobby or job may take priority over studying. Both values are important, but one is, at least for the moment, more important to you than the other. Values encompass our beliefs, goals, and objectives. Priorities apply to the ranking of choices, goals, or objectives in order of their importance at a given time. The messages we send in our personal and public communication reflect our values and priorities.

Classifying Values

Because values are personal, no single list of values will be common to all of us. However, four major categories of values—moral values, social values, individual values, and practical values—are common to most people. These categories can be conveniently used to consider how personal values can influence communication. It is important to remember that some values may fall into two or more of these categories. Sometimes the priority we place on a value influences the way in which it might be categorized.

Moral values

Moral values provide a basis for making communication choices. Included in this category are our beliefs and principles concerning what is "right" and "wrong" in behavior and communication. Cultural or religious heritage, for example, may provide a foundation for our views of what is moral or right and what is immoral or wrong.

Social values

Social values include values related to people and to our interactions with others. Interpersonal relationships and the worth we attach to these relationships reflect social values. On the public level, we concern ourselves with issues that affect the general welfare of humanity. We may take stands on ecological issues or nuclear weapons because of our concern for people in general or for society as a whole. We may communicate support for school, civic, or patriotic activities because we value the group, the community, or the people from our state or nation.

Individual values

Individual values may strongly influence our communication choices. "I have my rights!" and "You can't do that to me!" are statements that reflect values concerning the worth and dignity of the individual. We may take stands

Social values
influence our
interpersonal
relationships.

on issues related to the belief in our own individuality or to the belief in the protection of the rights of others.

Practical values may also serve as a basis for making choices. Many individuals place priority on being efficient, thrifty, or healthy. People save money and organize their time. Some people take pride in keeping their property in clean, tidy order or in good repair. People eat nourishing food, get plenty of exercise and rest, and practice good hygiene in order to keep their bodies healthy and in good condition. People may value education and learning as a practical means to an end, implying personal reward or accomplishment.

Practical values

Values and priorities provide a basis for intrapersonal choice and, to a large extent, fashion our lifestyles. It becomes important, therefore, for us to realize the impact of value choices and to develop awareness of the role values and priorities play in interpersonal, group, and public communication.

Analyzing Values and Priorities

Unlike needs, which seem to be innate, values and priorities are acquired from a variety of sources. They seem to stem directly from our experiences, and they relate directly to our communication and interaction with others. Basically,

experience is made up of a stimulus plus a response. If it were a mathematical formula, it would look like this:

$$(S + R) = E.$$

Attitudes, in turn, result from a series of experiences. If our self-talk tells us an experience is positive, our attitude is likely to be positive. If self-talk tells us an experience is negative, our attitude may be negative.

In order to alter our values and priorities, our attitudes must change. Therefore, experiences must change. Experiences *do* change, of course. We grow older; we acquire more education; we leave home; we travel; we make new friends. All of these experiences influence our attitudes, which in turn influence our values and priorities.

Our values and priorities come from a variety of sources, and are influenced by our experience and communication with those sources. As our experiences accumulate and overlap, our priorities change. Our families are a principle source of our values and continue to influence them as we grow and change. Values and priorities are also influenced by people, organizations, cultural and religious heritage, and regional origin.

Applying Values to Communication Choices

It is important to realize the impact of values on our lives and our communication with others. We can develop an awareness of this impact when we understand that we become the product of our values and priorities, and that we should be willing to accept responsibility for them. An understanding of values and priorities can be applied to communication on all levels—intrapersonal, interpersonal, and public.

Intrapersonal Communication Choices

Even when you do something as simple as purchasing a tube of toothpaste, you are applying values to your communication choices. Consider Brand A. This toothpaste promises white teeth, fresh breath, and an attractive smile. Brand B offers healthier gums and cleaner teeth. Cavities will become a thing of the past. Think of the money you will save with fewer dentist bills!

Brand C is on sale. It makes no real claims, but look at that huge tube for a cheaper price! After all, toothpaste is toothpaste. Brand D has stripes. One stripe is for a sparkling smile and fresh breath, one is for cleaner teeth and elimination of gum problems, and one is for stain removal. Brand D is more expensive than the other brands.

You stand at the toothpaste counter as a receiver/sender who will now provide a response to these four messages. Which brand will you buy? Some of the messages were designed to appeal to your social values (being clean, being socially acceptable); others were meant to appeal to your individual values (being attractive and healthy); and others were meant to appeal to your practical values (saving money). Your intrapersonal choice will reflect which of these values has priority to you at the moment.

Values may cause intrapersonal conflict. If we hold two strong values that are of similar priority, conflict can occur. If we work all summer to save money (practical value), we may then have to decide whether to buy new clothes for the school term (individual value) or to spend the money to do fun things with our friends (social value). We make decisions and choices to resolve intrapersonal conflict.

Interpersonal Communication Choices

We make choices based on values and priorities when we decide how and when to communicate with our friends, family members, and others. We may want to be popular and part of a certain crowd or group. Therefore, we try to communicate in a way that is acceptable and pleasing to others in that group.

If we place priority on a relationship with a friend or family member (social value), we may sacrifice our own wishes (individual value) to protect the relationship and please the other individual. We place more priority on the social value than on the individual value at that time.

Understanding values and priorities can be useful in communicating to resolve interpersonal conflict. Often, two people may share a value but place different priorities on the value. Through communication, each person can indicate an awareness of his or her personal values and priorities,

We make interpersonal communication choices when we interact with others in school, work, and social groups.

We can express our public communication choices through voting.

and can learn about the values and priorities of the other individual. They can then make choices that help to resolve interpersonal conflict.

Public Communication Choices

Values and priorities influence the stands we take on public issues. Arguments concerning public issues that are addressed in public speaking and debate often stem from value assumptions and priorities. Understanding the role of values in public communication is essential to understanding the democratic process. Because of who we are, the groups in which we are involved, or the way we are affected by economic conditions, ecological issues, or social pressures, we take stands on public issues.

Farmers may argue for an increase in prices for farm products, while consumers may argue for lower prices. Students may prefer a relaxed dress code; teachers may prefer stricter rules. The values and priorities underlying these communication choices can be related to the different perceptions and experiences of the people involved.

Making Choices

Several steps can be taken in applying our insights about our values to making effective communication choices. First, of course, we should carefully consider our needs, values, and priorities so that we can determine what our real desires and goals are. ("What do I want? Why do I want it?") Second, consider the possible short-term and long-term consequences of your choices. Third, determine whether or not you are willing to assume the responsibility for your choices and their possible consequences.

Fourth, ask yourself whether or not you are willing to support your value choices consistently or systematically. Defending values can be compared to dieting. Unless you are willing to form a plan and follow it consistently, you may not realize the results you want.

Fifth, as a final step, take the precaution of asking yourself "Is this really a priority?" and "Have I made my choice after considering the alternatives, rewards, and consequences?'' You may find it useful to consider whether or not a priority is worth taking a public stand on, or if you feel you can take action to implement your choice. It is one thing to say you are in favor of something, and quite another to take action on it. You may say, ''I believe we should do something about litter and abuse of school property.'' It is another thing entirely to form a committee and organize a clean-up campaign.

Checkpoint *Find a magazine and select three advertisements in which you can see a clear appeal to moral, social, individual, or practical values.*

Developing Ethical Standards

"This above all: to thine own self be true,
And it must follow, as the night the day,
Thou canst not then be false to any man."
(Wm. Shakespeare, *Hamlet,* Act I, Sc. 3)

The term *ethics* is sometimes associated with moral practices and behavior; however, we are going to use the term in a more specific manner to apply to communication behavior.

In order to understand the concepts of ethics, ethical choices, and ethical communication interaction, we will first examine the Greek concept of *ethos.* Aristotle used ethos to describe the image a speaker presents to an audience. Aristotle believed that to be an effective persuasive communicator, a speaker should have sound qualifications and a knowledge of his or her topic. The speaker should also possess competence, or be capable of making and rendering the judgments given. Speakers should also be of good character and of good intent. Good character implies openness and honesty, while good intent implies fair play, concern, and consideration for the audience to be addressed. **Ethics**—as a derivative of ethos—can be defined as a code or system of choices and behaviors through which we communicate with others.

Ethos

Ethical communication involves being knowledgeable about our choices and actions. Ethics also implies making choices and expressing opinions only in areas we are capable

Ethical communication is usually effective communication.

Ethical choices

of assessing. Ethical choices are first of all free choices. In a democratic system, individuals have the right to determine their own destiny and to make choices for themselves. Second, free choice—in order to be effective—should be informed choice. When we make choices, we want free access to complete, accurate, unbiased information to use as the basis for those choices. Access to information is essential for truly ethical communication behavior.

Ethical intrapersonal and interpersonal communication is rooted in the belief that every individual has dignity and worth. Choices on the intrapersonal level begin with being true to ourselves as persons of worth and dignity. Ethical intrapersonal choices are based on positive self-concepts, realistic perceptions, an understanding of personal needs, and a clear understanding of personal values and priorities. Ethical intrapersonal choices also imply making informed choices for which we are willing to assume responsibility.

Unethical communication

Interpersonal communication is ethical to the extent that it protects others' rights to gain accurate information to use as a basis for their choices. Communication is *unethical* when it interferes with other individuals' freedom of choice by denying them access to information. Unethical communication either forces others to make choices they would not normally make, or forces others to decline to make choices they would normally make. Our communication is ethical to the extent that we guarantee others the same right to make free, informed choices we would like for ourselves.

You are going to buy a new computer. You want to know exactly what you will get for your investment. You have questions about the operation of a particular unit. You want to know about any optional equipment, special features, software, and service. In other words, you want the facts— all of them—so you have complete and accurate information upon which to base your choice. If information is withheld just to make a sale—for example, if this particular unit were about to be discontinued—you would probably consider the salesperson to be unethical.

In summary, several behaviors can be found in the ethical communicator. As senders of messages, we should assume the responsibility for the messages we send. This implies that we should have a knowledge of our statements so that we can answer questions and support our statements with facts. Ethical communicators present fact and opinion fairly, and not only tolerate but encourage alternative views. Such diversity is essential to the democratic process.

*Ethical
behaviors*

Recognizing Unethical Behavior

On the intrapersonal level, choices based on insufficient information or without careful consideration of needs, values, and priorities can be unethical. Such choices are frequently made in haste and may not be in our best interests.

In interpersonal communication, withholding information in order to influence another person's choice is unethical, as is distorting information by exaggerating or minimizing facts. Lying is unethical because it gives others a false basis for making their choices. Failing to take a stand on issues that affect you may be unethical because you are not being fair or honest with yourself or with others. Letting others come to harm when we can prevent it is unethical (as well as irresponsible).

Examples of unethical behaviors used in public communication include the presentation of false or distorted claims and the excessive use of emotional appeals. Negative appeals such as fear, hate, and prejudice may indicate that a speaker is trying to gain acceptance of his or her ideas without using proper logical reasoning.

Recognizing Barriers to Ethical Choices

Ethical interaction suggests that making open, honest choices would benefit everyone. Such choices lie at the very heart of our democratic system of government. Why then are we not always ethical?

Lack of Assertiveness   Sometimes we simply lack the confidence to take a stand on our own behalf or for others. The choice not to act on important matters may, in this instance, be unethical. Have you ever agonized over not saying what you thought when it was important? Have you ever regretted letting others "run over you" and make choices for you instead of standing up for what you believed was right? Were you in these instances being fair or ethical with yourself.

Defensiveness   When we become concerned about the actions of others and how they may affect us, we may react defensively. We adopt an attitude of "Do unto others *before* they can do unto you!" When self-talk tells us that others do not have regard for our interests or that someone intends to harm us, we may respond unethically. "After all, if he's double-dealing, why shouldn't I?" "What is fair for one is fair for another!" "All's fair in love and war!"

Defensive communication can be unethical when we withhold information or otherwise attempt to influence the rights of others. Defensive communication is usually less open and honest than ethical communication, because we feel we must protect ourselves. We may end up in a communication situation that is not effective, productive, or pleasant.

Competitiveness   Despite the fact that we are taught that competition is beneficial, it can be harmful to human relationships because it might undermine trust. Trust is essential to effective ethical interaction. If you and your best friend both become interested in running for president of the student body, you may find your relationship in jeopardy.

Competitiveness
influences
communication
choices.

Jealousies may appear; loyalties of mutual friends may be divided. Trust is diminished. You may begin to employ unethical tactics in relating to each other.

We are often surprised after competing against a team from a rival school to find out that a member of that team is someone we can like. He or she seems different as an individual from the way he or she appeared in the competitive arena of athletics.

Businesses sometimes resort to unethical advertising to compete with their rivals for your dollar. Nations may be suspicious of one another and cannot reach ethical agreements because their competitiveness prevents mutual trust. Competitive communication is usually self-defeating and destructive. Despite the many benefits of competition, we must approach it very carefully to avoid unethical communication.

Making Ethical Choices

Being true to themselves and to others is not always easy for people to do. People are frequently caught in ethical dilemmas that can present almost unsolvable situations. A **dilemma** is a situation in which someone cannot find a desirable or acceptable solution. Individuals are frequently caught in the dilemma of what they *want* to do and what they *should* do. People are also caught in ethical dilemmas when they confront what is good for them in contrast with what may be good for someone else who will be affected by their choices.

We can consider two levels of ethical choice. Are people being ethical with themselves when they compromise their values, goals, or beliefs and make self-defeating choices? And are people ethical with others when they make choices from which they will benefit at someone else's expense? Let's consider some examples of ethical dilemmas.

Rick's best friend is the victim of gossip being spread by a third mutual friend. The gossip is damaging, and his friend is unaware of the rumors. Rick knows his friend would be terribly hurt on being told of the gossip and its source. On the other hand, his friend will be equally hurt upon finding out about the rumors and Rick's role in concealing them. Either way, Rick feels he will betray one friend or the other.

Eva has a quiz in English. It is important that she makes a good grade, but she has no time to study. A friend tells Eva that her teacher usually gives the same test on that particular unit each year. Eva's friend scored "100" on the test last year and still has a copy of the test. Eva may borrow the copy.

Myong is running for student council, and is to make a speech to a group of her classmates. Getting their votes is critical to Myong's election. She knows that her position on a particular issue is different from theirs. She knows that if she is elected, she could not favor her classmates' position personally. Myong's choice is to support the position of her constituents and compromise her own values, or to defend her own moral and ethical position and not support her classmates' stand on the issue. Myong is aware that she will be asked about this particular issue and the stand she will take.

In each of these dilemmas, individuals must make ethical choices. The individuals must consider what they *want* to do and what they *should* do. People should try to consider their own ethical standards in making difficult communication choices.

Checkpoint Consider Aristotle's concept of *ethos*. Why is it important for public speakers to behave ethically? Can you think of a speaker in your experience who demonstrates ethos?

Summary

The effectiveness of our communication depends on the choices we make. Therefore, choice is the basis for interaction. Once we are aware of our options and the choices that are available to us, our communication should improve.

Some of the choices we make depend on our needs. Most of our personal needs must be recognized on an intrapersonal level before they can be satisfied. Very few of these needs can be met, however, without the assistance of others. Survival, security, and social needs are usually realized on an interpersonal level, through interaction with others. Esteem needs are most commonly met through public communication.

Values and priorities also affect our communication choices. Once formed by our experiences and attitudes, our values influence those with whom we choose to communicate and what we choose to communicate. The priority we place on a specific value will direct whether we defend it on an intrapersonal, interpersonal, or public level.

Ethical considerations also affect our communication choices. Intrapersonal communication is ethical when—after considering your own self-concept, perceptions, needs, and values—you remain true to yourself. Our interpersonal communication is ethical when we protect the rights of others to accurate information and freedom of choice. Ethical public communication is an extension of ethical interpersonal communication. We should be well informed about any statements we make and accept the responsibility for them.

Any choices we make that affect our communication should be conscious, informed choices. We owe it to ourselves as well as to the others involved in the interaction.

Check Your Knowledge

1. Identify and define the needs represented in Maslow's hierarchy.

2. Identify four value clusters that form a basis for intrapersonal, interpersonal, and public communication.

3. What are two criteria for ethical communication?

4. What are three types of unethical communication?

5. What are three barriers to ethical communication?

6. What factors usually account for ethical dilemmas?

Check Your Understanding

1. Explain choice as the basis for all communication behavior.

2. How do needs influence communication choices?

3. Explain how value appeals are used in advertising.

4. What role do values and priorities play in intrapersonal, interpersonal, and public communication?

5. Why is lying an unethical communication behavior?

6. Explain the relationship between openness as a characteristic of ethical communication and lack of assertiveness as a barrier to ethical communication.

7. Apply Shakespeare's quotation to the criteria for ethical communication.

Check Your Skills

Henry and Elaine are out with some people they really admire. They would like to be accepted into the group. The group wants to have a party at the home of a member whose parents are out of town. Henry and Elaine feel uneasy about the plan, but they know that if they disagree, they will not be accepted by the group. Henry and Elaine must make some communication choices.

1. Brainstorm with a classmate about the process Henry and Elaine might go through in making their choices.

What are the possible needs, values, priorities, and ethical issues present in their situation? How do they relate to communication?

2. Write a script for the dialogue between Henry and Elaine as they make their choices.

3. Write a script for Henry and Elaine to use in communicating their choices to the members of the group.

Mass Communication and Mass Media

Mass communication occurs through print and/or electronic *media* instead of directly between people. The word *medium* connotes a channel, or means, of transmitting messages. The media of mass communication include magazines, newspapers, books, films, recordings, radio, and television. They bring us up-to-the-minute news stories from around the world, foreign literature and films, and coverage of sports, cultural, and social events. We expect our mass media to inform and entertain us.

The nature of mass communication and its effect on society is an important area of study. Research helps us to understand the differences between mass communication and other levels of communication, and the enormous force that the media are in our lives.

In mass communication, feedback is always provided less directly than in other levels of communication. There is a distance between the senders and the receivers. Because of the separation, feedback is not immediately provided to the message senders. Eventually, television and radio stations receive feedback in the form of ratings; recording studios and publishers receive feedback in the form of sales figures. The message senders then respond to the feedback, over distance and time, as the communication process continues.

As consumers of the media, we choose whether or not to receive a message and we choose how much attention to give to it. In our own homes, we can decide to leave the room briefly or permanently without being rude to the cast of the television drama. In direct communication among people, you cannot exercise a similar kind of control over the communication process.

The mass media are used more than any other communication channel to persuade listeners. Think of the advertising that you encounter daily in the press and on television. Advertising is big business and supports the ongoing operation of most media. Because of the enormous impact of advertising on our world, it is important that you use everything you know about communication to evaluate the appeals that are made through the media.

The mass media do not have the same effect on everyone. Each of us responds to communication according to our own perceptions and our own self-concept. The mass media are different from other forms of communication. Understanding them and their potential effect allows us to be more informed decision makers and more effective communicators in our roles as students, friends, workers, and citizens.

TOWARD EFFECTIVE
Interaction

Part

3

Senders and receivers exchange messages in a variety of ways to carry on interpersonal communication, one of life's most dynamic activities. Nonverbal messages are seen and heard in a person's appearance, movement, and voice. Verbal messages are made up of words, and so effective speaking involves making effective language choices. Skills in listening can be developed along with speaking skills. Both speaking and listening are most effective when they are appropriate to the communicators and to the context of the message.

Skills in nonverbal communication, making language choices, listening actively, and providing appropriate feedback are essential to the communication process. In this Part, we will look at ways to develop these important skills and how to apply them to effective communication in personal and public relationships.

CHAPTER 6

Using Nonverbal Communication Skills

After reading this chapter, you should be able to:

1

Define nonverbal communication and explain its importance.

2

Describe nonverbal communication as message about message.

3

Explain the kinds of silent messages and their impact on communication.

4

Describe how sound is used as nonverbal communication.

5

Explain the concept of voice as nonverbal communication.

6

Explain paralinguistic cues and their influence on messages.

7

Describe how nonverbal communication can create a barrier.

Key Terms

Nonverbal communication
Silent language
Sound language
Silent cues
Sound cues
Paralinguistic cues
Respiration
Phonation
Resonation
Articulation

What do you think of when you think of nonverbal communication? You probably think of body language, because you have read about messages sent by crossed arms, crossed legs, and hands on hips. Body language is an important aspect of nonverbal communication, but there are many other types of nonverbal communication.

Understanding Nonverbal Communication

We define **nonverbal communication** as all communication behavior *other than* speech. Nonverbal behavior can be divided into two general categories: the language of silence and the language of sound. **Silent language** includes all behaviors or messages that are transmitted silently and are acquired through sight, touch, smell, or subconscious processes. **Sound language** includes all messages or behaviors that are transmitted by sound and are acquired through hearing. Language is *not* part of nonverbal communication.

The Significance of Nonverbal Communication

It would be difficult to overestimate the importance of nonverbal communication. Studies indicate that approximately 90 percent of what we communicate is nonverbal. We tend to react first to what we see (silent language), then to what we hear (sound language), and, finally, to what we understand (verbal language). The old adage "actions speak louder than words" definitely seems to be true.

A second observation on the importance of nonverbal communication is that nonverbal messages are generally *believed*. For example, when we send conflicting messages (when our words say one thing and our body and voice say another), the receiver is apt to discard the verbal message and believe the nonverbal message.

What nonverbal messages are these people sending?

*Conflicting
messages*

A three-year-old watches as his father assembles a rocking chair just purchased for the child. The little boy reaches for a screwdriver, which the father quickly retrieves. "Sit right there and watch while I fix your chair, but don't bother my tools!" Simple instructions—but the voice is harsh and commanding, and the father's face is hard and contorted. The little boy, with the astuteness and sensitivity of the very young, looks at a visitor and announces: "My father is angry with me." Anger is what the child receives as message—not hearing the words, but instead responding to the nonverbal cues given in the father's voice and facial expression.

A teacher reprimands someone for misbehaving in class, warning of the consequences of repeating the behavior, but the teacher is smiling and relaxed, and her voice is soft and friendly. What message is received from the conflicting cues? If we are given a choice between what we see and what we hear, we probably will choose to believe what we see!

*Ongoing
communication*

A third reason to support the claim that nonverbal behavior is important to our effectiveness as communicators is that nonverbal behavior *always* communicates. This is significant, since we spend so little time really thinking about all the aspects of our nonverbal behavior. Whether we intend to send nonverbal messages or not, others observe and, consciously or subconsciously, assign meaning to our actions.

Just as significant is the observation that each of us is probably assigning meaning to the nonverbal behavior of those around us right now! We may be totally unaware of the fact that we are processing and interpreting nonverbal cues and recording them as fact (*and* we may or may not be correct in our assessments).

Let's analyze the following scene: Someone walks into a classroom, chooses a seat on the back row, noisily lays down her books, and slumps into the chair. She may not mean anything by her behavior. She may be tired; she may not feel well; she may be upset by something that happened during her previous class. The teacher, however, may observe the behavior and assign the meaning that the student is uninterested in the class or that she is belligerent. Other students may be confused by her actions and may be thinking, "Hey, what's wrong with you?" Nonverbal messages may or may not be intentional, but meaning will be assigned by observers who may or may not be correct.

The real significance of nonverbal communication lies in the fact that it affects relationships. As we begin to understand the impact of nonverbal behavior on our messages, we can begin to understand why we choose to be around people whose behavior we find pleasing. People whose nonverbal cues we perceive as ''relaxed'' make us comfortable. People whose nonverbal cues scream ''tense'' make us uneasy. Those whose nonverbal cues say, ''Hey, I like you!'' are perceived as friendly; those whose cues indicate avoidance, we might leave alone.

Nonverbal Communication and Barriers

Nonverbal cues can reinforce, distort, or present barriers to effective communication. Nonverbal cues can support verbal messages when verbal, silent, and vocal messages say the same thing. Nonverbal cues can distort or contradict verbal messages, too. If your body sends one signal, your voice another, and your speech still another, your nonverbal cues can present communication barriers.

Sometimes, cultural differences influence nonverbal communication and result in barriers. A person from a culture that often communicates by touch may be confused by a person from a culture that limits touching to close relationships. A person who is brought up to understand that eye contact is an important aspect of sincerity may be uncomfortable with someone who has learned to lower his or her eyes to indicate respect.

Stereotyping and prejudice can influence our reactions to nonverbal cues. We should be aware of our preconceptions. Considering nonverbal behavior in light of a person's background is important to effective communication. Stereotypes can develop by observing physical characteristics and nonverbal cues and then leaping to conclusions about an individual. Concluding that carrying a briefcase equals businessperson equals wealthy is an example of stereotyping, which is a barrier to nonverbal communication.

Checkpoint *Why is it important that attorneys are able to reject potential jurors who might be prejudiced against the defendant in a court of law?*

The Nature of Nonverbal Communication

Another way to understand nonverbal behavior is to think of it as message about message. As you may remember from earlier reading, the sender—to the best of his or her ability—may initiate and transmit an intended message to the receiver. The receiver filters and interprets the message, and _then_ determines the meaning of the message that is received. Unless the receiver is skilled at sorting out levels of message, nonverbal cues may dominate the assigned meaning.

Facial expression, eye contact, body tone and tension, voice, touch, and "spatial communication" all convey how we feel about the people with whom we are speaking. Thus the relationship component of message is often communicated nonverbally. We may say something as simple as "Would you close the door?" but how we sound and how we look implies message about message, and influences the meaning assigned to the intended message. When assigning meanings to nonverbal behavior, we should also remember that meanings are highly related to context.

Imagine that you are walking down the hall of your school and you meet an attractive new student who has just enrolled in your history class. She sat on the third row and answered most of the questions the teacher asked her. She has also admitted to being on the debate team at the school she previously attended. You muster your cheeriest voice and greet her with an enthusiastic "Hi!" as she approaches. However, she ignores you, turns away, and walks on. "That snob!" may be your response.

Now imagine you are walking down the hall of your school and you meet a person who sits on the back row of your history class. He doesn't talk much in class and, to the best of your knowledge, doesn't participate in school activities. Deciding to be friendly, you muster your best smile and in your cheeriest voice greet him with an enthusiastic "Hello!" as you approach. He ignores you, turns away, and walks on. Your response may be, "How painful it must be to be so shy!"

These are two identical situations, yet you may assign different meanings to them based on perceptions you have already formed about the people involved.

Understanding that nonverbal communication is learned behavior, which is acquired by imitating the people we are

By changing our nonverbal messages, we can make very different first impressions.

around the most, often helps us to understand its personal and cultural aspects. The messages we send and receive are highly personal because each of us is unique. We have each acquired our nonverbal habits and mannerisms through our unique experiences and interactions with others. Family, friends, and people we admire influence our nonverbal communication the most. Mothers and daughters frequently have the same vocal characteristics. In fact, some callers may have difficulty identifying each on the telephone. A small boy may stand with both hands in his hip pockets just as Dad does. Many high-school students adjust their nonverbal behavior to be like their peers.

Cultural aspects of nonverbal communication may account for the fact that the open nonverbal expression of someone from one part of the country may seem rude to someone from a more "reserved" region. Likewise, the clothing of some young people may be offensive to older individuals. In many ways, nonverbal behavior may enhance our social relationships or may, on the other hand, present barriers to effective communication.

Nonverbal communication is both highly personal and strongly related to the situation.

Checkpoint _Try to think of an instance when your initial impression of someone changed. What nonverbal cues possibly influenced your first impression? What nonverbal behavior possibly caused your impression to change?_

Understanding the Language of Silence

Silent language has many components. A number of **silent cues** influence communication. A person's general appearance, as reflected by dress and grooming, is assigned meaning by others. We are labeled by what we wear, how we style our hair, and how neat or disheveled we appear to be.

Posture also sends messages. The position of someone's body (standing, sitting, slouching, slumping, squatting, reclining) tells others about his or her attitude and relationship to a situation or to the surroundings. An erect body is "read" as an alert body. Slumped posture, on the other hand, may suggest disinterest, illness, or dullness.

Movement—a change of position from one space to another—conveys meaning. How we walk (the rate, intensity, and directness) will be assigned meaning. Running implies rushing; strolling implies leisure. _Gesture_ is a movement of the body that supports, reinforces, or indicates meaning. It is important to note that gesture is a movement of the entire body rather than a movement of an isolated part of the body, because the body moves as a unit. A raised eyebrow, a shrug of the shoulders, a pointed finger, and a nod of the head are all gestures. Each is assigned meaning by others.

Posture, movement, and gesture are important aspects of silent language.

Facial expression has been indicated in some studies as the most important element of nonverbal communication. Even though, as just indicated, a raised eyebrow could be considered a gesture, facial expression merits a separate category. A smile, a frown, or a stare can outweigh dress, grooming, and posture in conveying the emotional or relationship dimension of message.

Facial expressions reflect the personal nature of nonverbal communication. What do you think each of these people is expressing?

Adults communicate a great deal to children with touch as well as eye contact.

Eye contact is an important element of nonverbal communication. A wink can emphasize a joke when it is well timed. A twinkling eye usually accompanies a warm greeting. We include or exclude others from our interactions with eye contact. Teachers use eye contact in the classroom to control activity. Eye contact, like other silent cues, is highly personal and cultural. Misunderstandings can occur when cultural expectations are not met.

The following chart gives examples of several other kinds of silent messages. You will see that a wide variety of behaviors can be interpreted as nonverbal message about message. All of these silent messages are perceived, interpreted, and assigned meaning. Our senses may be bombarded by many silent cues simultaneously.

Silent messages can be sent in a variety of ways.

Some Ways People Communicate Nonverbally

Body Tension and Movement (known as kinesics)
Examples: Tightened jaws, stiff shoulders may indicate anger or stress. Relaxed body may convey ease or comfort.

Spatial Relationships (known as proxemics)
Examples: American culture follows some general spatial guidelines.

Intimate distance—used for very private conversations and close relationships—6 inches to 18 inches
Personal distance—used for friendly conversations and relationships—2 feet to 4 feet
Social distance—used in public settings or in groups of friends—4 feet to 7 feet
Public distance—used in formal settings, public speaking, and presiding—12 feet to 15 feet

Touching (known as haptics)
Examples: Can be used for numerous purposes, such as in demonstrations of tenderness, affection, or approval. Can also be used for restraint or reprimand.

Objects
Examples: A businessperson carries a briefcase; a construction worker wears a hard hat. Others include sportscars, jewelry, furniture, books, houses.

Color
Examples: Kings wore purple to indicate royalty; red sometimes indicates anger or aggressiveness. Others include cheerful, bright surroundings or dull, dark places.

Time and how time is used (known as chronemics)
Examples: When a student says, "I didn't have time to do my assignment," the message may be, "I found something more important to do." When a clerk ignores someone to assist another customer, that person may feel slighted or unimportant.

Odor
Examples: Strong perfume can keep others from coming too close; a familiar smell (like that of a Thanksgiving turkey) can bring back memories of past holidays.

Checkpoint *Think about your teachers. How do they use the language of silence? Are there similarities and differences among your teachers?*

Understanding the Language of Sound

Close your eyes and concentrate on the sounds around you. You may become aware of sounds that provide an almost constant background for your daily activity. There may be the sound of traffic on the street outside—the screech of brakes or the squeal of tires. Somewhere, a locker door slams. The wind whistles around the corner of the building. Music is playing somewhere down the hall. There are voices: the commanding voice of the teacher across the hall; laughter from students outside the door; and maybe the voice of the person across the aisle.

Sound cues play important roles in our daily routines. Sound wakes us up in the morning when the alarm clock rings. Bells ring to summon us to answer the telephone or report to class. Chimes or knocks announce visitors at the door. Music "gets us going" and "calms us down." Sirens scream warnings. These sound cues, if noted, are assigned meaning depending on the context for communication.

In order to begin to understand sound, we should be able to identify the components of sound. *Pitch* is the highness or lowness of a sound on a musical scale. *Volume* is the loudness or softness of sound. *Duration* is the length in time of the sound unit. *Tone* is the quality of the sound as mellow, flat, thin, resonant, or metallic.

It would be impossible to assign meaning to every sound cue in the environment.

Remember those sounds you heard when you closed your eyes? The wind? The soft music? The alarm clock telling you to get up? How did those sounds make you feel? Not only are sounds assigned meaning, they also affect our mental and emotional state. Often the sounds we have been exposed to during the day account for the way we feel in the evening.

Think about pitch. Do you respond more favorably to high or low pitch? Do you prefer bass or treble? What about volume? How do you feel when sound is too loud or too soft? What is the effect of prolonged sound like the moaning of the wind? How do thin, metallic sounds affect you, compared to mellow, resonant sounds? Sound cues—like silent cues—affect our perceptions because we assign meanings and respond with our emotions.

Checkpoint   *Think about your favorite movie. How did the background music enhance the intensity of the mood or emotion?*

Voice as the Language of Sound

Many of us fail to separate voice from speech. *Voice,* however, is the medium for speech and is generally classified as a nonverbal mode of communication. Voices, like silent cues, give us message about message. Also, like sounds in general, the voices of the people around us have a direct impact on our emotions, perceptions, and responses.

The emotional dimensions of message are revealed through **paralinguistic cues.** (*Paralinguistic* means "along with language" or "accompanying language.") These cues include the various qualities of voice that convey direct or implied meanings and feelings along with the message.

Paralinguistic Cues

In order to work with our voices as receivers and senders of message, we need to become aware of paralinguistic cues. The sound of voices includes the pitch, volume, duration, and tone already mentioned. These qualities have additional meaning when applied to voice.

High *pitch* usually communicates surprise, excitement, or tension. Medium pitch is used in most ordinary conversations. Low pitch usually implies extreme emotion or a desire for seclusion or intimacy. Loud *volume* may indicate a desire to be noticed or excitement or urgency. Softness can imply courtesy and consideration. Soft volume may also indicate fatigue, illness, weakness, or a desire for privacy.

Prolonged *duration* may be a matter of regional dialect, or may indicate a desire for undisputed emphasis. A rapid succession of short, clipped sounds often communicates matter-of-factness or abruptness.

Tone is often an indicator of physical or emotional state. Hoarseness can indicate illness; harshness can indicate anger. Lightness or airiness can indicate happiness, and a mellow, rich tone can indicate emotional favor. Tone can also become a matter of subconscious imitation of the voices around us. Even though nasal tones may result from physical conditions, they can also be a reflection of regional vocal patterns.

Vocal characteristics can contribute to the impressions we have of people.

Because speech, like music, is fluid and continuing, it takes on additional paralinguistic qualities. *Rate* refers to how quickly or how slowly we speak. In other words, rate refers to the succession of sounds. Rapid speech may imply urgency or excitement. Slower speech may mean hesitancy, uncertainty, or apathy.

Force refers to the energy or intensity of the voice. Force can be a balancing factor to volume. Actors learn to project their voices, using energy and vocal power. They learn that yelling or shouting at an audience is not the same as using energy to project even a whisper. Interesting voices usually reflect energy and an enthusiasm motivated by a real desire to communicate.

Inflection is the rising and falling of the voice on the musical scale. A pattern of lively inflection or variation of pitch usually communicates enthusiasm. A monotone may indicate disinterest, dullness, or illness. Inflection seems to relate directly to force or energy. *Melody,* as in music, is a pattern of pitch, volume, and inflection. Melody sends messages about personality, mood, and attitude.

Resonance actually means "re-sounding" and, in the instance of voice, refers to the vocal variations reinforced by the resonating cavities of the chest and head. Resonant voices are usually described as deep and rich because of the amplification of tone. Resonant voices are also usually considered pleasant by listeners.

Pause can also be considered a paralinguistic cue because pause or lack of pause punctuates our speech. Pauses indicate grammatical structures such as sentences, phrases, or clauses. Pause—silence—can be used for special implied meanings or for dramatic impact.

Tempo is made up of rate, force, and pause. It may consist of accent and stress. Speech has accents, rests, and beat, just like music. Tempo, like melody, makes speech interesting and reflects personality and attitude.

Quality can be thought of as the unique characteristics of the individual voice. Quality is often used to describe the most noticeable characteristics of voice such as hoarse, feeble, husky, shrill, or nasal. The term can, in that instance, be interchanged with *tone* as described earlier.

Effective communicators "tune in" to sound. We can listen to ourselves and others, carefully noting how we sound, how others sound, and how we can modulate and improve our own voices.

The Steps of Voice Production

How is sound produced? How do we set vibrations in motion to produce sounds? To produce musical sound, we strike a bar or board with a hammer, we pluck a string or wire, we beat a drum, we strike a key on a piano, or we blow into the mouthpiece of a reed instrument. In each instance, an object is struck to set vibrations in motion that are amplified and projected to a receiver. These same steps are involved in the production of voice.

Respiration, or breathing, is the first step in voice production. We must breathe to speak. Air is inhaled into the lungs and exhaled with the power provided by the *diaphragm* (a muscle stretched across the chest cavity).

The anatomy of voice production.

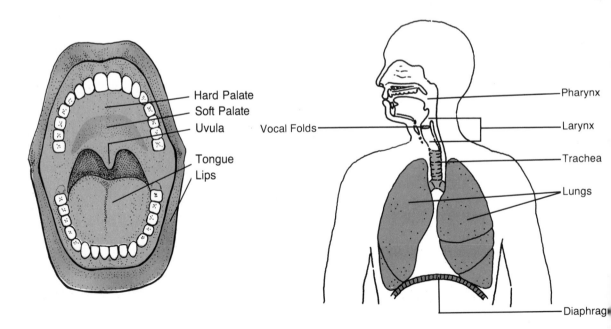

Phonation occurs with respiration. As air is exhaled, it passes through the vocal folds. As the air strikes these bands of tissue located in the larynx, they begin to vibrate and produce sound. These feeble sounds would hardly be recognized as voice.

Resonation is the next event in voice production. As the vibrations re-sound in the bony framework of the chest and head cavities, the sound is enriched and amplified. Think about what happens when a string is plucked on a guitar. The sound of a plucked string would be thin and feeble if it were not stretched across the wooden cavity of the guitar where re-sounding, or resonation, occurs. So it is with the respiration, phonation, and resonation steps of the vocal process.

A fourth step in the production of speech is **articulation** (the forming of speech sounds). The lips, tongue, gums, teeth, uvula, and the hard and soft palates serve as articulators, enabling us to shape sound into speech.

Checkpoint *Think about your favorite DJ. What vocal characteristics make him or her pleasurable to listen to? How are these characteristics different from those of other DJs in your area?*

Building Effective Nonverbal Skills

To promote effective nonverbal communication, you may apply a skill-building process. By observing others and monitoring your responses, you can set personal communication goals and take one step at a time toward achieving them.

Sending and Receiving Silent Messages

Seven steps can be used to improve sending and receiving of silent messages.

1. Observe the behavior of others.

2. Note your response to specific silent cues. How are you affected by gestures, touch, odor, and color?

3. Monitor your response carefully for accuracy. Compare the possibilities of the intended message to the meanings

you attach to the message. Ask yourself: "Is that what the person means to imply or is this meaning originating inside me?"

4. Begin to analyze your own silent behavior. What kind of feedback do you get from others? Are you pleased with this feedback? Is the feedback based on nonverbal cues? Does feedback indicate that your messages are clear or contradictory? Does feedback indicate that others accurately interpret your silent messages?

5. Set goals, and develop a model of the silent communicator you wish to become.

6. Take one step at a time. Establish priorities and start at the top. Are you friendly, sensitive, and caring? What silent behaviors denote these qualities? How can you adapt your behavior to send these messages to others?

7. Practice and be patient. Changing behaviors you have used for a long period of time is not easy. It takes time!

Sending and Receiving Vocal Messages

How do we develop flexible voices capable of expressing a wide variety of feelings? We do not sound to ourselves as we do to others. Since we are sensitive to the reverberations of sounds within the resonating cavities of our own bodies, our voices usually sound lower in pitch and richer in tone to us than to our listeners. You might exclaim, upon hearing your voice on a tape recorder for the first time, "That doesn't sound like me!"

Think about the phases of skill development for silent messages and begin to apply them to your vocal messages. Listen! Really tune into sounds and listen to the voices of those people around you. Note your responses to individual voices. Be aware of your perceptions and interpretations of oral cues and messages.

How do voices affect the meaning you assign to others and to their oral messages? Is the person who must always claim "center stage" by being loud just trying to get attention, insensitive, or disguising insecurity? How did you record this person's image and message—positive or negative? What about a person with a soft, unintelligible voice? Does the softness reflect shyness or sullenness or, perhaps, fear?

A tuning fork can be used to identify your natural pitch.

Listen again. Begin to construct a list of the vocal behaviors and characteristics you find pleasing. Also construct a list of the behaviors and characteristics you find annoying. Also listen to yourself. Really try to hear yourself! Select behaviors you want to adopt in order to communicate more effectively.

Take one step at a time. Establish priorities and start at the top! Decide to avoid being too loud, or to use enough force and volume to be heard and understood. Decide to get rid of a nasal "twang" or to develop more inflection. Remember to practice. There are vocal exercises to assist you. Use a tape recorder, and use feedback from others. Practice breathing exercises.

Remember, few people have physical vocal problems, and there are usually physicians and therapists available to those who do. Most of us simply have not yet learned to use our bodies like musical instruments to produce rich, pleasant voices capable of expressing a wide range of thoughts and feelings for interpersonal and public communication. But all of us *can* learn!

Checkpoint *While watching the news on television, note some of the silent cues used by the reporters. Then, with your eyes closed, listen for sound cues. How do these cues provide message about message?*

Summary

We usually process silent and vocal cues simultaneously, or in such rapid succession that we are unaware of separate cues. We normally react first to what we see (visual or silent cues) and then to what we hear (vocal or sound cues). If we like what we see and what we hear, we may listen to the words of the sender (verbal cues). If we don't like what we see or hear, we can easily "turn off" and block out the message. As receivers, we may not even be aware of the factors that play such a vital role in fashioning our perceptions of others. It is entirely possible for visual and vocal messages to conflict or contradict one another.

Public speakers consider how they look, how they stand, and how they move as well as how they use gestures, facial expressions, and eye contact to capture the attention and interest of their audiences. Speakers must speak clearly, distinctly, and articulately in order to be heard and understood. Speakers must also communicate in a sincere, enthusiastic manner to convey their messages.

The same criteria apply in interpersonal communication. When we "get our messages together," we present ourselves in the manner that we choose and to convey clear messages to others.

Check Your Knowledge

1. What are the various types of silent message?

2. What are the components of voice as nonverbal communication?

3. What are the components of sound as nonverbal communication?

4. How is voice produced?

5. What are some barriers to effective nonverbal communication?

Check Your Understanding

1. Why is nonverbal communication important in daily interactions?

2. How is sound used as communication?

3. Why is voice a form of nonverbal communication?

4. When Helen Keller was asked what sense she would have restored if only one could be restored, she chose her hearing. Why do you think she chose this sense over others?

5. Why might a rich, pleasant, sensitive voice contribute to professional success?

6. What is the impact of silent language?

7. Why do personal perceptions, cultural influences, and stereotyping present barriers to communication?

Check Your Skills

1. Analyze a relationship you might like to change in terms of silent language behaviors. Focus on your own behavior as well as the behavior of the other person or persons. Record your perceptions and construct a list of behaviors you could change to improve the relationship.

2. Keep a "sound log" for one day. List sounds you found to be pleasing, irritating, and so on. Try to analyze the components or qualities responsible for your responses.

3. Tape record a conversation or class discussion. List the qualities or characteristics you note for each voice. Cite your response to each.

4. Tape record your own voice in a variety of situations. List qualities that please you or displease you in each situation. Write goals for the improvement of your voice Use exercises from class activities to help you reach these goals.

CHAPTER 7

Using Language Skills

After reading this chapter, you should be able to:

1

Define language.

2

List and define the four components of language.

3

Define four common terms used to describe speech sound.

4

Explain the four criteria for determining language appropriateness.

5

Explain the concept of language repertoire.

6

Describe the five language functions as a part of repertoire.

7

Explain the six levels of language usage.

Denotation
Connotation
Diction
Articulation
Formal usage
Standard usage
Informal language
Colloquial usage
Temporal language
Slang
Jargon
Profanity
Obscenity

Although we spend more than seventy-five percent of our waking time speaking and/or listening, little attention is given to the development of oral language skills in school. Most of our language training has been devoted to reading and writing. As a result, we seem to lose our awareness of spoken language skills as we focus on the formal study of written language.

We somehow get the idea that we should speak as we write, and as a result, we may miss the pleasure and creativity of experimenting with our language. The development of speaking skills is often brushed aside with the explanation that good speaking skills just come naturally.

Understanding Language

In this chapter we will take a look at language from the perspective of speech communication. Perhaps we can create a new awareness of what language is and, consequently, develop some new ideas and approaches from which we can develop language skills.

Language skills continue to be developed throughout life, through training, experience, and communication.

What is Language?

Developing a new perspective on language can lead to more creative, satisfying, and effective oral language skills. Language is any code that carries meaning and it involves symbols.

Symbol

Language can be defined as *symbol.* A word, for example, is a symbol for an object, an action, an idea, or a feeling, in the same sense that a trophy is a symbol for an accomplishment or victory. Words in this sense become a convenient "medium of exchange" as we use them to convey messages to others. The word is not the concept, but a symbol for the concept.

Code

Language can also be defined as a *code* for exchanging messages. In communication we speak of "encoding," to mean putting a message into code or assigning meaning. We use "decoding" to indicate the process of taking a message out of code to formulate our own thoughts or ideas. You may have, at one time, designed a code to exchange messages within your group of friends, so that no one else could understand what you were saying or writing. The military sometimes use secret codes to disguise messages for security reasons. In this sense English becomes a code, French a code, and Spanish a code. A code is a system for using language symbols in order to exchange messages. Individuals or groups must agree on the code in order to understand each other.

Understanding Oral Language

You may not have thought about the fact that language always begins in the *oral* (spoken) mode. No one invents a written set of symbols or code and says "Now, let's learn to speak this language!" Rather, language arises from the fact that people need to exchange messages orally. When we are prevented from *talking* to the person with whom we need to communicate, we write. We may also write when we wish to preserve our ideas. Poets, historians, and scholars write essentially to preserve our heritage, culture, and knowledge for future generations.

Dialect

When the Brothers Grimm travelled in Germany during the 18th and 19th centuries, they discovered that fairy tales varied very little from one state or section of the country to another. They did, however, discover that the speech of the German people varied from one place to another, to the extent that individuals from one section could not understand or converse with individuals from another. The brothers made some important discoveries about **dialect,** a term used to define oral language. It is important to understand the Grimms recognized that there is no superior dialect. The speech within a particular culture is correct within that culture, because it is *understood* within that culture.

Today, dialect describes the unique characteristics of a group or their oral language. We may then speak of British dialects, southern dialects, Brazilian dialects, and so on. Dialect can also refer to a language that has not yet been codified into writing and exists only in an oral form. There are several tribes in Africa and South America who speak their own language but do not write it.

The living language

In this light, the oral code of communication is considered the living language. It is immediate, fleeting, and practical. We talk when we need to talk for some immediate reason. "May I borrow your book?" "Come here!" and

Oral messages often reflect an immediate need to communicate.

"Who called?" are simple examples of talking to meet immediate needs. Long conversations may begin with "I need to talk to you. . . ." The key word is *need;* we usually initiate oral messages when we need something.

Since oral language arises from the people and is immediate and urgent, it is subject to change. As our lifestyles change, language changes to meet our changing needs. Our ability to use oral language effectively to meet these needs is related to our effectiveness as individuals. For this reason, an examination of oral language as a medium of exchange is important to us in our private and professional lives.

The Components of Language

Having defined language as symbol and as a code for exchanging messages, we can move to an examination of the components of language. Exactly what is "language"? What characteristics or components does it possess? What are its parts?

Meaning

Language has a meaning component. When we process stimuli from the world around us, we encode and decode information. Encoding is a language-related function used to organize, classify, and apply names or labels to objects, ideas, people, actions, and/or feelings. In other words, we use mental, language-related processes to organize and assign meaning to our perceptions. This represents *semantics,* or the meaning components of language.

Semantics

It is important to realize that words have no permanent meaning of their own. The meanings assigned to words are the result of use. In fact, in speech communication we frequently say "Words do not mean; people mean." A word means something only once. If we talk about a book, the next time we say "book" we may mean *another* book. This point is reinforced in Lewis Carroll's *Through the Looking Glass* when Humpty Dumpty tells us "I can make a word mean exactly what I want, no more and no less."

A distinction related to the semantic component of language is that between denotation and connotation. A

denotation is the direct, literal meaning of a word. A **connotation** is the implied or suggested meaning of a word. For example, the word *flat* denotes a level surface, but can connote dullness or a lack of variety.

Structure and Grammar

Syntax

Language has *syntax,* or linear structure. We learn structural rules applying to prefixes, suffixes, phrases, clauses, subjects, and verbs. Structure, like other components of language, may vary. Also like other components, it must be agreed upon if we are to communicate.

There are, of course, differences in language structures. For example, in English we place adjectives before nouns ("the large table"). In Spanish, the noun precedes the adjective ("la mesa grande"). In English most of us say "Are you going with me?" Those of Scandinavian descent, however, might say "Are you going with?"

Prefixes change the meaning and function of words, as do suffixes. By rearranging the order or linear structure of language, we can change its meaning and function. Consider the sense and non-sense of the changes implied in the following structural arrangements affecting the root word "norm": normal, abnormal, alnormal. The first two arrangements make sense, but *alnormal* is meaningless. When a structural rule is violated, the sense is lost.

Grammar

Language has a grammatical component. Even though oral language seems to provide more opportunity for flexibility than written language, we are obliged to conform to grammatical rules. Subjects must still agree with verbs, and words such as "ain't" are avoided in standard speech. A basic knowledge and use of *grammar* is essential to effective communication.

Sound

Language has a *phonological* component. That means that language has the characteristic of sound. Speech sound can actually be described in several ways.

Diction is a term sometimes used in a broad sense to mean language in general, as in the instance of the *dictionary,*

*Diction
and
articulation*

*Enunciation
and
pronunciation*

which describes our language. Diction is also used to describe the clarity of a person's speech. If we say someone has good diction, we usually mean the person has clear, easy-to-understand speech. **Articulation** usually refers to the clarity, distinctness, and correctness of a person's consonant sounds. If you substitute a "d" sound for the "t" sound in "butter," for example, you have made an error in articulation.

Enunciation refers to the clarity, distinctness, and correctness of vowel sounds. If you substitute an "i" sound for an "e" sound and say "git" instead of "get," you have made an enunciation error. *Pronunciation* usually refers to the general sounding of a word as described in the dictionary—a reflection of how most educated people prefer to pronounce the word.

We are often judged, at least on first impression, by the quality of our speech. We cannot overestimate the importance of clear, precise speech in determining the messages we convey to others.

Choices

Language is a system that includes choices. There are sounds, structures, and vocabulary within each language system that are consistent and, in many instances, unique. Within each system, therefore, there are choices that permit us flexibility and specificity. We have words with different denotations and connotations from which to choose. "Blouse," "shirt," "sweater," or "top" might be chosen to describe a particular garment. "Walk," "amble," "stagger," "stumble," or "prance" might be chosen to describe a movement.

We may choose to make statements or ask questions. Our language system includes many elements from which we may choose to convey our messages. Making choices within the system becomes a key to self-expression.

Checkpoint

1) Listen to a recording of speakers using several dialects. Try to describe each dialect using the terms in this chapter. 2) Select a short poem or a scene from a play that is written in dialect. Read the section aloud. Try to describe the dialect using the terms in this chapter.

Understanding Language Functions

As we begin to understand what language is and what it consists of, another logical sequence of questions emerges. What does language *do?* How do we *use* language? What functions does it serve? If we use language to express ourselves, what are we attempting to express or accomplish? What kinds of messages do we send?

The Speech Communication Association, in attempting to deal with these questions, relates the concept of language function to a collection of options and choices. The asso-

All languages have meaning and structural components. Choices are possible in American Sign Language, as they are in speech.

Language skills can be developed in all five functional categories.

ciation described language as serving the following purposes or functions. We should develop appropriate strategies and skills for effectiveness in each area.

1. We use language to inform—to give and seek information. Making clear, concise statements and asking clear and relevant questions certainly relate to our goal of wishing to learn to "express ourselves."

2. We use language to express feelings. We often experience difficulty in explaining how we feel. Perhaps this is due to the fact that society sometimes imposes a penalty for expressing feelings openly and freely. Perhaps it is due to our own inhibitions. Most of us, however, readily admit the need to share feelings with others.

3. We use language to control—to direct, command, request, and comply. We tell others what to do and we are told what to do.

4. We use language to ritualize. We make and acknowledge introductions and greetings. We participate in interviews and in meetings that demand correct parliamentary procedure. We follow the rules of etiquette, in order to succeed socially and professionally.

5. We use language for imagining. We talk about our dreams and ambitions, and we sometimes verbalize our wildest imaginings and creative urges. In so doing we expand our world and increase our capacity as individuals.

The S.C.A. research reinforces the idea that developing flexibility in self-expression involves acquiring a keen sense of language function or purpose. If we wish to develop language skills, we can begin to refine our choices for informing, expressing feelings, controlling, ritualizing, and imagining.

Checkpoint

Begin with a simple statement. For example, "Who is Stacey?" Now, write sentences or paragraphs to fit each of the language functions: informing (Stacey is a member of the senior class), controlling, ritualizing, imagining, and to express feelings. You may want to role play each function and note the language used in each instance.

Understanding Levels of Usage

If we are to use language effectively in a variety of situations, we must consider the levels of language usage. Real skill in using language as a means of self-expression involves the ability to adapt our language strategies to meet our needs.

This concept implies building a language *repertoire* (a term that usually refers to a collection or group of pieces for performance). As an acting company may have a repertoire of plays that it performs in a season, so must a speaker have a repertoire of language. This repertoire may include several levels of usage.

Formal and Standard Usage

Formal usage is appropriate for special tasks and occasions that take on a definite form or format, or that dictate the use of highly specialized language. Debate, for example, involves using terms and language strategies peculiar to debate. Parliamentary procedure uses formal statements: "I move that John be elected by acclamation."

Standard usage is the language most frequently understood and used by educated people. Standard usage and pronunciation are usually provided in a dictionary. Standard usage is appropriate for public speaking, interviews, and in most public situations. It is generally considered appropriate for communication in the classroom. Standard usage is what most of us consider to be "correct" speech. For example, a job applicant would not respond "It's groovy!" when asked by a personnel manager what he or she thought of job description. A far more appropriate response might be "The job sounds interesting and really exciting."

Informal and Colloquial Usage

Informal language (or *casual language*) is used for casual conversations and in close relationships where a relaxed, personal style is appropriate. Often, social groups develop their own special forms of communication. "How're ya doin'?" may substitute for "How are you?" "Can you fix this gadget for me?" may replace the more standard "Can you repair this machine for me?"

Informal language is often creative and free. It can, in fact, be considered "fun" language and is frequently experimental, following a very flexible form.

Colloquial usage is unique or peculiar to a particular area or region. It can be defined loosely as the "grassroots language of the people." Colloquial speech may vary to the extent that people in one part of the United States may have difficulty communicating with those from another.

A southwesterner, for example, who confronts a waitress in the midwest with the fact that the glass of milk she ordered is "blinky" will be met with a frown of confusion. Finally, upon being asked to taste the milk in question, the waitress could respond, "Oh, you mean it's tainted." Blinky or tainted, sour milk is sour milk, but colloquial usage confuses the message.

From the 1930s to the 1950s, "standard American speech" was an ideal, to the extent that people encouraged the use of standard diction and pronunciation as well as the elimination of informal expressions from their language choices. In the 1960s, people began to recognize the richness of their heritage of regional and cultural differences. Today, we acknowledge colloquial speech as part of our lore, and respect its place in the language and culture of the United States.

The situation often determines whether formal or informal language is more appropriate.

Temporal Language

Language is sometimes characterized by *temporal* influences. This means language changes with time — often to the extent that we can almost identify a person's age by what they call a particular object. For an example of **temporal language,** what do you call the electronic device you use to listen to your favorite music? A ghetto-buster? A boom-box? A walk-man? Chances are your parents call their maker of music a "hi-fi," a stereo, or a transistor. In the 1950s, before many changes in technology, rock-and-roll tunes may have blasted from a record player, while in the 1920s, flappers had to wind their Victrolas to listen to their favorite crooner or dance the Charleston.

Slang

Slang is temporary language. It is the language of intimate relationships and changing times. We will give examples of slang words and terms, but by the time this book is published, these words or terms may have become obsolete. What was "in" last year may be "out" today. Last year we may have said that something was "cool" or "neat;" this year it may be "hot," or we may say it "jives" or "jams."

Slang seems to arise from a need to express ourselves in fresh, new, creative ways. It also seems to arise from a need to be included in a group—members of a clique or a crowd often begin to speak the same "lingo." Slang can tell the world that you are "in." Slang can also exclude.

Slang has proliferated from space technology, from the ghetto, from the C.B. craze, and from song lyrics. Slang adds newness and freshness and "pizazz" to our language, but if we rely too heavily on slang, it can seriously limit our ability to cross cultural lines and communicate effectively.

Jargon

Another type of language that can be categorized as slang is jargon. **Jargon** usually refers to a specialized vocabulary shared by people within a group or profession. Jargon is often difficult for "outsiders" to understand. (In fact, the primary definition of *jargon* in most dictionaries is "gibberish.") Some people assert that communication in some professions would be impossible without jargon, while others say that jargon is a negative kind of language because it excludes communicators who are not in the group.

Profanity and **obscenity** can be defined as ugly talk. The use of profanity or obscenity may arise from a sense of frustration, anger, or hostility. It may simply reflect the lack of more appropriate verbal skills. In many instances, however, "ugly talk" is used for effect or impact.

It can take awhile to understand the jargon someone uses.

Choosing Levels of Usage

The concept of *repertoire* implies that we should develop skills for choosing from a variety of verbal strategies in order to communicate effectively in a variety of situations. If you're thinking, "Fine, but people seem to understand me. Why do I need to know about or to use different language in different situations and with different people?" we might clarify our point by using an analogy.

Let's consider the nonverbal concept of choosing a wardrobe. How do you choose your clothing? Chances are that you choose it to meet the needs of your lifestyle. You want different kinds of clothing for different occasions and activities, or to meet the approval of yourself and/or others. The point is that you should give the same care and consideration to choosing language strategies in a particular instance as you give to choosing your clothing.

We like to have clothes that are pleasing and appropriate to us as individuals, that help us to "express ourselves," and that project the image we would like to have. We also choose clothes that are pleasing to others. We choose clothes for the occasion, task, or activity.

Think of building a personal and attractive repertoire of language strategies with the same careful consideration as you use in building a personal and attractive wardrobe. What kind of language strategies do you now need or can you visualize yourself needing in the future to accommodate your personal, professional, and public needs?

Checkpoint *Rewrite the sentence "This soup is delicious!" (standard usage) changing the adjective "delicious" to indicate formal usage, colloquial usage, slang, and jargon.*

Evaluating Language

It is important in any type of skill development to set criteria for evaluating the skill. How can you evaluate your language effectiveness? Written language is evaluated, as you know, by standards of "correctness" as specified by grammatical rules. We learn that we must write correctly to communicate well.

The guidelines for speaking are more open and flexible than those for writing. The primary criterion is appropriateness, which suggests using some different standards for the evaluation of speaking strategies and skills.

Essentially, there are four standards to consider in determining or assessing appropriateness. First, is the language

Appropriate to speaker?

appropriate for the speaker? Since you are a unique individual, your language should reflect your personal style. Language choices are critical in enabling you to present yourself in the manner you wish. These choices also become a critical factor in determining how others perceive you as a person. You should take care to select language and language strategies that express who you are and what you want to say.

Second, is the language appropriate to the listener? We

Appropriate to listener?

learn to adapt our speaking to our listeners. You probably speak differently with your friends than you do with a person of authority. A doctor may use technical language when addressing other members of the medical profession, but must use standard terminology when speaking with a patient.

Language should be appropriate to the speaker, the audience, the occasion, and the task.

Appropriate to occasion?

Third, is the language appropriate for the occasion? Your lifestyle is composed of a variety of relationships and activities. In a single day you may have a hurried discussion with a parent before leaving for school, take part in a class discussion, visit with your friends at lunch, go for a job interview, and make a speech at a public meeting in the evening. All of these are different situations or occasions, and the criteria for appropriate language are different in each instance.

Appropriate to task?

Finally, is the language appropriate for the task? For example, the language used for teaching a class is different from the language needed for talking with a friend. The first task demands clear, specific, and standard usage; the second instance may imply casual and unstructured language strategies.

When you consider the four criteria for language appropriateness, you can begin to understand the need for building a repertoire of speaking skills and strategies in order to communicate your messages. As you apply your communication skills you will be using these criteria to evaluate your language choices in each communication situation.

Checkpoint *Make a list of all the activities in which you are involved for one week (going to class, working in a public place, participating in a formal meeting). Think about how you would introduce yourself to a stranger in each instance. How do the criteria for appropriateness change from one activity to another?*

Applying Language Skills

For all practical purposes, language becomes more than a medium (or means) for conveying a message. It becomes *part* of the message. Our messages are interpreted, evaluated, and responded to depending upon the language strategy we use to transmit the message. Few people bother to sort out the possible differences between language used to express the message and the actual intent of the speaker.

Let's assume that you discover a mistake has been made in a bill you have to pay. If you approach the person in charge and say, even politely, "I think you have made a mistake . . .," it will seem to be an accusation. The response will probably be defensive. If, on the other hand, you ask a question such as, "Can you help me? I think there is a mistake . . .," the response will probably be more positive. You have chosen a language strategy that focuses attention on the actual issue—the mistake—rather than on who made the mistake. The difference in the response (and the effectiveness of the communication) can be explained by the language strategy chosen to convey the message.

In addition to applying the criteria for appropriateness in selecting language strategies, you can begin to apply some of the following simple rules in sending effective verbal messages.

Use Descriptive Language

As a rule, use *descriptive language* (which relates observations) rather than *evaluative language* (which relates judgments) when reporting judgments or stating opinions or preferences. It is more effective to say "The play was unusually funny!" than to say "It was a good play." It is better to say "Bull's eye! That shot was right on target!" than to say "That was a great shot!"

You will note that descriptive statements report more information and give a greater basis for the judgment than evaluative statements, which merely state an opinion.

Use Supportive Language

Supportive language is characteristic of productive relationships.

Use language that lends itself to a supportive rather than a defensive climate. _Supportive language_ is characterized by openness and equality, and usually leads to productive relationships. _Defensive language_ is usually characterized by domination and secrecy, and tends to lead to unproductive relationships.

Supportive language can be characterized as descriptive and information-giving. It denotes ownership of feelings. Supportiveness is implied in statements like "I did not enjoy the play." rather than "That was a boring play." Supportive language focuses on observable and reportable data.

Supportiveness is also characterized by _provisional language_ (statements prefaced by "if," "sometimes," and "often"). Information-seeking questions, which imply careful listening and interest, are also considered supportive. Questions beginning with "what," "who," "where," "when," and "how" are usually not perceived as probing or threatening. A real problem can result from the overuse of "why" questions. These questions are usually probing and immediate defensiveness.

Language that tends to produce defensiveness is usually evaluative, judgmental, and accusatory. For example, overuse of "you" statements such as "you need to pay attention" and "you are late" will probably result in a defensive, nonproductive response. Statements that reflect certainty may also produce defensiveness ("this is always true" or "he never does that").

Avoid Killer Statements

Killer statements are "dead ends" that block communication. Imagine this dialogue: A student asks "What time is it?" The teacher, concerned with the work at hand, responds "Would you get busy?" Why is this statement—no matter how positive the intention—a real "put down" or "killer"? The answer is found in recalling that messages have both a meaning component and a personal or feeling component. The answer "Would you get busy?" acknowledges neither the meaning nor the feeling aspects of the student's question. The student will perceive the teacher's response as negative and may not risk asking another question. If this pattern is repeated, what will happen to the relationship?

Effective speech is often tied to personal effectiveness. As a speech student, you can use your knowledge of language to assess your skills, set goals, develop skills, and use your language skills for your own personal accomplishment.

Checkpoint *Role play a scene between two students in an argument over the fact that one has borrowed a book from the other without permission. The owner of the book may only use "why" questions when addressing the other student. The other student must begin every sentence with "Because."*

What happens to the relationship? What role does language play? How could using "How," "When," or "What" questions have changed the situation?

Summary

A very important insight is gained from the concept of appropriateness and choice in verbal communication. The concept allows room for regional speech within a region and cultural or ethnic speech within a culture.

The height of effective verbal communication could be achieved if each of us were, in a sense, multilingual. If our language repertoires were extensive enough and flexible enough, we could make choices permitting us to communicate effectively in a variety of situations—at school, at work, with our families and friends, and with people of different ages and social backgrounds.

We need to invest in acquiring a repertoire of language skills to meet our needs and to accommodate our lifestyles.

Check Your Knowledge

1. What are two definitions of *language*?

2. What are the components of language?

3. What are the functions of language?

4. What are the levels of language usage?

5. What are the four criteria for determining the appropriateness of language?

Check Your Understanding

1. Explain the concepts of language as a symbol and as a code.

2. Explain the statement: "Words do not mean, people mean."

3. Explain the statement: "There is no superior dialect." Why is this statement true? How does it apply today?

4. Why is it important to build a language repertoire to meet the needs of your lifestyle and relationships?

5. Explain how language can become a part of the message. Give examples of how evaluative language or "killer" statements can change messages.

6. Make a list of guidelines, based on the criteria for appropriateness, for your use in oral communication.

7. Explain the statement "To some extent we should all be multilingual within our first language."

Check Your Skills

1. Use the skill-building process from Chapter 2 to begin to build your own language repertoire.

2. Try to use descriptive rather than evaluative language to describe a speech in your class or to discuss an assembly. What differences do you notice in the responses of others?

3. Experiment with using the lead "In my perception . . ." when stating what, to you, is fact. Note the differences in others' responses.

4. If you find yourself having a negative reaction to a conversation, listen to the statements of others. Try monitoring your responses. Are you responding to the intended message or to the language used to convey the message? Do your interpretations make a difference in your behavior? How?

Communicating by Telephone

Americans use telephones quite a lot. According to the National Exchange Courier Association, the average American spends thirty minutes a day on the telephone. Some playful arithmetic tells us that during a seventy-year life span, the average American spends 12,775 hours on the telephone! Despite frequent use of the telephone, many people do not know how to use this familiar instrument skillfully. This activity, to which we devote so much time, and which is so important to personal and professional functions, deserves some attention.

You can learn to interact effectively in all telephone communications, if you become aware of the limitations of the time and technology. Because you are not with the person you are talking to, you cannot see his or her environment and nonverbal posture or movement. You must rely instead on your clear, articulate language skills and on your sensitivity to this particular communication channel.

For example, have you ever stopped to think that you might be interrupting someone when you call? There are times when an answerer definitely does not welcome the interruption. It is impossible for you to anticipate that reaction. But if the answerer seems irritated or abrupt, don't take the reaction personally. The response is probably related to the interruption, not to you as an individual.

Another related perspective may be gained from thinking about the use of telephone answering machines. They are increasingly common, even through many callers are uncomfortable with them simply because they are *machines*. However, answering machines are designed to facilitate communication, not hamper it. When a machine answers your call, remember that a real person installed and programmed that machine. Think of that person saying, ''I cannot be interrupted right now because I am away or busy, but I appreciate you calling and would like to communicate with you soon.'' The individual is saying that he or she will respond to you when time is available.

Your ability to use the telephone skillfully can affect your success on the job and in your personal life. A telephone connection is a mechanical channel in the process of communication. Effective communicators develop strong telephone skills.

CHAPTER 8

Listening and Responding

After reading this chapter, you should be able to:

1
Distinguish between *hearing* and *listening*.

2
Explain the importance of good listening skills in interpersonal communication.

3
Explain the uses of the four different kinds of listening.

4
List some poor listener habits to avoid.

5
List some good listener characteristics.

6
Recognize some common listening barriers.

7
Describe the role of feedback in good listening.

8
Improve the feedback you give while listening.

Hearing

Listening

Recreational listening

Informational listening

Empathic listening

Critical listening

Reasoning errors

When considering communication, people sometimes think of sending a message, and forget that *receiving* the message is equally important. Although we spend more of our time listening than speaking, we are more likely to take listening for granted.

We listen more than we speak.

We speak more than we read.

We read more than we write.

We learned the four skills in the same order. We listened before we could speak; we spoke before we could read; and we read before we could write.

In the schools, however, the time spent teaching communication skills has been given the opposite priority:

Writing is taught more than reading.

Reading is taught more than speaking.

Speaking is taught more than listening.

Listening, the most-used communication skill, is taught very little. Listening and responding are the activities that give the communication process its circular nature, so it is important to consider them carefully.

The Nature of Listening

Everyone knows how to listen, right? There is a general misconception that listening is a process that comes naturally. The truth is, few of us are really good listeners, and most people confuse *listening* with *hearing,* although they are not the same.

Listening is More Than Hearing

What is the difference between listening and hearing? **Hearing** is the physical process of receiving sound from the environment. It happens without effort if the ears and brain function normally. On the other hand, **listening** is a part of the perceiving process and requires concentrated effort. It is the mental process of focusing attention, interpreting, and understanding what is heard. While you must be able to hear in order to listen, productive listening requires much more effort.

Listening requires
concentrated attention.

In addition to the ability to hear, there are other basic requirements for listening. Physical and emotional factors influence attentiveness. If you are tired, or not feeling well, you will need to make a greater effort to listen effectively. You need adequate sleep and good health to do your best at listening and remembering.

Another factor that separates listening from the physical hearing process involves the need for language skill. Listening requires comprehension, so listeners need to understand the code or language the speaker uses. Also, the listener and the speaker must have similar vocabularies. Since limited vocabulary can interfere with the ability to *think with* a speaker, good listeners work continually to enlarge their vocabularies. Vocabulary building and listening skill are two of the best ways to improve study habits and learning ability.

Listening is Faster than Speaking

Researchers have measured listeners' abilities to comprehend messages at different speeds. They have found that human beings can *hear* and *understand* messages at the rate of 400 to 500 words per minute. However, the average rate of *speech* is only 100 to 200 words per minute. Since we can decode and think much faster than most messages are spoken, it is important to learn to use the extra time efficiently. What do you do with your extra time when you listen?

Since a lot of time is left over in the listening process, we all "tune in" for a time, and then we "click off" and daydream because it takes less effort (and may be more entertaining). What you do with the extra time available while listening to a teacher or some other speaker has an enormous effect on your listening effectiveness.

Barriers to Effective Listening

Listening requires focusing attention on one message and ignoring others. This is a process of overcoming noise and barriers. You will recall that we defined *noise* as any temporary interference in the communication process. A barrier is an obstruction to communication, and may be a distraction within the listener (such as worrying over a problem in another class).

Barriers may also be external (such as an uncomfortably cold room or the sound of a truck outside the window). A barrier or kind of noise may occur in the message itself, as when a speaker does not speak clearly or when words are confused. Great effort is needed to screen out noise and barriers.

Earlier, when we discussed barriers inside the receiver (listener) and the sender (speaker), we mention closed-mindedness, stereotyping, and prejudice. Lack of interest can also interfere with listening. Daydreaming can reduce listening effectiveness, particularly when the time could be used to listen more carefully. Negative attitudes about the communication situation can also interfere with listening, and should be adjusted if possible.

Checkpoint *Explain the difference between hearing and listening. Can you recall some barriers to listening that you have recently observed?*

Purposes and Levels of Listening

The purpose of your listening differs from situation to situation all day long. Every time your purpose changes, the need for your attention and the level of your thought involvement changes also.

Perhaps you listen to music on the radio while you get ready for school. You are listening for entertainment. If the music is interrupted by a weather bulletin, you may shift more of your attention to the broadcast in order to understand and remember information that may influence your plans for the day. You are listening for facts.

Between classes a friend may talk to you about a problem, and you listen to understand what your friend is feeling. At lunch, if someone tries to persuade you to help with a "Learn to Swim" campaign, you listen to weigh alternatives and to decide what action you should take. You listen critically.

Throughout the day, you will shift from one listening situation to another, giving little thought to the changes in your listening purpose. Each purpose requires a change in your concentration or listening level. Successful communicators are able to recognize the different situations and apply the appropriate kind of listening.

Certain situations call for very careful listening.

Listening for Recreation

You listen for recreation when you attend a play or a concert. Your purpose is enjoyment of the event, and listening does not require great mental effort unless noise interferes. Your listening is focused enough to make you resent any major distraction. Unlike hearing quiet background music, **recreational listening** requires your attention, and any intellectual task attempted at the same time will suffer in quality. For example, you cannot divide your attention between television and reading a textbook (another purpose) without lowering your reading concentration considerably. You probably would not remember much of either the television show or the textbook material.

Listening for Information

Another level requires taking a major step in focusing attention. It is the process of listening for main ideas or for information to be remembered. The attention required for lectures, on-the-job instruction, assignments, or directions to a place across town reflects **informational listening.** At this level you must "tune out" noise. You will know you have listened well at this level when you can recall major facts or details in their proper sequence, repeat a message in your own words without distorting it, or accurately follow the directions you have been given. When comprehension is added, you will be able to recognize and explain the relationships between the facts, identify the main ideas, ask meaningful questions about the information, and draw accurate conclusions based on the information you have received.

Informational listening often requires that we remember details in their proper sequence.

Listening for Interpersonal Understanding

Empathic listening requires tuning in to the emotional component of a message.

The next listening level is listening for interpersonal understanding, and another ingredient must be added to your focused attention at this point. The addition is *empathy*. Empathy is the process of feeling *with* others and of seeing the world as they do. It requires tuning in to the emotional part of messages from others as well as to the factual part.

For this level it will be helpful to recall that messages have emotional as well as informational components. You will need to be especially receptive to nonverbal information. When we discussed nonverbal communication and the use of silent cues, you learned that nonverbal messages add an important dimension to words. You must stay aware of what the other person is saying with facial expression, gestures, posture, and bodily motion.

Empathic listening requires mental, physical, and emotional alertness. You will know you have been successful when you have listened attentively without permitting interruptions, making judgments, or offering advice, and when you can restate the feeling expressed and have *understood* how it feels. When you have been able to restate the feeling, the other person usually lets you know if you have interpreted it well.

**Listening for
Decision Making**

The highest level of skill is required for **critical listening,** or listening to evaluate ideas and make decisions. This is the focused attention needed to evaluate persuasive speeches. At this level, you must consider the idea or claim the persuader wants you to accept, but you must also test the evidence or factual information used to support the claim for its believability. You must also pay attention to the reasoning used to connect the claim and the supporting evidence, and evaluate the logic of the speaker's reasoning. It is important for you to be aware of the appeals the speaker makes to audience members emotionally. You may argue silently with the speech, asking yourself questions about the speaker—why he or she offers the argument, what his or her motives are, and whether he or she should be believed. Finally, you will decide what action to take or whether to accept or reject the speaker's message.

Critical listening is essential to evaluating persuasive speeches, and involves a high level of skill.

We will discuss criteria for evaluating speeches in detail later. For now, you will know you have listened critically when you recognize the major issues that are raised, evaluate the reasons the speaker asks you to accept his or her arguments, test the connection between the speaker's claims and the facts used to support them, and recognize the emotional appeals used in the speech.

Checkpoint *Explain the characteristics of listening for four different purposes. How can you know when you have listened well for each purpose? What activities are needed in informational listening that are not needed in listening for recreation? Why is empathic listening more difficult to carry out than recreational listening?*

Guidelines for Listening

Good listening requires preparation. It is important for you, the listener, to be physically, mentally, and emotionally ready to listen. If you are in class, get paper and pen ready for taking notes before the lecture begins. Adopt an alert posture, and if possible, move your chair to get a clear view of the instructor. Next, tune out the noise. Get ready to listen for central ideas and information that you must understand, apply, and remember.

Rule 1 for good listening is *do not prejudge.* It is a common mistake to decide a subject is dull before you listen to a presentation. Keep an open mind, and work for a positive attitude about what you will hear. Tell yourself the information will be interesting, important, or useful. Be alert and enthusiastic.

Rule 2 is *set a goal* for yourself. Goal setting is really a part of getting ready to listen positively. Establish what *you* want from the listening experience, such as, "I want to learn everything I can about comets," or "I'll try to understand why she thinks I have been unfair." Be determined to search for the part of the message you need to meet your goal.

Rule 3 is *identify the kind of listening that is needed* as quickly as possible, and adapt to it. Once you have decided which kind of listening is required for the situation at hand, don't forget it. For example, an entertaining class lecture sometimes makes it easy to forget that active steps must be taken to organize and remember important information. Be careful *not* to apply critical thinking skills to every situation, or accept everything you hear as fact without applying critical listening skills at all.

Rule 4 for good listening is *focus attention on the content of the message.* You are capable of opening some message channels and closing others at will. Focus on the message, not the speaker, and try not to let the speaker's mannerisms or poor delivery habits take your attention away from the central message.

You probably bring distractions to class with you in the form of memories from a previous class, questions about a conversation in the hallway, or concern about the exam you must take after lunch. Mental preoccupations are a kind of noise that must be put aside to allow you to focus attention on the message you are about to hear. Of course, if there are external noises (an unruly classmate or a lawnmower), you cannot make them go away, but you can decide not to *listen* to them.

It may be difficult to focus attention on the message when internal or external noise is persistent.

Rule 5 is *use your extra time productively while listening.* Real listening is an *active* process and it is hard work. Since you only use a third or less of your listening time for receiving the spoken message, what you do with the rest of the time is very important. When you listen for recreation, you probably use much of your extra time for daydreaming, and that is fine. When your purpose changes to listening for comprehension of facts and ideas that must be remembered, listening empathically in an interpersonal situation, or listening critically to make a decision, the use of time becomes more important. Now we want to suggest some techniques you can use to improve your listening in each of these situations.

Checkpoint *Think about the way you usually "get set" to listen in class. Now, review the guidelines for listening. What would you need to change in order to improve your listening readiness?*

Testing and Improving Listening

Let's look at some specific techniques to apply as you begin to improve your listening skills. Since a large portion of your listening is done in school, we will begin with listening for information and ideas. Some techniques for improving your empathic listening with friends and family follow, and then some specific ways to apply critical listening skills are discussed. You may find that some of the techniques presented will be useful in certain recreational listening situations. However, we will focus here on listening activities that require more concentrated levels of energy.

Applying Informational Listening Skills

If you are listening for ideas and information to be remembered, first try to listen for main points or central ideas and index the subpoints or details under them. Main headings are often phrased with "signal words." Be alert for words or phrases such as "first point," "next," "most important," "in summary," "finally," and "review" as signals that can help you organize the message into a mental (or written) outline.

Look for the interesting parts of dull topics to help yourself stay tuned in. Delay evaluating information until later. Instead, try to predict what the speaker will say next. Avoid reacting to emotional words and phrases. If you let yourself become angry or resentful, your attention will be diverted from the information you need. Argue with the ideas you hear only *after* you have heard the entire message.

Review the main ideas frequently and check your progress through the topic. Mentally summarize or paraphrase ideas occasionally. Form mental pictures to assist you in remembering the message, or relate the information you are hearing to things you already know. Finally, resist the impulse to "turn off" the message momentarily and let your mind wander. Look interested and alert. A speaker tries harder when the audience is attentive.

Applying Empathic Listening Skills

When empathic listening is required, try first to avoid making judgments of the speaker or of the message. Watch the speaker closely for nonverbal cues about how he or she *feels* about the message. Listen closely to the speaker's *paralinguistic cues*—changes in vocal pitch, rate, or volume—to learn about his or her emotional state.

Try to hear the message from the speaker's point of view. Set aside your own viewpoints while listening. Remember, you communicate your attitude and response to the speaker while you listen. Show your support and concern (but not judgments) with your nonverbal feedback.

Applying Critical Listening Skills

If you are listening to a persuasive message, you are required to evaluate the message and make decisions. You may have to act on the decisions or choices you make. Persuasive communication is intended to bring about a change in your thinking or behavior. Because of this, it is very important to develop and apply critical listening skills.

Watch the speaker's verbal and nonverbal behaviors for cues about how convinced the *speaker* is of his or her own message. Can you believe what the speaker says? Ask yourself what motive the speaker has for trying to persuade you. Does the speaker know the subject? Are the speaker's views based on facts or on unsupported opinions? Restate the

School elections offer opportunities to practice critical listening skills.

speaker's ideas in your own words. Do they still seem true? Do the ideas fit together and work as a whole?

Test the ideas presented. Do they agree with your experience and with other things you know about the subject? If not, why not? Examine the evidence offered by the speaker. Is it from a reliable source? Does it sound authoritative? Does it "prove" the claim it is supposed to support? Analyze the speaker's appeals. Does the speaker rely mostly on reasoning or on emotional responses? Try to apply the speaker's ideas and claims. Can you transfer the ideas or claims to another situation effectively?

Evaluating Reasoning

A good listener must learn to evaluate a speaker's reasoning. **Reasoning errors** occur most frequently in persuasive situations, when someone is attempting to influence the ideas and actions of others. Be alert for such errors, which may be misleading. Ask yourself what the speaker's reasoning is. What logical connections does the speaker make between the evidence and the claim?

Some reasoning errors occur in speeches because of poor preparation, and are not intended to mislead the audience. Such errors include making hasty or false generalizations. Hasty generalization is reflected in the following reasoning: On visiting another high school, you see four students wearing suits and ties. Without learning that they are debaters on their way to debate before a civic club, you say, "Students here sure dress up for school." You have assumed too quickly that what seems true for a few is the general rule.

Misleading reasoning errors include appealing to the ignorance or prejudice of listeners, concealing important items of information, making false comparisons, and making false cause-and-effect statements. It is also misleading for speakers to try to convince people to support an idea or action "because everybody is doing it," or to make an attack on a person rather than on ideas or actions. Reasoning errors can lead the audience to make the wrong decision. Recognizing errors in reasoning will be helpful when you plan speeches of your own. It is also important, especially in critical listening, to be aware of the speaker's reasoning and to detect any errors that may occur.

Applying Standards

Think of the standards you feel should be used to evaluate the speaker's central idea. When you apply the standards, does the idea still stand?

Angela is trying to persuade you to take history with her next semester. She says, "Mr. Browning is a great teacher. He's easy. He almost never gives exams, and everyone gets good grades. In class he just tells funny stories and doesn't talk about history at all." The standards by which your friend Angela has decided Mr. Browning is a "great teacher" are 1) he's easy, 2) he gives few exams, 3) he gives everyone good grades, and 4) he entertains instead of teaching history.

While listening, you should apply *your standards* to Angela's appeal, considering her claim that Mr. Browning is "a great teacher" and her supporting evidence. Do Angela's criteria for "a great teacher" match yours? If so, you may be persuaded. If, however, *you* have criteria for good teaching that include factors such as 1) the teacher motivates students to work hard and to learn, 2) the teacher gives regular tests, 3) grades fairly according to each student's effort, progress, and quality of work, and 4) uses class time well and makes the subject interesting, your application of standards will not match Angela's and you probably will not agree to her appeal.

Developing a System

Obviously, you will not be able to apply all of the techniques immediately. In fact it will not be easy to change your old habits, but keep working, because better listening will make you a far better communicator. Choose one or two techniques from each of the three types of listening discussed. Think of some situations in which to try each technique, and over the next two days, try them.

Each time you apply a technique, review afterward and set new goals for applying the technique more effectively. Next, choose one or two more from each list and *add* them to your goals for the next few days. Review often and continue to add techniques until you have become an efficient, skilled listener.

Some listening behaviors are desirable and some are undesirable. They are listed in the "Checklist of Listening

A Checklist of Listening Habits

A Good Listener	*A Poor Listener*
☐ Sets goals	1. Wants to be entertained
☐ Gets set, prepares	2. Avoids the difficult
☐ Expects the subject to be interesting	3. Expects the subject to be boring
☐ Keeps an open mind	4. Hears what he or she wants to hear
☐ Tunes out internal and external noise	5. Pays attention to noise and is easily distracted
☐ Tunes in to find useful information	6. Plans a response while listening
☐ Is aware of his or her own feedback	7. Criticizes the speaker's appearance or speaking style
☐ Focuses attention on the topic	8. Lets his or her mind wander
☐ Seeks an overview before taking notes	9. Listens only for facts
☐ Organizes ideas when the speaker fails to	10. Tries to outline everything
☐ Divides information into significant and insignificant points	11. Fakes attention
☐ Uses voice cues to help attach importance	12. Blocks out the unpleasant or uninteresting
☐ Avoids evaluating the speaker until later	13. Lets emotion-laden words and phrases sway him or her
☐ Stays alert	14. Daydreams during spare time
☐ Stays attentive even to difficult or unpleasant material	15. Tries to punish a speaker by "tuning out"

Habits'' as things good listeners and poor listeners do. See how many good listener habits you recognize in yourself. When you are through, you should have a list of your listening strengths. Then, before you decide you have mastered listening, go through the list of poor listener habits and test yourself to see how many of them you may need to consider.

Good listeners use their extra listening time to do some important things. Try the "Suggestions for Using Extra Time in Listening Situations'' to improve your listening skills. Keep working. You will begin to notice a difference in your listening effectiveness very quickly.

Suggestions for Using Extra Time in Listening Situations

Because the listener processes messages more rapidly than they can be sent by another person, there is time for additional activity in most listening situations. Consider using your extra "listening time" in the following ways.

Informational Listening
1. Paraphrase (translate the message into your own language).
2. Compare and contrast information.
3. Put information into needed sequence.
4. Consider the implications and applications of ideas.
5. Develop questions.
6. Summarize.
7. Test ideas for consistency with other ideas and experiences.

Empathic Listening
1. Recognize levels of meaning or components of the message.
2. Set aside your own perspective and try to see ideas and situations from the speaker's point of view.
3. Prepare to give supportive feedback.

Critical Listening
1. Separate supported facts from opinions.
2. Separate evidence from unrelated information.
3. Evaluate the speaker's biases, qualifications, and motives.
4. Recognize and evaluate the speaker's use of emotional appeals.
5. Test ideas and solutions for effectiveness and appropriateness.
6. Recognize the speaker's reasoning in connecting claims to evidence.
7. Evaluate any errors the speaker may make in reasoning.

Communicating a Response

Responding is a natural part of listening, and it is an important part of the entire communication process. A *response* is the receiver's reaction to the message. There is always a response, but it may never be known to anyone except the receiver. The response is based on the receiver's interpretation of the message, which is largely a product of individual perception.

When the receiver's response is seen, heard, or perceived by the sender of the message in some way, it is called *feedback*. Feedback is a necessary ingredient of communication, because the process of communication is circular. The only way you, the sender of a message, can know your message has been received by the person you intended it for is by feedback. Feedback tells whether the receiver's interpretation of your message matches your intended meaning.

Feedback Influences Communication

Feedback is always occurring, but it is most important in informative, persuasive, and interpersonal sharing situations. Feedback tells you, the speaker, if your message has been received and gives you clues about whether it has been understood. It can also tell you whether your persuasion or interpersonal sharing has been accepted. Feedback lets you know what to expect of a listener as you continue, and influences you to continue speaking as planned or to alter your message or communication style in some way. Experienced public speakers learn to read audience feedback as they speak, and to vary the speech as the response dictates.

As a listener, your attentive feedback can encourage a public speaker to do his or her best; your interest can inspire a teacher to teach better and to be more energetic; and your look of boredom can discourage speakers or cause them to stumble over words nervously. Regardless of its form, feedback influences the speaker, the continuing message, and the relationship between the communicators. Speakers are more animated and entertaining when listeners give positive feedback.

A speaker sometimes has to sort out different kinds of audience feedback before adapting the speech to create greater interest.

Teachers rely on student feedback as an important part of the teaching process.

Feedback Influences Speakers

As you listen to a teacher's explanation of an assignment, you are continually giving the teacher feedback. In class, much of your ongoing response will probably be nonverbal, and you may be unaware of the messages you are sending. Your teacher will look for and recognize visible feedback, however, and may alter her or his explanation because of your nonverbal message. A puzzled look is likely to cause the teacher to repeat or expand an explanation. It may cause the teacher to ask a question such as, "What is it you don't understand?," or "Are you confused?" in an effort to understand your perception of the explanation.

Feedback Influences Messages

We have stressed the value of clarifying messages. A question to clarify the meaning of a message (a perception check), such as "Do you mean . . .?" followed by a paraphrase, is one kind of verbal feedback. The role of the listener and of supportive, nonjudgmental feedback helps to make sharing easy and productive. There are many other kinds of feedback, of course, like verbal or nonverbal responses to show agreement, disagreement, questioning, or simply to show you are attentive and are actively _thinking with_ the speaker. Some feedback messages indicate the receiver has selected some part of the message to probe or to consider further.

Feedback in the form of questions can encourage a teacher to explain concepts in several ways.

Feedback Influences Relationships

In interpersonal situations, the listener's response is critical. Negative, judgmental responses may stop a friend or family member from sharing personal information altogether. Such responses may also add unnecessarily to any negative feelings someone has about himself or herself, since all feedback has the potential for becoming a part of self-concept. A good empathic listener develops skills in giving supportive feedback to others.

Appropriate responses to interpersonal sharing often sound like these:

When Someone Shares Good News:
"I know you must be very proud."
"That's great! Congratulations."
"I'm glad you had that opportunity."
"That must have been fun. Tell me about it."
"You must have studied very hard to do so well."

When Someone Shares Painful Information:
"I can see you are upset. Can I help?"
"That must have been frightening. I'm glad you were not hurt."
"I'm sorry that happened to you. I'm glad you don't have to worry about that any more."

Feedback Improves Listening

One of the best ways an audience member can give feedback is through eye contact. In our culture, an active listener is expected to look at the speaker. When a classmate (or your teacher) addresses your class, remember that your direct eye contact and your active listening can be helpful.

Your eye contact and energy that accompanies it will improve *your* concentration and retention of information as well. You will understand more of what you hear because you are receiving messages through the visual channel as well as through your ears. You are even less likely to be bored when you contribute the energy of eye contact to active listening.

Giving Effective Feedback

Effective feedback can be nonverbal as well as verbal.

Just as you, the listener, can choose to listen, not listen, or listen only to selected parts of a message, you can also choose the kind of feedback you will give. A skilled communicator will check his or her verbal feedback before uttering it, to be sure it is appropriate for him- or herself, the person or people who will hear it, and the situation or occasion. You have the same opportunity to choose nonverbal responses, but you will not always stop to choose. A nonverbal response may happen quickly, and it is likely to precede a verbal response. It may happen so quickly you do not even know it has occurred.

Remember that when nonverbal and verbal messages do not say the same thing, the nonverbal message will be perceived as more accurate. For example, suppose you tell a friend you cannot keep a date the two of you have been looking forward to for some time. The immediate look of disappointment on her face may be followed by a statement like, "Oh, that's okay, I really needed the time to study for tomorrow's exam anyway." Which reaction do you believe? The disappointment, of course. Nonverbal responses are more reliable indicators of feeling than words. When the two conflict, we usually accept the nonverbal response as truth.

You have discovered that positive feedback can improve the speaker's attitude toward the audience, motivate the speaker to be a better speaker, and improve the quality of the listener's own listening. You have also learned that positive feedback can improve interpersonal relationships and make it possible to help those who need your caring. Throughout this book, you will find suggestions for giving appropriate feedback in different communication situations.

Some Basic Rules

The following are some very basic rules for giving feedback in interpersonal situations that involve informing, persuading, or sharing empathically.

1. Give feedback as quickly as possible. Be sure that the other person is ready to receive feedback.

2. Be honest and accurate in giving feedback.

3. Give positive feedback whenever it is appropriate.

4. Send the clearest possible message in giving feedback.

5. Try to take responsibility for your own thoughts and feelings in giving feedback. Avoid labeling people and making judgments that influence your communication.

6. Give only as much feedback as a person can apply at one time.

7. Use supportive and descriptive language (rather than evaluative language) whenever possible.

Using Feedback

If you want to be a better communicator, watch and listen for feedback from your listeners. With practice, you can learn to interpret feedback accurately and adjust your communication accordingly. It is also important to be able to select the feedback that is most useful to you. You can, of course, choose interpersonal messages to cherish and repeat to yourself to reinforce your self-concept.

Try not to ignore messages you do not enjoy hearing. Attempt to recognize feedback signals (usually nonverbal) that tell you you are talking too loudly or have overstayed your welcome. By paying attention to such signals, you can improve communication. Remember that you can also ask for feedback. When you ask, your listener knows that you are applying your communication skills and trying to be as effective as possible. Asking for feedback can also encourage others to request feedback from you, reinforcing the communication process.

Checkpoint

1. *Explain how feedback is different from response.*

2. *Can you think of a nonverbal cue that told you to change something about your communication? Can you recall some positive feedback that has helped your communication?*

Summary

Listening requires more energy than hearing. It is an essential part of the communication process. Listening requires readiness; the speaker and listener must have similar vocabularies; and effective listeners focus on the speaker's message, recognize barriers, and tune out noise.

Four kinds of listening—recreational listening, informational listening, empathic listening, and critical listening—are useful in a variety of situations. Students use informational listening in class. Empathic listening takes place between friends and relatives. Critical listening is appropriate for evaluating ideas and making decisions.

In all listening, it is important to 1) avoid prejudging, 2) set a goal for the listening experience, 3) identify the kind of listening that is required, 4) focus attention on the content of the message, and 5) use extra time productively. Try to consider the guidelines for good listening whenever active listening is needed.

Responding is an important part of communication. Providing feedback completes the circular communication process. Feedback can influence interpersonal and public speaking situations. Learning to listen to and use feedback is important to the development of effective communication skills.

Check Your Knowledge

1. What are the four levels of listening? Which ones do most people have to work at learning?

2. List the five basic rules for good listening of any kind.

3. List some common barriers to effective listening.

4. Name some reasoning errors to listen for in persuasive situations.

5. How does feedback effect communication?

Check Your Understanding

1. List some situations in which *you* would use each kind of listening.

2. How is critical listening different from informational listening?

3. Why are good listening skills important in interpersonal relationships?

4. Explain what happens when verbal and nonverbal feedback do not agree.

Check Your Skills

1. Can you think of an example of verbal-nonverbal disagreement?

2. What are some ways a listener can help a poor public speaker?

3. Which kind of listening do you think is most difficult? Why?

4. Considering the rules for giving feedback, see if you can revise these responses to make them better.
   "You won? You must have cheated."
   "I'm glad that didn't happen to me."
   "How do you expect us to get these problems right?"
   "You'll have to say that some other way if you expect me to understand it."
   (To a classmate) "That was a little bit better today."

5. What kind of listening would you use for these situations:
   a. a musician giving a concert
   b. a driver-education teacher giving instructions
   c. a vendor at a baseball game selling food or drinks
   d. a flight attendant giving emergency instructions
   e. a parent telling a story about his or her childhood
   f. a politican making a campaign speech
   g. a salesperson promoting an automobile
   h. a friend sharing a personal experience
   i. a friend who wants help with homework
   j. an assembly speaker recruiting volunteers for a community service

6. People who live near airports, railroads, or busy intersections learn to ignore—to hear but not listen to—noise. Do you live or work in a place where you must "tune out" some sounds? What are they?

CHAPTER 9

Communicating in Relationships

After reading this chapter, you should be able to:

1

Define *relationship*.

2

Explain the importance of communication in relationships.

3

List the three emotional levels possible in relationships.

4

Describe the three stages of building relationships.

5

Relate communication strategies to building relationships.

6

Describe the communication choices that can resolve conflicts.

Relationship

Communication
attraction

Conflict

Coercion

Avoidance

Accommodation

Negotiation

Confrontation

Collaboration

Walking down a busy street, sitting in a class, or having lunch in the cafeteria, you are surrounded by people. Although you are among these people, physically present with them, can you say that you have a relationship with all of them? No, that would not be so. We cannot build personal relationships with everyone we meet, so we are selective and build relationships with a small number of people. The central component of building and maintaining relationships is communication.

The Nature of Relationships

A **relationship** can be defined as a bonding between two or more individuals, which is a result of interaction between those individuals. Just being together in the same place does not denote a relationship, nor does physical separation denote the absence of a relationship. Shared feelings of unity and commitment must bind individuals together before a relationship can exist.

Earlier we discussed communication as a process through which we form and maintain relationships. It follows that the effectiveness of our communication choices influences our relationships to a great extent. Likewise, the effectiveness of our nonverbal and verbal communication behaviors affects the quality of our relationships. Even though developing effective communication skills is a rewarding and valid goal in itself, communication can also be viewed as a means to an end. Communication is the process; our relationships are the product.

Relationships meet our needs for belonging and esteem. They provide outlets for exercising our values, for developing our individuality to its fullest potential, and for becoming contributing members of society. We need other people. We need family and friends to provide us with love and affection. We need authority figures to provide security and support. We need individuals and groups with whom we can form meaningful relationships to ensure feelings of happiness, well-being, and personal worth.

Emotional Levels

Relationships have emotional (or feeling) levels. Each level requires that the individuals involved use certain kinds of energy. Relationships can be positive, neutral, or negative.

We can have intense relationships with people we do not like as well as with people we love.

Positive relationships can be characterized by like, love, care, respect, nurture, enjoyment, trust, cooperation, support, and acceptance. Neutral relationships are characterized by neglect, indifference, and lack of concern. Negative relationships can be characterized by fear, envy, guilt, dislike, distrust, hate, competition, grief, and regret.

Positive relationships are usually healthy relationships that are mutually rewarding. Neutral relationships quickly become non-relationships. We are not willing to invest the necessary energy to maintain a relationship for which we have neutral feelings. Negative relationships can be destructive and damaging, not only to the individuals involved but also to others around them.

Long-term, meaningful relationships are characterized by both positive and negative influences. Positive aspects of relationships require commitment and care. Negative aspects of relationships require careful analysis regarding the causes and effects of perceived problems. When such analysis occurs, individuals can make communication choices about solving problems and redefining the relationship.

Categories of Relationships

Relationships, as a product of the communication process, play a large part in our personal lives, in our success at school and in the job market, and in our roles as citizens. If we examine relationships, we find that they may be placed into two broad categories: personal relationships and public relationships.

Personal Relationships

Personal relationships include those with family and friends, as well as relationships with other individuals who are important in our lives. In many instances, we have role models with whom we identify or special people who meet our needs in a unique way. For example, you may have a fulfilling personal relationship with an elderly person or a small child. You may have an adult who has become your mentor, who guides your decisions in special, caring ways. Each of these is a personal relationship, a bonding for personal enrichment.

Personal relationships are maintained through ongoing, effective communication.

Public Relationships

There are at least two kinds of public relationships in which we can be involved. The first are occupational relationships, which we form at school or at work with our peers, subordinates, and superiors. Usually, these are relationships formed outside the home, family group, or neighborhood. Sometimes they exist solely in school or in the work place, never leading to contact on a personal or social level. At other times, an occupational relationship may eventually become a personal relationship as well.

Another kind of public relationship is formed as we perform citizenship roles in the community. Community relationships are usually broader based, shorter in duration, and less personal in nature than those formed at work. They involve activities such as serving on a city council, participating in a community project, working for an election campaign, working within a civic organization, and forming grassroots committees to work for a particular decision on a public issue.

Happy, productive relationships at both the personal and public levels are important to our effectiveness as individuals, as professionals, and as citizens. Effective communication is the key to productive relationships.

Participation in town meetings helps to develop effective community relationships.

Checkpoint _Think about your favorite book or television show. Are there people in the book or show who have both public and personal relationships? Would you characterize these relationships as positive, neutral, negative, or a mix of all levels? Can you see how communication influences the relationships between the characters?_

Building Relationships

Relationships usually proceed through several stages or growth periods. There is a first meeting, called the _first-impression stage_. This is followed by the exploring of common interests and testing of the initial attraction, or the _stabilizing stage_. Then there is the time during which conflict, possible deterioration, and even termination of the relationship may occur. This is called the _evaluation stage_.

Just as individuals grow and change, relationships must grow and change so that they continue to meet personal needs and provide outlets for self-expression. In order to understand how our communication behaviors influence the way our relationships develop, we can examine these stages in the growth of relationships.

Stage One: First Impressions

Relationships (obviously) begin with an initial encounter, a first meeting or a first impression. First impressions are so important that some people believe that the ultimate nature of a relationship is established in the first five minutes of interaction.

Communication Attraction

When we want to communicate with someone we have just met, a type of interaction begins. Occasionally, we experience an instant liking for a new acquaintance. This kind of "chemistry" is called **communication attraction.** Communication attraction means more than responding to physical attractiveness. It is an immediate sense of wanting to interact with another individual; it is willingness to communicate.

You may remember a specific time when you experienced this communication attraction. It might have been intellectual, when you discovered a classmate with whom you enjoyed studying, or a person in your debate class with whom you loved to argue. The attraction might have been social, when you discovered a person whose idea of a "good time" was the same as yours, a person with whom you could go dancing, or a person whose passion for baseball you shared. The attraction might have been romantic. Whatever its nature, when communication attraction is mutual—when both individuals are willing to communicate with each other—the building of a relationship can begin.

First impressions

First impressions do not always lead to communication attraction. You may recall from your study of perception (Chapter 4) that first impressions strongly influence our perceptions of another person or group. In some cases, it may be necessary for us to develop a relationship with someone who does not initially appeal to us (for instance, with a doctor, a principal, or a teammate). In order to build a relationship, we will probably have to work at changing the perceptions we have based on your first impressions. This takes effort, but it can be done! One of the best ways to change our perceptions is through ongoing communication.

Communication and First Impressions

The opening moments between two strangers are extremely important in building relationships. Therefore, we need to understand the kinds of communication choices that lead to making a good first impression.

It is almost always advisable to use your positive verbal and nonverbal skills as a first step to making positive first

Work relationships often begin with an interview, and these first impressions can strongly influence later communication patterns.

impressions. It may help to remember that most people react first to what they see (general appearance, grooming, posture, gesture, and eye contact). Then they react to what they hear (voice and paralinguistic cues, for example). Third, people react to what they understand (verbal messages, diction, grammar, and language). Therefore, using guidelines for appropriate nonverbal and verbal behavior can help to make a good first impression.

Introductions

Think about the last conversation you had with a person you had just met. If that person seemed to be at ease, was it easier for you to talk? If that person seemed interested in you, was it easier to begin a conversation? When we meet strangers, it may help to think of the communication behaviors that put us at ease. We can then employ them to put others at ease and encourage their willingness to communicate with us.

In many initial encounters, communication may begin with the ritual of an introduction. When you are introduced to someone, it is important to try to communicate in a relaxed, appropriate, empathic, interested, and helpful way in relation to the other person. These communication behaviors are important in building and maintaining relationships over time.

If you are introducing two people to each other, consider the following suggestions.

1. Be sure to say both names distinctly.

2. Try to add some information about each person, to give the individuals a conversational starting point.

3. Present an older person or the person with more authority and status first.

5. When possible, stay and participate in the first part of the communication interaction.

In any introduction, use your communication skills to increase the possibility that a sense of communication attraction will develop.

Stage Two: Stabilizing

Not all first encounters result in either personal or public relationships. Sometimes, because of circumstances, we do not even follow up on initial encounters in which communication attraction was present. However, through either accidental or intentional continued contact and communication, we do form relationships with selected individuals. When we form a relationship, the second stage of communication is a dynamic phase of experiencing, responding to, adjusting to, and stabilizing that relationship.

Characteristics of Positive Relationships

Our ultimate goal is that each relationship we have will be a positive one. Communication behaviors are the key to positive relationships. Positive relationships are characterized by trust, commitment, equality, openness, supportiveness, and empathy. When these characteristics exist, we can usually maintain a truthful, ethical, comfortable, mutually productive interaction with others.

Trust   The key characteristic in stabilizing relationships is trust. *Trust* is a confidence in the words and actions of another person. It is a sense of knowing that the other person is truthful and dependable. Trust comes from experience with another person and faith in that person. Mutual trust is essential to the development of a positive relationship.

Lack of trust occurs when experiences with a person damage our faith in that person. Mistrust can result in defensiveness or competitiveness. These qualities have already been discussed as barriers to effective communication (Chapter 1), as barriers to making ethical choices (Chapter 5), and as barriers to effective listening and responding (Chapter 8). Consequently, we can also say that defensive and competitive communication choices can be barriers to positive relationships.

Commitment   A relationship with another person demands a *commitment,* which is an investment of time and energy in the relationship. A relationship without commitment will wither. If we take relationships for granted—with family, friends, mentors, or bosses—we are forgetting that relationships grow because the people in them work to meet each other's needs.

Trust and commitment may be as important in occupational relationships as in personal ones.

If we recall the three possible levels of relationships, we can imagine the kinds of communication energy that are necessary to stabilizing and maintaining a relationship. People can devote positive communication energy to a relationship to move the relationship forward. Minimal energy means that no effort is made at effective communication. Negative energy is seen in communication choices that are self-serving or keep the relationship from moving forward toward mutual goals. Only when positive energy is exerted by all parties in a relationship will the relationship flourish.

Other Communication Behaviors   In stabilizing and maintaining relationships, it is important to remember to use communication skills that encourage interaction and effectively sustain the circular communication process. In this book, we have discussed communication choices in relation to self-concept, perception, and the influences of needs, values, priorities, and ethics; we have also identified some important nonverbal and verbal communication skills. In each case, we have emphasized that being aware of variables in the communication process can lead to greater effectiveness in building relationships.

Using communication skills

When you are making choices about communicating in a positive relationship, remember to keep your communication appropriate to yourself, the situation, and the other person as much as possible. Try to be relaxed and open whenever possible. One of the most constructive ways to relax is to concentrate on putting the other person at ease. Be empathic in listening and giving feedback. Try to communicate both an intellectual and an emotional understanding of the other person's messages. This leads easily into showing interest in the other person. Use your verbal and nonverbal skills to show that you are willing to listen and respond effectively.

Stage Three: Evaluation

Relationships change. Therefore, when a relationship is formed and stabilized, it must be constantly evaluated to determine if it is still meeting needs. This is because each individual in a relationship is constantly changing, and so are the needs each person brings to the relationship.

Generally speaking, if relationships are nurtured and maintained, and if the people in them grow and change together, the relationships will change accordingly and will endure. Communication is essential to dealing with change in relationships. If relationships do not change as the people in them change, they may deteriorate. Conflicts within the relationships may increase, and choices about the continuation of the relationships must be made and communicated. Evaluation and communication may result in a redefinition— or even a termination—of a relationship.

Checkpoint *Think about a positive relationship you know about (public or personal). What verbal and nonverbal behaviors seem to enhance and maintain the relationship? Is there ever any evidence of negative energy in the relationship? Has the relationship reached an evaluation stage? What happened if it did?*

Conflict in Relationships

In your study of literature, you have learned that conflict is a necessary ingredient in a short story or novel. Very simply, literature teachers define **conflict** as a struggle between two forces. Under such a broad definition, communication itself is full of conflict—the sender struggles to recreate a message in the mind of the receiver, against the force of the barriers in the channel that may interrupt or distort that message. Life is a series of conflicts or struggles, and no relationship can endure without experiencing conflict.

The Nature of Conflict

There are several words commonly associated with conflict. *Frustration* is related to the uncertainty that arises from an inability to make choices and resolve problems. *Stress* is strain or pressure resulting from unrelieved frustration. *Burnout* reflects a state of hopelessness or alienation resulting from unrelieved stress.

All of these conditions can be mild or severe, and all affect the way we feel about the forces at work in our lives. Few of us go through a day without experiencing some conflict, and the conflict is often reflected in our communication. The way we communicate in our relationships is affected by conflict, whether the conflict is within the relationship or outside of it, affecting one of the individuals in the relationship.

Conflict is a natural outgrowth of the effort expended by individuals to meet needs, make ethical choices, and achieve goals. Conflict does *not* have to be negative. When conflicts occur in a relationship, communication skills can help to resolve them.

Conflict may be positive

Conflicts can often produce positive results. Frustration, for example, is also a part of accomplishment. Few great things were ever accomplished without moments of frustration that related to the conflict between what was and what could be. Think of Beethoven, who became deaf while still composing his symphonies, or of Marie Curie who battled radiation burns while uncovering the mysteries of uranium. Conflicts may often spur us to try harder to meet our goals.

Perceptions can be clarified through conflict. New truths may emerge through sharing and discussing conflicting perceptions. If teammates argue about how to win a close game, their individual perceptions may reveal that they are reacting to the competitive communication of their opponents. By concentrating, instead, on effective communication among team members, the team may have a better chance of winning. People who work their way through conflict together may also develop a stronger relationship as the result of their efforts.

Analyzing Conflict

Conflicts occur in the best of relationships. Conflicts can result from clashes between individual perceptions, goals, or beliefs. Some usual subjects of conflict are values, power, resources such as space, money, or time, policies, and facts.

Conflicts need not damage relationships. The way conflict is handled is far more important than the fact that conflict occurs. Handling conflict constructively depends on communicating about it accurately. Some steps to take in analyzing conflict in order to resolve it may be helpful.

Diagnose the Conflict

The first step is to *diagnose* the conflict. Because conflict can become emotional, the real cause of the problem may

When conflict occurs, it is important to try to identify the issue despite negative emotions.

*Sources
of conflict*

be masked by an emotion. Resolving a problem cannot occur until everyone involved can properly identify the problem and verbalize it.

If conflict is present in a relationship and neither party makes the effort to identify its cause, each will carry around unformulated and vague notions about the problem. No attempt at resolution can begin until the problem can be talked about as well as felt.

Identify a Level

Having diagnosed the problem, people next need to *identify the level* at which the conflict exists. Sometimes the conflict will exist only intrapersonally. We may be struggling with a choice between two values or two needs, and our struggle is creating a conflict in a relationship. Knowing that will enable us to resolve the conflict within ourselves and take it out of the relationship.

The conflict may be interpersonal. This commonly occurs when two individuals in a relationship want the same thing but only one can have it. A typical expression we use is, "You always want your own way!" Having two individuals in a relationship who both "want their way" means conflict.

Another common source of interpersonal conflict comes when two individuals have different goals or values that are operating on the choices they are trying to make together. If the question in a friendship is, "What shall we do tonight?" and one friend values a good time and the other values making good grades, the conflict over the night's plans will relate to their different values.

The conflict influencing a relationship can also be environmental. If a person in the relationship is uncomfortable or generally unhappy in the environment, the communication in the relationship can become negative and inappropriate, resulting in conflict. A high-school student whose parents have relocated during his or her senior year may be so miserable in the new school that he or she introduces conflict into the family relationship.

Identify the People Involved

The third step in conflict resolution is to *identify the people involved* in the conflict and those affected by it. The choices that will lead to eventual resolution of conflict sometimes have to be evaluated in terms of the impact a specific action or reaction will have on others.

Before decisions about what to do can be made, a clear understanding of who is affected must be achieved. We are usually able to identify the primary actors in a conflict, but we may overlook others who will also be involved or affected by its resolution.

Find a Focus

Fourth, having verbalized the problem, determined on what level it is operating, and identified the people affected by it, we need to determine the real *focus* of the conflict. What are the issues? Do they relate to resources (time, space, money, or supplies), to procedures (how something can be handled or achieved), or to people (how one person's behavior affects another's)? Sometimes this is the most difficult step of all, because we sometimes repress the real issue involved in a conflict and try to deal with the "symptoms" instead.

Part of the process of finding the focus or issue in a conflict is to think in terms of facts, beliefs, values, and policies. Are these things at the heart of the conflict? Or is the real issue the appropriate role for someone, cultural differences, differences in priorities, or differences in communication styles? Whatever the real issue or focus is, it must be identified and faced realistically if we wish to analyze the conflict.

Managing Conflict

If you think about two toddlers playing with one another and both wanting the same toy, you will see interpersonal conflict in its simplest and most basic form. A toddler may often resolve the conflict by banging the other child on the head, thus gaining the desired object, or by finding another toy and retiring from the conflict. As we mature, we become more sophisticated in our responses to conflict and our ability to manage it. We develop an understanding of the communication options open to us.

There are several communication strategies available to a person who is working for the resolution of a conflict. When you decide on which of those strategies to follow, you are deciding on the outcome of the conflict. Consequently, a close examination of each strategy, the communication behaviors it requires, and the usual outcome it brings will assist you in making a choice of which to use.

Coercion

A conflict can be resolved through **coercion** or force. This force can be physical, psychological, or emotional. It resolves conflict by forcing one individual to bow completely to the will of another, not because the individual chooses to do so, but because he or she believes there is no choice.

The communication behaviors employed in coercion may involve unethical choices and reasoning errors. Coercion is generally unacceptable because it is unethical. Its effect on a relationship will always be negative.

Avoidance

Another strategy for resolving conflict is **avoidance** or repression. This strategy does not remove the source of the conflict; it merely allows one or both persons to repress or hide the conflict. The communication behaviors employed in avoidance are refusal to discuss the conflict, open denial that there is a conflict, or talking about surface "symptoms" or behaviors rather than real issues.

If the issue that caused the conflict is not really important (or if the relationship is not important), avoidance may be a practical communication choice. When either the problem or the relationship is important, avoidance is not a good choice. It prolongs the conflict, moves the stress to an intrapersonal level as "bottled up" anxiety, and may even cause the problem to grow. It will almost always cause the conflict to be communicated eventually in an inappropriate and unproductive fashion.

Accommodation

Accommodation—giving in to the wishes of the other person—is another communication strategy for resolving conflict. There is no unique communication behavior in this strategy. One party merely communicates verbally or non-

Negotiation is a healthy strategy for resolving conflict if communication remains ethical.

verbally, "You win!" This is a one-way resolution and can establish an imbalance in the pattern of communication in the relationship. If the issue of the conflict is relatively unimportant, accommodation can be acceptable. However, if a balanced and healthy relationship is important, repeated accommodation may not be wise.

Negotiation

When resolving conflict, **negotiation** is often used to good advantage. This strategy involves making a trade to get what we desire. It is a bargaining process. Usually, each individual gets something he or she values. Occupational relationships often involve negotiation, whether in a formalized manner such as labor unions use, or in an informal way such as exchanges in committee deliberations or board meetings.

People in interpersonal relationships also use negotiation. If we want an extension on our weekend curfew, we may offer to check in by telephone so our parents will not worry about our safety. If a friend wants us to help with a difficult homework assignment, he or she may offer to type the final copy of our English paper in return. In communicating in a negotiation, we clarify exactly what we want before beginning, and we must be sure of which elements in the conflict are negotiable and which are not. Negotiation is a healthy communication strategy that can resolve conflicts productively.

Confrontation and Collaboration

Confrontation and collaboration, when used together as a single strategy, can be the best method of resolving conflict. **Confrontation,** in this sense, is a time during which the parties in a conflict communicate openly and honestly about the conflict, the issues in the conflict, and the options for solution. The confrontation occurs with the prior understanding that the purpose is not to assess fault but to examine alternatives. A prior commitment to cooperation is essential to success.

The process moves quickly from confrontation to **collaboration** when creative thinking about the alternatives begins. The greatest advantage to this approach is that while communicating about alternatives, collaborators may discover new solutions that had escaped them as they thought individually and in isolation.

Checkpoint *Explain each of the communication strategies for resolving conflict.*

Coping with Unresolved Conflict

Through the skillful use of communication strategies, most conflicts in relationships can be resolved. However, we sometimes encounter conflicts that, for a variety of reasons, cannot be resolved. When this occurs, we must cope successfully. Intrapersonal communication, or self-talk, is the key to that coping.

People with strong self-concepts who have established effective intrapersonal skills will use them. First, we will need to examine the value of the relationship involved. Next, we should make an honest assessment of the nature and importance of the unresolved conflict. Finally, we must determine just what alternatives are available. Throughout, remember that unresolved conflicts demand creative skills.

Redefining Relationships

Because of unresolved conflicts, unproductive communication patterns, or natural changes in needs, relationships sometimes end. In the first two situations, redefining a relationship is usually painful. In the third, it may be a gradual and natural process.

Sometimes the choice to terminate or redefine a relationship will be yours. At other times, it will be a choice made by the other person. No matter whose choice it is, the choice will usually follow conflict. It will occur during the third stage of the relationship—the time for evaluation. If you have analyzed the conflict, and have used the communication strategies available to you in trying to resolve the conflict without success, redefinition of the relationship is not only unavoidable, it is healthy.

Once more, communication skills become vital in redefining or terminating a relationship. Being open and honest with the other person may not be easy, but it is essential.

Having arrived at a decision about the relationship, it is appropriate to share that decision and avoid, as much as possible, extreme emotionalism, anger, or hostility.

Five guidelines for communication in redefining a relationship can assist you:

Five guidelines

1. Choose the time and place to allow for privacy and time for open communication.

2. Consider the feelings of the other person, using firm but empathic strategies in stating your feelings.

3. Be willing to listen to the other person's feelings and allow the other person to understand your reasons.

4. Consider discussing options and alternatives, but do not prolong the discussion needlessly.

5. If emotional conflict begins to arise, disagree without being disagreeable and end the conversation quickly.

If the decision to end a relationship has been made by the other person, your task is to accept that choice without damaging and negative emotions. Using some of these same communication guidelines can help you do that.

Regardless of whose choice it is to redefine a relationship, the important thing to remember is that the relationship is still a part of your total experience and has been a meaningful part of your life. Strictly speaking, no relationship is ever ended; it is redefined.

Checkpoint

Can you think of several historical events (such as wars, scientific discoveries, political debates, etc.) in which the resolution of conflict had positive results? What role did communication play in the resolution of the conflict? What relationships were strengthened or terminated because of the conflict?

Summary

Relationships, which reflect a bonding between individuals as a result of their interaction, are central to our lives. We have both personal and public relationships. Communication is central in the formation and maintenance of relationships.

Because relationships are dynamic, they evolve in stages: first impressions, stabilizing, and evaluation. In each of these stages, communication skills and strategies allow for the development of the relationship. Conflict is a natural part of relationships, but conflict can be resolved through the application of communication strategies. When these are not successful, relationships must be redefined.

Check Your Knowledge

1. Define *relationship.*

2. What are some communication characteristics of positive relationships?

3. What are some communication characteristics of negative relationships?

4. List the stages involved in building relationships.

Check Your Understanding

1. Explain why a combination of confrontation and collaboration is the best communication strategy for resolving conflicts in relationships.

2. Why is conflict in a relationship *not* always negative?

3. Why is communication essential to positive relationships?

Check Your Skills

1. Think of two acquaintances you could introduce to each other, and write a script for the introduction that would give their initial meeting a good start.

2. Think of three personal relationships you have and of three public relationships. List the differences in your communication in them.

3. Think of a conflict that has been successfully resolved in one of your relationships. Determine which of the communication strategies you or the other person used.

Communicating Across Cultures

Because communication is a product not only of our own selves but also of the total culture in which we develop our communication skills, we each reflect our culture's unique communication characteristics. Those characteristics can be imbedded in our languages, our nonverbal symbols, our expectations for group behavior, and in a vast number of ways we interact with each other. When we find ourselves communicating in a brand new culture, such as a new school or another state or country, we experience dramatically the importance of what has been called cross-cultural communication.

One way in which American students have traditionally been given the opportunity to learn and practice effective cross-cultural communication is through studying abroad or inviting foreign students into their homes. When such opportunities are available, a "communication laboratory" results, which, if one is alert, can be a rich experience for everyone involved. The following quotes are from an essay written by an American student who had the opportunity to study abroad.

"The summer I spend as a student ambassador provided me with many learning experiences about the differences in world cultures. . . . Even though we were from completely different worlds, I learned to stay open to experience and not judge others by my own standards. As a result, I had a wonderful time."

It is important to remember that cultures do not differ just between countries. We do not have to travel to need skills in communicating with people who are different from us. In your classroom, each person represents many cultural traditions. A truly effective communicator attempts to understand the perspective of everyone involved in a communication situation.

Communicating across cultures then, comes down to being sensitive to and interested in others and to being aware of your own heritage. In this way, exciting opportunities exist for sharing and learning about the endless variety of cultures that interact in our world.

TOWARD EFFECTIVE
Group Communication

Groups come in all shapes and sizes. They may be formal or informal, small or large, private or public. People participate in a wide variety of groups throughout their lives. Each role a person plays as a group member provides an opportunity for interaction and depends on effective, dynamic communication.

Effective group communication produces effective organizations and results in effective problem solving. Whether a group exists to accomplish tasks, provide social interaction, or encourage public discussion, the communication among its leaders and members involves making appropriate choices. From families to formal parliamentary groups, communication is central to effective, productive interaction. An understanding of the ideas in this Part will help you develop valuable skills to increase your effectiveness as a communicator in groups.

CHAPTER 10

Understanding Group Communication

After reading this chapter you should be able to:

1

Define *group.*

2

Describe the importance of groups in our society.

3

Distinguish between casual and formal groups.

4

Identify the group categories.

5

Describe the process of gaining group membership.

6

Describe the two kinds of group membership.

Group

Norms

Primary or
predetermined
group

Reference group

Social group

Casual group

Formal group

Task-oriented
group

Consensus

Nuclear member

Marginal member

You are probably a member of far more groups than you realize. How many can you list? Some of the groups you are part of are permanent, and some are temporary. They are all an essential part of your life, and you must learn to communicate in small groups to become educated, to have a quality family life, to be employed, or to be a part of the governmental and social affairs of your community. One can live a whole lifetime without ever making a formal public speech, but few people can survive a week of ordinary living without interacting in at least one group. For most of us, every day is a continuing series of group communication situations.

The Nature and Importance of Groups

Most of us would say that a group is a collection or congregation of people. But, is every bunch of people a communication group? In the context of communication, it is helpful to have a precise definition. A communication **group** is 1) a collection of more than two people who 2) communicate face-to-face, 3) work together toward a common goal, 4) think of the group as a unit, and 5) recognize group rules (or *norms*).

In order to test our understanding of groups by this definition, let's apply each of these tests to the following groups of people: students in the cafeteria line, students standing in line to see a movie, a Student Council committee, and students in detention hall. If you applied each of these tests, you'll know that only one of those groups functions as a communication group—the Student Council committee.

Test the definition

The people who talk while standing in line at the cafeteria or who sit in detention hall are not a group. Another example is the people who chat while standing in line for two hours to buy concert tickets. The ticket buyers lack a common goal (each one's goal is separate—to buy his or her own tickets), and they have no feeling of unity or oneness as a group of people. A ticket buyer could be expected to speak of those in line as "*I*" and "*they*," not "*we,* the line." On the other hand, a family or a regular crew of coworkers can both probably be called groups for our purposes. Both family and crew must communicate. They are also more likely to speak of what they achieve as a group as something "we" are working for together, and in which "we" will have pride *as a group.* They have a group identity.

The line of ticket buyers, the family, and the crew of coworkers all acknowledge some group rules. The one major rule for those people wanting to attend the concert is, "stay in line and wait your turn." For them, there are few added rules, but there are usually many rules that families and coworkers follow to make living or working together successful. A group's rules may be standards of conduct or ways of doing things that are accepted without discussion. A phrase frequently heard about them is, "That's just the way we've

Norms

always done it." We call those rules **norms.** Norms exist in every group, and some group norms influence all of us. Our wish to be included in the group motivates us to conform, and conforming to the norms helps us to be accepted by the group. You can remember the word *norm* and its meaning by thinking of it as what is *normal* or typical for the group.

Groups influence the ideas and actions of their members, because members think of the group as a unit. That is, the members feel a part of the group, try to behave as other members do, and therefore make decisions according to group rules. Group influence is usually strongest while a member

Various influences

is actively taking part in group activities. In some cases, however, that influence continues long after the group has disbanded or the member has left. The former member simply continues to use the group's norms in making decisions. During a lifetime, many group memberships will affect the decision-making habits of most people.

We live in a culture that depends on group communication and group systems for many activities. The family, church, and school all work in groups, and our entire government runs by group process. Our legislature works primarily through small committees, which study and recommend legislation to the larger group for action. Our courts leave many legal decisions to a group of twelve jurors. In large businesses and industries work is done by crews, teams, or management groups. A hospital, for example, uses shifts of workers, groups of managers and supervisors, staffs for some areas, and teams for specialized kinds of work.

Communication skills are essential to the group process, no matter what the purpose of the group is.

Because group process is so important to us in our daily lives, we need to learn all we can about groups. We need to know how our group memberships influence us. We also need special skills to be sure we can communicate well in groups, because through communication group members influence each other. Because we participate in different kinds of communication groups, we need special knowledge and skills to be effective members in each group.

Checkpoint *How many groups have you been a member of during the past 24 hours? Can you identify some norms that are accepted by one of those groups?*

Categories of Groups

By our definition there are several categories of groups. The categories we will describe here are 1) primary or predetermined groups, 2) reference groups, 3) social groups, and 4) task-oriented groups. The first three categories will be explored primarily because of their influences on us, and task-oriented groups will be considered as special situations in which we communicate.

*We Are
Born into
Predetermined
Groups*

Groups like families, cultural or ethnic groups, and people living in specific geographic areas are called **primary** or **predetermined groups.** Ordinarily a person does not need to work at becoming a member of a predetermined group. Membership usually dates from birth. You may be a member as the result of who you are or where you were born or live. Predetermined groups usually include some lifelong commitment. Often these groups give the individual his or her first sense of identity and belonging. They are a primary source of physical and emotional support. They influence growing young people and teach them what they should and should not do through examples and feedback.

Families are important, primary reference groups.

We Evaluate Ourselves by Reference Groups

Consider the groups that are important to you. We care more about being accepted by some groups than others. Any group that is significant in your life is a **reference group.** We evaluate the things we do and adapt our behaviors to meet the expectations of our reference groups. Reference groups may be groups you have been a member of in the past, groups of which you are currently a member, or any groups you wish to be a member of in the future. Predetermined groups serve as reference groups for most of us. The longer a group relationship lasts, the more likely it is to be a *referent* (the object of reference) for its members.

When we discussed the development of self-concept, we explained that we modify our conduct and our images of ourselves to meet the expectations of the people around us—a reference group, like a family or a group of classmates. You learned from your family some behaviors that were considered appropriate for you as a family member, and you learned in other groups a different set of expected behaviors or norms. As a small child, when you first went to school, you probably learned there were some things you did at home that were not allowed at school. As you have grown older, you have adjusted to the expectations of numerous groups, and have realized that we all need to be an accepted part of a group or groups.

We Join and Leave Social Groups

In the third category are **social groups.** The primary purpose of a social group is companionship for its members, although some social clubs have more serious purposes as well. Social groups may be casual (unstructured and unplanned), or formal and carefully organized, often with strict *parliamentary rules* (parliamentary groups will be discussed in Chapter 13). The work of a social group is likely to be the planning and preparation of entertainment events for its members. A travel club, a social organization at school, or a few close friends who get together regularly to play golf, fish, shop, restore old cars, dance, or to enjoy some other recreational activity are all informal social groups. Fraternities and civic organizations are formal social groups.

Casual Groups

A **casual group** develops spontaneously and exists only as long as it is beneficial or convenient to the members. A casual group relationship may last a few days or a lifetime. For example, a close group of high-school friends may gradually lose contact with each other after graduation, or they may be close friends forever.

Sometimes casual groups arise accidentally out of situations that were not primarily planned to create or organize groups. Examples are the close relationship of friends who first came together because they were assigned to work on a class project, or a close social group that developed in a coffee shop or small restaurant because the members ate or had coffee there on a regular basis. In spontaneous social groups there are no formal rules, elections, or assigned titles, although most groups do label certain behaviors acceptable or unacceptable as the need arises.

A social group may hold special meetings to recognize contributions made by individual members.

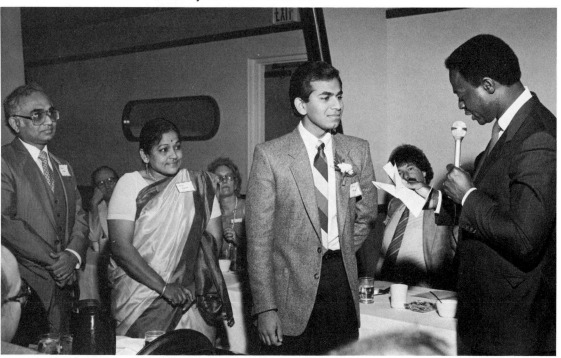

Formal Groups

Formal groups (or parliamentary social groups) have a more organized structure and tend to be larger than casual social groups. The group usually has a name, may have a clearly defined statement of purpose, and often has rules (or *bylaws*). In some formal groups, participants are voted into membership. Leaders are elected or appointed, and meetings usually follow parliamentary procedure. Often, social groups with a more structured organization focus on one kind of entertainment or recreation. They are special-purpose social clubs.

Dual-purpose groups

Some formal social groups have two purposes. Each exists for companionship *and* another purpose, which is often a benevolent one. Service clubs, civic or professional organizations, political groups, or amateur athletic groups fit in this category. Some examples are: Rotary International, the Booster Club for a local athletic team, or The Young Republicans or Democrats. We are surrounded by groups of this type. There are dozens of clubs in your town that fit in this category, and you probably belong to at least one of them.

These dual-purpose clubs may have either service or companionship as a priority, and some are more task oriented than others. Most of these groups exist to do some particular kind of work or activity. They may be organized to accomplish special goals for themselves or others. In that case companionship is secondary. The organization of Shriners is a clear example of a dual-purpose organization. The public may see the Shriner clowns or motorcycle riders in parades or at a Shriners' circus and assume the group exists only for fun and companionship. What many do not know is that one of the group's primary goals is raising money to build and operate children's hospitals and to fund medical and surgical care for children. A similar combination of social and task purposes exists in many groups.

Task-Oriented Groups

Task-oriented groups exist to do work, to fill a specific need, or to perform a particular function. Some groups that fit in this category because of their concern with a task are groups that exist for therapy, study, information sharing,

Task-oriented groups might also be dual-purpose formal groups.

political action, policy making, problem solving, and committee work of all kinds. The type includes both casual groups (like an information-sharing review session just before an examination), and formal, parliamentary groups (like the Executive Board of the Family Outreach Center).

All types of task-oriented groups have a *communication focus* within the group itself, although the task they discuss may be related to something outside the group. Public discussion groups (which will be discussed in Chapter 13) have a primary communication focus that is external, with the audience. Instead of discussing problems within the group, public discussions are designed to inform or persuade an audience.

Focus

The goals of task-oriented groups often center on making decisions or choosing policies or courses of action that will solve problems. These are sometimes casual groups, but predetermined groups and formal parliamentary groups may engage in problem-solving discussions, too.

Goals

Group discussions to develop policies or new ways of doing things must begin with identifying the problem that makes a change necessary. The discussion will not be productive unless it moves through some orderly steps, from the problem to the solution. It is important to know that the group attempts to arrive at total agreement about the policy or solution that results from the discussion. Total agreement in groups is called **consensus.** Even though consensus is not always possible, it is still often the goal for task-oriented groups.

Checkpoint *Can you name the four kinds of groups we have just discussed?*

Select a group you are a part of or are familiar with. Decide which kind of group it is and explain why it fits the definition.

Achievement of Group Membership

Our definition of *group* says members "communicate face-to-face"—in the same place at the same time. The word *communicate* is central to the whole idea of groups and group membership. Our definition does not mean that group members must *always* be in the same place at the same time, but it does suggest that face-to-face communication will happen. Group members must communicate with each other, and without communication, no group membership can develop.

Group membership also requires sharing some common goal. We seek memberships in groups of people we see as being like us in some way or with whom we share some common ground, such as an academic interest, involvement in sports, forensics, or a church, a vocational goal, politics, or another activity.

Changing for acceptance

As children we tried to look and act like an older brother or sister or some teenager we admired and thought important. In a similar way, we will change in order to be accepted into a group, but only when the membership is *important* to us. If the group is very attractive to us, the number and importance of the changes we will make increase.

An illustration of change to achieve group acceptance is a student who wishes to become a member of some elite social group. He or she may first observe the obvious differences between himself or herself and the group members, and attempt to be enough like the others to gain acceptance. Suppose that at first the student notices the elite group has a different style of dress and hair fashion. The first change may be to look more like the group. Next the aspiring member may try to be in the same place at the same time as the group, and so may begin to "hang around" wherever the group usually is found. If the group is involved with some hobby, the student may begin to practice that activity in his or her ongoing effort toward gaining acceptance. The changes continue until membership is gained, or until the further changes required seem too costly (and the group is not attractive enough to make the effort worthwhile). Then the changes stop.

Negative changes

In an effort of the kind described, people sometimes are willing to change too much of themselves. People with healthy self-concepts will only make minor changes, in habits or language, for example, to gain membership in a group whose members are not extremely different from them. People who aren't sure they are acceptable *as they are,* however, may make enormous effort to change for a group that appears powerful or attractive, even if they have little in common with the members. Their tactics for gaining acceptance may take them further and further away from the behaviors considered appropriate by their families or other reference groups.

Some people may assume that membership in a powerful group will prove their acceptability (If the group accepts me, I must be okay). Unwholesome groups may take advantage of an aspiring member's felt need, and subject new members to cruel or degrading initiation requirements. Street gangs, for example, sometimes require an awesome "price" for membership. A last proof of "worthiness for membership" may be some act which is a complete violation of the potential member's past values or standards of conduct.

If group members go along with acts that are contrary to their past beliefs and standards (and which may even be dangerous or illegal), then they must alter their self-concepts accordingly. They must also replace the standards of their primary and reference groups with the standards of the new group. This may cut them off from their first reference groups completely. They may even cling to a new group that is undesirable or punishing just because they are no longer sure of who they are by themselves. If they have given up all other reference groups for the new one, there may be no one else to supply a sense of belonging.

Positive changes

On the other hand, if we carefully select the groups to which we want to belong, we may make very positive changes in our lives. The indifferent student who wants to be accepted as a part of a group of academic achievers may find a new excitement in becoming an achiever, too. The student who takes up a hobby because of an admiration for others involved in it might even discover a talent that could be both profitable and enjoyable. In any event, group membership can have either positive or negative consequences, and we must give careful consideration before we join a group to those possible consequences.

Checkpoint *Can you think of a group you wanted to be a member of sometime in the past, and later decided the cost was too great?*

Kinds of Group Membership

Nuclear members

In a group that stays together over a period of time, there is a central cluster of members who are important to the group. They are **nuclear members** because they form the nucleus, or core, of the group in decision making. Nuclear members have power. The group listens when they speak and accepts their ideas or plans more readily than they accept ideas from others.

Members become a part of the group's nuclear unit gradually. They become accepted, gain the group's trust, and prove their loyalty and value to the group. They may prove their worth to the group by solving a problem or supplying leadership. In return, the group gives them a higher status. In formal parliamentary groups, nuclear members hold offices, chair committees, and serve on executive councils or governing bodies. Think of the casual or spontaneous social groups in which you have memberships. Can you identify the nuclear members in each? In how many groups do *you* have nuclear membership?

Marginal members

Another kind of group membership is marginal membership. A **marginal member** is one who is not a nuclear member, and who has only a kind of limited acceptance by the group. Marginal members have little power, and when they make suggestions, they are not given as much consideration as nuclear members. They may be involved with the group to a limited degree, either because they choose to remain on the edge of the group or because the group only partly accepts them. In formal parliamentary groups, marginal members may be those who attend meetings only now and then, or who attend regularly but are never given leadership roles of any kind. Their opinions are rarely sought regarding important decisions.

Marginal members may choose to limit their involvement in a group, or may be only partially accepted by other group members.

Some members may *choose* marginal status, however, because they enjoy the group or its activities, but do not want to make a great commitment to it. They may have limited amounts of time to devote to the group. Serious students who work more than a few hours a week at outside jobs, for example, will have little time or energy left over for clubs or social groups. Another person may choose to be a marginal member because it is easier to participate in several groups when he or she has fewer leadership roles. Whether you are a marginal or nuclear member of a particular group may depend on the group's purpose or reason for existence.

Checkpoint

You are probably a marginal member of some groups. Do you know which of your group memberships are marginal? Can you sort your group participation into nuclear and marginal memberships?

Summary

The characteristics that define a group are:

1. More than two persons

2. Face-to-face communication

3. A common goal

4. Group identity

5. Group norms

Our culture is basically group oriented, and all of us must communicate in groups. The categories of groups we are likely to be concerned with are predetermined groups, social groups, reference groups, and task-oriented groups. We gain membership in groups by conforming to group norms, and we acquire status or a central power position as nuclear members by proving our worth to the group. Members with little status or central position are called marginal group members. Our membership and effective communication in groups are essential to participation in society.

Check Your Knowledge

1. Define *group.*

2. What is a reference group?

3. What is a group norm? How do norms influence members?

4. How do people become members of predetermined groups? How is the achievement of membership different for social groups?

5. What is meant by *consensus*?

Check Your Understanding

1. If you want to know whether a cluster of people you observe is a group by our definition, what characteristics should you look for?

2. Think of some group norms in your family or another predetermined group. How do the norms influence your behavior when you are with that group? Is the influence different when you are away from the group?

3. Are there some dual-purpose clubs in your school? What are their purposes?

4. Groups respond differently to the ideas communicated by nuclear and marginal members. What is the difference?

5. Think of a group you aspire to be a member of someday (a teacher on a school faculty, a staff member of a hospital, etc.). What changes will you need to make in the way you communicate before you become a member of that group?

6. Make a group participation inventory.
   a. List your predetermined groups.
   b. Name your social groups.
   c. List your present task-oriented groups.
   d. Look over the lists you have created, and put an *R* beside each group which is also a reference group.
   e. Go over the groups again and write the length of your membership beside each (2 weeks, 15 years, etc.).
   f. From the list, choose the three groups you think have influenced you the most. Mark them *I, II,* and *III,* making *I* the most important.

Check Your Skills

1. a. Share the discoveries you made in completing the Group Participation Inventory above with a classmate.
   b. Compare the groups each of you marked *I, II,* and *III.*
   c. Are the groups similar? Are some the same?

2. a. What predetermined groups were you "born into"?
   b. How do you think the predetermined groups have caused you to think and act differently from others?

3. Can you identify some casual groups you have been a part of in the past? What ended your participation?

4. In your school are there some groups whose members can be recognized by some styles of dress, by meeting in some particular place, or by some other identifying factor? What do the identifying factors tell you about the group norms?

5. Can you think of someone you know or have known who changed so much for acceptance in a group that he or she "lost" a previous reference group?
   a. Give the person a fictional name.
   b. Write a brief account of what happened. Be sure to protect the person's identity by avoiding giving any information that would identify him or her.

6. Look at the photograph on page 192. What type of group do you think this is? Why? Which people in the photograph do you think are nuclear members? Marginal members? What kind of topic do you think they are discussing?

CHAPTER 11

Participating in Group Discussion

After reading this chapter you should be able to:

1
List some rules for giving feedback to prevent group conflict.

2
Explain the organizational leadership role in groups.

3
Describe three leadership styles.

4
Explain the task roles in groups.

5
Explain the maintenance roles in groups.

6
Identify and describe negative roles in groups.

7
Describe common communication patterns.

8
Observe a group situation and diagram its interaction pattern.

Key Terms

Organizational leader
Autocratic style
Laissez-faire style
Democratic style
Task roles
Maintenance roles
Negative roles
Interaction pattern
Interaction diagram

Many of the groups in which we are involved use discussion to reach decisions or solve problems. Important roles are played by all group members, in leading and participating in discussion. In this chapter we will discuss a variety of behaviors that contribute to a healthy group atmosphere.

Group members can play both positive and negative roles, of course, so it is important to understand feedback, conflict resolution, and general problem-solving steps in participating in groups. It will also be helpful to you to understand the common interaction patterns groups can follow, and to learn how to establish or change patterns to ensure positive, productive group communication and decision making.

When to Use Group Process

Knowing how different the perceptions of each person can be, how can any group arrive at total agreement about a controversial topic? We know that individuals can make decisions faster than groups. That means group process can be more time consuming. Does it mean that group discussion is an inefficient way to solve problems? No, it only means group process is not *always* the best way to proceed.

If, for example, time is very short or, if the decision to be made is highly technical and most of the group is uninformed, it is sometimes better to delegate decision making to one or two informed leaders. Questions that should be considered in choosing to use group process are:

1. Is there adequate time for discussion?

2. Is the group sufficiently informed?

3. Is the group willing to work cooperatively?

4. Is the group willing to accept responsibility for the decision?

When time permits and conditions are positive, group discussion has two important advantages. It yields high-quality decisions that make use of the problem-solving skills and creativity of the whole group; and it will result in higher group morale, cohesiveness, and dedication to carrying out whatever action the decision requires. The first of these advantages relates to the quality of the resulting work or

How might group process change in this situation? How might the interactions you see here influence later group discussions?

product. The second concerns the quality of the group's human relationships. We use these advantages to measure the success of group discussion.

Discussion is successful when it results in a high-quality decision with positive human relationships. This is in agreement with the goals of good interaction we set up earlier; we feel good about the decision and about ourselves. The more you understand about the group-discussion process and your participation in it, the better you will be able to use discussion for problem solving.

Checkpoint

Suppose you were the president of a club that had to make three immediate but small decisions and one very large decision (perhaps the choice of a service project for the school year), and your meeting time was very short. Do you think it would be better to a) allow the same amount of discussion time for all four topics, b) delay discussion of the large topic until a later meeting, or c) appoint a committee to make recommendations about the service project? Explain your decision to a classmate.

Requirements for Participation

Group members must be willing to discuss topics openly. The group must begin with a desire to cooperate (rather than compete) and to arrive at the best possible solution. As each member shows his or her willingness to cooperate and to contribute to the group honestly, he or she will be trusted. The building of interpersonal trust is essential to a healthy group atmosphere, in which ideas can be offered and tested through feedback.

Participating in Discussions

If you are inclined to listen and accept the ideas of others without ever sharing *your* ideas, remember that it is essential that every group member share ideas and assist in evaluating them. When you are reluctant to persuade others of your ideas, you let someone else persuade. Although that may seem cooperative, it delegates the responsibility for making decisions to someone else, and the "someone else" may not be offering a solution as workable as yours. In group discussion, all members share equally in responsibility for the outcome.

Constructive disagreement

Don't be afraid to disagree. Learn to use disagreement constructively to solve problems. After all, if everyone thought alike, no group communication would be necessary. There is a popular misconception that the absence of spoken disagreement means a group is in harmony. That is not always true. You already know that people often withdraw and decide to remain silent instead of arguing. Have you ever noticed that strangers are more likely than old friends to nod politely when someone voices an opinion contrary to their own?

As group members become more comfortable with each other, they often disagree aloud more frequently. They feel safe enough with each other to say they disagree without fear of losing friendship. Remember that feedback is a vitally important part of the communication process. If you are to be a helpful discussion-group member, you must continue to discuss important positions, even when you are not in complete agreement.

In general, we are afraid to state opposing views because we have had unpleasant experiences when we did not know how to state opposition or give feedback without competing. Three things are very important to remember in making your views known: 1) state your position as your own perspective; 2) do not label people because of their views; and 3) do not try to tell others what *they* think or feel. Keep an open attitude of *sharing* views rather than *arguing* them.

Feedback and Conflict Resolution

In group discussion, skillful feedback can keep a group functioning harmoniously and can often prevent serious conflict from occurring. When conflict does occur, the skillful use of feedback can often bring about its resolution. As we discussed earlier, when no complete resolution of conflict is possible, it must be managed in a way that permits the group to continue its work.

Let's see if you can improve your ability to prevent conflict. Remember that when trust wavers or conflict seems unavoidable, it is time to use the rules for empathic replies discussed in Chapter 8, and the conflict-resolution feedback rules listed in the following chart. The use of good feedback will help to create an atmosphere in which group members

---

Conflict Resolution Through Feedback

In group or interpersonal situations, when feedback seems necessary to limit further conflict or to improve the group atmosphere, you should observe certain rules.

1. Give feedback for improvement *only* when someone indicates a readiness for it. (Don't try to reform others.)
2. Give only as much feedback as someone can apply at one time. No one wants to hear a long chronicle of his or her errors. Try a single suggestion, such as "Well, when you interrupted to argue before Sam had finished stating his position, he seemed to give up and withdraw. How about listening carefully until he finishes before you reply?"
3. Be nonjudgmental. Never use ridicule. Focus feedback on an idea or a problem and its resolution, not on people. Label behaviors and ideas, not people.
4. Identify the *behavior* you wish changed, and phrase requests clearly. Take responsibility for your own feelings and actions—do not blame them on another person. Avoid phrases like, "you make me so mad . . ." Instead, try a request like this: "We really need to hear what you think about Margie's plan. When you don't talk at all, I begin to think you're not interested in solving the problem, and I find myself getting annoyed with you."
5. Give feedback quickly after an incident that produces conflict. The longer you delay in giving feedback, the more confusing a situation can become. Do not assume conflict will "go away." Give feedback about the here and now. Avoid ancient history.
6. Give honest, accurate feedback. Do not distort or exaggerate. For example, avoid phrases like "You've never done anything to help another person in your whole life!" (*Never* is rarely accurate.) Try instead, "This is your opportunity to help someone else who really needs you."
7. Question your own reasons for giving feedback. Be sure feedback is given for positive reasons, and is not destructive in purpose.
8. When you ask for change, and your partner or another group member tries and *shows* change (even minimal change), be sure to give *positive* feedback.

Feedback can be provided in many different ways.

feel safe in sharing their creative ideas. That means they must be willing to disagree at times.

Leadership in Groups

In order for every group member to play a part in creative problem solving, there must be leadership. Think of leadership as a specialized *service* a member supplies for the group and its work. Usually, the person who presides over a group is easily identified. We will call that person the *leader,* but it is important to keep in mind that he or she only supplies one *kind* of leadership. All group members can provide leadership, by playing important group roles, as well.

Organizational Leadership

An **organizational leader** is usually someone who speaks up when a new group is forming to say something like, "How shall we begin?" or "Let's begin by introducing ourselves." He or she is nearly always someone who thinks in a well-organized fashion and understands the problem-solving steps that must be followed in order to achieve a quality result and group consensus. In a formal parliamentary group, the presiding officer is the organizational leader. In a formal group structure he or she will have a title like President, Moderator, or Chairperson.

Whether a leader has a title or not, the role and purpose of the position are the same: 1) to apply a problem-solving sequence; 2) to give all members and their ideas a fair hearing in order to reach quality decisions; 3) to avoid distorting ideas; and 4) to keep a few people from controlling the discussion or manipulating others. The function is essential to any democratic group discussion.

When no one supplies organizational leadership, a group may arrive at a poor solution to a problem; a bully may dominate the group; the best ideas may never be heard; or the discussion may go around in circles, never arriving at a conclusion. The earlier an organizational leader emerges when a group discussion begins, the more efficiently the work of the group will proceed.

Styles of Organizational Leadership

A leader is likely to use a certain style in doing his or her job. The basic styles of leadership are autocratic, democratic, and laissez-faire. The three leadership styles rarely exist in "pure" forms; the leadership style of an individual leader tends to be more like one of those described than others. Each style is based on a different belief or philosophy about leadership, and each has both advantages and disadvantages.

The Autocratic Style

The **autocratic** (or authoritarian) **style** is carried out by a leader who feels he or she must keep firm control of the group to keep members from making errors. Autocratic leaders believe that they are better prepared to make decisions for their groups than the groups are. They share decision-making authority reluctantly, and are inclined to make decisions and announce them, rather than encourage the group to develop the decision or solution.

A dictatorship in government is an excellent example of autocratic leadership. The primary advantage of the autocratic system is that it can be highly efficient (that is, a decision can be made with an economy of time and energy) if the autocratic leader makes wise decisions. (Remember, it may

Autocratic leaders do not invite group members to participate in decision making.

be *faster*—but not always *better*—when one person decides and announces his or her decision to the group than when the group decides by discussion.

There are several disadvantages to the autocratic style. Members of groups led by such leaders usually have lower morales than members of other sorts of groups. Group members are less dedicated to carrying out the leader's decision, and their commitment is short-lived. A revolution of some kind may occur when the group becomes disenchanted with the leader, and when that happens a whole new leadership program (or government) must be built from scratch. (Autocratic leaders rarely find it easy to give up their roles, and they seldom make it easy for new leaders to get started.)

The Laissez-faire Style

The **laissez-faire** leader is one who feels the person holding a leadership title (President, Chairperson, etc.) should not interfere in whatever group members want to do. The advantages of this leadership style are great freedom for the group's members and great potential for creativity. Since creativity flourishes in an atmosphere where there are limited or flexible rules, laissez-faire leadership provides an environment where originality and expressiveness occur often.

This is also the disadvantage of laissez-faire leadership. It is important to understand that total freedom can cause chaos, because in a situation without rules, every person

Laissez-faire · leadership encourages independent work and creativity, but some direction is usually helpful in most group situations.

must be his or her own leader and create personal rules. When that happens, the rules or choices of each individual may clash with the choices of every other individual.

While an autocratic leader directs or decides too much alone, the laissez-faire leader directs too little. The resulting disadvantage is a frustrating lack of leadership, which hampers the group in accomplishing work or reaching decisions.

The Democratic Style

In the **democratic style,** the organizational leader encourages all members to participate in the responsibility for group decisions. Such leaders base their style on the belief that groups can diagnose problems and make sound, responsible decisions for themselves. They also feel groups need a leader to help bring about group decisions. Democratic leaders may best be called **facilitators,** or leaders who make the work of the group easier.

The advantages of democratic leadership over other styles are higher group morale, a feeling of group responsibility for and commitment to decisions, the use of the intellects and creativity of all, the ease of changing to a new leader when the time comes, and, in general, a group that stays together longer and is happier. One disadvantage is the greater time required for discussion and group decisions. Another is that the decisions made and the problems solved are only as good as the group members' ability, responsibility, honesty, and dedication.

Some structure for making rules must exist, and some authority must be delegated, for an orderly society to work. For example, through our delegated legislators we make

In the democratic style, the leader encourages all members to take part in reaching group decision.

laws, and by general consent we delegate the enforcement of those laws to our police personnel. In doing so we have, as a society, voluntarily limited our freedoms (to injure others, to take what is not ours, etc.), and we have delegated to others (law enforcement bodies) the authority to enforce those limits for the protection of us all.

Combining styles

Not only have we found a governmental democracy to be a good overall system, but we have found the democratic leadership style to be workable in situations such as discussion groups. Although leaders rarely adhere completely to autocratic, laissez-faire, or democratic styles, you will readily recognize the democratic leader, working somewhere between the autocratic and the laissez-faire style, as being more consistent with our description of a good organizational leader.

The ideal leader guides, but does not dictate. Such a leader protects the right of each member to have a say. He or she allows as much freedom for creative expression as possible without threatening the personal rights of individuals, the well-being of the group, or its future. He or she values and understands order and organization, and considers it his or her responsibility to assist the group in orderly decision making.

Checkpoint

Can you compare what happens in small groups with an autocratic leader to what happens in a government with a dictator?

_**Leadership Roles
of Group
Members**_

Now let's consider the parts group members play in keeping a group atmosphere comfortable and bringing about strong solutions to problems. As groups work, their members play certain membership roles. The roles are actually kinds of leadership responsibilities needed to keep the group going. Sometimes two or more persons share a role, and often a single member acts in more than one role. The longer a group stays together, the more likely each member will be to perform the same role regularly. After a time, the group expects each member to carry out his or her usual role.

In an informal group, it is important for each member to realize that the responsibility for supplying leadership functions belongs to everyone. Group problems should be identified by the first person in the group who becomes aware that a problem exists. If that person is _you,_ don't wait for someone else to supply the leadership. It is possible that you are the only one who recognizes the problem. To wait for someone else to notice it may cause delays and handicap the work of the group.

_Task and
maintenance
roles_

There are two general kinds of helpful roles group members can play, and several negative roles that work against the group or its goals. Examples are given in the chart on the following page. The helpful kinds of roles are _task roles_ and _maintenance roles._ You can remember them easily by thinking of roles related to the task the group must do, and others related to maintaining the human group itself.

Task roles all focus on helping the group reach its goal or get its work done. The **maintenance roles** are all centered on making the group's work pleasant and comfortable. Each role does something to improve the personal climate of the group, such as building morale, resolving conflict, or offering encouragement. Without having members to carry out task and maintenance roles, most groups would fall apart without completing their tasks. Discussions would be disorganized; someone would become angry and leave; or the group members would become uncomfortable with and distrustful of one another and become nonproductive. Maintenance roles help in achieving a healthy group atmosphere.

_Negative
roles_

Negative roles (or not-so-helpful roles) work against the group. You can probably remember some group situations

Membership Roles in Groups		
Task Roles	**Maintenance Roles**	**Negative Roles**
Supplying information	Relieving tension among members (often with gentle humor, never with ridicule)	Blocking the group's progress by arguing and objecting to other members' contributions for ego-centered reasons
Asking questions to get new information or to clarify facts	Offering encouragement or emotional support to another member	Competing for authority and recognition
Offering new solutions or ways to finish tasks	Resolving conflict by offering compromises or by agreeing to go along with the group	Giving aggressive replies or making personal attacks on members, rather than dealing with their ideas
Seeking opinions from others	Keeping watch to see that members are satisfied with their places in the group	Attempting to dominate or manipulate the group
Supplying details, examples, or definitions to clarify or help members make decisions	Balancing the discussion to see that no one monopolizes the time	Pleading some interest that is for personal advantage rather than the group's
Summarizing the group's progress occasionally as it proceeds	Accepting all members and listening to each respectfully	Telling jokes, making trivial remarks, or taking attention away from the task (do not confuse this with the maintenance role of relieving tension)
Suggesting a new direction or orientation for the group to pursue		
Probing into the ideas or philosophy behind a problem or its solution		
Taking care of routine tasks, such as handing out materials		
Keeping minutes or records of the group's work		

in which a negative role created conflict. If your group was fortunate, some member knew how to supply a positive leadership role to improve the situation and move the discussion along smoothly.

In general, a trusting group that works well will involve few negative roles and enough positive task and maintenance roles to offset the negatives. In such a group, views can be expressed safely, ideas offered freely, and feedback given honestly.

Many times a group member will appear to assume some helpful role in such a way that it seems to come almost naturally to him or her. In all probability, that person has learned to carry out the role function to meet the needs of another group. If you learn the characteristics of the group roles and watch groups carefully, you will soon be able to recognize the role behaviors when they appear.

Checkpoint _Do you regularly play a particular membership role or roles for the groups to which you belong? Do you play the same role no matter which group you are in?_

Communication Patterns in Groups

You are already familiar with the term _network_ as a group of interconnected broadcasting stations. A broadcast network allows for direct communication between stations, and makes it possible at times for the entire group to send out the same program as one unit. Although a network may communicate as one voice, it is made up of parts that are all capable of sending their own messages independently to each other and to the outside.

We apply the term _pattern_ to small group process in much the same way. We call the network of communication between members of the group an **interaction pattern.** We sometimes diagram the pattern, to give us a picture of who speaks to whom while the group is interacting. There are five common patterns that can develop in any group. We can diagram the lines of communication in almost any group situation, and identify the pattern as similar to one of the five designs, which are described in the following chart.

We hope you will observe the groups around you and try diagramming their interaction. You can only do this by employing good listening skills, so continue to practice good listening while you learn to identify patterns. With practice you can become skilled at identifying and diagramming them. Often a diagram of the lines of communication will show clearly why a group is or is not working together well.

Patterns such as the ones illustrated are visible in small groups, businesses, and other kinds of organizations. Even in large companies we can diagram the general network and see that it is similar to one of the five patterns. Patterns are not basically good or bad, but each one works better for some situations than for others.

Common Group Interaction Patterns

Wheel

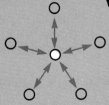

The wheel pattern is a network in which one main person serves as the hub. That person can and does communicate with everyone, but all other people speak directly only to the main person. For a long time schools have used this pattern for lecture classes to put the teacher at the "hub," making it easy for her or him to lead or control communication in the room.

Chain

In the chain pattern, messages pass from person to person in a chainlike sequence. This is a leaderless pattern. As a message is passed along, each person changes it as he or she repeats it, even when he or she tries very hard to tell exactly what he or she heard.

Circle

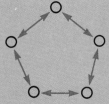

The circle pattern is basically like the chain in that each person relays messages to the persons on either side of her or him. Most of the communication is limited to the people inside the group (the circle). When face-to-face discussions cannot be arranged, we often rely on circle patterns.

Y

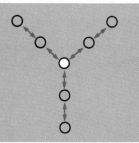

The Y pattern is similar to the chain in some ways, but leadership is more apparent. Everything depends on the reliability of the person at the point where the Y becomes a chain. Any time messages must pass through a single relay point or person, the person must be a good listener and completely trustworthy. This pattern is commonly used in business situations.

All-channels

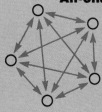

When it is possible to use an all-channels communication pattern, it has many advantages. It is especially useful in face-to-face discussions. In the all-channels pattern, everyone can communicate directly with every other person. The all-channels group can operate well even if one member is not a good communicator.

**Following
Interaction in
Discussions**

*How to
diagram*

One way to analyze the communication pattern in a discussion group is to diagram interaction as it occurs. An **interaction diagram** is a picture of the pattern that is developing in a group. It can be helpful in identifying membership roles, and often helps in diagnosing problems. You can observe a discussion taking place and diagram the channels.

First, take a seat that gives you a clear view of the group. Then draw circles to show the seating position of every group member. Put a first name or initial in each circle. Now *watch* and *listen* carefully as the group begins. If Aaron speaks first and looks directly at Mona as he does, draw a line from Aaron to Mona with an arrow to show who "sent" the message. If Mona answers Aaron directly, put an arrow on the other end of the same line. Now, with an arrow on each end you have shown a message sent and received, and feedback returned. If a group member looks at the whole group and makes a comment that is clearly directed to everyone, draw a short line to the center of the group. Put an arrow on the center end to show the statement was made to all.

As the discussion continues, your diagram may begin to look like this:

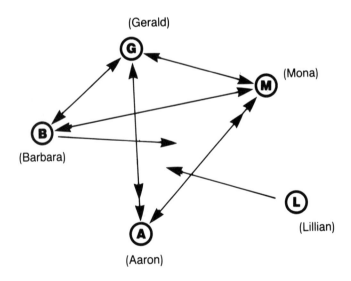

With a diagram, a group may be able to see a pattern of which they were totally unaware. The group in the figure has obviously excluded Lillian. She spoke to the group once, but no one ever spoke to her.

At first, if the discussion moves rapidly, you may have trouble keeping up, but with practice keeping up becomes easier. Begin to practice diagramming whenever you have an opportunity to observe a discussion. You will probably discover that each group follow a pattern.

Seating to Improve Discussion

Earlier, we discussed the impact of space on communication. The space in which a group of people live and work influences the communication network between those people. Architects must consider this fact when designing buildings. If a row of offices is built to make it easy for some workers to visit together often (perhaps around a drinking fountain or a copy machine), you may expect their frequent communication to become a part of the informal company network. (We call the flow of communication in an informal network a *grapevine.*) If one worker inhabits an office in some out-of-the-way location, you can expect that person to receive some information later than others do, if he or she receives it at all.

Effects of seating

Rooms to be used for informal discussion need to be big enough to allow for comfortable seating in a circle. Chairs should be alike. Taller or fancier chairs sometimes have the effect of giving one group member extra status. Chairs must be positioned so every member can see every other member easily. A circular seating arrangement is the natural shape of a democratic group.

Chairs can be arranged in a manner that makes it difficult for one or two members to participate well. Other seating arrangements can create partnerships or suggest leadership. A seating pattern can make it easy for a strong member to dominate the group or difficult for a quiet person to be included in the discussion at all. Circular seating, which allows all members to see and hear each other, encourages an all-channels pattern. To give members equal power potential, they need equal seating, space, visual contact, and position.

Seating arrangements can go a long way toward encouraging effective group discussion.

Watch for poor communication patterns in small groups that result from poor seating. You may be able to improve the situation by saying something like, "Jimmy, can you turn your chair around so I can see you better?" or "Let's pull our chairs closer so we can all see and hear each other."

Look at the arrangement of furniture in the living area of your home. Are chairs or sofas placed to allow for easy conversation? Furniture should be positioned to suit the purpose of the room. If you wish to encourage communication, position chairs so group members look at each other. We are more likely to talk to people when they are in our direct line of sight.

Correcting problems

When a poor communication pattern results from the way an entire building is designed, correction will be much more difficult, of course. A business having serious communication problems often calls in a communication consultant. One of the things a consultant will examine is the network created by the space in the building itself and by its furnishings. Perhaps you can improve your own communication environment by applying the following rules to encourage open communication:

1. Arrange seating to allow all members of the group equal opportunity to speak to each other.

2. Avoid barriers between people (large furniture or excessive space).

3. See that chairs face each other.

4. Make the seating equal in height and style whenever possible.

Checkpoint *See if you can diagram the pattern of interaction in a group you participate in today. Watch for these things:*

> *Does one person dominate?*
> *Is anyone left out?*
> *Do some members speak only to one other person?*
> *Do some members speak regularly to the whole group?*
> *Is the pattern you diagrammed the result of some space or seating factor?*
> *Can you improve the pattern you see?*

Summary

Using group discussion for making decisions should be done only when there is ample time and an informed, responsible, and cooperative group. Once the decision is made to work as a group, each member must be willing to discuss issues openly and work toward the best decision for the group, even when members disagree. Conflict may often be avoided by the skillful use of feedback.

Organizational leadership must be supplied in order to ensure an orderly progression from problem toward solution. The three possible styles of organizational leadership are autocratic, laissez-faire, and democratic. Although each style has advantages, the democratic style has the greatest number of advantages and fewer long-term disadvantages. The group members are equally responsible for supplying the group's leadership functions to maintain positive human relations, accomplish the task, and counteract any negative activity.

By observing who speaks to whom in communication groups it is possible to diagram the pattern of interaction that develops. There are five common patterns: the wheel, the chain, the circle, the Y, and the all-channels pattern. Each pattern has advantages and disadvantages. When possible in small groups, the all-channels pattern is most desirable. Patterns are diagrammed by using lines and arrows to show where messages go. Some patterns result from the space and seating used by the group. Altering seating arrangements may improve the group's communication.

Check Your Knowledge

1. What questions should be answered before deciding to use group process for decision making?

2. How many of the eight rules for giving effective feedback can you state?

3. How may the organizational leader in a small group be recognized?

4. Can you draw and label diagrams of the five patterns of communication?

Check Your Understanding

1. Do you know someone who is a good tension reliever? Someone who usually works to include everyone in a discussion? Someone who usually asks questions to clarify meanings? Someone who helps resolve conflict?

2. Can you name some people who help you feel accepted because they give you positive feedback?

3. Discuss why it is important to recognize efforts to change with positive feedback, even when the change is not perfect.

4. Which interaction pattern do you think has the greatest number of disadvantages? Why?

5. Can you think of some situations in which only one pattern is possible?

6. Can you diagram the communication networks in some of your classes? How do they differ? Are the networks determined by the subject being studied? How?

Check Your Skills

1. Can you think of some phrases that could be used in giving feedback to request a change in behavior?

2. Can you think of some phrases to avoid?

3. Continue your own program for improving your communication in groups, monitoring group discussions while you participate. See if you can identify your own helpful roles, and carry out others deliberately when you recognize a need for them. When a discussion ends, see if you can remember which roles each person carried out. You will gradually be able to diagnose group problems as they occur and correct them early.

4. What is the pattern in each of the following situations? Can any of them be changed? How?
   a. In a restaurant, the customer orders, the waiter gives the order to the cook, the cook prepares the order, and the waiter gives it to the customer.
   b. In a business, the owner gives an instruction to a manager, the manager instructs shift managers, and each shift manager instructs his or her work group.
   c. In a business, a sales manager sends a written message to six district salesmen, and each one replies.

The First Amendment

*Communication
Essay*

The year was 1787, the place was Philadelphia, and the event was the Federal Convention to write a constitution for a new nation. George Washington served as the presiding officer against his wishes, and each of the fifty-five delegates had strong ideas about the document they were to draft.

The circumstances appeared to be set for failure. The group was too large and too diverse to work rapidly or politely. Disagreements were fierce, the delegates were spirited, and they argued about subjects ranging from the rights of states to the African slave trade, from qualifications for office to taxation. Who could have predicted that the emerging experimental Constitution would be a work of genius and a crowning achievement in creativity?

Even those whose ideas were defeated worked to see that the creative process did not end until the Constitution was the best document possible. Their efforts went on even after the original document was completed. Something was missing, they said. That "something" was a Bill of Rights.

The first article of the Bill of Rights (or the First Amendment) protects us from any law "abridging the freedom of speech or of the press; or the right of the people peacefully to assemble . . ." The First Amendment has been tested many times and continues to serve us well. You do not have to look over your shoulder before saying you disagree with some aspect of our government, or that you feel we need to have a new executive officer. This right to open communication is an essential American freedom.

With every freedom comes a responsibility, however. The success of our 200-year-old constitutional experiment has always depended on the efforts of the American people to stay informed and get involved. Citizens must know how to communicate within our parliamentary system to bring about change. They are obligated to develop the communication skills to speak out effectively against injustice, and to be effective persuaders for change when necessary. The serious undertaking of those communication responsibilities guarantees that the First Amendment will continue to serve us well.

CHAPTER 12

Problem Solving Through Group Communication

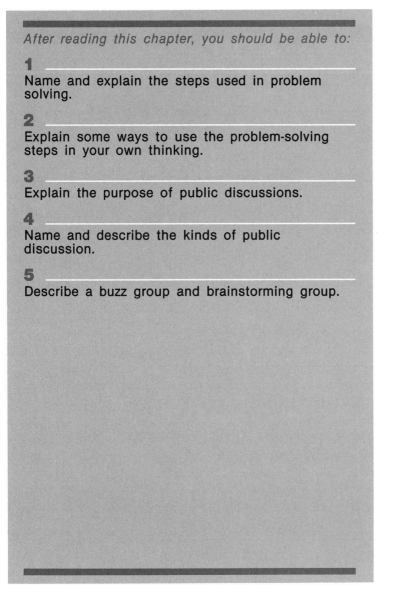

After reading this chapter, you should be able to:

1

Name and explain the steps used in problem solving.

2

Explain some ways to use the problem-solving steps in your own thinking.

3

Explain the purpose of public discussions.

4

Name and describe the kinds of public discussion.

5

Describe a buzz group and brainstorming group.

Key Terms

Presiding officer
Moderator
Buzz group
Brainstorming
Panel discussions
Symposium
Agenda

Task-oriented groups, as you know, exist to do work. In fact, most organized group discussions are carried out to accomplish some particular task. Discussion occurs in research groups, political action groups, therapy groups, committees of all kinds, juries, and city councils. Some are public discussion groups, some are formal groups, and some are very small casual groups.

We will begin this chapter by discussing the problem-solving steps that must be used by all of these groups in order to do their work well. We will also explore participation in small, task-oriented groups that exist to solve problems or make decisions, and discuss participation in public problem-solving discussions.

Accomplishing Tasks Through Discussion

The small task-oriented group involves all of its members in discussion to make a decision within the group, and in public discussion a group plans and carries out a discussion before an audience, to help the audience make decisions. You will find that small group discussion is an excellent way to solve a problem or create a plan to meet a particular need. For committees or policy-making groups, the all-channels pattern will be useful as long as the group is small. Even then, you will find it helpful to have a chairperson who acts as the organizational leader to keep the discussion moving from problem toward solution.

Presiding Officer

As group size increases, the need for an organizational leader becomes more apparent. In groups that are fairly small, a person to fill the organizational role may emerge naturally with no formal selection process; in large groups, someone should be elected. We call the elected person a **presiding officer.** In some groups the exact title will be *president,* in others *chairperson.* When a new group meets to discuss a problem and its solution, the first thing to be done is select a chairperson to preside. In public discussions the organizational leader is often called a **moderator** and is chosen in advance.

An organizational leader must know the steps in problem solving and be able to keep the group moving through them.

As the group reaches a general agreement about each step, a good organizational leader will recognize the general agreement. To check for agreement about the definition of the problem, for example, the leader may say, "Are we in agreement that . . . ?" or "It sounds to me like we all think the basic problem is . . .—is that correct?" When agreement is clear about one step, the leader will move the discussion to the next step. We will discuss other responsibilities of the chairperson or moderator (in public discussion) later.

The Problem-Solving Steps

Whether you are the leader or a participant you will find the problem-solving steps an asset to you and your group. You will also find them useful in your own thinking, in improving the orderliness of your personal problem solving. Later, you will find the problem-solving steps important in the research and organization of persuasive speeches. If you study debate, you will find the steps absolutely necessary in building a debate case.

In any kind of problem-solving group, it is useful for members to be aware of all of the basic problem-solving steps.

To progress from problem to solution in an orderly fashion with efficient use of time, some basic steps should be followed. They are highlighted in the following chart.

Steps in Problem Solving

1. *Define the problem.* You should answer some basic questions:
   Does a problem exist?
   What is the nature of the problem?
2. *Describe the significance of the problem:*
   How serious is the problem?
   What are the bad results of the problem?
   Are the bad factors that exist really a direct result of the current situation or course of action?
   Is the problem serious enough to justify a major change?
3. *Analyze the problem:*
   What is the history of the problem?
   What are the main parts or aspects of the problem?
   Who does the problem affect?
   What are the main issues (points of major disagreement) about the problem?
   Can the problem be solved?
   Will the problem persist no matter what plan is tried?
   Will the problem go away without a change in policy?
4. *Develop solution criteria:*
   What must a proposed solution accomplish to be acceptable?
   Using the bad results listed, what "harms" must the plan solve?

5. *Suggest possible solutions:*
   What alternative solutions are there?
6. *Evaluate the solutions:*
   Is each of the proposed solutions practical?
   Which ones can be put into operation without major disruptions?
   Which ones are most workable?
   Which ones are most capable of solving the problem?
   What are the advantages and disadvantages of each plan proposed?
   Which solutions only meet some of the criteria?
   Which ones can potentially create more problems than the original situation we wish to solve?
7. *Select the best solution:*
   Which proposed plans should be discarded?
   Which plans have the greatest potential for solving the problem with the fewest disadvantages?
   Which one of the plans will we choose?
8. *Try the solution* (*if* the group has the authority to put the chosen plan into operation):
   What should be done first to implement the plan?
   What sequence of steps should be taken?

Checkpoint *Can you think of some situations other than discussions in which the problem-solving steps would be helpful?*

Problem Solving in Small Groups

There are several kinds of small problem-solving groups. What we say here will apply to decision-making groups, committees, and policy-making groups that follow the problem-solving sequence. Later we will consider brainstorming groups and buzz groups, each of which uses a portion of the sequence. Problem-solving group discussions usually center on questions like, "how can we cope with international terrorism?" In order to develop a workable solution to the problem, the group must pursue it in an orderly fashion.

Decision-Making Groups

A successful group will arrive at a decision or develop a policy by using the steps already outlined. Let's explore the steps in relation to discussions in small problem-solving groups.

Define the Problem "What is the current terrorist situation?" If the problem has not been clearly indicated or described in advance, it should be clarified early in the discussion. The group should first ask if a problem exists. ("Is terrorism a problem?" or "Is our present policy for coping with terrorism working?")

Sometimes the problem has been identified by a large organization, and a committee (the small group) has been named to find a solution. In that case, the committee chairperson may begin with a statement like, "We have been asked to develop a new policy for selecting members," or "The committee is charged with the task of finding a money-raising project to pay for our spring dance." If a teacher has assigned a problem for the group to discuss, it may be a question, such as, "Should capital punishment be abolished (or, in some states, reinstated)?"

Describe the Significance of the Problem What are the results of the situation, and how do they effect us? In debate we call "bad results" *harms*. The group must decide whether the problem is serious enough to make a change necessary. With the terrorism question, deaths, injuries, loss of property, and other "bad results" should be identified. The number of terrorist attacks, the increased frequency of attacks, and the international locations of attacks should be considered at this point.

Analyze the Problem   The group should be certain the negative effects really are a result of some policy (or lack of one) or of some specific way of doing things. Will the problem still exist no matter what plan is developed? Will the harms be taken care of soon, without a new plan?

Develop Solution Criteria   When the group agrees about the nature of the problem and its significance, they know the new plan, whatever it is, must correct the harms or bad results of the old plan without creating problems just as bad or worse. The description of the problem should become the standard or checklist for measuring any solution suggested. To be acceptable, the solution must meet the criteria of solving each harm described. Usually there are other criteria also. Sometimes these are factors like ''The new solution must not cost any more than the old plan,'' or ''It must be a plan we can have in operation by July.'' Other criteria may relate to some extra benefit to group members or to someone outside the group.

Suggest Possible Solutions   Once the group has set criteria for the solution, they are ready to begin offering creative ideas. They should try to identify as many workable solutions as possible. (What possible solutions to terrorism can you think of?)

Evaluate the Solutions   The group should examine each plan proposed and measure it by the criteria developed in Step 4. In addition, members should check each plan to be sure it will not create greater problems than those they wish to solve.

Select the Best Solution   Some possible solutions will be eliminated in the process of checking them against the criteria. The remaining solutions should be compared until an obvious choice emerges. The plan or policy chosen should be the one with more advantages and fewer disadvantages than the others.

In decision-making groups, members should all work to maintain the focus on the problem and its possible solutions.

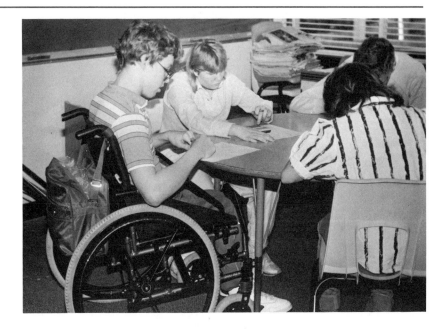

Try the Solution   The last step in the problem-solving sequence is testing the plan selected by putting it into operation.

Buzz Groups

Sometimes a large organization wishes to investigate a topic thoroughly, but there is not enough time for everyone to be heard in a general meeting. One solution is to divide the large group into a number of smaller discussion groups called **buzz groups** or cluster groups. Usually, each buzz group is assigned a portion of the topic (perhaps one part of the problem or one part of the solution) to discuss and report on to the larger group. Sometimes a buzz group is assigned one or more of the problem-solving steps to carry out. In this way, everyone has an opportunity to raise questions and voice opinions.

One of the advantages of using buzz groups is that the creativity of all group members can be tapped. The purpose of the buzz group is to give all members a chance to have input on the topic, and to explore the portion of the topic assigned them as completely as time permits. A report to the main group is written or outlined, to be sure the will of the buzz group is accurately presented to the entire membership. Reports are often made orally as well.

Brainstorming Groups

The group process we call **brainstorming** is a way to generate many creative ideas in a short time. A brainstorming group often exists to carry out the fifth problem solving step—to suggest solutions. The leader usually asks the group members to mention as many solutions as they can think of without stopping to evaluate them. Each member should offer only one solution at a time. The ideas may come as rapidly as they pop into the heads of members. Sometimes a tape recorder is used to capture all the ideas for future reference, and sometimes a member will scribble the ideas on paper or on a chalkboard. Occasionally, a group simply relies on memory to preserve whatever worthwhile ideas emerge.

It is important to avoid pausing to criticize or discuss ideas as they are offered. When that happens, members become reluctant to offer new ideas for fear they will be judged. It should be understood that some of the ideas tossed out in brainstorming will sound a bit foolish. Occasionally, however, an idea that appears "crazy" at first suggests another solution that is not absurd at all. Selection and evaluation of solutions comes at the end of brainstorming.

Checkpoint

How do the functions of buzz groups, decision-making groups, and brainstorming groups differ?

Problem Solving in Public Group Discussion

Public discussions are held for the benefit of the audience. They may inform the audience of various aspects of a problem to help them arrive at a solution. Public discussions may also present persuasive aspects of the problem and its possible solutions, so the audience can decide which to choose. Panel discussions and symposiums serve these purposes.

The Panel Discussion

Panel discussions, like all public discussions, inform or persuade an audience and assist the audience in making a decision about a particular topic. For a panel there must be a small group of participants and an organizational leader (who is usually called a moderator or chairperson). Four or six panelists and a leader are common. The panelists may

Panel discussions are a popular form of public communication.

be selected because they are familiar with the topic, or they may be assigned to research the topic in advance. They sit in front of the audience. The moderator opens the discussion by announcing the topic. (He or she may also briefly provide background on the problem to be discussed.) Then the panel discusses the subject. No one makes formal speeches, and each panelist keeps his or her comments brief. After a prearranged amount of time (thirty minutes is common and the discussion seldom lasts more than an hour), the moderator asks for questions or comments from the audience before closing the discussion.

Panel discussions are useful for considering many controversial topics. This discussion method can be used to educate audiences, and in many instances to show a variety of viewpoints that may be overlooked when audience members are uninformed or unskilled in the decision-making process. Panels are used frequently by the media. You have probably seen a number of panel discussion on television, in which the moderator is a central figure who hosts the program and moderates regularly. Often the participants selected for television panels are well-known individuals who have extreme differences in points of view. The controversy ensures that the discussion will be lively and that some important alternatives will be discussed. Such controversy also keeps the audience attentive (and sometimes entertained).

Why not try planning a mock television panel discussion for a school assembly program or for your class. Choose a topic that will be certain to interest the audience, and choose panel members who have different views. We will discuss the leader's responsibilities later.

The Symposium

The symposium, too, is a method of discussing a topic before the public in order to educate the audience. In the **symposium,** a group of speakers (usually experts) are chosen to participate. Each makes a short speech to explore one specific part of a topic. Sometimes, each offers a possible solution to a problem, but in a symposium the participants do not ordinarily argue or oppose each others' positions. A chairperson is required, and usually the audience is permitted to comment and ask questions at the end of the presentations.

The Role of the Leader in Public Discussion

In symposiums or panel discussions, rules are applied by a formal organizational leader who is usually called a chairperson or moderator, and who is addressed by that title rather than by name while the meeting is in progress. The chairperson sits on the platform with the expert participants and guides them through their presentations (symposium) or discussion (panel). During the participants' portion of the meeting, the chairperson keeps order and keeps the discussion moving along smoothly. He or she calls the session to order, introduces the topic, and introduces the panel or symposium members.

The chairperson also asks for questions or comments from the audience and keeps order during the audience-participation portion of the meeting. Audience members must be recognized and called on by the presiding officer before they can speak. Only one may speak at a time. If more than one audience member is seeking recognition, the leader chooses one, and the others sit quietly while that person speaks. When it is time to end the meeting, the leader should thank the participants, make whatever closing statements are necessary, and adjourn the meeting.

When large groups meet to solve problems or reach decisions, an organizational leader serves many important functions.

Preparing an Agenda for Public Discussion

The person who will preside prepares a written outline of the meeting called an **agenda.** For a public discussion, the chairperson's agenda should include the topics to be discussed and the order in which they will be considered. The agenda a chairperson follows could look like this.

Sample agenda

1. Call to order

2. Introduce topic—"A solution to the local water shortage"
   a. History of the problem
   b. List of studies made by engineers
   c. List of solutions under consideration by city council

3. Introduce panel members
   a. Howard Phillips, Registered Professional Engineer, from the firm of Morris, Mangess, and Phillips, Consulting Engineers
   b. Dr. Ellen J. Lendquist, Associate Professor of Petroleum Engineering, Southregion A & M
   c. Maynard O. Rosen, Regional Director, Corps of Engineers
   d. Sidney P. Norris, Strongtown City Councilman

4. Start discussion with questions—What can we expect the water supply for the Hamilton Valley Area to be during the next fifty years? What long-term plan should be adopted to meet the growing demand for water?

5. Supply follow-up questions when needed concerning
   a. Time factors
   b. Cost factors
   c. Effects on
      1. Agriculture
      2. Population growth
      3. City water and sanitation
      4. Industrial growth

6. Stop panel at 10:45 and open floor to audience questions.

7. Close meeting with
   a. Summary of views
   b. Announcement of next panel discussion topic

Participating in Public Discussion

To be an effective participant in the types of discussions described above, you will need to follow these rules:

1. Research the topic in advance.

2. Use the problem-solving steps whenever possible.

3. Be open minded and consider ideas presented by others.

4. Be cooperative and polite to the other participants.

5. Work with the other participants toward a common goal.

6. Think clearly and check your reasoning before presenting it.

7. When you see they are needed, carry out the task and maintenance roles discussed in Chapter 12.

8. Pause often to review.

9. Ask questions to clarify statements.

10. Ask questions to learn the opinions and suggestions of others.

11. Listen carefully and give clear feedback.

During the question-and-answer period that involves the audience, panel and symposium members respond to questions from the audience. Each audience member who wishes to ask a question should wait to be recognized by the moderator or chairperson. The audience member stands to state the question. He or she may address the question to a specific person on the platform. If the audience member does not specify a person, the leader should refer the question to a panel or symposium member. The response is then stated to the audience. With audience participation, public discussion becomes a valuable public communication form.

Checkpoint

What is a symposium? What is a panel discussion? Can you recall some rules for participation in public discussion?

Summary

Most organized group discussions share a common purpose: to accomplish some task or to solve a problem. In small problem-solving groups, the group members choose a solution or make a decision. In public discussion, the group discusses the problem before an audience to assist the audience members in making a decision. For either kind of discussion, an organizational leader is needed. In public discussions the leader is called a moderator or chairperson.

There are eight steps that should be followed by problem solving groups. The steps, in sequence, are: 1) define the problem; 2) describe the significance of the problem; 3) analyze the problem; 4) develop solution criteria; 5) suggest possible solutions; 6) evaluate the solutions; 7) select the best solution; and 8) try the solution. All of the steps are applied in small group discussions when a decision must be made.

In large organizations, members are sometimes divided into buzz groups to discuss problems and/or solutions. Buzz groups often apply only a few of the problem-solving steps. Another kind of task-oriented group discussion is called brainstorming, and it is especially useful in suggesting solutions.

Public discussions are carried out by a small group of participants and a moderator in front of an audience. Usually a problem and a solution are involved. The two basic types of public discussions are panels and symposiums. In each kind of public discussion, the participants rely on the moderator and his or her agenda to ensure an orderly progression of discussion and question-and-answer periods. Public discussions are often used for media presentations. Regardless of the occasion, a problem-solving group must apply the problem-solving steps, and the members must follow some simple rules to be effective participants.

Check Your Knowledge

1. What is an elected organizational leader called?

2. What are the questions that should be answered in defining a problem?

3. What kind of discussion group is useful for generating a lot of ideas in a short time?

4. Which of the early problem-solving steps is essential to the development of criteria for a solution?

Check Your Understanding

1. What is the purpose of the problem-solving steps? What would happen to a problem-solving discussion if the sequence of the steps was scrambled?

2. If you were asked to develop an inexpensive solution for the parking problem at your school (or some other school problem), how should you proceed?

Check Your Skills

1. Plan a symposium with two or three of your classmates to help the other students understand a topic covered in this textbook.

2. See if you can apply the problem-solving steps in a class discussion of a current national problem. Take turns serving as organizational leader.

3. Choose one of the topics below and try brainstorming to see how many things you and your classmates can think of in five minutes. Remember not to stop and evaluate the ideas until after the brainstorming period is over.
   a. potential ways to make one banana split big enough tor the entire student body
   b. possible slogans for a clean-up campaign for your school or town

    c. potential ways to publicize a band concert to raise money for new band instruments

    d. possible programs for your class to present to the rest of the school

    e. some people in your town who should be given an Outstanding Citizen award

    f. ways to increase attendance at school basketball games

4. Divide a timely topic into parts for buzz groups.

5. Apply the problem-solving steps to some problem situation of your own. Jot down your answers to the questions related to each step. Avoid the temptation to skip over some steps!

6. Plan an imaginary panel discussion. Choose a controversial topic and four famous participants. Next, write ten questions the moderator could use to start the discussion and keep it going through the problem-solving steps.

CHAPTER 13

Participating in Parliamentary Groups

After reading this chapter you should be able to:

1

Explain the purpose of parliamentary procedure.

2

List the basic principles of parliamentary procedure.

3

Describe the responsibilities of the president in conducting meetings.

4

Make a motion properly.

5

Explain the four classes of motions.

6

List the precedence of motions.

Key Terms

Parliamentary rules

Majority decision

Order of business

Motion

Second

Main motion

Subsidiary motion

Privileged motion

Incidental motion

Precedence

Committee

We have explored the way informal groups operate, the role of leadership in groups, the styles of leadership seen in group process, and the patterns in which groups communicate. We have discussed the steps by which groups solve problems and the way the organizational leader of a problem-solving group works. We have examined the responsibilities of the chairperson or moderator who presides over public symposiums and panel discussions. Now it is important to know about organized groups, the parliamentary rules by which they operate, and the role of the parliamentary leader.

The Purpose of Parliamentary Rules

Parliamentary rules are a system for working together in groups. The purpose of the rules is to protect the rights of freedom of speech, freedom to hold meetings, and freedom to form organizations based on common goals. The name for the rules comes from England's Parliament, a legislative body that long ago developed a brief set of rules, which have been updated over the years. New rules have been added when needed. Today the common parliamentary rules we use in our organizations are not the same as the rules of Parliament, the United States Congress, or our court system. They are similar, however.

Uses of Parliamentary Rules

Most of the groups we belong to are not *legislative* (to make laws), but rather *deliberative* (to discuss or debate important issues or business). Without set principles and a formal set of rules, most large groups would not stay together for very long. For that reason, common parliamentary rules are used in all organized groups where the rights to meet, discuss, decide, and act are valued. Businesses, student congresses, clubs, churches, professional groups, labor unions, and government committees or agencies all use the rules. You may already know some parliamentary rules from your experience in groups.

These rules are not difficult to learn, because they are based on common sense. When we discussed leadership in informal groups, you learned that organizational leaders may emerge naturally. Formal groups are often much larger,

United States legislators meet in parliamentary groups.

however, and the larger the group, the more difficult it becomes to reach total agreement about leaders or anything else. (Think how it would be to select a President of the United States if we just waited for a leader to emerge!) Common sense tells us we need another way. When a group is too large to use common consent *or* when it wishes to be very certain that the rights of everyone are protected, it uses the parliamentary rule of majority decision.

Majority decision means that after voting to determine what most of the group wants, the rest of the group will consent to follow what the majority wishes. A *simple majority* consists of at least one more than half of the total group membership (for example, 6 if your group has 10 members, 51 if your group has 100). If six members of a ten-member club vote *for* a proposal, the other four are called the *minority*. The minority agree to abide by the outcome of the vote, but they still have the right to speak and make their wishes known.

Checkpoint   *Can you explain in your own words the purpose of parliamentary rules?*

The Principles of Parliamentary Procedure

There are seven basic principles of parliamentary procedure. All the rules are based on these seven principles, and there is much to be studied and learned about each of them. We are going to be concerned with all of the principles in a very general way, but we want to discuss some of them in greater detail than others.

If you want to learn parliamentary procedure thoroughly, you should consult *Robert's Rules of Order Newly Revised* by General Henry M. Robert. This book was first published in 1876 and the "newly revised" edition was published in 1970. This is the principle resource of parliamentary procedure. We also recommend *Sturgis' Standard Code of Parliamentary Procedure, Second Edition* (1966) by Alice Sturgis. Of the two, *Sturgis* is perhaps easier for a beginner to understand. If you are developing a personal library, you will certainly want a copy of one, or both, of these books. You will find them valuable reference volumes to use for a lifetime. Regardless of the resource you choose to study, the time you spend mastering parliamentary rules will be rewarding.

Seven principles

The seven principles of parliamentary procedure are:

1. The purpose of parliamentary procedure is to facilitate the transaction of business and promote cooperation and harmony.

2. All members have equal rights, privileges, and obligations.

3. The majority vote decides.

4. The rights of the minority must be protected.

5. Every member has the right to full and free discussion of every proposition presented for decision.

6. Every member has the right to know the meaning of the question before the assembly and what its effect will be.

7. All meetings must be characterized by fairness and by good faith.

As you read the principles you may have been reminded of *The Declaration of Independence* and the *Constitution of The United States*. Parliamentary principles are the basis for democracy itself, and rules based on them are developed to protect our human rights and liberty. We apply the principles by using the rules when we meet for discussion in formal organized groups, _and_ when we conduct public discussions.

Checkpoint _Can you name the seven principles of parliamentary procedure?_

The Role of the Parliamentary Leader

The presiding officer recognizes group members who wish to speak.

It is always a compliment to be elected presiding officer by a group. The election means the group has respect for your ability and confidence in you to lead them well. In addition to presiding, there are responsibilities that go with the honor. The first responsibility of the leader is in planning and organizing. If the leader is disorganized, the group will suffer. Second, the leader must be enthusiastic and must work for unity within the group. The leader should never create a split among members or take sides in disputes. Third, the leader needs to know the history and current affairs of the group and be acquainted with its members.

Next, since the presiding officer often speaks for the group publicly, she or he must be able to speak well and make a good impression when representing the group. Finally, confidence and sufficient knowledge of the rules must be combined with public speaking ability when the leader presides over meetings.

The president always presides over meetings of the organization or its board of directors if he or she is present. Only when the business concerns the president personally does he or she step aside to let someone else preside. For example, during a discussion of presenting a special award to the president, the vice president should preside. The president _does_ preside over elections when he or she is a candidate.

The Order of Business

In conducting meetings, the president must know and follow the _order of business_. The **order of business** is a master plan that is established by parliamentary law. It lists the sequence in which each division of business will be handled at every meeting, but does not list the specific items of business to be considered.

Order of Business

I. Call to Order

The president stands, calling the meeting to order at a designated time. The president may use one tap of gavel and says, "The meeting will please come to order."

II. Opening

(Optional: varies among organizations. Can be invocation, the pledge to the flag, a welcome, or an introduction of the Head Table or guests.)

III. Reading and Approval of Minutes

"The secretary will read the minutes of the preceding meeting." The secretary stands and reads the minutes. The president asks, "Are there any corrections?" (The president does not ask for additions or deletions.)

The president says, "There being none, the minutes stand approved as read."

    or

(following corrections), "If there are no further corrections, the minutes stand as corrected."

IV. Statement of Treasurer

The president asks, "Are there any questions? This report was read for your information."

No action is taken on the unaudited report of the treasurer.

V. Correspondence

Bills—action is taken on their payment.

Communications are read by the secretary—any action that may arise from them is taken up under the proper part of business.

VI. Reports & Their Disposal

  A. Executive Committee

  B. Standing Committees

  C. Special Committees

    1. Reports that contain only facts, opinions, or a report of work do not require action.

    2. Action must be taken on recommendations or resolutions.

VII. Unfinished Business

The president presents for consideration:

  A. Business postponed from previous meeting to this one

  B. Business on which action was not complete at previous meeting

VIII. New Business

Must be introduced by a motion or resolution.

  A. Member rises and addresses the chair

  B. Member is recognized by chair

  C. Member says, "I move that . . ."

  D. Seconded by another member, without rising or being recognized (name not recorded in the minutes)

IX. Adjournment

The president says, "The meeting is adjourned."

The order of business used in the business meetings of parliamentary groups appears here to guide you in your parliamentary group participation. Learning the proper order of business will also prepare you for your time as a presiding officer.

The Agenda

Using the order of business, the presiding officer of a parliamentary group must also prepare and follow an *agenda*. The president's agenda (sometimes called "the Chair's Memorandum") includes all the specific items to be announced, discussed, or included in any way during a business meeting, and the order in which they will occur. The agenda helps ensure that the meeting will progress in an appropriate sequence. It contains more detail than the order of business, since it serves for only one meeting.

Rules for the Presiding Officer

A gavel is often used by presiding officers to call a meeting to order, and is sometimes used to signal the end of a meeting.

Many of the general rules for chairpersons of public discussions apply to presiding officers of parliamentary groups. Here is a summary of rules for presiding officers of parliamentary groups to follow when conducting meetings:

1. Refer to yourself by title—"The Chair, the President, the Moderator." *Example:* When several people are raising hands or asking to speak in a meeting, "The Chair recognizes Mr. Goode."

2. Call the meeting to order.

3. Welcome, state the purpose of the meeting, introduce honored guests.

4. Keep the meeting moving along at a steady pace, but remain flexible.

5. Speak clearly and audibly so that all can hear.

6. Encourage each member who speaks to speak so he or she can be heard.

7. Sum up what members have said (restate when needed).

8. Prevent confusion and maintain firm but gentle control. (Stop disturbances quickly before they grow!)

9. Speak to the whole assembly, not to individuals on the platform or in the audience.

10. Encourage open discussion and see that no action takes place without an opportunity to discuss and decide.

11. Stop aimless or off-topic discussion without stifling meaningful discussion.

12. Remain neutral, never argue, and let the group decide.

13. Defend the rights and privileges of all, and know the rules well enough to keep out-of-order members from taking over and to keep out-of-order motions or comments from being discussed.

14. Stay aware of the physical surroundings and members' comfort (heat, light, external noise, etc.).

15. Preside impartially and always state the facts in an unbiased way. (Be courteous, patient, and tactful to all.)

16. See that every motion raised is disposed of properly.

17. State the results of every vote.

18. Adjourn the meeting.

Checkpoint *What are the major parts of the order of business? Can you list them in sequence?*

The Role of Members

Just as the presiding officer has a certain role to play in how well a parliamentary meeting goes, members, too, have special functions. In order for a meeting to be purposeful and orderly, members need to be familiar with parliamentary procedure, the specific rules of their organization, and their rights as members. In addition, they need to participate fully in the presentation of motions, discussions of issues, and the group decision-making process.

Motions

All business is brought before an assembly through a **motion,** which is a formal proposal for group action. There are eight steps to remember in presenting motions. When you wish to offer a motion, stand and address the presiding officer by saying, "Madam Chairman" or "Mr. President." Wait to be recognized. The chairperson will call you by name, or will nod to show that you have the floor. Make the motion. The proper wording of a motion is, "I move that . . ." or "I move to . . ."

Seconds

Another member **seconds** the motion. He or she is not required to rise or address the chair. The chairperson restates the motion for the group by saying, "It has been moved and seconded that. . . ." The chair then asks for discussion. Following the discussion, the chair asks, "Are you ready for the question?" The chairperson then takes the vote, saying, "Those in favor of . . . say 'Aye'; and those opposed, say 'No'." The chair counts the vote and announces whether the motion carried or failed and what the effect of the vote will be ("The motion passes. Ninth grade students are now eligible for membership in this organization.")

Classification of Motions

Main motions

The motions made in any organization can be divided into four groups or classes. The four groups are main motions, subsidiary motions, privileged motions, and incidental motions. Motions of these kinds are used to carry out most of any organization's work. **Main motions** are used to propose business on which the maker wants the group to decide. They must be seconded, and they are debatable. A main motion may sound something like this: "I move we hold a garage sale to raise money for a scholarship fund."

There are also three frequently used *specific main motions* that have somewhat different rules. They are: 1) a motion to *reconsider* another motion that has already been voted on; 2) a motion to *rescind* or cancel a motion that has already passed; and 3) a motion to *resume consideration* or discussion of a proposal that was previously postponed.

Subsidiary motions

Subsidiary motions are used to change a motion that has been proposed, or to change the way a motion is being dealt with. Some subsidiary motions are made to *postpone* ("I move we postpone consideration of the garage-sale topic until after the fair"). Subsidiary motions can also be used to *limit debate* on the motion ("I move we limit debate on the topic to twenty minutes"), to *refer the matter to a committee* ("I move to refer the motion to a research committee to be appointed by the president"), to *amend* the main motion in some way ("I move to amend the motion by inserting the words 'three-member' before the word

Participation in parliamentary groups can provide members with excellent decision-making experience.

'research' ''), or to *vote on the motion immediately* (''I move to vote immediately on the motion'').

Privileged motions

There are three motions that are called **privileged motions** because they relate to emergency situations that should be dealt with quickly. They are motions to *adjourn,* motions to *recess,* and *questions of privilege.* Questions of privilege are usually for the purpose of correcting some problem, such as a room that is uncomfortably noisy or cold.

Incidental motions

Incidental motions are used to do things like *appeal* a decision made by the chair. If, for example, a presiding officer announces that a motion has failed after hearing a voice vote that to others sounded too close to decide, a member may say (without being recognized), ''I appeal from the decision of the chair.'' The chair announces, ''The decision of the chair has been appealed from.'' The chair then states the reason for his or her decision, and the appealing member states his or her reason for appealing. A vote is taken to determine whether members sustain or overrule the decision of the presiding officer.

Incidental motions may also be used to *suspend* rules (''I move to suspend the rules requiring the reading of the committee reports—we have printed copies—and go directly to the unfinished business''), or to *raise a point of order:*

MEMBER: ''Ms. President, I rise to a point of order.''

CHAIR: ''State your point of order.''

MEMBER: ''There was no call for opposing votes on the motion.''

CHAIR: ''Your point of order is well taken. All those opposed to the motion to . . . say no.''

You can also use an incidental motion to _withdraw_ a motion. After the presiding officer has restated a motion, if the proposer wishes to recall it, he or she says—without recognition—"I wish to withdraw my motion." The chair says, "(name of member) wishes to withdraw his/her motion. Is there any objection? If not, the motion is withdrawn." If there is objection, a vote is taken on the withdrawal of the motion. Finally, an incidental motion can be used to _divide the question_ under consideration ("I move to divide the motion into two questions: 1) that we hold a garage sale and 2) that we establish a scholarship fund").

Precedence of Motions

In addition to being classified, motions are ranked or given a priority level. The priority of motions is called **precedence,** and the purpose of giving motions an order of precedence is to make the chairperson's job less confusing. Look at the following list of motions, which shows their order of precedence.

If your organization is considering a main motion of some kind, such as a motion to build a float to be entered in the annual parade, another member may interrupt the discussion with any one of the kinds of motions that appear _higher up_ on the list in order of precedence. During the discussion following the main motion about float building, another motion could be proposed amending the main motion to read, "to build a float _jointly with the Boosters Club_ to be entered in the annual parade." An amendment is acceptable because it is a motion of higher precedence than a main motion.

Order of Precedence

Privileged motions
1. Adjourn
2. Recess
3. Question of privilege

Subsidiary motions
4. Postpone temporarily
5. Vote immediately
6. Limit debate
7. Postpone definitely
8. Refer to committee
9. Amend
10. Postpone indefinitely

Main motions
11. Main and specific main motions

Rules Pertaining to Motions

All motions are considered according to some basic rules. Only one _subject_ may be discussed at a time. While a motion is being discussed, only motions of a higher precedence may be proposed. When more than one motion is before the organization, they are voted on in the opposite order from their proposal. The most recently proposed is considered first (for instance, the amendment), and then the main motion is considered. Urgent motions (questions of privilege) may interrupt a speaker.

Some motions must be seconded by another member. When you second a motion you say, "I second the motion," to show that you think the motion merits discussion. It does *not* mean you support the motion as seconded, and it does *not* obligate you to vote in its favor. Motions that could be called *requests* (points of order, withdrawing a motion, and others) do not require a second. Seconds are not required in committees or boards of directors.

Main motions, amendments, appeals, and postpone-indefinitely motions are debatable. Motions to postpone *definitely* (to a specific time), recess, refer to a committee, and to limit debate are debatable only to a limited degree. The discussion regarding motions open to limited debate must be confined to a few specific points. Certain other motions are not debatable. They are voted on immediately with no discussion. Some motions may be amended; others may not, because the motion can be stated only one way.

Most motions require only a simple majority (11 of 20, 51 of 100) to carry, but motions to limit debate, suspend rules, and to object to the topic in consideration all require a two-thirds vote. The reason is that the motions' outcomes would limit the rights of members.

Committees and Their Work

The president appoints **committees** when needed. There are numerous advantages to using committees. Many of them must already be obvious to you from reading the chapters on group process and discussion. The following outline, prepared by the American Institute of Parliamentarians, describes the advantages of committees well:

1. Size

2. Can work quietly and effectively

3. Greater freedom of discussion

4. Informal procedure

5. Members are experts

6. Delicate, troublesome, or embarrassing questions may be handled by a committee without publicity.

Everything you have learned about discussion, problem solving, and small group process can be applied to participation in committees. If you make use of your knowledge, you can be a very effective committee member.

Table of Parliamentary Motions

Motions	Need A Second?	Amendable?	Debatable?	Vote Required?	May Interrupt Speaker?
Motions With a Sequence of Precedence					
1. To adjourn a meeting	yes	no	no	majority	no
2. To recess a meeting	yes	yes	no	majority	no
3. Question of individual or group privilege	no	no	no	chair*	yes
4. To postpone consideration of a topic temporarily	yes	no	no	majority	no
5. To vote on a motion immediately	yes	no	no	2/3 majority	no
6. To limit debate on a motion or topic	yes	yes	no	2/3 majority	no
7. To postpone consideration definitely (to a specific time)	yes	yes	yes	majority	no
8. To refer a proposal to a committee	yes	yes	yes	majority	no
9. To amend a motion	yes	yes	yes	majority	no
10. To postpone consideration indefinitely (to kill a motion)	yes	no	yes	majority	no
11. Main motion to bring business for consideration	yes	yes	yes	majority	no
Incidental Motions With No Sequence of Precedence					
Parliamentary inquiry concerning the rules	no	no	no	chair*	yes
Objection to consideration of an inappropriate topic	no	no	no	2/3 majority	yes
To raise points of order to conform to rules	no	no	no	chair*	yes
To appeal from the decision of the chair	yes	no	yes	2/3 majority	yes
To suspend the rules temporarily	yes	no	no	2/3 majority	no
To withdraw a motion from consideration	yes	no	no	majority	no
To divide a motion for consideration	yes	yes	no	majority	no

Order of Precedence

*Requires only decision of chair; no vote unless appealed
Adapted from J.W. McBurney and K.G. Vance, _The Principles and Methods of Discussion_ (New York: Harper and Brothers 1939, p 283.)

Summary

Parliamentary law is a system of rules based on common sense. There are seven basic principles of parliamentary procedure. The presiding officer of an organization is expected to have numerous leadership characteristics. He or she has some determined responsibilities, and is required to apply parliamentary rules in conducting meetings. A specific order of business should be followed in meetings.

There are four classes of motions: main motions, subsidiary motions, privileged motions, and incidental motions. Incidental motions have no priority, but all others have a set order of precedence. There is a proper form of presentation for all motions, and there are established rules for dealing with motions and their disposal.

Some business can be taken care of more effectively by a committee than by an assembly. A committee is a small, task-oriented group, and participation in committees can be improved by applying principles of problem solving and group process to participation.

Check Your Knowledge

1. What is the order of precedence for motions?

2. What are the advantages of referring some matters of business to a committee?

3. What are the responsibilities of the presiding officer? Can you recall some rules for the chairperson to follow?

Check Your Understanding

1. Why do you think the seven principles of parliamentary procedure are so important to a democratic way of doing things?

2. Why are privileged motions important? Why are they acted on immediately?

3. Why is there no order of precedence for incidental motions?

Check Your Skills

1. Choose a member of your class to preside and conduct a meeting on choosing a parliamentary project for your school (teaching a parliamentary workshop for clubs; performing a demonstration for the freshman class, etc.).

   Use parliamentary rules to conduct the meeting. Ask one student or your teacher to serve as the parliamentarian.

2. Apply what you have learned about parliamentary procedure to your participation in an organization outside class. Write down problems you notice and look up answers to them in *Sturgis'* or *Robert's Rules.*

Participating in Committees

Communication
Essay

Some people have suggested that the only way things get done in complex organizations is through committee interaction. In schools, community organizations, and businesses, committees are given responsibilities to make decisions and solve problems that the entire group would be unable to communicate about effectively.

Committees are small groups that complete tasks or solve problems through relaxed, but focused, small-group discussion. They are usually made up of three to twelve people. Committees that are too small may not represent enough of the larger group. Committees that are too large may have difficulty communicating and arriving at a consensus. A good committee size is five members. Larger committees may be divided into subcommittees to encourage further focusing and effective communication behavior.

The appointment of an organization's committee members is usually the direct responsibility of the president. Some committees are required by a parliamentary group's bylaws. They are called *standing committees* and members serve for set terms to do continuing committee work. These committees exist to allow a few people to give special attention to some aspect of the organization's work. *Ad hoc* committees are appointed to attend to a special event or problem. The committee exists only until its assigned work is completed. In school, such committees may be formed to plan social events or special projects for classes or clubs.

A committee usually has a chairperson who presides as leader if the committee is a formal one, or who coordinates the group's progress if the committee is less formally organized. The chairperson reports on the committee's work to the larger organization and may be given the authority to make decisions when the committee is not able to meet.

Committee membership involves work and all members must participate in order for a committee to serve an organization. In school you probably have been a member of a committee to plan a dance or an assembly, to study a particular policy, or to elect someone to office. These committees are remarkably like those on which you will serve as an adult. They exist to serve a purpose and they give you the chance to develop sharp communication skills that you will use throughout life. Committees are essential to government, business, industry, and social service organizations. Effective committee participation depends on using effective interpersonal, problem solving, discussion, and public speaking communication skills.

TOWARD EFFECTIVE
Public Speaking

Public speaking involves planning and creative use of a full range of communication skills. In this Part, you will look at the preparation, presentation, and evaluation skills needed for effective public communication. Understanding and acquiring these dynamic skills is a worthwhile effort; they will be of value to you throughout your life.

Preparing a speech involves a logical, ten-step process. It includes selecting and limiting a topic, selecting a purpose, investigating the topic, assessing the collected information, creating an outline, preparing a brief, writing a manuscript, adapting the manuscript or notes, and rehearsing.

Public communication offers opportunities to make responsible communication choices. Through presenting speeches in class, you will refine your message-sending and receiving skills and you will learn much about evaluating the speeches of others.

CHAPTER 14

Beginning the Speech Preparation Process

Key Terms

After reading this chapter you should be able to:

1

Explain or relate instances in which public speaking has influenced history.

2

Explain six basic responsibilities you should assume in exercising your right to free speech.

3

Explain four responsibilities a listener should assume in exercising his or her right to listen.

4

List five criteria for selecting a topic.

5

Explain the importance of each criterion.

6

List three processes involved in limiting a topic.

7

Explain the importance of each process.

8

List three general purposes for speeches.

Selection
Organization
Style
Memory
Delivery
Ethos
Persuasion
Urgent message
Transient message
Thesis statement
Definition
Classification
Informative speech
Persuasive speech
Ceremonial speech

As we begin a study of public speaking, we should devote some attention to the important role public speaking has played in the shaping of history and Western thought.

At the heart of a democratic system lie our abilities to analyze and question issues, speak out on issues of concern, participate in formal and informal groups, and evaluate messages. The responsible citizen is an informed, assertive critic and an articulate spokesperson. Skills presented in public speaking (research, organization, analysis of issues and information, and the use of language) provide the basis for participation in public communication.

Most of us are unaware of the time we spend in public communication because of our conscious apprehension of speaking in public. One study on fear revealed that the item most feared by respondents was speaking before an audience. Yet in another study, a majority of blue-collar workers said they had spoken in public at least once in the previous year. What does this tell us? It tells us that, while most people fear speaking to an audience, most of us exercise our rights and assume the responsibility of giving a speech more frequently than we might imagine.

You probably speak before your classes, for church groups, for community groups, or for organizations to which you belong. You probably listen to speeches every day; a teacher's lectures, sermons, radio and television addresses, town meetings, and special addresses on special occasions are all types of speeches.

Gaining a Perspective

There is no disputing that we exercise our rights as speakers and as listeners in the democratic process, where the exchange of ideas and information is vital. It is therefore important that, in order to benefit the most from public communication, we develop competencies and skills in public speaking, listening, and evaluating that will enable us to exercise these rights effectively and responsibly.

Students sometimes wonder about the difference between a speech and a report. Giving a report usually involves reading what someone else has written or said, while speeches are prepared from the speaker's perspective, using a variety of source materials. In other words, a report usually reflects someone else's thoughts, while a speech is always *you!*

Speeches reflect the numerous choices speakers make in preparation for self-expression.

Understanding the Speaker's Responsibilities

Selection

You will be pleased to know that there are only five basic clusters of skills or canons that you should master in order to speakffectively. The first is the idea of **selection**. In order to assume your responsibility as a speaker, you must carefully select a topic and ideas to support your topic, and must conduct sufficient research to gain valid information to support your topic. The classical title for this canon is *invention,* and this label still seems appropriate. Speakers invent speeches. Invention suggests that preparing and presenting a speech represents creative processes.

Organization

Speakers must use careful **organization.** Beginning speakers are sometimes surprised to learn that a speech is a literary *form* just as a short story or a poem is a form. Form refers to how something is "put together" and to what its particular attributes are. For example, what makes a chair a chair? Its form—the fact that the object has a flat surface to sit on, a back rest, and, usually four legs to support it. In your English classes you learn about the form for five-

The preparation process involves making choices about selection, organization, style, memory, and delivery.

paragraph essays, short stories, and lyric poetry. In this section you will discover that speeches also follow a basic organizational form. Knowing about speech form will assist you in composing speeches and in listening to the speeches of others.

Style

Speakers must develop **style** or skill in using language. You learned earlier that choosing language is like choosing clothing. Speaking is a formal (adhering to form) activity, and speakers should apply standards to using language. Developing an effective style—a system of language choices—is a basic skill.

Memory

Speakers should have a ready command of ideas and information while speaking. There are many advantages to learning to "think on your feet." Speakers develop special kinds of **memory** that are essential to convincing audiences they have knowledge on their topics. Memory skills also provide a flexibility that allows speakers to adapt to the needs of their audiences.

Delivery

Speakers must also develop skill in verbal and nonverbal presentation. The actual **delivery** of the speech is critical to success. You may have an important topic; you may have conducted impeccable research; the speech may be well organized; and your language may be carefully selected. You may have absolute command of your ideas and information, but *all* of this can be lost in ineffective delivery.

Ethos

Learning and applying these five basic skills are vital to speaking effectiveness. Aristotle reminded us, however, that the speaker must be a "good" person if he or she expects to be believed. Another important aspect of public speaking is *ethos*. There are three dimensions of **ethos** (speaker image), or *ethical behaviors,* speakers should consider.

1. Speakers should have sound qualifications for speaking on their chosen topics. Being well informed and using valid and complete information is essential.

2. Speakers should be of good character. Our credibility as individuals is important if we want our ideas to be accepted—no matter how informed we may be.

3. Speakers must demonstrate good intent. Simply stated, a listener must feel that the speaker is sincerely interested in the topic, is presenting information fairly, and is putting the listener's best interests ahead of his or her own.

A fourth dimension—personalism—is sometimes added as an ethical consideration. Generally speaking, listeners tend to believe speakers who demonstrate that they are real and open. Personal, human qualities increase a speaker's effectiveness. Ethos is considered to be the most important and influential aspect of **persuasion,** in which a speaker tries to change listeners' perceptions, attitudes, beliefs, or values. The speaker who demonstrates sound qualifications, good character, and good intent is more apt to be believed than one who does not demonstrate these qualities.

Understanding the Listener's Responsibilities

Learning about speaking skills prepares the listener for active listening and effective critical evaluation. Listening and critical skills can be developed along with speaking skills. You can learn to listen and evaluate a speaker's ideas and supporting information. You can follow the speaker's pattern of organization, and observe his or her language strategies and presentation. Listeners have a responsiblity to develop skills in active listening and in the critical evaluation of messages in order to fulfill their role in a democracy.

The study of public speaking and critical listening can provide an important basis for you to realize your full potential as an individual and as a citizen. Exercising your freedom to speak out on issues important to you is not only your right, but is also your responsibility in many instances.

Checkpoint *Speakers and listeners in the public forum have the same shared reasons for speaking and listening that they do in interpersonal or group interaction. Think about a public speaking situation that you have recently observed. Were the speakers and listeners fulfilling their responsibilities? In your opinion, was the communication effective?*

Beginning Your Speech

You're probably thinking, "Okay, so what do I have to know? What do I have to do to give a speech?"

There is a logical, systematic process that can ensure success in developing a speech. You will discover that there are a total of ten steps in our process, each step designed to focus on one or more of the basic skill clusters we have discussed. Constructing your brief, for example, combines the results of your research and analysis (selection) with your outline (organization).

The 10-Step Process

The ten steps in our speech preparation process are: 1) select a topic; 2) limit the topic; 3) select a purpose; 4) investigate the topic; 5) assess the information; 6) create an outline; 7) prepare a brief; 8) write a manuscript; 9) adapt your manuscript and notes; 10) rehearse your speech. The strength of the step-by-step approach to speech preparation is that, if you focus clearly on only one aspect of the process at a time, you are free to think about only that phase of development. The results are usually clear and concise. If you have a problem in selection, organization, or style, you can solve it quickly by returning to the appropriate step in the process.

First three steps

The first three steps of the process will provide a base from which you can begin to build your speech.

1. Select your general topic.

2. Limit your topic! Make it specific.

3. Select your purpose.

These steps in the invention process will form the foundation for your speech and start you on your way.

Selecting a Topic

There are several guidelines for you to consider in selecting your topic.

Select a Topic that Interests You Your audience will assume you are well informed on your topic, that you have had experiences that relate to your topic, and that you are vitally interested in your topic. A good way to begin selecting a topic is by asking yourself: "Who am I? What can I do? What are my interests? What do I know about? What experiences can I share."

The answers to any of these questions can give you ideas for topics. Preparing the speech can provide personal growth by expanding your experience, interest, or knowledge. In order to make the speaking experience interesting and rewarding, you should choose a topic in which you are already interested and about which you want to know more. Ask yourself, "Why do I want to speak on this particular

Step 1

Select a Topic

Selecting a topic offers many opportunities for creative thinking!

topic?'' You can probably determine by your answer whether or not the topic is worth pursuing.

We should note that your topic may be chosen for you. On some occasions you may be asked to speak because you are known to have experience or expertise on a particular topic or because an audience wants to hear your ideas. In that instance, focus on your particular audience and the purpose and constraints of the occasion. You may have a responsibility to a club or organization that involves speaking. The occasion may dictate what topic you need to address.

Select a Topic that is Appropriate to the Audience   Audience analysis lies at the heart of what the speaker's task is really about. After all, speakers do not speak to fill their own needs alone; they speak because they are concerned about the audience's response to their ideas.

Who will your listeners be? What are their interests, attitudes, and values? What are their concerns and needs? What does your listener have to gain from listening to your speech? Answers to these questions, especially when combined with insights gained from probing your own interests, should assist you in choosing a topic.

Make sure your topic is appropriate for the audience!

Select an Important Topic   Your speech can be no better than your topic. A prominent professor of speech communication used to chide his students with the statement, "You can't make a great speech on garbage cans!" His point, of course, was that the topic must have potential for development. There must be provocative ideas related to the topic and pertinent information available.

Selecting topics for speaking is somewhat different from selecting topics for writing. An essay may be written on any topic, for a reader to read at leisure. A speaker, on the other hand, has a captive audience to whom he or she has a specific responsibility. Consequently, we sometimes call a speaker's message an **urgent message.** Urgency implies that a speaker's topic should be timely. It should pertain to right now! It should also relate to the particular audience's immediate or felt needs.

Importance does not necessarily imply that a topic must have dire consequences. You don't have to speak about weighty national concerns such as poverty or pollution. You can talk about local issues, your school or school activities, personal topics—your hobbies or things you like to do. You can explain how to make things or perform a task.

Relevance

It is only essential that you choose a topic of immediate interest that meets a need for your particular audience, at that particular time, in that particular place. In other words, in order to be interested, the audience must perceive the topic as relevant. You would not choose to talk about the latest techniques in skateboarding to the ladies' afternoon sewing circle. As interesting as skateboarding may be to you, the ladies just might not find your topic important because it doesn't relate to them.

Select a Topic that is Appropriate to the Occasion   Audiences come together and speakers speak on a variety of occasions. You should always assess the constraints and implications of the speaking situation in selecting topics.

Time

Time, for example, is always an important consideration for a speaker. At what time of day will you give your speech? Will it be in the morning when the audience is alert and capable of following a complex presentation? Is the speech scheduled for the afternoon? An "after-dinner speaker" should

Make sure your
speech is appropriate
for the occasion and
time of the
presentation!

know that speaking at a banquet or luncheon does not lend itself to exploring complex issues at length.

Place

Where will your speech be given? Is the setting formal or informal? How will this affect your plans? Will a large audience be assembled in an auditorium? Will the setting be in an informal room with distractions due to overcrowding?

Purpose

What is the purpose of the occasion? What interests and values have prompted the event to be scheduled? Is it a celebration? Is it a meeting designed to arouse enthusiasm for a campaign? Is it a meeting of citizens concerned with local affairs? Is it a social gathering? Considering the implications of the occasion is important for your success.

Determine What Information is Available   This is of special concern to those who may be speaking from limited knowledge or experience. It is, however, important that *all* speakers—no matter how knowledgeable or experienced they may be—have sufficient information. It is vital that you have an in-depth understanding of your topic, as well as current information. Checking on sources of information should be a part of the topic-selection process.

Start a list of interesting topics and ideas for speeches. As you encounter new topics, ideas, or experiences, add them to your list. Think about exploring new, unusual, or unique ideas for added interest. Think about topics about which you are qualified to speak because you are *you*!

Limiting Topics and Making Them Specific

Step 2

Limit the Topic

A speech is not only considered to be an urgent message, in that it must be designed to meet the particular needs of the speaker, the audience, and the occasion; it is also a **transient message.** _Transient_ implies that a speech is a live performance for a live audience. Both speaker and audience, in most instances, have one brief opportunity to accomplish their respective purposes for speaking and listening. Electronic media have changed this somewhat, but for the most part, when we think about public speaking, we think of a speaker speaking to a live audience in a live situation.

Speaking and listening again impose different demands from reading and writing. Unlike readers and writers, speakers and listeners cannot "replay" the experience to clarify the message and its implications in case of confusion. They have one fleeting opportunity to accomplish their purpose. For this reason, speakers must limit and clarify their topics so that listeners can follow, understand, evaluate, and remember what has been said. The observation of the following guidelines will be helpful in limiting your topic.

Draft a Thesis Statement   If you had to reduce your message to one clear and simple sentence or question, what would it be? Perhaps you could compose a list of several statements from which to choose, but it is important that you be able to verbalize what you want to say in one concise, clear, grammatically simple statement or question that reflects the precise point you wish to make. The statement you choose may become your **thesis statement,** and will serve as a base from which to construct your speech. Each ensuing choice can be made based on its relevance to this first statement.

Define Your Topic   When you think of **definition**, you probably think of a dictionary. Standard definitions are important for clear communication; it is important for you to know exactly what you mean and to be able to limit, clarify, or explain your topic according to your own specifications. You cannot possibly cover an entire topic in a speech, because the message must be simple, concise, and relatively brief. Therefore, it becomes important to define and personalize your topic so that your audience will understand precisely what you want to say.

If you are talking about football, what particular aspect of the game do you want to discuss? If you are talking about friendship, what do you mean by *friendship*? If you are talking about skiing, do you want to talk about the benefits of the sport, the equipment needed, important skiing events, or famous skiers? Perhaps you want to tell us how to ski. All of the items named pertain to skiing, but each limits, defines, and personalizes the topic in a different way.

Classify your Topic   One way to further limit your topic is to classify it according to the approach you want to take. **Classification** will provide you with a variety of possible choices and will simplify your research. You can think more clearly about possibilities for developing your topic, and you can evaluate research materials more quickly according to their potential usefulness if, at this point, you place your topic in a specific class or category.

Almost any topic can be classified in one of the following categories:

Places	Processes
People	Problems
Things	Policies
Events	Concepts

Let's say you want to give a speech to a civic club about the high school you attend. What do you want to talk about? Is the _building_ of great interest or historical importance? You might want to talk about your school as a place. In your speech you can take us on a verbal tour of the building and grounds. Perhaps your school is outstanding because of the _people_ associated with it: the administration, faculty, and student body. You could classify your topic as people.

Events? You could talk about unique activities at your school or unusual festivals or workshops your school hosts. _Processes?_ Your speech could be an orientation speech for an incoming class. You might want to inform them about procedures for enrollment, attending classes, and/or participating in activities. _Concepts?_ Your school may be an experimental school, a vocational school, a private school, or magnet school. You may want to talk about its particular philosophy or approach to education.

It is also possible to combine categories in classifying topics. For example, you might wish to address a particular problem and offer a solution. In this instance you are covering a problem and suggesting a policy. These examples reinforce the idea of classifying your topic. You can simplify your research when you know specifically what kinds of information you need. Relevant and irrelevant information can be sorted out immediately, saving time and effort.

The real significance of limiting topics prior to making other choices lies in the fact that you will analyze your topic and consider your alternatives before proceeding with your speech. With your topic clearly in mind, you can contemplate your purpose.

Selecting a Purpose

Speeches can be defined by purpose by placing them into one of three general categories: **informative speeches, persuasive speeches,** and **ceremonial speeches.** You should ask yourself what you want to accomplish and what response you want from your audience when selecting first a general purpose, and then a specific purpose.

You may choose to inform your audience. In that instance, you want your audience to know about something

You may choose to inform (a), to persuade (b), or to entertain (c) your audience. You will consider a variety of strategies before deciding how to communicate your message most effectively.

a

c

b

Step 3

Select a Purpose

of which they have no knowledge, or you want to give them new and unusual information and ideas on a topic about which they have some knowledge. In either instance, you will want to be sure that your ideas and information create further interest in your topic.

You may wish to persuade your audience to change their perception of facts, change their attitude or feeling about a topic, become concerned about the significance of a problem or issue, or take action to implement a policy or program. Many of the speeches you hear on the radio or television are persuasive, and persuasive speeches are frequently given in speaking events.

You may wish to inspire or unite your audience in a common cause, or to entertain.

The specific purpose depends on the response you want from your audience. You may want support for a political campaign; you may want the audience to embrace a particular philosophy or share an opinion. Just as a comedian must want a laugh and know how to get it, you must establish a specific objective for your audience and choose and implement appropriate strategies to ensure the response.

Checkpoint *Make a list of words that describe you (student, friend, gymnast, brother or sister, actor, violinist, golfer, etc.). Be creative! Then, using the list as a guide, develop three possible topics for a speech. Which of those topics would be of special interest to your audience? What aspects of the topic would be most interesting to you and your classmates? What speech purpose would be most appropriate for your class?*

Summary

Public speaking provides an opportunity for speakers and listeners to participate fully in the democratic process. The right to the free exchange of information and ideas is essential to democracy as we know it. In order to protect our democratic system, it is important that we as individuals and citizens exercise our rights of articulate expression of ideas, and of critical listening and evaluation, in assuming responsibility for productive public dialogue.

A speaker must think about a topic, select a message carefully, and be well informed on the topic. A listener must possess knowledge about a speaker's role and responsibilities in order to listen effectively and apply valid criteria for evaluating the speaker's message.

In order for your message to be clear and meaningful, you should give careful consideration to the first three steps in the preparation process. Select a topic. Limit the topic. Select a purpose.

Check Your Knowledge

1. What are six responsibilities an effective speaker should consider?

2. What are the five basic speech skills or canons?

3. List four qualities that contribute to speaker ethos or image.

4. What are four responsibilities involved in listening to speeches?

5. List, in order, the first three steps of the speech preparation process.

6. What are five things you should consider in selecting a topic?

7. What are three processes to use in limiting topics?

8. What are the three purposes for speaking?

Check Your Understanding

1. Explain the importance of public speaking in local, national, or world affairs.

2. Give current examples of speakers and speeches that are influencing public opinion.

3. Why is it important in a democratic system for a speaker to exercise the right to free speech?

4. Why are effective listening and critical skills as essential to public dialogues as they are to effective speaking?

5. Explain the statement, "A speech is no better than its topic."

6. Why must a speaker limit his or her topic to one central idea or issue?

Check Your Skills

1. With your classmates, choose a recent school event as a potential speech topic. Then, limit the topic. How will you define it? How will you categorize it? What particular aspect of the topic is most interesting to all of you?

   Now, decide how the topic could best be presented considering each of the three possible speech purposes—informing, persuading, and uniting or inspiring an audience.

2. What topics do you feel strongly about or have an intense interest in? Can you think of three topics about which you believe it is your *responsibility* to speak?

CHAPTER 15

Conducting Effective Research

Key Terms

Primary research

Secondary research

Card catalogue

Standard tests for evidence

Logical proof

Ethical proof

Pathetic proof

Citation

After reading this chapter you should be able to:

1

Explain the importance of using primary resources in conducting research.

2

Give specific suggestions for conducting interviews and informal surveys.

3

Give specific suggestions for preparing to investigate secondary sources.

4

List questions useful in guiding investigation of secondary sources.

5

List specific resource guides found in most libraries, and explain how to use each in locating secondary sources.

6

List kinds of resource materials found in most libraries and explain the use and application of each.

7

Explain the purpose of standard tests for three kinds of evidence and/or proofs needed by speakers.

8

Give specific suggestions for recording information to be used in speeches.

As citizens and as consumers of public messages, we should expect speakers to present complete, accurate, and unified information when they speak. In order to meet these expectations, you must realize that no matter how knowledgeable you may be or how much experience you may have in the area on which you are speaking, you must still conduct research.

Responsible speakers know they must find the most recent information, and that they need qualified sources to reinforce their own observations and beliefs. You will need to verify facts regarding background or details. You will need to consider arguments from sources that may not share your perceptions or agree with your positions on issues. You will need to find quotations, analogies, or anecdotes to add interest and appeal to your speech.

Research is the fourth step of speech preparation. Armed with your topic and your purpose, you can begin to conduct primary and secondary research.

Step 4

Investigate Your Topic

Gathering Information from Primary Sources

We will define **primary research** as the gathering of information from personal sources. Don't forget that you are an important repository of information and experience. You should review your own memories and insights for possible use as examples to personalize your speech.

You may also want to compose a list of resource people with whom you can discuss your topic. You can conduct an interview or an informal survey.

Conducting an Interview

If we continue our example of making a speech about the high school you attend, you can see that you might want to interview your principal, discuss your speech with your teachers, and conduct a survey of the student body. The information you gather from primary sources will broaden your perception of your topic and will give you human perspectives to consider. You should follow some basic procedures in conducting an interview to ensure positive results.

Planning and Preparation

Since you are going to involve another person or persons in your interview, you should plan carefully. Arrange conversations or interviews early. If planning an interview, make your appointment several days ahead of time. If you simply want to discuss your topic informally, you still need to arrange a time and place convenient to the other people involved.

Know what you want to gain from the interview or conversation. You are requesting the meeting, so it is your responsibility to know exactly what information you want to get. You may want to interview your principal about the overall goals, objectives, and governance policies of your school. You may want to discuss school background and traditions with one of your experienced teachers. You may want to discuss impressions of your school with a first-year teacher. In each instance, you will want the individual to know ahead of time why his or her insights are important to your speech.

When you arrange for an interview, remember that the impression you make may influence the interviewee's expectations!

Do your homework. Write out questions before the meeting. The success of your interview or discussion will relate directly to the questions you ask. You will want to be sure your questions are clearly worded and sharply focused on the information you hope to gain. Try to avoid questions that can be answered "yes" or "no," because such questions do not yield sufficient information. Instead, ask questions that focus on what you want to know but are open ended enough to encourage others to talk.

Instead of asking your principal, "Does our school offer a sufficient variety of courses to accommodate student needs?" ask, "How does our school curriculum accommodate the wide range of student needs?" In the first instance the principal could answer "yes" or "no." Where do you go from there? In the second instance, your principal would probably say that your school does or does not offer a variety of courses and provide examples. If examples are not given, you can ask for them.

An additional step to take in planning your interview or discussion is to limit your number of questions. A few appropriate, relevant, concisely stated questions will serve your purpose more effectively than a long list of loosely structured questions.

The Interviewing Process

When conducting your interview, remember to be flexible. One of the delights of conducting an interview is the surprise that may lie in store. Your resource person may disclose interesting bits of information of which you are unaware. In that case, be interested and encourage the person to talk or tell a story. In most instances, your time will be well spent. You may also want to pursue the answer to one of your original questions with another question (for clarification), or to encourage your interviewee to talk in more depth in order to pursue a new lead for additional information.

Use your verbal and nonverbal communication skills to show a positive attitude, enthusiasm, and courtesy. When you seek out others to gain information, you want to extend courtesy and appreciation for their efforts.

Listen actively and ask meaningful questions during an interview. Be open to the other person's verbal and nonverbal messages.

Keeping records

Be on time! Listen attentively! Let the resource person talk instead of dominating the conversation yourself. Take notes discreetly. If the individual has said something you wish to quote, ask permission and then read the quote in order to be sure it is correct. Keep the meeting on schedule and bring effective closure to the discussion.

If you would like to tape the interview so that you are sure to have a record of all that is said, be certain to ask your resource person for permission to use a tape recorder. Test the recorder and the tape before beginning the interview. You may also want to play the tape back to your interviewee. One advantage of taping an interview is that conversation may occur more easily when you are not concentrating on taking precise notes.

Be sure to thank the person for his or her time and information. If you want to extend an extra courtesy, you could write a note of appreciation. This would be a nice touch, and excellent public relations for you (and your speech communication department!) You could also invite the resource person to hear your speech, or send the person a copy.

Conducting Informal Surveys

Informal surveys can be interesting to prepare and conduct, and can yield timely information. Surveys usually indicate current opinion and, like interviews and discussions, can add personal or timely dimensions to your speech.

Careful planning will help you get the information you need from your survey. Of course, you should know your specific purpose and exactly the kind of information you are seeking prior to conducting your survey. You will need to draft a _thesis_ or _hypothesis_ stating exactly the claim you want to test. What do you want to know?

The format of the survey can then be decided. Do you want to use a "person-on-the-street" technique and ask questions directly? If so, write down your questions and prepare to take careful notes or use a tape recorder to tape responses in order to ensure accuracy.

Would you prefer to distribute a questionnaire? If so, questions need to be phrased clearly and briefly. Do you want simple "yes" or "no" answers, or do you want your respondents to indicate a degree of feeling or agreement?

In this case you may want to use a *semantic scale* such as this:

Do you consider yourself to be politically liberal or conservative? (Please indicate the degree of your response.)

very liberal	liberal	moderately liberal	neutral	moderately conservative	conservative	very conservative
1	2	3	4	5	6	7

Sampling and Analyzing

What kind of *sampling* do you need? Surveys can focus on a particular group, in order to test the responses of a particular segment of the population such as an age group or income-level group. On the other hand, random sampling is frequently used to focus on the general population. How many samples should you solicit? We sometimes evaluate the validity of a survey by whether or not sufficient sampling has been attempted and included.

When you take survey responses in person, be alert for new perspectives on your topic!

Computers offer exciting ways to analyze the information gathered in a survey.

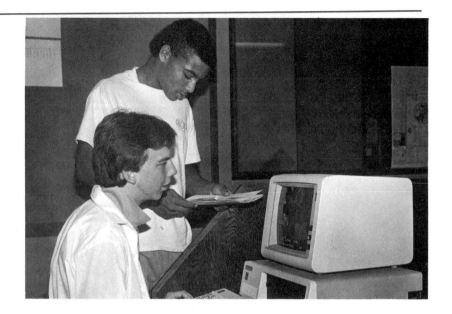

Assume for a moment that there are three members of your speech class named Ron. There are six girls and six boys in your class, for a total of twelve. Would this sampling support a conclusion that one fourth of the students in your *school* are named Ron? Depending on your school enrollment, the answer is, ''Probably not.'' The sampling is probably insufficient.

What factors should be considered in sampling? If you are surveying your student body, have you included sophomores, juniors, and seniors? Have you included boys and girls? Have you ensured an ethnic mix of those sampled?

What criteria will you use to analyze your data? How will you determine the results of your inquiry? You may want to enter your data in a computer. You may be surprised at what you can learn.

Many speech students enjoy conducting surveys because they encourage creativity in gathering and analyzing information.

Checkpoint

Conducting an interview or survey is enjoyable for the interviewer and provides an interesting personal touch for your speech. When you plan your primary research, ask yourself who might be a valuable and interesting source of information. What specifically do you want to learn in interviewing the person or conducting the survey? In class, discuss the questions you might ask in an interview or the format you might use for a survey.

Gathering Information from Secondary Sources

When most people think of research, they think of **secondary research,** which we are going to define as gathering information from print or electronic media. Books, periodicals, microfilm, microfiche, films, film strips, videotapes, recordings, and radio or television are valuable secondary sources of information. Computers have introduced us to new technology that can also yield valuable information for speakers.

Whether you conduct primary research prior to, after, or simultaneously with secondary research, you will find combining research strategies advantageous. The human experiences and perspectives from primary research personalize and amplify; the factual information, anecdotes, and experiences from secondary sources are more formal and precise.

Preparing for Secondary Research

In order to ensure success in conducting secondary research, you should consider the following steps of preparation. Much time can be lost in a library or media center if you are unfamiliar with the facilities, unaware of the resources and services that are available, and uncertain about the kind of information you need. A trip to your school library or media center is invaluable. If you live in a city with a public library, research center, or college or university library, you will want to visit those facilities to find out what services are available to you.

Media centers and libraries are full of secondary sources.

A class visit arranged by your instructor during which the librarian or media specialist has an opportunity to conduct an informational tour would be valuable. If such a field trip cannot be arranged, you should arrange to meet the librarian or media specialist yourself. Explain that you are a speech student interested in a wide range of topics and materials, and that you will be doing research and would appreciate whatever assistance he or she can provide. You should use your primary research processes and skills to discover potential for conducting secondary research.

Before actually beginning your investigation of secondary sources, list aspects of the subject about which you need to find information. Consider your classification of the topic (event, problem, concept) and think about possible avenues of inquiry. Knowing exactly the kind of information you need, and knowing how to locate information, are major aspects of research.

Asking Some Questions

Depending on your classification of your topic, you should find these general questions useful in guiding your investigation.

1. What is the present status of my topic? Gather all the current information available.

2. What is unique or unusual about my topic? You may take for granted that everyone knows what you know about your topic, but finding new and unusual information on your topic may increase your own interest and spark the interest of your audience.

3. What is the background of my topic? In order to put a topic in perspective, you need to know something of its history. You need to know the origin of the topic, how it came to be, and how it arrived at its current state.

4. Who are people who have been associated with my topic? What contributions have they made? What influence have they had? How has my topic affected them?

5. What forces have contributed to or hindered the development of my topic? Topics are not isolated or independent; other forces give momentum to, provide barrier

to, or shape the character of related topics. Exploring the interrelationships of forces can provide valuable insights about your area of interest.

6. What are the inner workings or parts of my topic? This information gives you ideas about various aspects of your topic and their relationships; you can also identify the strengths and weaknesses of your topic.

7. To what other topics does my topic relate? What are its effects on other areas of society, for example?

8. What is the real significance of my topic?

9. What is the value or worth of my topic?

In finding answers to the last two questions, which are basically evaluative in nature, you should make a special note of the significance and worth of the topic for you personally. Why did you choose the topic? How does it relate to you?

You can use these questions in the initial stages of your research to generate ideas about the kinds of information you will need. As you find information, other avenues of investigation will become available to you, increasing your alternatives in making final choices for your speech.

Locating Research Guides

Your librarian or your instructor will provide valuable assistance in locating sources of information. Most libraries offer certain standard resource materials. You can consult the library's **card catalog** for major books on your topic. In the card catalog you will find author cards that will help you locate the works of particular writers. You may also consult subject cards to find information about your topic. Be sure to *cross reference*; for example, if you are looking for information about shyness, you will also want to look under communication apprehension, stage fright, and assertiveness.

The Reader's Guide to Periodical Literature includes references to articles in most recognized periodicals. Information related to your topic can be found by consulting annual editions of the *Reader's Guide.* If you already know key dates related to your investigation, you will want to consult that edition. If you want information about writer

Subject card (a), title card (b), and author card (c) from a card catalogue.

```
        INTELLECT--PROBLEMS, EXERCISES, ETC

153     Salny, Abbie F
SAL         The Mensa think-smart book / by Ab-
        bie Salny and Lewis Burke Frumkes. 1st
        ed. New York : Harper & Row, c1986.
            124 p. : ill. ; 21 cm.

        "Perennial Library."


            1.Intellect--Problems, exercises,
        etc. 2.Puzzles. 3.Questions and an-
        swers. 4.Mensa. I.Frumkes, Lewis
        Burke. II.Title.

                                         153
ISBN 0-06-091255-3
                     003 198          LC-MARC
                          © 1960 BRODART
```
a

```
            The Mensa think-smart book

153     Salny, Abbie F
SAL         The Mensa think-smart book / by Ab-
        bie Salny and Lewis Burke Frumkes. 1st
        ed. New York : Harper & Row, c1986.
            124 p. : ill. ; 21 cm.

        "Perennial Library."


            1.Intellect--Problems, exercises,
        etc. 2.Puzzles. 3.Questions and an-
        swers. 4.Mensa. I.Frumkes, Lewis
        Burke. II.Title.

                                         153
ISBN 0-06-091255-3
                     003 198          LC-MARC
                          © 1960 BRODART
```
b

```
153     Salny, Abbie F
SAL         The Mensa think-smart book / by Ab-
        bie Salny and Lewis Burke Frumkes. 1st
        ed. New York : Harper & Row, c1986.
            124 p. : ill. ; 21 cm.

        "Perennial Library."


            1.Intellect--Problems, exercises,
        etc. 2.Puzzles. 3.Questions and an-
        swers. 4.Mensa. I.Frumkes, Lewis
        Burke. II.Title.

                                         153
ISBN 0-06-091255-3
                     003 198          LC-MARC
                          © 1960 BRODART
```
c

Larry McMurtry, who you know received the Pulitzer Prize for literature in April 1985, you would want to consult the 1985 edition of _Reader's Guide_ for information. The publication is usually six to eight weeks behind in publishing information about periodicals. If you do not know related dates, start with the most recent edition and work back through previous editions.

Two cautions in using _Reader's Guide_ are important. First, be sure to use the "See also" notes in the _Guide._ Also check your library's holdings in order to learn which periodicals are available.

Your librarian may have compiled a vertical file of a variety of kinds of information from special sources. Vertical files often yield unique or unusual information not otherwise available. Also in the "Ask your librarian!" category, you can inquire about other special indexes or files that may be available, including library loan services, media sources, and potential for conducting computer searches for information.

The Reader's Guide to Periodical Literature is the starting point for investigating magazine coverage of your topic.

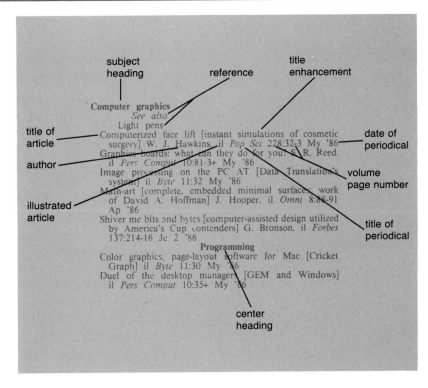

Using Resource Materials

In addition to indexed materials needed for locating sources of information, most libraries provide traditional sources of information that may be relevant to various aspects of your topic. Encyclopedias, dictionaries, and almanacs may prove valuable. *Facts on File,* if available, can give you a condensed account of the most recent information available on your topic.

Books on your topic and related topics may or may not provide the most recent information, but will include the history of your topic and possible in-depth analyses that can be helpful. Books are usually, but not always, written by authors with sound qualifications and considerable experience.

Periodicals include magazines and newspapers, and offer endless potential for information and topic development. Periodicals may not offer in-depth analyses but will provide timely information. You should be aware, however, that many periodical publications represent a particular political, social, or religious bias, and their articles and editorials will most likely reflect that bias.

In many libraries, back issues of newspapers and magazines are kept on *microfilm* or *microfiche*. Your librarian can assist you in locating and using these materials.

Speakers should also become familiar with a periodical called *Vital Speeches of the Day*. This bimonthly publication of current important speeches is absolutely essential for speakers and listeners. Not only can you become informed about current issues through current speeches, you can also use the speeches for quotation in your own speech. Speech students should read speeches, just as athletes read the sports pages or actors read plays.

Other sources

Films, film strips, and radio and television broadcasts will vary in usefulness. When using electronic media sources, survey the credits for the producer or sponsor of the material. The date of the filming or programming is also important.

You may wish to investigate other miscellaneous sources of information. The Yellow Pages of your telephone directory can provide a list of organizations or local, county, state, or national agencies that offer free brochures, publications, or films. Office personnel from these agencies or organizations may be available for interviews. Government documents may provide an additional source of information. Experts on your topic who live in your community may have materials or know of special sources of information you can use.

Vital Speeches of the Day, bound copies of periodicals, and books are sources rich in logical, pathetic, and ethical proof materials.

After finding standard information on your topic, you will want to find special sources you can use to make your speech lively and interesting. Your librarian or teacher can advise you about collections of humorous anecdotes, speakers' handbooks, or books of quotations. Consulting these sources will help you develop a collection of fables, analogies, literary quotations, jokes, or quotations from famous speakers that you can use to personalize your speeches.

One thing you can usually count on is that if your topic is timely and important, information is available! Remember, however, that determining the accessibility of information in your particular instance is an important aspect of the topic-selection process.

Assessing Information

Once you have located books and articles relating to your topic, you will probably begin to wonder which particular pieces of information will prove most valuable in developing your speech. You can ask yourself several questions at this point.

Is the information appropriate for my topic and purpose? Reconsider your classification of your topic. Think about the kind of information you need. For example, in a speech about your igh school, if you are talking about school personnel you can give cursory attention to information concerning the building or the school dress code. If you are speaking about the history of your school, information on current custodial problems will be of little use. By asking this question you can begin to sift, sort, and select information as you scan or read. However, one word of warning: Do keep an open mind to discovering new ideas. You may be surprised at what you find, and it *isn't* too late to shift the focus of your topic.

Is the information credible? Remember that your information is no better than its source. Before investing a large amount of time reading from one book or magazine, you may want to investigate the author or publisher for qualifications, credibility, or bias.

Some periodicals found on newstands are known to exploit the public with their exaggerated and false claims. Newspapers and news magazines often have an editorial bias, and most authors of books report their opinions and perceptions along with fact.

Standard Tests for Evidence

Along this line you will want to ask some other questions. What qualifies this author to write on this topic? What bias does my author or source represent? Is the author or source believable and of sound reputation? Is the source competent and capable of making the judgments? When was the material written? What is date of publication? Is the information still relevant?

Such questions represent **standard tests for evidence.** You will want to use these in evaluating your sources as well as in choosing the information you use in your speech. Standard tests include a source's qualifications, credibility, and competence. The timeliness of information may also be important to you.

Proofs

The information you gather in your research will be used to support the points you will make in your speech. You will use the results of your research to develop _proofs_ that represent evidence. There are three kinds of evidence you will want to consider using in your speech, and you should keep them in mind as you conduct your research.

Logical proofs include statistics, specific instances, and testimony. **Pathetic proofs** include anecdotes, examples, descriptions, and other types of materials that are used primarily for emotional appeal. **Ethical proofs** include your own personal experiences or insights, which personalize your speech and demonstrate your sound qualifications and intent. Audiences usually appreciate learning how the topic relates to the speaker. Logical proofs sometimes double as pathetic or ethical proofs. For example, a quoted or personal anecdote about the experience of skiing down a snowy slope can be a form of testimony.

As you survey your resource materials, you will also want to be aware of your need for humorous or dramatic materials to add feeling to your speech. Speakers and listeners agree that emotional appeals are an important element of persuasion, because both our thinking selves and our feeling selves are actively involved in speaking and listening.

Checkpoint *Who is your favorite musician or actor? Make a list of questions you'd like to ask about that person. Then, for each question, note the secondary sources you can consult to find the answers.*

Recording Information

A final phase of the research process involves recording information. Certainly you can check materials out of the library. You can duplicate information for speaking purposes on a copy machine in most instances without violating copyright laws. You can take general notes.

Keep materials organized during the research process. You can use large envelopes or manilla file folders to organize copied information by points or categories. This process allows you to focus on one category at a time as you consider and choose the proofs to include in your speech. It can be extremely frustrating to remember a particular anecdote you want to use, but not be able to remember where you read it!

Be Systematic

It is important to keep careful, organized records.

Systematic recording of information will prove invaluable to you. In doing this, some speakers use note cards. Some record information in a notebook under different headings. Some assemble organized "worksheets" for the purpose of recording information. Regardless of the form you choose, you will need to observe three guidelines.

1. Be sure to copy information exactly as it is written.

2. Record a complete citation of your sources in each instance. Complete **citation** includes the author, the title of the publication, the title of the article, date of publication, and the page number. You may also have to include volume numbers, publishers, and places of publication. Your teacher can give you special instructions about the information you need and the citation form you should use.

Notes should include exact source information.

Kwakiutl Indians

"Their civilization was built upon an ample supply of goods, inexhaustible, obtained without excessive expenditure of labour. The fish, upon which they depended for food, could be taken out of the sea in great hauls. Salmon, cod, halibut, seal, and candlefish were dried for storage or tried out for oil."

<u>Patterns of Culture</u>, Ruth Benedict, © 1934 (Houghton Mifflin edition), page 173.

3. Record information about the author's qualifications and the context of the information. If you are quoting from *Vital Speeches,* for example, noting information about the occasion and the audience for whom the speech was given will be useful.

How many sources should you consult? How much information do you need? The answers to those questions depend directly on how much you already know about the topic, your topic itself, your specific purpose, the audience you are addressing, and the occasion on which you are speaking. It is generally wise, however, to consult several sources (preferably of different types) in order for you to have alternatives from which to choose as you compose your speech. Consulting several sources will also be important to you in fulfilling your ethical responsibilities as a speaker.

While open to new and creative information sources, speakers should always remember to use the standard tests of evidence to evaluate them.

Summary

In order to meet your responsibility as a speaker, you will need to conduct research on your topic.

Consulting primary sources allows you to examine the perceptions of others, broadening your own perspective and appreciation.

Exploring facts and opinions reflected in print and electronic media brings the world of research, inquiry, and knowledge of your fingertips, allowing you to investigate and analyze the topic for yourself.

As a speaker you want to make the most informed, articulate presentation of your speech possible in order to get your point across to your audience and accomplish your purpose.

Check Your Knowledge

1. Define primary research.

2. What are three steps in planning an interview?

3. List three guidelines for conducting an interview.

4. What are three considerations in conducting a survey?

5. Define secondary research.

6. Explain three ways to prepare for secondary research.

7. What are three kinds of secondary sources found in most libraries?

8. What are three tests for evidence.

9. List three ways to record information to be used in speeches.

Check Your Understanding

1. Why is primary research important to both the speaker and the listener?
2. Explain the importance of consulting a wide range and variety of secondary sources in meeting your ethical responsibility to your audience.
3. Explain the statement, "Your information is no better than your source."

Check Your Skills

1. Usually when we are really interested in something, we want to know more about it. Choose a favorite topic and explain step by step how you would go about finding useful and interesting information in your school library.

   Now, think about the topic you have chosen for your speech. List some questions you can use to help you look for information. List some sources of information you think will be useful. You are ready to begin doing research for your speech.

2. With several of your classmates, arrange to interview a teacher or administrator at your school. Prepare your list of questions before the interview, and decide on a way of recording the answers to the questions. After conducting the interview, discuss how it was similar to a one-on-one interview and how it was similar to a small group discussion.

3. Select a major event in the history of your region about which you'd like to know more. Read about the event in an encyclopedia or history book. Which aspect of the event would you like to investigate further? Where can you look for more information? Who in your community can you interview about the event?

CHAPTER 16

Organizing Your Message

After reading this chapter you should be able to:

1

Explain the importance of analyzing the audience before making final choices for your speech.

2

Explain the importance of analyzing listener values and needs before making final choices for your speech.

3

Explain the importance of analyzing the occasion before making final choices for your speech.

4

Explain the concept of speech form.

5

List and explain the major functions of each of the parts of the classic speech outline.

6

Explain the importance of the statement: "Each point must support the thesis statement and relate to other points in the body of the speech."

7

Outline your speech.

Key Terms

Speech form

Introduction

First transition

Definition

Background

Motivation device

Preview

Body

Chronological order

Spatial order

Topical order

Problem-solution order

Second transition

Summary

Second thesis statement

Conclusion

Selecting your topic, limiting your topic, selecting your purpose, and gathering information through primary and secondary research are the first four steps of the speech preparation process. Throughout our examination of these steps several words important to communication, and to public speaking and critical listening, have emerged. The words *process, choice, effectiveness, rights,* and *responsibilities* are vital on all levels of communication, but they are especially important for public speakers and their listeners.

The desire to communicate, which prompts a speaker to devote time and effort to the preparation and presentation of a formal speech, and the desire demonstrated by listeners who invest their time and effort to hear the speaker's message, require that both speaker and listener know what a speech is.

Does that statement sound strange to you? Of course we all know what a speech is! Not necessarily! A speech is not just a speaker talking to an audience that listens. A speech is a classical literary form intended for oral presentation to an audience. The word *form* is a key word in this definition. After examining the **speech form,** you will probably agree that a knowledge of form makes the speaker's choices much simpler. Knowledge of a basic formula is also useful to the listener.

In order to proceed with your task as a speaker, you now need to verify your first basic choices. Then you will make use of a basic structure or outline that will help you organize your speech.

Verifying Initial Choices

Reconsidering your own objectives, when you are, at least for the time being, satisfied with the information gained through research, is important. First you selected a topic. You then thought of various aspects of that topic you might choose for your speech, or you considered various approaches you could take. You then limited your topic to the area you felt had the most potential for you and your audience.

Now, is the choice reflected by the limitation of your topic what you *really* want to talk about? Just to be sure, look through your research materials carefully. After all, you limited your topic before you began investigating it. Perhaps your research revealed a new approach for you to take.

Step 5

**Assess
Your
Information**

Suppose you planned to talk about a congresswoman from your home town. You classified your topic (general) as a politician (still general, but a bit more specific). You chose to limit your speech to various aspects of her political career, including her offices on the local, state, and national levels. You could, with this limitation, trace her political career or contributions chronologically. You might also focus on her record—on legislation she has written or causes she has supported.

Perhaps your research led you to an interest in the congresswoman's rise within her party, so, instead of classifying your topic as "politician," you now want to limit it a bit further to focus on a Democrat, Republican, or Independent. This further limitation can make your speech more interesting.

You should also verify what it is you *really* want to accomplish with your speech. If you chose as a general purpose "I want to inform my audience about the congresswoman," you may find that choice a bit vague after conducting your research. You have learned new things about your topic, and your purpose may have shifted as you gained new knowledge and insights. Your original purpose may

---

Verification Checklist

Limit the Topic
- Is the choice reflected by the limitation of my topic what I *really* want to talk about?
- What was my basic limitation?
- Can I limit my topic further within that class to make my speech clearer and more interesting?

Select a Purpose
- What do I really want to accomplish with my speech?
- What do I want to happen as a result of my speech?
- How do I want my audience to respond to my speech?
- Exactly what do I want my listener to know?
- Exactly what do I want my listener to understand?
- What do I want my listener to think?
- How do I want my listener to feel?
- What do I want my listener to do?

have been to convince, persuade, inspire, or entertain. That general purpose guided you through your research, but at this point more fine tuning is in order. You will need to formulate clear listener objectives based on your general purpose to serve as a base for choices in formulating your speech.

Analyzing the Audience and Occasion Further

In order to be realistic about your final topic limitation and your specific objectives, you will need to perform some audience analysis. You will find answering the questions in the following Audience Analysis Guide helpful in determining your final topic limitation and specific purpose. The Guide will also provide a basis for choices you will want to make later in developing your speech.

You may also reconsider the occasion for the speech before making final choices regarding your topic and purpose. Why has the audience come together at this time and in this place? Several questions can help you adapt your speech to the occasion.

1. What is the purpose of the meeting?

2. What values underlie the occasion and unite the audience?

3. What are the implications of time and place?

4. What are the implications of other activities also on the agenda?

5. How can I adapt my message to be appropriate for the occasion?

After reconsidering your own interests and purpose, the implications of your research, and what you know about the values, knowledge, interests, attitudes, and needs of your audience, you are ready to formulate clear and specific choices for your speech.

Clarify objectives

Review the original thesis statement that guided your research. Since you probably want to further limit your topic and draft clear objectives for your audience, you will need to reassess your thesis. After consulting your audience analysis guide and considering the implications of the occasion, write a clear, simple sentence that best states your topic and purpose.

Remember what you want your audience to learn, to understand, and to feel. State in one sentence what you want your audience to do as a result of hearing your speech. Do you expect action? If so, what action do you want audience members to take? Do you want them to be more knowledgeable and interested so they will seek more information on your topic?

Audience Analysis Guide

1. To whom will I be speaking? (Describe your audience.)
2. What do my audience members have in common?
   Age:
   Gender:
   Ethnic Identification:
   Organizational Affiliation:
   Commitment to interest or cause:
   Other:
3. What do I know of their common interests, attitudes, or values?
4. What is the reason for the occasion of the speech?
5. What expectations does my listener hold for the occasion and for my speech?
6. Why would my listener want to hear my speech?
7. How much does my listener already know about my topic?

very knowledgeable	knowledgeable	somewhat knowledgeable	relatively unknowledgeable	ignorant
1	2	3	4	5

8. Where did my listener obtain his or her information?
9. What is the interest level of my listener?

enthusiastic	interested	disinterested	uninterested	hostile
1	2	3	4	5

10. How does my topic relate to the particular audience?
11. How is the audience affected by my topic?
12. What is the probable attitude of my listener toward my topic?

very positive	positive	neutral	negative	very negative
1	2	3	4	5

13. What can I realistically hope to accomplish in my speech within the framework of my own desires and my knowledge of my audience?

Checkpoint *Think about your class and their needs as an audience. What kind of an occasion would it be if you were speaking to them? Do you want them to be more knowledgeable and interested so that they will seek more information on your topic? How would you formulate a message for this audience?*

Understanding Speech Form

With your thesis statement to serve as the foundation of your speech, you are ready to formulate your message.

Just as a contractor needs a blueprint before beginning to build a house, you need a basic plan or structure to serve as a guideline for constructing your speech. The contractor will use bricks and mortar as basic materials. You will use your knowledge of your topic, your purpose, your knowledge of your audience and occasion, and your thinking and language skills to construct your speech.

You have already been introduced to the idea that a speech is a form. A speech is not an essay or a short story; a speech is a speech. The implications of the urgent and transient nature of the oral message require that you give special attention and care to the formulating of message. For that reason, the sixth step of speech preparation is the construction of an outline.

You are probably already familiar with a three-part plan of organization.

Constructing an outline

I. Introduction

II. Body

III. Conclusion

However, as we begin the second basic speaking skill—organization—we will introduce you to a classic five-part speech outline. The outline introduced in this chapter is a basic outline. It provides for clear, systematic analysis of your topic and arrangement of your message. Later you will discover ways to adapt the outline to serve special purposes, but it can always be used to ensure a well-organized oral or written message.

Because clarity of topic and purpose are so very important to you and your listener, we will use a five-part general plan that allows for clear analysis and completely accommodates the needs of your audience. You will notice the emphasis on transition areas.

The five-part outline consists of:

I. Introduction
II. First transition
III. Body
IV. Second transition
V. Conclusion

Basically, the first transition is intended to prepare the listener to better understand the points you wish to develop in the body of your speech. The second transition puts your ideas in a final focus or perspective before concluding your speech.

As a means of introducing you to the basic parts of the speech, we will focus first on the function of each part, then on materials you might want to consider in developing that particular section of your message.

The Introduction

The **introduction** serves several important purposes. First, the introduction should get the attention of the audience. It should lead into the topic and create interest in the topic. The introduction is the place to establish good will and a positive climate of communication. The introduction should set a basic mood or tone for the speech, in order to prepare the audience for the listening experience.

Opening remarks set the tone for your speech and encourage listeners to become interested in your topic.

Startling statements
can be used to gain
attention.

The introduction consists of any opening remarks or devices you choose to meet your specific purpose. The introduction may consist of two parts, an "address" or salutation and an attention-getting device. We hear speakers say, "Ladies and gentlemen, I am happy to be speaking to you today." The speaker may then proceed to compliment the audience or talk about the importance of the occasion. This is an address.

Special attention-getting devices may include literary quotations from poems, songs, short stories, novels, plays, cartoons, or essays. Startling questions or statements of fact can be used to get attention and build interest. Speakers can make a positive first impression by quoting from the speeches or written works of a well-known scholar, social leader, or member of government.

The First Transition

The **first transition** provides a link or bridge between the introduction and the body of the speech. It consists of a series of logically related parts designed to prepare the listener to understand the speaker's message. The first transition includes statements and information chosen to orient the listener to the speaker's topic and purpose and to motivate the audience to listen and accept the speaker's message.

Thesis statement

The _thesis statement,_ as you know, is the main idea of the speech. It is use to clarify, from the beginning of the speech, the basic message you wish the audience to receive. It is the statement you would make or the question you would ask if you could only present one sentence instead of a whole speech. The thesis statement is a simple, clear statement of your topic and/or purpose. A simple sentence or a question may be used.

Definition

You may choose to include definition as a second element of the first transition. The purpose of **definition** is to clarify what you mean or focus the attention of the audience on the topic precisely as you desire. Basically, a definition limits the topic and places it sharply in focus. Definition can be used when words within the thesis statement may be new to the audience, or if you plan to approach your topic in a unique manner.

Dictionaries can provide definitions; on the other hand, you may wish to offer a personal or descriptive definition of your own. After all, you can, within reason, choose the personal meanings and limitations you impose on a topic. You may, in fact, use a kind of negative definition. You could say, "When I speak of Central High School, I am not talking about buildings or school policies or traditions, I am talking about people." In so doing, you limit the scope of your topic and focus the expectations of the audience.

Background

Now, ask yourself "What does the audience need to know before I proceed further, in order to be able to follow and understand the information and ideas I want to present in the body of my speech?" The answer to this question provides your approach to using **background** in your first transition. The background section can be a point you wish to make or a claim you want to support but, because it does not directly support the thesis statement, it is placed in the first transition section rather than in the body of the speech. Also, background can introduce an idea or provide information the audience needs before hearing your major points.

The background usually consists of one or more of the following: history of the topic; current status of the topic; or the philosophical stance or value position you want the audience to adopt in listening to your speech. In each instance, you would have concluded in your audience analysis that the listener needed a knowledge or understanding of the past, or needed to be informed of the most recent facts (especially if those facts are unusual or shocking), or needed to know the value base of your presentation.

Motivation devices

If you analyzed your audience as uninterested or negative in their feeling or attitude toward your message, you may want to include a **motivation device** in the first transition. This device may be used instead of or in addition to background. You want to begin the major portion of your speech—the body—on a positive note. Therefore, ask yourself ''What do I need to tell the audience in order to help them to be interested in my ideas?'' ''How can I help them gain a more open or accepting attitude about my ideas?''

You might say, ''You may be wondering how our present immigration policy affects you. After all, there aren't many immigrants coming into this area. Actually, all of us are affected socially and economically by this vital issue.'' You could then proceed to show the particular listener how he or she is affected by immigration policy, advantageously or disadvantageously, depending upon your thesis statement. You would, in so doing, motivate the audience to listen to what you have to say.

The first transition orients and motivates listeners.

Preview

You should include a **preview** of the points in your speech in the first transition, in order to provide the audience with a plan for listening to your points. The transient nature of the oral message makes it important to include clues or "memory hooks" that facilitate effective listening. Redundancy is usually built into the speaker's message for this purpose. Generations of speech teachers have instructed their students to "tell them you are going to tell them, tell them, and tell them you have told them." In other words, you should preview your points, present your points, and summarize your points. You could say, "I will show you the part immigration played in this town's history, describe current immigration policy, and discuss the implications of the policy."

Sign posting

The only alternative to using a preview in your first transition is to label your points in the body of the speech. This "sign posting" can help listeners follow your speech. For example, you could say, "The first point I'd like to discuss is the role immigration has played in the history of our town. . . ." Then, "My second point concerns current immigration policy," and so on. Can you see why a preview might be helpful?

The Body of the Speech

The body of the speech consists of several related points that communicate your main idea and accomplish your purpose. You will probably find that using two or three main points to support your thesis statement is sufficient. In fact, you should try to "uncover" a limited number of points rather than trying to "cover" more points than can be adequately developed in the speech.

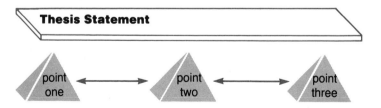

In choosing points to be covered, you should limit the points to those that directly support your thesis statement and relate directly to each other. The body of your speech can be organized in one of several ways.

Patterns of Organization

The most common patterns of organization include chronological, spatial, topical, and problem-solution. The order you use will relate closely to your topic and your purpose. There are certain patterns of organization that are particularly useful in informative or persuasive speeches. Ceremonial speeches are usually inspiring and can be basically informative or persuasive, as the speaker chooses.

Patterns for Informing

Points may be arranged in **chronological order** according to time—past, present, or future. If you have chosen to inform your audience, chronological order would seem especially appropriate for explaining about things, people, processes, concepts, places, or events. Let's assume you want to inform your audience about (and create interest in) an organization to which you belong. For practical purposes, let's apply our model.

"I'd like to tell you about the growth of our organization."

point one — point two — point three

"We began five years ago with only a few members."

"Today we have a large membership and a variety of civic projects."

"We anticipate expansion in the future."

Your points follow chronological order, and relate to one another in that each focuses on the number of group members.

Points may be arranged in **spatial order.** The spatial pattern of organization is most applicable to talking about places or things. You could arrange points from top to bottom or north to south, for example. Let's resume the example of a speech about the school you attend. You want to talk about Central High School as a unique building or facility. How many spatial divisions can you think of? Will you talk about the first floor, second floor, and third floor? Will you say, "When you enter the front door you will see to the right (point one), to the center (point two), and to the left (point three)"? Again, let's apply our model.

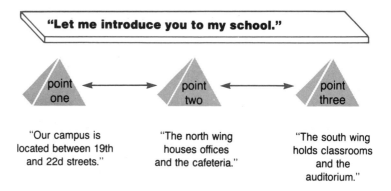

"Let me introduce you to my school."

point one — "Our campus is located between 19th and 22d streets."

point two — "The north wing houses offices and the cafeteria."

point three — "The south wing holds classrooms and the auditorium."

Speakers may also choose to use a **topical order.** If your purpose is to inform, you may wish to simply divide your topic into the parts or aspects you plan to address. Topical arrangement is appropriate for informative speeches about places, people, concepts, or things.

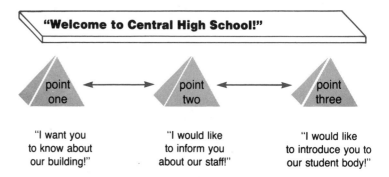

"Welcome to Central High School!"

point one — "I want you to know about our building!"

point two — "I would like to inform you about our staff!"

point three — "I would like to introduce you to our student body!"

Patterns for Persuading

When you want to persuade an audience to accept a fact as true or false, a value as good or bad, a problem as significant or insignificant, or a policy as wise or unwise, you will want to consider your pattern of organization very carefully. In persuasive speaking, you will be addressing topics on which individuals hold differing perceptions or views, and this makes audience analysis for persuasive speeches especially important. In formulating and organizing your ideas you must consider facts, values, and a variety of points of view or perceptions.

In policy-oriented persuasive speeches, you will want to draft your thesis statement carefully and then proceed to select and arrange points to reflect clear analysis of your topic and purpose. You can arrange your points in a **problem-solution order.** If you want to convince your audience that a change in school policy is needed, you might choose to use this pattern of organization, which moves from fact, to problem, to solution.

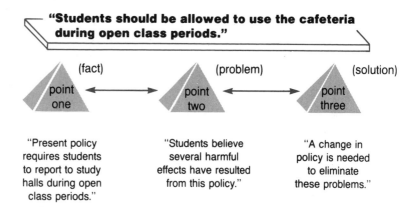

Variations on the problem-solution order are possible. You can also arrange your points from cause, to effect, to solution. Or you can explain the effects first, and then explain the cause as background for the solution. When you want the audience to accept a value assumption, you may decide to focus on only one aspect of the problem, for example, the effects. See the following model.

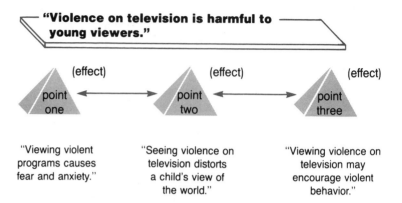

"Violence on television is harmful to young viewers."

(effect)   (effect)   (effect)

point one   ↔   point two   ↔   point three

"Viewing violent programs causes fear and anxiety."   "Seeing violence on television distorts a child's view of the world."   "Viewing violence on television may encourage violent behavior."

Monroe's Motivated Sequence

One other organizational pattern proposed for persuasive speeches may be useful for you to consider. *Monroe's Motivated Sequence* relates to an overall strategy for presenting a topic persuasively. The sequence applies to the total speech (not just the body) and represents an alternative to the model used in this text. This pattern is frequently used by salespeople.

  I. The Attention Step (get the audience's attention in your introduction!)

 II. The Need Step (show audience members that they have an unmet need)

III. The Satisfaction Step (suggest a policy or solution that will meet the listeners' need)

IV. The Visualization Step (encourage listeners to imagine that their need has been satisfied by your suggestion)

 V. The Action Step (tell listeners what *they* have to do to bring about the change you have suggested)

Thinking about Monroe's Motivated Sequence can help you in planning each section of your persuasive speech.

The Second Transition

Just as you must prepare your audience to listen to your speech by using appropriate attention-getting, orientation, and motivation materials in your first transition, you must review what you have said and put your message into perspective in the second transition.

Summary

The **second transition** usually consists of two parts, the summary and the second thesis statement. The **summary** can be a simple restatement of points. You could say for example, "And so today we have looked at several causes of terrorist activities. We have examined the many harmful effects of terrorism, and have explored possible solutions to the problem." In so doing, you have restated the three points covered in the speech. The summary may also be an eloquent description of a central value or idea, in which you use strong appeals to put your message in perspective.

Second thesis statement

The **second thesis statement** is a final statement of your topic or purpose. It should clearly relate to the first thesis statement and pull your entire message together.

Let's suppose you use a question for your first thesis statement. In one of the sample speeches we will examine, Karen Cochran uses the question, "What is dyslexia?" as a first thesis statement. She answers the question in her second thesis statement: "Dyslexia is a perceptual problem, but not necessarily a disability."

You may use a general statement as your first thesis to lead into the topic; you can then use a related, specific statement as a second thesis to pull the message together. For example: "Everyone should assume a share of responsibility for the project" (first thesis); "We need your contribution of ten dollars to ensure success" (second thesis).

A subject statement could be used as a first thesis; a purpose statement for a second thesis. For instance: "The crime rate is increasing;" "We need your support to stop the rising crime rate."

You may develop a summary to be followed by the second thesis statement, or you may choose to restate your thesis, then develop your summary. Use the strategy that best serves to put your message in perspective.

The Conclusion

In the **conclusion,** you end the speech by "rounding out" the topic and meeting the needs of the audience. Conclusions often include strong emotional appeals to encourage acceptance of the message.

One conclusion strategy often used by speakers is to return to the introduction. If, for example, you choose a poem for your introduction, you might use an opening verse or a few lines in the beginning. In the conclusion, you might use the same lines or perhaps a last verse.

Different devices can be used. You may use a literary device in the introduction and a quotation from a recognized authority in the conclusion. You can end your speech with a question or statement that encourages your audience to think about the points raised in your speech. Concluding devices should be carefully chosen to highlight your message and leave a lasting impression with the audience.

Checkpoint

What is your favorite television commercial? Identify the form of communication used in the commercial. What is the purpose of the commercial? Does the commercial follow the five-part speech form? How does the structure of the commercial work to convey the message?

Organizing Your Message

Your outline should consist of a maximum of twelve clear sentences, arranged in the form you've studied. Placing your ideas in a clear format is a prerequisite for clear speaking.

The Basic Outline
I. Introduction
II. First Transition
A. Thesis statement
B. Definition (if needed)
C. Background
D. Motivation (if needed)
E. Preview
III. Body
A. Point one
B. Point two
C. Point three
IV. Second Transition
A. Summary
B. Second thesis statement
V. Conclusion

Step 6

Outline Your Speech

Use the outline diagrammed here to organize your own speech. The following suggestions will help you be clear and specific.

1. Begin by writing the thesis statement exactly as you want to state it in your speech.

2. State your points in complete sentences exactly as you want them in your speech.

3. Place your points in a logical order using an appropriate pattern of organization.

4. Check your points carefully to determine that each point supports your thesis statement and that each point relates to other points.

5. Examine the thesis statement to see if you will need a definition. Consult a dictionary or other reference if necessary, and write your definition.

6. Ask yourself what your audience needs to know in order to understand your message and write your background statement.

7. Consider the need for a motivation statement to establish a link between your topic or purpose and your audience. If necessary, write the statement.

8. Write your preview—stating the points you will cover in your speech.

9. Write your summary statement.

10. Write your second thesis.

11. Consider your choices for introduction and concluding devices.

12. Write your introductory statement.

13. Write your concluding statement.

Checkpoint

Write an outline for a speech on your school, as you'd like to present the topic. What is your purpose? How have you limited your topic? What research would you like to have done?

Summary

Effective message organization requires that you have a thorough knowledge of your topic, and that you consider your own goals and needs in choosing your topic and purpose. Your final choice of topic and purpose must also reflect careful analysis of the audience and occasion for your speech.

Clear organization is an indication of clear thinking. You will want to put your ideas into an appropriate speech form, in order to present a message your listeners can follow, interpret, and understand. The classic speech outline provides a logical format to meet your purpose!

Check Your Knowledge

1. What are the specific criteria for analyzing an audience?

2. What are the specific criteria for analyzing an occasion?

3. What are the five main parts of the speech outline?

4. Describe the functions of each part of the speech outline.

5. What are some devices that can be used in introductions?

6. List three types of background.

7. Explain four main patterns of organization.

Check Your Understanding

1. Why is it important to re-examine your own choices after conducting research?

2. Why is it essential to analyze the audience and assess the occasion prior to organizing your message?

3. Explain why each point must support the thesis statement and relate to the other points in the body of your speech.

4. Why is repetition important in organizing your speech?

Check Your Skills

1. Using the information processes and guidelines in this chapter, outline your speech.

2. Using the guidelines in this chapter, check your product.

CHAPTER 17

Developing Your Message

After reading this chapter you should be able to:

1

List and explain three steps for developing a point.

2

List, define, and give examples of three kinds of logical proof.

3

List ten tests for logical supports.

4

Cite reasons for using ethical appeals in speeches.

5

Cite suggestions for using pathetic appeals in speeches.

6

List, define, and give examples of five kinds of amplifying devices.

7

Construct a brief for your speech.

Key Terms

Statistics
Specific instances
Testimony
Amplifying devices
Description
Comparison
Contrast
Example
Visual aids
Brief

With a fresh new outline that represents your choices, research, and analysis, you are ready to develop your speech. In essence, your task is to combine your information and the ideas reflected on your outline. On the one hand, you have your blueprint or pattern; on the other hand, you have the materials you are going to use to support your message.

A review of the data you accumulated in your primary and secondary research is in order. As you survey your notes, keep in mind the fact that you want to choose the most *interesting* and *relevant* information possible. If the process of verifying your initial choices has resulted in a need for new or different information, you may want to make an additional trip to the library. If you are speaking on a current topic about which there are new developments every day, you will want to use the most recent information available in your presentation.

Having given thought to the emotional tone you want to develop in your speech, you will need to find special materials to assist you. Wise speakers know that every speech should be interesting and entertaining, regardless of its purpose. Finding the right anecdote to add a touch of humor, or finding that dramatic instance that will give a tug to the listener's heartstrings, may provide the touch you need for real success.

A summary of your information and the goals you have set for audience response will be most helpful as you begin to develop your speech.

Developing a Point

As you choose the information to use in your speech, remember that there are three basic steps for developing a point: State your point; support and amplify your point; and restate and relate your point.

In writing an outline, you developed clearly stated points that support your thesis statement and relate logically to each other. The statements on your outline should reflect clear thinking and logical analysis. You also know that it is your ethical responsibility to be well informed on your topic and to present complete, accurate information to support your claims. In public dialogue, no statement stands unless it is supported. In other words, the unsupported statement is automatically unacceptable because it has no support. We can also say that a point or claim is no more valid than the information that supports it, and that the support is no better than its source.

After clearly stating a point and giving adequate support and amplification, you should restate your point and relate it to your thesis statement and/or other points in the speech. In other words, "wrap up" one point before proceeding to the next. Restatement does not necessarily imply repetition. You don't have to repeat what you said in the original wording; you might strengthen the point, in fact, by stating it in a slightly different fashion.

State Your Point

Support and Amplify Your Point

Restate and Relate Your Point

Checkpoint *Working with a classmate or a friend, choose a magazine advertisement that makes a clear, strong claim for a product. What are three points you can imagine making in relation to this claim? How could you support or amplify each point? How could you restate and relate each point?*

Using Proofs   In conducting research, you learned that your information would be used as evidence to amplify and support the points you make in your speech. There are three kinds of specific information you will need for use in your speech—logical proofs, pathetic proofs, and ethical proofs.

When Karen Cochran, in her speech "Color Me Dumb" (complete text in Appendix A), tries to help us grasp the answer to the question: "What does it mean to have dyslexia?" She says:

> It means not being able to learn to tell time. When I was six the attempt made by my sisters to teach me to tell time, turned into a disaster. They became angry with me, because when I read the clock backward, my sisters thought I was not trying to learn.
>
> For Woodrow Wilson, it meant not learning the alphabet until the age of nine and not learning to read until he was eleven. It meant only fair grades at Princeton University.

Karen has offered specific instances (logical support) in an effort to help us learn about dyslexia. Her first instance (ethical proof) and her second instance (pathetic proof) really help us to understand what it means to have dyslexia. A mere description or example would not be so effective!

Knowing that a speech contains adequate proof encourages a confident presentation.

Using Logical Supports

Statistics

Instances

In conducting researching and organizing your speech, you should look for three types of logical support to provide evidence for your points.

Statistics may be used as support. Frequently we need to quantify our claims in order to gain their acceptance. Studies and records yield numbers that can be used for this purpose.

Specific instances may be used to support a point or claim. Instances consist of *verifiable* accounts of actual events or occurrences, and can make claims seem real to us. When the numbers given in statistics may be difficult for listeners to comprehend, a specific instance can make the numbers more meaningful.

If your evidence states that five million people in your state live below the poverty line, we may somehow know that five million is a large number, and that living in poverty represents hardships, but we will not know exactly what you mean. A specific instance can help make your statistical evidence meaningful. If you give us a documented account of one family living in poverty, we can grasp the significance of the statistic.

An additional advantage in using instances lies in their pathetic appeal. We not only understand what the speaker is talking about because the instance clarifies the point for us; we also feel the impact of the point and can relate to it emotionally. We can empathize with Karen and her frustration, and we can imagine how difficult learning must have been for Woodrow Wilson. The point becomes more real for us because we are dealing with the idea on a personal, human basis.

Logical supports can be presented in a visual aid, which allows the audience to ponder them and permits the speaker to refer to them.

Testimony

Testimony lends support and credibility to a speaker's claims. We certainly know that experts disagree, so for each quotation we can find from one government official, philosopher, or scientist, we can often find another that discounts it. However, quoting from recognized and respected authorities can lend weight to your statements.

When you use testimony, what is known in advertising as a *transfer device* is at work. After all, if your favorite sports star eats a particular breakfast cereal, just think what can happen to you if you eat the same cereal! If your favorite actor or actress uses a particular cologne, think how glamorous or alluring you can be when you douse yourself generously with the same fragrance. In speaking, the transfer is a bit more subtle and sophisticated. We can enhance our expertise by quoting a well-known, highly respected source.

How can you go wrong quoting from Thomas Jefferson or Abraham Lincoln to support a claim relating to democracy or justice? How can you fail when quoting Geraldine Ferraro when talking about being female and running for national office? We literally borrow credibility when we use quotations from respected sources.

Use recognized authorities as sources of testimony.

The other advantage of using testimony—more important than the first—is that you can improve your own *ethos* by showing that you have thoroughly researched your topic. Quoting from qualified, respected sources helps you to sound informed and literate, which adds to your own credibility.

Checkpoint *Read Karen's speech "Color Me Dumb." Identify the kinds of logical supports she uses. Would her speech be strengthened, in your opinion, if she had cited her sources in every instance? Why or why not?*

Testing Evidence

Speakers and listeners should be aware of, and should apply, the logical tests for evidence presented here and in Chapter 17. As you choose supporting evidence, you should remember that the claim you make is no stronger than the evidence that supports it. Listeners should question your claims by applying tests for evidence used as support.

1. Is the source qualified?

2. By what means is the source qualified?

3. Is the source biased?

4. What is the philosophical bias of the source?

5. Is the source reliable? Is the source known to be of sound reputation and character?

6. Is the information given by the source consistent with other sources? If not, what conditions account for the discrepancies?

7. Are sufficient instances included? Are the instances typical? Are negative instances included?

8. Are statistics based on a sufficient sample?

9. Are statistics accurately and completely reported?

10. Is the information recent?

As a speaker you will want your evidence to pass scrutiny. As a listener you will want to listen critically to the statement of the speaker's point and to his or her use of supporting evidence.

Checkpoint

What questions do you most often ask when someone tells you something surprising or unusual? . . . Who told you that? Did you actually see this happen? How does she know? When did he tell you this?

These natural responses are tests for evidence. During the next few days, listen carefully to the questions you use or you hear others use to check the validity of claims.

Attend a session in court, or watch or read a courtroom drama. How do attorneys use tests for evidence in questioning witnesses?

Using Ethical and Pathetic Proofs

Ethical and pathetic proofs are strong appeals.

In addition to using logical supports for the points of your speech, you will want to use ethical and pathetic proofs. When you share a personal experience related to your topic, you demonstrate that you are uniquely qualified to speak on the topic. Karen's instance about learning to tell time establishes her qualifications and provides a link between the speaker (Karen) and her topic (dyslexia). We know that she is sincere and that she has a real reason to give her speech and a real concern for her listener's response.

If you have chosen a topic about which you are knowledgeable, and you have experiences, observations, and stories to share, you will give your speech a real touch of authenticity and interest.

Ethical proofs can also double as pathetic proofs, lending strong emotional appeal to the speech. Speakers sometimes share funny experiences with their audiences for a humorous touch, or share tragic or moving experiences for emotional impact.

Pathetic proofs can appeal to compassion, dignity, justice, pride, love, and generosity as well as to other emotions. Fear, prejudice, or anger may be used to motivate an audience to accept or reject an idea. Pathetic proofs can include specific instances, testimony, literary devices, and quotations. The common element is that pathetic proofs lend an emotional tone to the speech and invite the listener to react to the claim on an emotional basis.

In order to be interesting and entertaining in a speech, you can refer to the objective you set for your audience by answering the question, "How do you want your listeners to feel?" Then you can choose pathetic and ethical proofs accordingly.

Avoid overusing emotional appeals. Listeners, in general, should be skeptical about a speaker who gives strong emotional appeals to support ideas without using many logical supports. Be especially careful when using (or listening to) appeals to negative emotions such as fear, hate, anger, or prejudice.

Checkpoint _Note the use of ethical and pathetic appeals in Karen's speech. What impact does her use of personal experience have on the speech? What kind of person do you think she is? Would you like to know her?_

Using Amplifying Devices

In addition to supporting points with logical, ethical, and pathetic proofs, we can add depth and interest to speeches through the use of **amplifying devices.** Amplification refers to the enlarging, extending, or clarifying of an idea through the use of several kinds of devices.

Descriptions

Description can be used to amplify a point or idea. If you want to convince your listener that skiing is exciting, help your listener to experience the excitement vicariously, through you. Think of the details that make skiing exciting to you. Then write a description to help your listener imagine the experience. Help your listener feel the chill of the wind, see the glint of sparkling snow, feel the anticipation of the ride up the lift high over the trees, and feel the thrill of the speed of descent down the winding trail.

Comparisons

Comparisons can clarify meaning for your listener. If you want your audience to understand an unknown experience, compare it to an experience with which the audience is familiar. Understanding how one thing is like another can help the listener gain insight into what you mean.

The _analogy_ is an anecdotal device that provides an especially interesting comparison. Telling us the story, for example, of the little boy who cried "wolf" once too many times, could help us understand the overuse of threats or "scare tactics" in some other instance.

Contrasts

Contrasts can aid a listener's understanding. Just as comparisons can help a listener to grasp a speaker's meaning through showing how two things are alike, contrasts can sharpen a listener's perception by pointing out differences. Telling listeners what something is *not* can be just as important as indicating what something *is*.

Examples

Examples are useful as tools of amplification. One way to help a listener understand is to give examples. Examples may be real, hypothetical, or literary. Interesting examples can add personality and appeal to your message. Frequently, examples are anecdotal; an interesting story used as an example can clarify as well as add interest.

Descriptions, comparisons, contrasts, and examples provide you with an opportunity to do some creative thinking and writing as you develop your speech. Using original amplifying devices affords the listener a more pleasurable listening experience.

Visual aids

Visual aids can be used to demonstrate or help the audience to visualize your point. Speakers can use charts,

---

Checklist for Choosing Supporting and Amplifying Devices

- ☐ What are the proof requirements of the point? What do I need to tell my listeners in order to win acceptance and command interest? Do I need a combination of proofs? Do I need to create interest or clarify my points with amplifying devices?
- ☐ Do my logical proofs relate directly to my point? Does each item of proof support the stated point?
- ☐ Have I chosen information from my most valid sources, as determined by the tests for evidence?
- ☐ Have I chosen the supporting and amplifying devices that hold the greatest potential interest and appeal for the audience?
- ☐ Are my appeals appropriate for the mood and tone of the occasion?
- ☐ Do my supporting and amplifying devices develop the mood or tone I want to convey?
- ☐ Do my supporting and amplifying devices reflect my personal style?
- ☐ Are my devices unique and fresh? Are my devices familiar to listeners, so that they will feel nostalgic or complimented?

graphs, photographs, drawings, models, or actual objects to help listeners understand the impact of their points or to assist listeners in understanding functions or processes. Visual aids can be used as amplifying devices to make speeches interesting for both speakers and listeners.

Remember that definitions can make meanings clear. Definitions that limit, describe, or personalize a point can make your intent clear to your listeners.

Checkpoint *Using Karen's speech, note her use of example and description. How does she use these devices to involve you in her message? What effect does this have on your ability to identify with her or remember what she has to say?*

Step 7

Construct a Brief

The seventh step of the speech-preparation process calls for constructing a rough manuscript or **brief.** The product of your efforts will not be a finished speech, but will be a logical combination of your basic outline and the supporting and amplifying materials you wish to use.

Constructing a brief is a step designed to assist you in developing a message resulting from your choices and for your purposes. There are different methods you can use. If you recorded your information on note cards, you can use your outline as your basic organizational device and arrange your cards in sections according to the points and sections in your speech. If you are depending on duplicated materials or handwritten notes, you may want to organize outline-related worksheets and copy your information onto your sheets or, better yet, try a cut-and-paste technique of taping information at the proper place on your worksheet. This works well for many students. You will find the following worksheet format helpful.

1. Begin with approximately five sheets of blank paper.

2. On the first sheet, as a reminder, make a heading at the top that states your topic and purpose.

3. Also on the first sheet, transfer the first part of the standard speech outline, leaving spaces for your introduction and first transition material. If you plan to use extended background or motivation material, you may want to use the back of the page or begin a second page.

4. On the next several blank sheets, depending on how many points you have, put the number of the point (1, 2, etc.) at the top of the page. You now have an entire page, front and back, on which to record or tape your supporting and amplifying information for each point.

5. On the last blank page, indicate space for your second transition, including summary and thesis statement. You will also want to leave space for your conclusion.

Your brief will look something like this:

Sample Brief

Subject statement: _____
Purpose statement: _____

I. Introduction _____
_____

II. Transition _____
   A. Thesis statement _____
_____

   B. Definition _____
_____

   C. Background _____
_____

   D. Motivation _____
_____

   E. Preview _____
_____

III. Body _____
   A. (State your point.) _____
IV. Second Transition _____
   A. Summary _____
_____

   B. Thesis _____
_____

V. Conclusion _____

As a speaker, you will want to sift carefully through your information, analyzing each piece for its potential value to your speech. For that reason, you will most likely want to record all relevant information in its proper slot on your worksheets. Then you have all your information organized, point by point. You can *then* choose the pieces of evidence and the amplifying devices you wish to use in your speech.

Summary

The speaker's choices in developing public messages stem from an analysis of the audience and from an application of classical communication skills in organizing, and then supporting, claims in a formal message.

You should keep in mind that a variety of proofs offered as support for a claim builds listener interest and responsiveness, as well as adding to the entertainment offered by the speech. Also, each piece of supporting and amplifying material should meet the proof requirements for the individual point.

The speaker who chooses claims carefully and arranges them strategically must use the same care in choosing supporting and amplifying materials that offer appropriate, relevant, and accurate proofs from reliable sources. At this point in the process, you should remember that the claim is no better than the information that supports it, and that the support is no better than its source.

Check Your Knowledge

1. What are the three steps in developing a point?

2. What are the three general kinds of proof?

3. List and define three kinds of logical supports.

4. What are the eleven tests for evidence?

5. Can you list and define five kinds of amplifying devices?

Check Your Understanding

1. Explain the statement, "In the public forum the claim is only as valid as the source of the information that supports it."

2. Why must speakers consider the proof requirements of each point before choosing particular supports?

3. Explain why analyzing the audience and occasion may be the key to choosing ethical proofs and emotional appeals.

4. Why are appropriate, interesting, and unique amplifying devices important in getting and holding the attention of an audience?

Check Your Skills

1. Choose a class member to write on the blackboard or take notes on a piece of paper. Imagine that you are all doing an informative speech on the history of Thanksgiving Day. For five minutes, brainstorm about logical supports you could use in the speech. Do the same for ethical and pathetic proofs.

2. Using one of Shakespeare's many plays or a copy of another play that your class has studied, find six statements that *could* be used as logical supports. Find six possible ethical proof statements and six possible pathetic proofs. How are the statements phrased? What is it about each statement that might make it effective in supporting and amplifying a point?

3. With the suggestion and guidance of your teacher:
   Analyze a speech model focusing on how the speaker has used logical, ethical, and pathetic proofs to develop the message.

4. Using the criteria you have gained from reading, discussion, and examination of models:
   Discuss your own needs for logical, ethical, and pathetic proofs in your speech.
   Choose the logical, ethical, and pathetic proofs for your speech.
   Construct your brief.

CHAPTER 18

Using Style Effectively

After reading this chapter you should be able to:

1

Define *style* and explain the importance of developing skill in oral language to speaking effectiveness.

2

Identify and give examples of three elements of style.

3

List and explain the importance of three kinds of devices used to provide continuity and to make ideas easy for listeners to identify and remember.

4

List, define, and give examples of four rhetorical strategies.

5

Explain the importance of using figures of speech and stylistic devices to make language vivid and memorable.

6

List, define, and give examples of three kinds of figures of speech.

7

List, define, and give examples of three kinds of stylistic devices.

8

Explain the importance of reading your speech aloud in perfecting oral style.

Key Terms

Style

Clarity

Force

Beauty

Signposts

Internal previews

Internal summaries

Rhetorical strategy

Rhetorical question

Parallelism

Antithesis

Climax

Figures of speech

Metaphor

Simile

Personification

Stylistic devices

Now that your speech is formulated and organized, and you have chosen your objectives, you are ready to think about choosing language in which to couch your message. Earlier we identified five basic speech skills as selection, organization, style, memory, and delivery. So far, you have devoted your efforts to the skills associated with selection and organization. The third skill cluster involves the use of language style. We will define **style** as the manner in which a speaker uses language to express ideas and feelings.

If you review the language model from our chapter on verbal communication, you will find that language includes vocabulary (word choice), grammar, and syntax (structural choices, in sentences and phrases). Your use of these components is our focus, as we examine some special strategies and devices speakers use to make their language appealing and memorable.

Understanding Style

Think about what we mean when we say a person has "style." We are usually referring to an "air" the individual has or to something unique that sets that individual apart. We say a singer new to the charts has style if the singer has a different sound or an unusual approach. Therefore, *style* can suggest uniqueness.

It is obvious that vocal style can be an important element of a person's success.

Barbra Streisand

The Beatles

Just as an artist uses paint, a knowledge of technique, and a personal theory of painting in creating a work of art, speakers use language, a knowledge of the communication process, and a personal theory of communication in creating an effective presentation.

Step 8

Write A Manuscript

Using Writing to Develop Oral Style

Style can be defined as "clear and consistent choices." If we consider this definition in relation to language, we can then think about choosing and implementing language strategies that reflect unique, appropriate, clear, and consistent choices.

In our discussion of selection and organization, we stressed the importance of clear thinking. You have now limited your general topic through definition. You have fine-tuned your general purpose into specific objectives for your listeners. You have forged a thesis statement to reflect your main idea. You have explored the use of a logical format for arranging the elements of your speech. You have examined each point to ensure its relationship to the thesis statement and to other points. You have analyzed each supporting and amplifying device. All of this can be lost, however, if your language is vague, general, or inappropriate for public speaking. Clear language indicates clear thinking. As a speaker, clarity and appropriateness of expression are obligations you have to yourself and to your audience.

A speaker should choose language as an artist chooses colors and textures. Your paints are words—language—and paper is your canvas. The speech is your work of art, your masterpiece. In developing style, you can play with words, experiment with sounds, and dabble in strategies that please you in order to attain the same feeling of creativity and satisfaction the artist achieves with paints and canvas.

After all, our language is critical to our civilization. Through the ages, language has enabled us to preserve our culture, our religion, our history, our legends, and our myths. Consequently, language should be approached respectfully and with delight—as a child learning to talk is delighted with each new addition to his or her vocabulary.

The question you are probably asking is, "Why would I need to write a manuscript when a speech is given orally?" There are several reasons. We choose language strategies more carefully when we write. Writing allows for polishing and refining thoughts and language. Writing is slower than speaking, permitting time for reflection and adaptation. Writing yields a tangible product for the speaker's satisfaction and a listener's verification. Writing facilitates memory.

William F. Buckley has a speaking style that reflects his training in the effective use of language.

Writing the speech means choosing language through a very tangible, visible medium that enhances the development of style and memory. Unfortunately, at least from a speech teacher's perspective, we have been taught to choose words and construct sentences carefully when we write, but we have had little training in choosing and structuring language for speech. By developing an awareness of style, applying our awareness through careful selection in writing, and examining the style of other speakers, we can begin to transfer the use of stylistic devices into our speeches. Our goal is for you to discover the pleasure of creating your own ''special effects'' by painting with words—through the precise and skillful use of language.

Time spent writing a manuscript results in a clearer, more artistic message. Time spent writing also saves you time in rehearsing or trying to memorize your speech. You will benefit from writing a manuscript even if you write in pencil and the copy is rough. Writing becomes, then, a means to an end.

Writing your speech can help you organize and remember the results of your research.

*Standard
usage*

In our earlier study of verbal communication, we discovered several levels of language usage. Because a speech is a "formal" (adhering to form) presentation, standard usage is the level most appropriate for public speaking. Standard English, if you remember, relates to word choices that most educated people use and understand. For your reference, standard English is usually recorded as the preferred form in recent dictionary entries.

Other language choices—colloqualisms, slang, and technical or formal usage—should be reserved for special effect and for use with special audiences and on special occasions.

Writing a manuscript will assist you in using standard language in your speech, since our writing is usually more formal than our casual speaking. Writing will also help you choose special language or special effects you want to create by employing other levels of usage.

Understanding the Elements of Style

In order to begin to develop language for speaking, we must consider three basic elements of style. These elements are clarity, force, and beauty.

Clarity is essential to effective communication. It is important as a speaker that you choose the most precise language possible in order to communicate with your listener. Clear word choice, clear sentence structure, and clear organization are all essential for speakers and listeners. Precision should be your goal. A review of the complexity of the communication process reminds us that, if the listener cannot decode the message, the message is lost.

Clarity can be found in nature. Why not strive for it in our communication?

Speakers should consider the denotations (literal limitations) and the connotations (emotional associations) of words in striving for clear messages. Speakers should also use grammatically simple sentences in order for listeners to follow the speech and understand the message.

Force is the energy or intensity of the message. If a speaker wishes to make an impassioned appeal for a cause, his or her language must reflect intense emotion. When Jenkin Lloyd Jones chooses words like "bulldozed" and "bedazzled" in his speech "Who is Tampering with the Soul of America?" his words reflect his desire to communicate strong feelings. Since word choice and sentence structure communicate intensity or strength of feeling, language can be "energized" depending on the effect the speaker wants to achieve and the audience response desired.

Beauty is the third element of style. Language choices range from ugly to beautiful, just as force ranges from languid to exuberant and clarity ranges from vague to precise. When we think of beauty in language, three things come to mind.

One is the image the language evokes. Writers and speakers can, as we noted, paint pictures with words; consequently, we may think of language as beautiful or ugly depending on the image the language conjurs in our minds. Another factor that may cause language to be thought of as beautiful, ugly, or plain and nondescript is that our choice of words, phrases, and sentences can create emotional reactions. *House* may be nondescript, while *home* arouses emotional responses. Short, rapid sentences can create a sense of impatience, while longer, more leisurely sentences are more relaxing.

A third element of beauty is sound. Poets are apt to choose words for how they sound as well as for what they mean. Since language is sound, it seems logical that the accoustic appeal of language is an important element of writing and speaking. Harsh words can grate against our ears and our sensibilities; tender words can soothe and placate.

Checkpoint *Think of a lullaby, a nursery rhyme, or a short song you remember from your childhood. Does it have elements of clarity, force, and beauty? Exchange discoveries with your classmates!*

Developing Continuity in Speeches

Your first task in transforming your brief into a polished speech manuscript is to write clear *transitions* (sentences that provide bridges or connections between the major sections of your speech and between your points), so that you and your audience may proceed from section to section or point to point smoothly and logically.

Writing Transitions

You can use several strategies for writing transitions. Remember that a transition may relate to what has just been said and serve as a summary or restatement before moving to the next point. Karen Cochran uses restatement as a transition in her speech when she says, "Even though most dyslexics learn to cope with, or compensate for, their handicap, they cannot escape the lasting scars of the condition." By wrapping up her point, Karen prepares us to change our focus on the topic, from coping to considering the scars.

Karen could have said, "Having just considered what it means to have dyslexia, let's look at the effects of dyslexia on the thousands who have the condition." In so doing, she would have provided a thought bridge, leading us from one point to another.

The language of transitions consists of transitional adverbs and conjunctions, such as: "Having just seen . . . Let's proceed," "On the other hand we can see," "In addition," "But," "While," "Secondly," "Finally," "In conclusion," and "Next." Statements or questions may also be used as transitions. Karen summarized one point, then asked: "_But what are the effects of dyslexia?_"—thus moving to a second point. She let the audience know that a shift in focus was taking place.

You can think of more transition strategies as you write your speech and encounter the particular gaps and shifts that need bridging. If you develop your statements and restatements carefully, clear transitions or thought bridges will emerge naturally.

A clear transition will: 1) clarify the relationship between the two thoughts it bridges; 2) bring closure to the previous point before beginning the next; and 3) alert the listener to the fact that the speaker is changing points. You may need to adapt your point statements and restatements to reflect these purposes, in order to provide smooth passage from one point to the next.

Using Signposts

Using **signposts** means labeling points as points. If you have a number of points, you may actually say, "My first point is . . .," "My second point is . . .," continuing for several points. Karen Cochran uses rhetorical questions as a kind of signposting. The audience catches on rather quickly to the fact that each point is revealed by a question, a strategy Karen chose to assist her audience in following her speech.

The transitional adverbs and conjunctions listed as helpful in developing smooth transitions can also provide signposts or cues for listeners, telling them that a new idea is being approached.

Using Previews and Summaries

Previews and summaries also provide listening cues or "memory hooks" for listeners. We've already established the classic tradition of the "tell them you are going to tell them; tell them; tell them you've told them." This kind of redundancy helps listeners follow and understand, and prevents them from getting lost in the verbiage of the speech.

Internal previews can provide memory hooks. If, for example, you have packaged your "problem" point into two subpoints, you may want to use an internal preview. You may say, "As we examine the problem, we will focus on two areas: the conditions that underlie the problem and their effects." Or you may say, "We are going to consider three major effects of the problem."

Internal summaries can be included in the same manner. A speaker may wrap up one segment of a point before proceeding to the next segment. An internal summary is often used between second and third points.

With preview and summary statements you have alerted your audience to the complexity of your analysis and have provided listening cues or memory hooks to aid the listener.

Clear transitions, signposting, and listening cues are evidence of clarity in speaking. While the strategies may prove useful in writing, they are essential to you and to your listeners as they attempt to follow and to understand your speech. The skillful use of such strategies is an indication of your appreciation of the listener's task and of smooth, clear speaking style.

Checkpoint

Using the brief of your speech as a basic form:

1. Write your transition statements.

2. Use signposts as needed for clarity.

3. Use memory hooks as needed for listener comprehension.

Using Rhetorical Strategies

Speakers can develop personal style and enhance the artistic quality of speeches through the use of special rhetorical strategies. Taking our cue from Aristotle's definition of rhetoric, we are going to define a **rhetorical strategy** as a device used for special effect in a particular instance.

The use of rhetorical strategies can add significantly to the clarity and aesthetic appeal of your speech. The clear and consistent use of special devices makes key ideas more memorable. Familiar quotations from well-known speeches are usually statements that include strategies that "sloganize" them into memorable sentences or phrases.

Using Rhetorical Questions

Rhetorical questions are questions to which speakers expect no immediate answer, with which they invite listeners to think a moment about a key point or central idea.

Karen Cochran chose to use a series of rhetorical questions as a structural strategy in "Color Me Dumb." She begins with the question, "What do Thomas Edison, General George Patton, President Woodrow Wilson, Hans Christian Anderson, and I have in common?" She chooses a rhetorical question "What is dyslexia?" as a thesis statement. Karen continues to use rhetorical questions to state each point throughout the speech. In so doing, Karen creates interest and curiosity by leading the audience from one point to another with a question-answer strategy.

You may not necessarily choose to use the rhetorical questioning to the extent Karen did, but you will find that rhetorical questions encourage active listening and audience involvement. They invite listeners to think as they listen to your speech.

Using Parallelism

Speakers use **parallelism** for emphasis and aesthetic effect. Parallel structures involve similar words, phrases, or sentences in a series of related ideas. Parallelism can make statements and ideas memorable.

In his 1972 acceptance speech at the Democratic National Convention, George McGovern used parallel structure to develop his theme with the use of the phrase, "Come home,

America . . .'' He was appealing to Americans to return to traditional values.

> . . . together we will call America home to the founding ideals that nourished us in the beginning.
>
> From secrecy and deception in high places, come home, America. . . .
>
> From the waste of idle hands to the joy of useful labor, come home, America. . . .
>
> From the prejudice of race and sex, come home, America. . . .
>
> Come home to the affirmation that we have a dream.
>
> Come home to the conviction that we can move our country forward.
>
> Come home to the belief that we seek a newer world.
>
> And let us be joyful in that homecoming. . . .

McGovern's call was met with an emotional outburst by delegates.

Using Antithesis

Speakers use antithesis for effect and appeal. **Antithesis** is a device that places two contrasting ideas into a similar structure. Antithesis, by using contrast, makes ideas emphatic, quotable, and memorable.

Both John and Robert Kennedy popularized the use of antithesis because it became such an obvious part of their style. What do you know about John Kennedy's Inaugural Address? Most people remember the statement: "Ask not what your country can do for you; ask what you can do for your country." Antithesis! We remember also that Robert Kennedy is credited with saying: "Some men see things as they are and say why. I dream things that never were and say, why not." Antithesis!

John F. Kennedy

Using Climax

Climax consists of a series of statements that lead the audience to an emotional peak or to a turning point. Martin Luther King frequently used climax as a rhetorical device. Through the use of climax (and parallelism), Dr. King brought the throng assembled at the foot of Washington Monument in August, 1963 to an emotional outburst.

Martin Luther King, Jr.

And so let freedom ring from the prodigious hilltops of New Hampshire.

Let freedom ring from the mighty mountains of New York.

Let freedom ring from the heightening Alleghenies of Pennsylvania.

Let freedom ring from the snow-capped Rockies of Colorado.

Let freedom ring from the curvaceous slopes of California. But not only that.

Let freedom ring from Stone Mountain of Georgia.

Let freedom ring from Lookout Mountain of Tennessee.

Let freedom ring from every hill and molehill of Mississippi, from every mountainside, let freedom ring.

And when this happens, and when we allow freedom to ring, when we let it ring from every village and hamlet, from every state and city, we will be able to speed up that day when all of God's children—black men and white men, Jews and Gentiles, Catholics and Protestants—will be able to join hands and to sing in the words of the old Negro spiritual, 'Free at last, free at last; thank God Almighty, we are free at last.'

Rhetorical questions, parallelism, antithesis, and climax may all be useful as you experiment to create the special effects needed for artistic and memorable language.

Checkpoint _Work with three classmates. Imagine you are giving a speech on pollution. Each of you should spend five minutes devising rhetorical strategies that could be used in the speech. One should work on rhetorical questions, one on parallelism, one on antithesis, and one on climax. Share your ideas! How might each of the strategies affect a listener?_

Using Figures of Speech

You can use **figures of speech** to make language artistic, visual, and memorable. Writers and speakers use figures of speech to "sensitize" language and to create images for their readers and listeners.

Metaphor

Speakers use metaphor to create artistic and memorable images. **Metaphor,** as you will remember from your English classes, is a stated or implied comparison. John Hightower, Texas Commissioner of Agriculture, spoke of the Federal Government's attempt to "sweep its nuclear trash under the lush green carpet of Texas farmland" in a 1985 speech opposing the government's plan to develop a nuclear waste disposal site in the Texas Panhandle. Texas farmland is being compared to a carpet. The use of metaphor makes the point visual, enabling the audience to understand and, consequently, to remember the point. Metaphors—by appealing to the senses—also evoke an emotional response that can make a point acceptable to an audience on emotional grounds.

Simile

Similes are used to evoke images and emotional responses. **Similes** are comparisons stated with "like" or "as." Carl Sandburg was invited to address a Joint Session of the House and Senate on February 12, 1959, to commemorate the 150th birthday of Abraham Lincoln. This moving tribute, "Lincoln, Man of Steel and Velvet," by an aging poet still stands as one of our greatest addresses. The introduction begins:

> Not often in the story of mankind does a man arrive on earth who is both steel and velvet; who is as hard as rock and soft as drifting fog.

Sandburg's use of figurative language adds beauty and visability to his message.

Carl Sandburg

Personification

Speakers use personification to add visual or human qualities to their topics. To indict what he perceived as unfair treatment of minority citizens, Martin Luther King used **personification,** the granting of human qualities or behavior to otherwise inanimate objects or concepts. He said:

> It is obvious today that America has defaulted on this promissory note insofar as her citizens of color are concerned. . . . America has given the Negro people a bad check, which has come back marked insufficient funds.

In contrast, President Ronald Reagan, in his State of the Union Address of February 4, 1986, also used personification when he said:

> Government growing beyond our consent had become a lumbering giant, slamming shut the gates of opportunity, threatening to crush the very roots of our freedom.

Carl Sandburg used personification in his tribute to Abraham Lincoln, when he described the journey from Washington, D.C., to Lincoln's burial place in Springfield, Illinois.

> In the time of the April lilacs in the year 1865, on his death, the casket with his body was carried north and west a thousand miles; and the American people wept as never before; bells sobbed; cities wore crepe. . . .

Hyperbole

Speakers can also use hyperbole (extravagant exaggeration) or metonomy (the granting of characteristics of part of an object to the entire object, as in "the kettle boils" or "the chimney smokes"). The artistic effect of the use of figurative language is usually appealing and interesting to listeners, as they find themselves not only hearing, but also picturing, what the speaker is saying.

Using Stylistic Devices

You can make speeches more appealing to your listener's ear by reading your speech aloud, listening carefully to the sounds of words, phrases, and sentences. You may like the idea of using *rhyme* for special appeal. You may want to experiment with *rhythm* or beat for special effect. You may want to use *alliteration*. The phrase, "Don't stare at the steps; step on the stairs!" used by a graduation speaker to inspire the class is memorable because of the play on words and the effect achieved by the repetition of the initial consonant sound. These represent **stylistic devices.**

Barbara Jordan is well known for her speech at the 1976 Democratic convention.

William Faulkner used language rich in accoustic and visual appeals in his Nobel Prize Acceptance Speech in December, 1950. A major point of his speech was to inspire young writers to choose noble themes for their texts.

> It is easy enough to say that man is immortal simply because he will endure; that when the last ding-dong of dooms has clanged and faded from the last worthless rock hanging tideless in the last red and dying evening, and then that there will be still one more sound: that of his puny inexhaustible voice, still talking. I refuse to accept this. . . . The poet's voice need not merely be the record of man; it can be one of the props, the pillars, to help him endure and prevail.

Checkpoint

If you had to compare your school to an animal, what animal would you choose? Write a metaphor or simile to draw your comparison. Can you include personification in your comparison? Can you include alliteration or another stylistic device?

Summary

As a speaker you can profit from experimenting with language in order to make your ideas and information interesting, meaningful, and acceptable to your audience. When writing a manuscript for your speech, you can "play with language," generating different forms of expression and creating effects to make your message clear, artistic, and memorable. Through practicing the use of rhetorical strategies, figurative language, and stylistic devices in writing, you can begin to transfer the devices that please you into your speaking, developing oral style and flexibility.

Parallelism provides an effective and pleasing format for listening by providing structure through repetition. Antithesis tends to sloganize and make statements memorable through tightly structured contrasts. Building a series of statements to a peak or turning point (climax) achieves an emotional response from the audience and makes a final or central point memorable.

Figures of speech can appeal to the senses and evoke images for an artistic impact. Stylistic devices, adding accoustic appeal, make messages pleasing and acceptable to the listener.

Check Your Knowledge

1. Define style.

2. What are the three elements of style?

3. What is a signpost?

4. What is a rhetorical strategy?

5. Describe four rhetorical strategies often used by speakers.

6. What are three figures of speech frequently used by speakers?

7. What are three common stylistic devices?

Check Your Understanding

1. From your reading in literature, cite examples of clear, forceful, and beautiful language. Describe the characteristics of the passages that support your choices.

2. Using a speech model provided by your teacher, find examples of transitions, signposts, and memory hooks. Discuss their use and effectiveness in helping listeners follow the speaker's ideas and remember what the speaker has said.

3. Using the same or a different speech model, identify and discuss the effectiveness of the rhetorical strategies used by the speaker.

4. From literary selections of your choice or from a model speech, give examples of how figures of speech are used to develop imagery and make ideas vivid to the listener.

5. Using a speech model or other selection of your choice, explain how stylistic devices are used to influence listener response through sound.

Check Your Skills

1. With your classmates or friends, conduct this experiment. Start with the sentence: "We should try to stay dry when it's raining." One group should try to add clarity, force, and beauty to the statement in a general way. Another group should try applying rhetorical devices to add special effect and drive the statement home. A third group should use figures of speech to change the basic statement into something visual and memorable.

   Compare the resulting variations on the statement. How are they alike? How are they different? What does this tell you about using style effectively?

2. Consider your own speech topic, and refer to your brief. Write down what (if anything) is beautiful about your topic. Describe your topic using antithesis. Compare your topic to something else and write a metaphor or simile. What other devices can you use to make your speech clear, forceful, and beautiful? How will you make your speech memorable?

3. Now using the guidelines from the chapter and your instructor's suggestions:
   (1) Write your final manuscript!
   (2) Check your product! A strategy you should use to practice choosing and implementing elements of style is to read your speech aloud concentrating on style by asking yourself the following questions:
     * Is my language clear and precise?
     * Does my language capture the tone and intensity of my feeling about my message?
     * Does my language capture the aesthetic qualities appropriate to my message?

CHAPTER 19

Preparing for Effective Delivery

After reading this chapter you should be able to:

1
Identify and define four methods of delivering speeches.

2
Cite the advantages and disadvantages of each method of delivery.

3
Prepare written manuscripts and notes to assist in speech presentation.

4
Explain the aspects and the importance of the speaker's visual message.

5
Explain the aspects and the importance of the speaker's vocal message.

6
Explain the aspects and the importance of the speaker's verbal message.

7
Use effective strategies for rehearsing your speech.

8
Approach presenting your speech with confidence and enthusiasm.

Extemporaneous delivery

Impromptu delivery

Memorized delivery

Manuscript delivery

Imaging

Posture

Movement

Gesture

Facial communication

Vocal message

Diction

Communication apprehension

With your completed speech in hand, you are now ready to make some final choices and to prepare for your presentation. One of the first things you will want to do is to choose your method of delivery. Just as speeches can be classified as to type according to purpose (informative, persuasive, or ceremonial), they can also be classified according to the speaker's method of presentation.

Choosing a Method of Delivery

Speakers have four alternatives in choosing their delivery strategy. At this point, three of the four methods will be of special interest to you. The preparation process you have followed is most applicable to extemporaneous, memorized, and manuscript speeches.

The Extemporaneous Speech

Extemporaneous delivery is considered by many to be the most practical method of delivery. Extemporaneous speeches are planned and prepared; however, the speaker speaks from a few well-planned notes and is free to adapt the speech during the presentation. Our process for preparation lends itself well to extemporaneous delivery.

Extemporaneous speakers may use notes, but they do not rely heavily on written reminders.

Advantages

As an extemporaneous speaker (well-versed in your topic, organization, and language), you are prepared for the speaking experience; you can adapt or adjust your remarks to the audience or occasion. The advantages of extemporaneous delivery explain its popularity. You are prepared and therefore confident. You are free to adapt, and have limited notes from which to speak. Extemporizing lends itself to effective communication because it is spontaneous. You can think, adapt, and verbalize to meet the needs of your audience.

The only disadvantage to extemporaneous speaking is that you might think too much time is required in rehearsal. Possibly, if you do not allow sufficient time and effort for rehearsing, you may have difficulty sustaining your planned continuity.

The Impromptu Speech

This "spur of the moment" type of speaking occurs in a meeting, gathering, or other group event when a speaker wishes to address an issue without having had an opportunity for formal preparation. For **impromptu delivery,** the preparation process obviously does not apply. You can use your knowledge of the process, however, to increase the odds for a successful presentation. In impromptu speaking, you should speak out only on issues on which you are knowledgeable, unless your purpose is to ask questions to obtain information or to clarify. (See Chapters 12 and 14 for a better idea of occasions for impromptu speaking.)

Formulate your speech before speaking. You will probably have writing materials of some kind with you. A note pad can be used to record notes. Think about the mood or tone of the meeting, the temper of your audience, and your purpose for speaking. Choose your strategies carefully.

Organize your statement. Take a moment to construct an opening remark. Write a subject or purpose statement, and list the points you wish to make in sequence. Plan effective closure for your speech. In other words, take a moment to organize an effective introduction, body, and conclusion.

If possible, rehearse your speech in your mind once or twice before gaining recognition to speak. Then be brief!

Avoid rambling. Use your knowledge of speaking with proper preparation to strengthen your impromptu speech.

Advantages

The advantage of the impromptu speech is that it allows you to speak out on issues important to you as opportunities arise. The disadvantage is the difficulty of organizing and speaking without preparation. If you use the thought and language processes you have learned from prepared speaking, you can, however, use impromptu speaking effectively.

The Memorized Speech

Some speakers wish to concentrate on polished language and performance. In order to practice for a smooth, perfected language and delivery style, you could memorize your speech so that it can be delivered without notes or manuscript. In this instance, you would concentrate on main ideas, usually reserving some flexibility in wording and detail. Students who enter original oratory as a contest event memorize their orations. Their speeches are usually well written and delivered in a smooth, articulate manner.

Advantages

The advantage of **memorized delivery** is the perfection that can be achieved through practice for memory and, consequently, the confidence that can be gained. The disadvantage is that the spontaniety that frequently accompanies effective communication may be lost. In addition, the speaker may perceive the time investment required for complete memorization and the nagging fear of forgetting the speech as problems.

Memorizing a speech may allow the speaker to concentrate on polishing language and performance skills.

The Manuscript Speech

Using a manuscript can ensure exact quotations.

Important speeches given to media or on special occasions are frequently performed from manuscript. One reason for using **manuscript delivery** is that the speaker does not wish to be misquoted—he or she wants the speech to be recorded and remembered exactly as presented. The printed page accommodates this concern. We should also note that important speeches are usually released to the press in advance of the presentation. In this instance, accuracy is critical. Speeches are often quoted and published as a matter of record, suggesting that a manuscript exists or is prepared after the speech is delivered.

The advantage of performing from manuscript is that the text is there as you speak. You can be confident that you will perform the speech exactly as you intended. The major disadvantage is in the loss of communication represented by the barrier of the printed page. The manuscript itself may be distracting to the listener. The possible loss of eye contact and liveliness caused by reference to the manuscript may interfere with effective communication. The temptation to read rather than speak from the manuscript may result in a monotonous speaking tone. The psychological impact on the listener (who may perceive that a speaker is reading the speech because he or she is unfamiliar with the content) may also interfere with communication.

Whereas speaking from manuscript may at first appear to be an attractive choice, in practice there are many problems. When it is appropriate or necessary to speak from manuscript, you should take care to prepare a legible manuscript and should practice for effective delivery.

The Speaker's Choice

Your choice of a method of delivery depends (as do other choices) on your own purpose and style. Some speakers find that they are more comfortable with one method than others. Ideally, however, you will become flexible enough to use any method, depending on the speech, the occasion, and the expectations of the audience. In time, you will most likely want to attempt each type.

After you have chosen the method of delivery most appropriate to the particular instance, you are ready to adapt and to rehearse your speech.

Checkpoint

As a speaker, you will want to try all four methods of delivering speeches. Each method has advantages and disadvantages for "particular" speeches, for "particular" audiences, and on "particular" occasions.

Think about a "particular" speech you are preparing to give! Which method of delivery is the most appropriate?

Adapting the Manuscript and Notes

Step 9

Adapt Your Manuscript or Notes

The ninth step in speech preparation is to write a normal, correct copy of the manuscript if you are using memorized delivery or speaking from manuscript. If you are speaking extemporaneously, you will need to prepare notes to use during delivery.

The step of adapting your copy marks the formal beginning of your memory process. It is essential that, in order to be convincing, you have full command of your information and use effective verbal and nonverbal communication skills in your presentation. Just as messages can be lost because of vague or general wording, messages can also be lost in indecisive delivery.

Preparing a Final Manuscript

It is useful to place a manuscript in a binder so that pages can be kept together as the speech is presented.

If you have chosen to memorize your speech, you should prepare two copies of your manuscript. One copy is a work or rehearsal copy, and the other is merely kept for your further use or records. Both copies should be typed or clearly written by hand. One reason for having a reference copy safely tucked away or filed is that if the work copy is lost or destroyed, you will have a second copy. Another is that you may find, as you rehearse from the manuscript for memorization, you want to make changes. The first copy is then available as a reference to your original plan.

The speech manuscript to be used for memorization should be written precisely as you wish to present your speech so that, as you rehearse, your text will be exact each time.

The manuscript to be used when you speak *from* manuscript is adapted in the same manner as that for memorization. It is important that you rehearse with the manuscript exactly as you intend to use it. In order to avoid the distraction of loose paper, you may want to encase your manuscript pages in plastic sheets. You may want to use a nondistracting notebook or binder to keep your speech organized for presentation. Manuscript speeches are frequently formal addresses, delivered from behind a podium, so you will want to arrange to have your script placed on the podium before making your speech.

Preparing Notes for Extemporaneous Delivery

In extemporaneous speaking you should plan to use as few notes as possible. You should know your information completely; therefore, your notes are used only for occasional reference and to keep your speech organized.

Speakers usually choose a 3″ × 5″ or 4″ × 6″ notecard. Notes should be written in ink and handwriting should be large and clear for easy reference. Most speakers use the numbers from their speech outline or brief as topic indicators, and record their notes on the card in a vertical position. Instead of a sentence outline, a topic outline is used.

Memorize your introduction and conclusion, thereby eliminating the need for notes in order to allow you to establish effective communication with your audience in the beginning and to intensify your communication in the conclusion.

Use brief reminders

Let's assume you want to give an informative speech designed to encourage your audience to play croquet. After your introduction, you state your thesis. Since you have rehearsed your speech, you only need brief reminders of the major points you wish to make.

In your definition, you define or briefly describe the game in case not everyone is familiar with your topic. In the background, you tell us something of the origin and history of the game. You then include a motivation statement to help each listener to understand that he or she can enjoy croquet as an inexpensive, entertaining recreational sport.

In making points in the body of your speech, you want to familiarize your audience with croquet equipment and demonstrate its use. You will then demonstrate how to play and explain the advantages and pleasure of the game. You will not want cumbersome notes to interfere with your demonstration; therefore, a brief topic outline will suffice.

The actual notecard would begin with a thesis statement. It will look something like the one on the next page.

II. A. Croquet is a game anyone can play
    B. Game/English origin (Pall Mall)
    C. Began in 16th century
            England
            France
            1850
    D. You can enjoy
    E. Preview
III. A. Equipment needed
            Mallet
            Wicket
            Ball
     B. Rules and procedures
            Object
            Rules
            Demonstration
     C. Advantages as a recreational sport
            Time
            Place
            Number of players
IV. A. Summary
    B. You too can enjoy croquet!

You should try to limit your notes to one notecard; however, you can use front and back if necessary. If statistics or quotations are involved, write a few key phrases to assist your memory. You can also record dates or difficult names or terms you might forget.

Notes may be used for reference and for your own confidence and security. They should be limited to as few words as possible and should be written and spaced for easy reference.

Checkpoint

Depending on the method of delivery you have chosen, you are now ready to prepare written materials for your speech. Write your manuscript—your copy can be rough. You may write in pencil on scraps of paper, but write! Read your speech aloud. Chances are it sounds pretty good! How is your memory at this point? Have you gained a command of the ideas and information in your speech?

Rehearsing the Speech

Rehearsing with others can provide you with useful feedback and support.

Imaging

The tenth step in the preparation process is rehearsing your speech. Rehearsal serves two important purposes. It helps in memorizing or "internalizing" your speech, and it provides a special time for experimenting with delivery strategies.

Ideally, rehearsals are conducted under circumstances that are as similar to performance as possible. Rehearse standing with the notes or manuscript you intend to use. If you are rehearsing for a completely memorized delivery, place your manuscript on a table where you can see and refer to it, but get your manuscript out of your hands so you are free to move and to gesture as you will in your speech.

Make each rehearsal a memory and concentration "workout." Work on small segments of the speech or for short periods of time at first, if you wish. As you begin to lose concentration, stop for a few moments. Give your mind a breather, then begin again with renewed energy and enthusiasm.

"Talk" your speech. Rehearse actively. Make each rehearsal a performance full of energetic, enthusiastic communication.

Try imaging. **Imaging** is simply a process of visualizing yourself actually giving the speech. Runners image themselves winning the race; they visualize themselves actually crossing the finish line ahead of their opponents. You can image yourself presenting your speech. See yourself making an entrance and greeting your audience. Image how you want

Step 10

Rehearse Your Speech

to look, how you want to sound, how you want to come across to your audience. Image for detail, noting the aspects of your behavior you find pleasing and feel would be effective in your presentation. Strive in rehearsal for that behavior.

If possible, and if your speech is for an audience other than your speech class, visit the room or auditorium where you are to speak in order to get a feel for the space, the lighting, and the accoustics. Begin to image yourself presenting your speech in that room or space. For added confidence, you may want to rehearse in your classroom or the room in which you will speak.

Experiment with your speech as you rehearse. Keep a pencil nearby to make changes in your manuscript or notes. Make changes that will improve your speech. You may discover a more effective rhetorical strategy you would like to use. Try it! Experiment with your ideas, and if they result in improvement, make changes.

Imaging can help you convey confidence and work for success.

Instead of thinking of rehearsal as routine repetition, think of rehearsal as a time for discovery and experimentation. Play with your speech and with your ideas. Have fun with your rehearsal. If you enjoy your speaking experience, chances are your audience will enjoy their listening experience, so rehearse with that in mind. Experiment with delivery strategies. Stay flexible; adapt as you feel a need. Move! Gesture! Rehearse in an animated manner, thinking about making your ideas interesting through delivery. Remember: As you rehearse, you also perform. If you provide yourself with short, enthusiastic rehearsals, you are preparing for an enjoyable speaking experience.

How much rehearsal is necessary? The answer to that question depends on the goals you have set for your speech and the method of delivery you have chosen. You are a better judge of how much rehearsal you need than anyone else, because you will know when you are confident and ready.

Rehearsal techniques vary. You may want to experiment with several to discover what works for you. Some speakers like to rehearse alone. Some like a responsive listener. Some use the "practice-before-the-mirror" technique. Others have access to video or tape recorders. All of these can be effective in rehearsal, and you may use a combination of several techniques to achieve the effects you desire.

Checkpoint *One of the main purposes of rehearsal is for you to begin to enjoy your speech. If you are sincerely excited about your ideas and interested in the response of your audience, you will demonstrate excitement and enthusiasm. Experiment with your speech and play with your ideas. Try something unusual or different in rehearsal. It may just benefit your speech!*

Controlling Communication Apprehension

Communication apprehension can be a barrier to effective speaking. All speakers experience what is commonly known as stage fright. In fact, we noted earlier that a recent study indicated that speaking in public ranked number one as a common fear.

The rehearsal strategies recommended in this chapter should eliminate much of your anxiety. The prepared and confident speaker usually has little to fear. However, confronting stage fright as a phenomenon that affects us all, and applying some procedures to reduce your apprehension, can be helpful.

We sometimes fear speaking because we fear rejection and we fear disclosure. Speakers want their ideas to be accepted. They wish to gain the approval and the support of their listeners.

The nervousness we call stage fright is the body's way of responding to our fear or stress. The adrenalin begins to flow to equip us to deal with a crisis. This nervous energy can be channeled into a positive source of power, providing the energy we need for communicating with our listeners.

Imaging can help alleviate anxiety. "Think positive" should be any speaker's motto. We need to be concerned if we do *not* experience excitement and anticipation! As speakers we need stimulation and challenge in order to generate the energy and enthusiasm for effective communication.

You can use physical or breathing exercises immediately prior to delivering your speech to reduce excess nervousness. You need to remember that most listeners are sympathetic and empathetic to your feelings and needs. Most listeners empathize with a speaker's natural anxiety and are intuitively supportive.

Checkpoint *Your preparation has guaranteed a good speech. You will come to your presentation with energy because you have made choices, organized, and rehearsed your speech! Remember that your listeners share in your energy. Establish communication with them, and exercise your rights to speak responsibly and effectively. Present your speech; maintain a note of confidence and certainty; and finish with assurance!*

Delivering the Speech

In preparing for delivery, a review of the chapters on nonverbal and oral communication will be helpful. As you rehearse and as you image, you will want to anticipate using your body and your voice to accomplish the best communication possible.

Considering Your Nonverbal Messages

Your Visual Image   Ask yourself, "What do I want my listener to see as I enter and approach the speaking area? What kind of image do I want to project in delivering my speech, as a speaker and a person?" As a part of your preparation process, you can think about what clothing you are going to wear to present your speech. You can also plan to be well groomed for your speaking experience.

As a rule, speakers should wear simple, tailored, becoming clothing for speaking. Clothing and accessories should not be distracting, but should help the audience focus attention on the speaker. Women should wear businesslike dresses or suits and shoes. Accessories should be simple and becoming. Men should wear suits, dress shirts, ties, and business or dress shoes. Sports coats and slacks are appropriate for some speaking engagements.

These suggestions refer primarily to speaking in public or competitive situations; however, you will find that making a little extra effort and taking a bit more time to look

Don't let your appearance be a distraction to your listeners!

especially nice the day you speak in class will pay off in added confidence. We usually perform better when we know we look attractive!

It naturally follows that grooming is important. Attention paid to hair, makeup, and the condition of your clothing contributes to your image as a speaker. If you want your audience to accept your speech as businesslike and well organized, you will need to *look* businesslike and well organized.

Your Entrance　The speaker's approach is important. You begin to convey a nonverbal message to the audience the moment you leave your chair to approach your position as a speaker. Again, think image. If you want to be perceived as confident and enthusiastic, your walk and posture must convey confidence and enthusiasm. As a part of your rehearsal strategy you should practice making an entrance; practice walking into position and facing the audience with the enthusiasm and confidence you wish to convey.

Your Initial Communication　Take a moment after reaching your speaking position. Pause! Take time to address your audience nonverbally. Look at your audience. Let your audience look at you. Establish a friendly nonverbal relationship before you begin to speak.

Too many speakers rush to the speaking area and, in their excitement or apprehension, begin to speak too quickly. The audience, unprepared to begin listening, may miss introductory remarks and may, as a result, feel rushed or anxious throughout the speech. The wise speaker knows that the listeners will not begin to listen until they have processed the visual message. In other words, since listeners can deal with only one message at a time, they won't listen until they have recorded a visual impression. If their visual perception is, "Hm, this person looks okay—looks as if this might be something worth listening to!" the audience is ready to begin to listen.

Also, give yourself a moment to size up your audience before you begin. No matter how much you have rehearsed, the speaking situation is going to make new demands. There are real people out there listening to what you have to say. Take a moment to "get set" before you start.

Good posture
communicates
confidence.

Your Posture   Get a good grip on the floor! Simply stated, good **posture** that communicates a confident, enthusiastic impression begins with good, firm foot position. If you begin speaking with your body off balance because of uncertain foot position, you may continue to shuffle or sway throughout your speech. Uncertain body position translates uncertainty or nervousness to your listener, neutralizing some of the effectiveness of your message. It can also make you uncomfortable and ill-at-ease as a speaker. You may want to move or shift your position as you speak, but a firm foot position at the beginning can provide a firm base for your speech.

Imagine that you have a string extending from your spine out of the top of your head. With that image in mind, pull your body to an erect position. This means head up, chest up, stomach and hips pulled in firm and tight. At the same time, arms and shoulders should be relaxed. Remember that listeners are especially sensitive to body tone and tension. A tense body communicates tension and anxiety that can make listeners uncomfortable. Practicing breathing or relaxation exercises can help; imaging yourself as confident or relaxed can help.

Rehearsing for confidence that you have your speech firmly in mind and are eager to share your ideas with the audience is the best insurance for a relaxed, anxiety-free presentation. You will not only look better, you will sound better. The separation between your rib cage and your hips will allow you to breathe more effectively for the projection you need in public speaking.

Your Movement   **Movement** in public speaking should be limited to motivated shifts in position. There may be times when you want to take a step to the left or right to emphasize a change in topic or to introduce a new point. If your audience members are seated to your extreme left and right, you may wish to move to address one segment of the audience or another. You do not have to take steps to suggest movement. You can shift weight or turn your body without actually changing your position. A major point is that you should move only when you feel _motivated_ to move.

As a general rule, speakers move to left or right to indicate shifts in points or focus. They normally do *not* move directly toward an audience. Doing so can be an intrusion into the listener's space and may be perceived as menacing or threatening. Generally, movement is more effective when it is motivated and, as a rule, it should not be anticipated or planned in advance. Just remember that a few relaxed, sincere, confident, motivated movements can enhance a speaker's message.

Your Gestures   **Gesture** supports and reinforces verbal messages. We have used *movement* to indicate a change in position from one place to another. It is important to remember that gesture is a movement of the body, not just of a part of the body. This simply means that a movement of your right arm away from the body can be felt in your left hip, thigh, and leg as your body shifts position. Remembering that the body moves as a unit can relieve some anxiety about gesturing. The question, "What do I do with my hands?" is no longer relevant. The question, "How can I use my body to assist me in communicating my message?" becomes relevant.

Gestures should be motivated by the content of the speech.

Some general guidelines for gesture may be helpful. As a rule, move arms away from the body for gesture. As a general rule, place gestures between the shoulder and waist for more effective communication. Gesture with palms up and open. Avoid overusing the same gesture. If you are using a manuscript or speaking from behind a podium, gesture may be limited. If you are using note cards, you should hold your notes so you can refer to them easily. You will want to avoid playing with your notes, but you will usually want to hold the notes naturally and easily in one hand.

Gestures, like movements, work best when they are motivated and spontaneous. Planned and rehearsed gestures tend to look planned and rehearsed and, as a result, detract from rather than enhance the speaker's message.

Your Facial Communication   Facial communication is an important aspect of nonverbal behavior. Public speaking texts without exception stress the importance of eye contact. Speakers must *look* at listeners, placing one thought here, another there, for emphasis. We like a speaker who develops personal communication with us. We want a speaker to talk "with" us, not "to" us or "at" us.

This *personalism,* which studies now indicate to be an important factor in determining speaker ethos, can best be achieved with interesting, personal facial communication.

The term *facial communication* certainly includes firm, personal eye contact for which there can be no substitute. When you "sweep the audience" with your eyes to establish communication before you begin to speak, you gain the attention of the audience from that moment. When you continue to touch audience members or segments of the audience with your eyes, you retain their attention throughout your speech.

Facial communication also suggests facial animation. If you greet your audience with a smile, you establish friendliness. When your face reflects the humor, tenderness, or seriousness of your verbal message, it mirrors the pathetic appeal of your words and reinforces the message for your listener. If your face reflects sincerity and a desire to communicate, you add to your personal appeal for your listener.

Like movement and gesture, facial communication should be spontaneous, not rehearsed. A planned smile often says

Facial communication, including eye contact, should be spontaneous, not rehearsed.

Facial expressions should not contradict the message of the speech.

"fake." Practiced attempts at facial expression usually cause a speaker to appear insincere or pretentious, and are seldom effective.

Ending the Speech and Making an Exit   Make sure to stay in control as you approach the conclusion of your speech! Maintain your eye contact with your audience as you finish, and stay in your speaking position for several seconds before returning to your desk or your seat. Even though you may be ready for your speaking experience to end, do not let yourself communicate nonverbally that you cannot wait to be done!

Your movement, gesture, and facial expression at the end of your speech should reflect the confidence and purpose you have had all along. You may wish to wait for questions from the audience, or you may wish to leave the speaking position. In either case, maintain interaction with your audience as you conclude your speech, and maintain your sense of assurance as you leave the speaking position.

Considering Your Vocal Messages

Your **vocal message** is an important aspect of delivery. Review Chapter 6 for some clear suggestions. Your primary responsibility to an audience is to be easily heard and understood. You must speak clearly and distinctly. Reviewing our chapter dealing with oral cues will help you prepare for the vocal presentation of your speech.

Your Vocal Projection   You must use adequate volume and force in order to be heard. A general suggestion is to speak to the listeners farthest from you. If you speak with listeners on the back row or to the extreme left and right, you can usually assume that closer listeners can hear. In developing force and volume, project your words, but do not shout.

Vocal *projection* is like throwing a tennis ball. How much energy does it take to throw a tennis ball to the listener on the back row? What is the effect of gravity on the ball you have thrown? Apply your answers to the amount of energy needed to project your voice.

The speaker's voice should be relaxed and responsive. A relaxed voice has a medium comfortable pitch, allowing

In developing vocal projection, be careful not to overdo volume.

for inflection and expressing the range of emotion reflected in the text of the speech. Just as your body should send a message of confidence and enthusiasm to your listener, your voice should be firm, interesting, and appealing. Since voice production is a physical process involving the muscles of the body, the voice takes on the tone and tension of the body. A monotone is uninteresting; a lively voice, characterized by animated inflection, is interesting because of the variety it provides.

Your Tone   Pleasant tone and warmth are desirable. Listeners respond more positively to conversational, friendly voices. They prefer, as a rule, to be "talked with" in a personal manner rather than "spoken to" in a formal way. Today, a conversational speaking style reflecting the speaker's personality is generally considered more effective than a more formal, rehearsed style.

Your Rate   Your rate should be slow enough to be followed easily by the listener, but rapid enough to hold audience interest and attention. Rate and tempo should reflect the mood and intensity of the message and can be easily adapted for emphasis or for clarity. An important statement can be emphasized by using a slow, deliberate rate, for example. Increasing rapidity can assist the speaker in building to an emotional peak or climax.

The voice is an important tool of expression. Volume, force, pitch, inflection, tone, and rate can all be adapted to provide emphasis and variety. You may want to experiment with recording your speech in order to develop a personal speaking style. Vocal flexibility is a goal worth striving for. Like other aspects of delivery, responsive vocal techniques motivated by your meaning, feelings, and desire to communicate are more effective than practiced and rehearsed strategies.

Considering Your Verbal Messages

Speakers need to use standard diction. Our definition of **diction** in this sense is limited to speech sounds or the shaping of syllables into intelligent speech, and the structuring of words into phrases and sentences.

We are judged by our speech. Our speech tells others about our regional background, our ethnic heritage, and our educational experiences. And if we wish to convey an image of intelligence and knowledge to our listeners, we must sound intelligent and informed.

Standard diction

Standard diction, like standard usage, is that used and understood by most educated people. Radio and television commentators strive for diction that is free of traces of regional or ethnic background in order to appeal to a wide range of listeners. Educated speakers attempt to eliminate idiosyncracies in diction that detract from their message.

Generally, diction can be divided into three categories: articulation, enunciation, and pronunciation. *Articulation* refers to the clarity and distinctness of consonant sounds. Common articulation errors to avoid include substitution, omission, and addition of consonant sounds. For example, substituting a "d" for a "t," resulting in "budder," instead of "butter," is an error in articulation. The omission of an "s," resulting in "wa'nt" instead of "wasn't," indicates a problem with articulation, as does the dropping of a final "g," resulting in "goin' " instead of "going." Occasionally consonants are added, resulting in errors such as saying "warsh" instead of "wash."

Enunciation refers to the clarity and distinctness of vowel sounds. Here substitution errors seem to be the most common. The substitution of an "i" for an "e," resulting in "git" instead of "get," or the substitution of the "e" for "u," resulting in "jest" instead of "just," are common enunciation errors. Such errors detract from our intelligibility and our credibility as speakers.

Pronunciation refers to the correct sounding of a word as reflected in a recent standard dictionary. A mispronounced word is usually a lost word, detracting significantly from the speaker's message. As a speaker you should assume the responsibility of determining the correct pronunciation of all words and terms in your speech.

Grammar

Speakers should also use correct grammar, since public speaking is a formal activity. Even though you probably applied a "grammar check" while writing your manuscript, the transfer from written to oral form may allow for discrepancies, especially if you are speaking extemporaneously. A grammatical error can severely reduce your effectiveness as a speaker; therefore, you will want to be certain of the grammatical structure of sentences you use in your speech.

Clear, articulate, correct speech requires practice. A general rule is to practice standard speech at all times, not just in speech class or when you are actually presenting a speech. To develop standard speech, you can apply the following steps for skill development:

1. Develop speech awareness.

2. Listen to the speech of others.

3. Begin to listen to yourself.

4. Set goals for developing standard speech.

5. Begin to attempt standard speech.

If you build effective memory strategies into your rehearsal, you should have no problem delivering your speech. If you experiment with the physical and vocal techniques that can best convey your message, and practice standard diction, your presentation should reflect your efforts. Your speech performance should, as a result, be characterized by animated, sincere delivery and should assist you in communicating your message to your listeners in an interesting and meaningful manner.

Your Presentation

Selection processes and organizational strategies have provided the basis of your message. During rehearsals you have gained skill in memory and delivery. You are now ready to approach your audience, confident in the fact that your speech is the result of your choices in each step of the preparation process.

In the actual presentation you will want to use all you have learned about effective verbal and nonverbal communication to ensure success for both you and your listeners. Remember also, as you speak, that you will want to be open and sensitive to the silent cues or feedback you receive from your audience, in order to adapt your message for effectiveness. Nodding heads, smiles, frowns, raised eyebrows, yawns, coughs, and alertness or restlessness send clear messages to you and deserve your sensitivity and adaptation.

Adapt your message

You may want to pick up your tempo. You may want to add examples for clarity. You may need to cut the length of your speech. On the other hand, you may wish to project your voice or use more animated movement or gesture. You may wish to request something be done about sound, lighting, or ventilation to make your audience more comfortable. The point is that the wise and confident speaker will adapt the message, the delivery, or the environment to improve the listener's opportunity to attend to his or her speech.

Successful presentations reflect time spent in rehearsal and communicate about the choices speakers have made in preparation.

Checkpoint _Observe the lecture given in one of your other favorite classes (it would be considerate to let that teacher know you are going to be paying attention to his or her public speaking performance). How does the teacher's nonverbal expression affect you? How about his or her vocal and verbal presentations? How can you use the insight you gain in preparing to deliver your own speech?_

Summary

Your final challenge as a speaker is to make an interesting and compelling presentation of your ideas. Delivery, the fifth public-speaking skill, can determine your effectiveness.

In the final steps of preparation, you want to be sure that your manuscript or notes are organized and written for effective use if needed for speaking. You will want to rehearse your speech, devoting attention to the image you want to create with your delivery in order to reinforce and enhance your message.

Your listeners will react first to what they see (your visual message) and second to what they hear (your vocal and verbal messages). You will want to rehearse for effective bodily communication, for a pleasant, well-controlled speaking voice, and for clear and correct speech. You will want to experiment with different approaches and strategies during rehearsals to provide the flexibility you may need to adapt to feedback from your audience or to the demands of the time and place.

Memory is an additional objective of rehearsal. With adequate rehearsal you should be confident that your ideas and information are firmly in mind and you are free to share your message with your listeners.

Your entire preparation process, by including in the ten steps a focus on all five speaking skills (selection, organization, style, memory, and delivery) has provided the ingredients for your success in public speaking. Your speech presentation is the product of that process. During your presentation your concentration should focus on only one element: communicating with your audience in lively interaction.

Check Your Knowledge

1. What are the advantages and disadvantages of four methods for delivering speeches?

2. List three reasons for using a manuscript.

3. What are three things to consider in adapting notes for extemporaneous delivery?

4. What is imaging?

5. List three ways of using the body effectively while speaking.

6. Define gesture.

7. What are the vocal aspects of public speaking?

8. List three elements of diction.

9. What is communication apprehension?

Check Your Understanding

1. Explain or discuss implications of each of the four methods of delivery for a variety of occasions or audiences.

2. What purpose do notes serve when used for extemporaneous delivery?

3. Explain why it is important to rehearse actively and experiment with your presentation.

4. How can imaging help to reduce or eliminate communication apprehension?

5. Describe your ideal speaker in terms of visual, vocal, and verbal choices and behaviors. Explain why you think each behavior lends itself to effective communication.

6. Why are conservative dress and "standard" speech appropriate in most speaking situations?

7. Explain the statement, "Practice does not make perfect; it makes permanent." Apply this statement to rehearsing your speech.

8. Explain why movement and gesture should seem to be spontaneous, not rehearsed.

9. Why is adapting to audience feedback important, regardless of your preference for a particular method of delivery?

Check Your Skills

1. Prepare your manuscript and notes.

2. Plan your performance method and rehearsal strategies.

3. Rehearse your speech.

4. Present your speech.

Using Visual Aids

Imagine your high school principal referring to a diagram of the school as he or she explains where the new gymnasium will be constructed. Then imagine a science teacher demonstrating an experimental procedure using test tubes and chemicals. Finally, imagine a television meteorologist pointing to a map while giving a nightly weather forecast.

These three scenes are examples of the effective use of visual aids. In public speaking, visual aids may be used to clarify detailed information for the audience, to demonstrate activities, or to lend greater impact to ethical and pathetic proofs.

Visual aids may add interest and support to your speech presentation. When you use visual aids, be sure to rehearse and practice with them so that using them will be a natural part of your delivery. Concentrate on speaking to your listeners (not to the visual aid).

Visual aids have impact and should be planned carefully. What facilities will you use? You may use a blackboard on which to list statistics or to diagram action. You may use a flip-chart for illustrating successive points with charts or drawings. You may want to make posters that state a strong, pointed theme or present statistics visually. You may use an overhead projector for transparencies or slide projector for photographs and maps. Would your presentation be enhanced by using objects or models to demonstrate things or activities?

Whether you are using a poster to put statistics in a pie chart or a projector to refer to a map, your visual aids should be easy for everyone to see. Writing should be large and clear. Photographs should be dramatic enough to be "worth a thousand words." Diagrams, objects, and models should be easy for you to explain and easy for the audience to understand. Remember that your visual aids should enhance or intensify your message, not distract the audience.

Preparation is vital. Organize your visual aids and rehearse with them repeatedly so that you can handle them naturally. When you select and limit your topic, conduct your research and organize and develop your speech, keep an open mind and consider the variety of aids that are possible. Devising and using visual aids can add creativity and flexibility to your presentation!

CHAPTER 20

Evaluating Speeches

After reading this chapter, you should be able to:

1

Give three suggestions for effective listening.

2

Explain the role of the critic.

3

Make five suggestions for effective criticism.

4

Explain four critical perspectives.

5

Explain the purpose for rhetorical analysis.

6

Describe the considerations involved in performing rhetorical analysis.

7

Explain how rhetorical analysis can assist you in improving your own speech.

8

Listen to or read speeches and render effective criticism and evaluations.

Key Terms

Critical listener

Critic

Critical perspective

Judgment by results

Judgment by ethical standards

Artistic judgment

Rhetorical analysis

E arly in our discussion of communication, we discovered that the listener ultimately determines the meaning and content of the message transmitted by a speaker. We have established that we have a responsibility as individuals, as consumers, and as citizens to become effective receivers of messages. Your civic responsibilities also strongly imply that you should become adept in the skills of rhetorical analysis, in order to objectify the persuasion of other speakers, to use the skills for more effective message formulation yourself, and to analyze the speeches that make up a large body of our literary heritage.

Developing Critical Listening Skills

We are going to assume that you as listener and critic have a sincere desire to gain the most from your listening experience. In order to do so, you will need to apply all that you have learned about communication and about public speaking. Just as we have studied communication as a group of skills and as a process, you can become a **critical listener** by improving your effective listening skills.

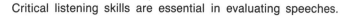

Critical listening skills are essential in evaluating speeches.

Listening Effectively

Learn about the topic

Be physically ready

Be emotionally ready

Get _ready_ to listen! Actually, a number of things are implied in this statement. We listen more effectively when we have some knowledge about the topic. If nothing else, having a vocabulary with which to listen is essential for effective listening. It may be helpful for you to do a bit of research on the topic in advance. If you are to listen to a speech on the effects of acid rain, for example, and you know nothing about acid rain, you may want to learn something about it. If your speech class is informed of upcoming topics, class members can inform themselves about the topics for more effective interaction during and after each speech.

Getting ready to listen also means getting physically ready to listen. As a listener you will want to sit in a position from which you can see and hear the speaker without effort. You will want to choose a chair or area where you can be physically comfortable and as free as possible from distractions. If you are in class, you will want to place your books and other belongings on the floor to avoid the distractions such objects sometimes provide. Take care of personal needs such as getting a drink of water before the speaker begins, so you can be physically comfortable, relaxed, and ready to listen actively to the speech as a full participant in the communication process.

Getting ready to listen may also mean being emotionally ready to listen. First, of course, you must decide you are interested in what the speaker has to say. A good starting point is to remember that there are no dull or uninteresting topics. Someone _is_ interested. The speaker is certainly interested, or he or she would not have chosen the topic. Decide that you are going to listen actively for areas of interest. If the speaker's first purpose is to gain your interest in the topic, your purpose as a listener is to find your areas of interest in the topic.

Second, you can lay aside attitudinal or emotional barriers to communication, deciding they can be dealt with at a later time. If you are preoccupied or concerned with a plan or problem, for example, you can lay it mentally aside until after the speech. You can concentrate on being an alert listener—think along with the speaker, and examine and attempt to understand each statement as it is made.

Establish objectives

Know what you are listening for! Just as you as a speaker must know exactly what you wish to accomplish in speaking, you as listener should establish clear objectives for listening.

What do you hope to gain from your listening experience? Do you want to discover a new interest or new information? Are you interested in knowing the speaker's point of view? Do you want to examine a new plan or policy? Do you want to celebrate a special idea, value, or occasion? You are going to invest a period of time out of your day or evening to listen to a speaker. What is your objective? It is just as important for you as listener to state your objectives as it is for the speaker to formulate and state a purpose and objectives.

Be open-minded

Listen with an open mind! You should attempt to remove common listener-related barriers from your communication process. Barriers such as lack of interest, defensiveness, or competitive listening can interrupt the flow of information and ideas. Reserve making judgments or formulating opinions and responses until you have heard all that a speaker has to say. Listen in order to ask questions that can further your knowledge and help you evaluate ideas. Do not listen just to agree or disagree.

The Role of the Critic

Understanding that you must be knowledgeable about the area in which you assume a critic's role is an important discovery. In other words, a **critic** (as in *criteria*) must be qualified to observe, to analyze, and, if necessary, to render a judgment!

A critic does not rely on personal responses in giving criticism. Nor is the critic apt to use evaluative language—"It was good" or "It was lousy." The critic probably uses descriptive language and assumes the responsibility for his or her own observation, saying, "I found the program entertaining."

Suggestions for Effective Criticism

Make specific observations! Formulate your listening. For example, you can generate an *order* for your listening, using what you know of basic speech form. You can listen for

Listen for form

the speaker's main idea or thesis, and for his or her limitation or definition of the topic. Listen to the introduction, noting the speaker's approach to the audience and topic. Listen, in turn, for how the speaker focuses your attention on the topic with background or motivation devices. The speaker is providing these devices as an aid to listeners. Listen carefully, and mentally record the information for later use.

Listen for supports

Listen for the cues the speaker provides in a preview or in statements of points. Listen for the speaker's main points, and listen carefully to the supports used—question each carefully, using your knowledge of the standard tests for evidence. Listen for ethical proofs to assess the speaker's bias, motives, or personal interest in the topic. Assess the emotional appeals the speaker uses to gain your acceptance of his or her ideas.

Listen for style

Listen, too, for literary devices and rhetorical strategies to appreciate the speaker's skill. Listen for stylistic devices and figures of speech, to appreciate the artistic expertise of the speaker. Observe the speaker's command of information and ideas, and observe his or her nonverbal behavior and special strategies, in order to appreciate the delivery.

Before you formulate judgments, apply the criteria in each area for speaking effectiveness. For example, you are familiar with criteria for effective introductions. You can

Apply criteria

ask yourself as you listen, "Did the introduction get attention? Did the introduction establish good will and a definite climate of communication with the audience? Did the introduction establish an appropriate mood or tone? Did it lead smoothly into the topic? Did it enhance speaker ethos?"

Just as a football coach or player uses first-hand knowledge of playing to watch and evaluate a football game, you can use your knowledge of speaking and the speaker's responsibilities to be an effective critical listener.

Respond

Register a response. After listening to the entire speech, following it step by step and applying the criteria for each step as the speaker proceeds, you will want to register your response as a listener. It is not necessarily the responsibility of the critic to determine whether a speech was "good" or "bad." When asked about a speaker's performance, simply saying "It was good!" or "It was lousy!" does not reveal very much about the speech or about your effectiveness as a listener.

Sports teams often watch tapes to evaluate their performance (and the performance of other teams).

A critic analyzes and responds. An effective critic assumes responsibility for his or her responses and uses descriptive, rather than evaluative, language in reporting those responses. For example, an effective critic might say, "I enjoyed your speech because it was easy to follow; your points were clearly stated and your supporting devices were interesting." In so doing, the critic would be taking responsibility for his or her response ("*I* enjoyed your speech . . .") and would, in descriptive terms—terms that are easy to follow, clear, and unusually interesting—support his or her evaluative statement with specific reasons based on criteria with which the speaker is familiar.

Statements that reflect effective critical listening might include:

"Your introduction really caught my attention."

"Your thesis statement made your subject and purpose clear."

"Your supporting information was recent and really up to date."

"Your physical presentation was enthusiastic and sincere."

Such statements indicate that the listener is applying criteria of evaluation with which the speaker is familiar. Speakers usually appreciate having their efforts rewarded by descriptive responses based on criteria they have strived to implement in their speeches.

Make suggestions or give praise

Give suggestion or praise. If you, as a critic, make an observation, apply criteria, and see need for improvement, you can give suggestion. In essence, this is what is known as constructive criticism. You literally say, "This is what I observe; this is the criterion; this is what I suggest." There are a number of ways in which constructive suggestions can be offered. You may register a response such as, "I would have liked to see you try a humorous anecdote in your introduction rather than a factual quotation, because the rest of your speech was so light and entertaining." You might ask a question, such as, "Did you think about using a humorous device for your introduction, since the rest of your speech was so light and entertaining?"

If no suggestion is warranted, you may wish to register praise, such as "I really enjoyed your humorous introduction; it really set the tone for the rest of your speech." In either instance—giving suggestion or giving praise—you as a listener are registering a positive response based on your own reaction, after applying a specific criterion for evaluation.

Understanding Critical Perspectives

Effective critics should be aware of the need for applying criteria and accepting personal responsibility for responses. They also should be aware that we base our critical responses on *different* criteria. Understanding those criteria helps in analyzing the criticism of others and also in understanding the criticism we give to others. There are four such **critical perspectives** we can use.

Judgment by results

First, we can judge by the outcome or results. This implies, of course, that if we won, we did well. If we lost, we did poorly. A speech student might complain after a round in tournament competition, "I gave the best speech I *ever* gave and still was ranked sixth in the round." Understanding the **judgment by results** provides insight into the student's complaint. It is entirely possible to give the best speech you ever gave and still rank sixth in a round of competition.

Second, we can judge by our own ethical standards. In other words, if we agree, it is good; if we disagree, it is bad. If a speaker takes a position on an issue that we happen to endorse, we like the speech; on the other hand, if the speaker presents a viewpoint we oppose, we dislike the speech. This **judgment by ethical standards** requires no critical thinking, just a personal response.

Judgment by ethical standards

We can also render artistic judgments. If we analyze a speech and formulate judgments by how well the speaker has assumed his or her basic responsibilities in using speech skills, we are making an **artistic judgment.** "The introduction got attention! The organization was clear! The information was interesting and up to date."

Artistic judgment

We can also use combined perspectives in criticism. Such responses might include "The audience really seemed to enjoy the speech. I personally found myself in agreement with and delighted by the speaker's fresh approach. The speaker's attention to detail was outstanding. The introduction got attention. The organization was clear. The information was interesting and meaningful. The use of humor added interest and appeal."

Combined perspectives

Now, ask yourself, as a speaker, how would you like to be evaluated? What criteria would you want to be applied, and by whom? Do you wish to be evaluated only on whether or not the listener agrees with your position (results)? Do you want to be evaluated only on whether or not your listener liked the values and/or procedures you observed in your speech (ethics)? Do you want to be evaluated on how well you met your criteria for speaking and your responsibilities as a speaker (artistic)? Would you rather be evaluated on all counts by an effective critic (Pluralistic)?

Most of us would appreciate knowing that our listeners are informed about our topic, open to new ideas and information, and aware of speech forms and strategies. We would appreciate having an opportunity to participate in a speaking-listening experience in which both speaker and listener assume full responsibility for their roles.

Critics observe, apply criteria, assume responsibility for personal responses, and give constructive suggestion when needed or praise when merited. Critics evaluate partially because evaluation or registering a final judgment seems unavoidable. Ultimately, we say, "I enjoyed it; it was an excellent speech," or we say, "You have really improved! Congratulations!" We should reach and render judgments, however, from a position of knowledge and awareness. In other words, we should be qualified to render the judgments we make.

Checkpoint

Critical listening skills can serve you in many ways. So tune in! Listen to the criticism of others and monitor your own.
Especially, apply your skills in listening to the speeches of other students in your speech class and to speakers you listen to in your community or on television. Exercise your critical listening skills!

Understanding Effective Rhetorical Analysis

Critical listening is a basis for **rhetorical analysis,** which simply means, in this instance, analyzing speeches. Usually, rhetorical analysis is used to analyze speech manuscripts; however, tape recordings or videotapes can also be analyzed. Rhetorical analysis can be compared to dissecting an insect in a laboratory, or taking a machine apart to discover how it works.

The Purpose of Rhetorical Analysis

We can accomplish several objectives through rhetorical analysis. For example, we can analyze several of a single speaker's speeches to discover his or her style. We can analyze speeches given within a particular timeframe to discover how speeches of that period differ from speeches today. We can learn how different speakers use basic speech forms, strategies, or appeals. We can improve our own speaking styles by observing and analyzing the speeches of others.

Before engaging in the analysis process, you need to determine exactly what you want to learn and gain from your analysis. You should establish an objective for your experience.

Rhetorical analysis is not reserved for public speaking. A recent article in a speech journal focused on the rhetoric of country music; another article focused on the social

People can evaluate televised speeches by listening carefully and critically.

comment of a particular comic strip. The process we are describing still applies, but you might enjoy analyzing the lyrics of a particular era or type of music.

You can analyze the rhetoric of the far left or the far right. You can analyze sermons. You can analyze contest orations for the use of anecdote of pathetic appeals. You can focus on any segment of public communication to "dissect" and, consequently, arrive at a logical conclusion about any element of the message.

Understanding the Process

We can use Aristotle's definition of rhetoric—"to determine in the particular instance what is the available means of persuasion"—as a basis for our process of analysis. First, let's determine the "particular instance"—the speaker, the speech, the listener, the occasion, the time, and the place.

Study the speaker

Who is the speaker? In order to analyze a speech, we need to know something about the speaker. We will need to know something of his or her background, education, and beliefs, and about the various influences on his or her life, his or her career, and his or her contributions to society in general. The first step you will need to take to prepare for rhetorical analysis is to do some research on your speaker.

Study the occasion

In each instance you will want to know about the background and occasion for the speech. Your investigation may include focusing on more than just the immediate occasion for the speech. If you are analyzing William Jennings Bryan's "Cross of Gold," for example, you need to know about important issues of the time. If you are analyzing Sacco and Vanzetti's plea for their defense, you will need to know about the events surrounding the trial and their relevance to the times, as well as about the particulars of the trial itself. If you are analyzing General Douglas MacArthur's "Farewell to the Cadets," you need to know the background in order to appreciate the drama of the moment.

Study the audience

Who is being addressed? Since speeches are designed for particular audiences, we need to know for whom the speech was intended. With this information firmly in mind, you can begin to observe how the speaker adapted his or her speech to meet the needs of the particular audience.

Study the time and place

Where and when was the speech delivered? What medium was used? Time and place sometimes have impact on the speaker's message. How did the speaker adapt his or her message in the particular instance to accommodate the demands of time and place?

With investigation of the "particular instance" accomplished—focusing on speaker, speech, occasion, audience, time, and place—you can begin your "dissection," using the information you gained to provide insight and understanding.

Read speeches

Second, you will need to read the speech—or several speeches, depending on your objective for analysis. If you want to analyze Henry Kissinger's use of rhetorical strategies, you will need to read several speeches by Henry Kissinger. If you want to analyze strategies used in acceptance speeches by Presidential candidates during the twentieth century, you will want to accumulate all the acceptance speeches given in the twentieth century. If you want to analyze the values

Children growing up in our society are given repeated opportunities to develop critical analysis skills.

Read criticism

addressed in graduation speeches in 1986, you will want to acquire copies of as many graduation speeches as possible, from as many different sources as possible.

As a third step, you can read what other scholars and critics have written. Few speeches of note are overlooked by reviewers and critics. Biographers analyze the speeches of their subjects. Speakers themselves write about their own works. You might enjoy using literary criticism as a basis for interpretation.

After learning about the speaker and the speech or speeches, you can begin your own analysis process. In so doing, you will apply all that you know about speeches, speech forms, and strategies to accomplish the purpose you chose as a reason for analysis.

Use a worksheet

In the analysis process, we will work from general observations to specific details. A procedure that can help you keep your efforts organized is to use worksheets much like those used in constructing the brief for your speech. You can then record your findings systematically. Use the following checklist to create your worksheet.

Rhetorical Analysis Checklist

- Determine and record the speaker, the topic, the occasion, the audience, the time, the place.
- Read the speech and write a brief synopsis or summary of the speech.
- Outline the speech. Using the basic speech form, analyze how the speaker has used or adapted the form for the particular instance.
- Determine the speech form (speaker's purpose).
- Identify logical proofs and sources cited by the speaker.
- Identify the emotional appeals and pathetic proofs.
- Identify the speaker's use of ethical proofs.
- Identify rhetorical strategies used by the speaker.
- Identify poetic devices or figurative language.
- Identify stylistic devices.
- Describe the speaker's use of words, phrases, and sentences to achieve clarity, force, or beauty.
- If using tape recordings, videotapes, or live experience, observe and describe the speaker's use of delivery strategies to reinforce his or her message.

*Make
statements
and
support them*

    With your findings recorded on your worksheets, you can now write some definitive statements about the speaker's text, which you can support with specific examples. The following questions will help you in your analysis.

1. What topics or causes does your speaker tend to choose?

2. How does your speaker adapt his or her purpose or form to meet the demands of the occasion and the needs of the audience?

3. What organizational strategies does the speaker tend to use (standard outline or adaptation)? Does the speaker use a preview, for example, or some other device to assist the audience in following the speech?

4. What kind of logical proofs does the speaker tend to use? From what sources?

5. What kind of emotional appeals does the speaker use?

6. What kind of ethical proofs does the speaker use?

7. Describe the speaker's style. Rhetorical strategies? Figurative language? What about sentence structure? Word choice?

8. Describe the speaker's delivery if appropriate.

9. Using the answers to these questions, evaluate the speech in descriptive terms on each point. Focus on how the speaker adapted his or her message to meet his or her own purpose as well as the demands of the occasion and the needs of the audience addressed.

    Rhetorical analysis is a very effective strategy for understanding and appreciating speeches and, in fact, for appreciating all sorts of communication. If you have ever studied a foreign language, you know that the translation of words into English is just one step in understanding what the writer or speaker has to say. In the same way, rhetorical analysis allows us to take a variety of factors into consideration when analyzing speeches. The speaker, the audience, the occasion, and the message are all important aspects of public speaking, and all contribute to the overall effectiveness and appeal of the communication interaction.

Checkpoint *How can you become a more interesting speaker by analyzing the speeches of others? You might begin by examining the speeches included as models in the Appendix. One of the real advantages of conducting rhetorical analysis is that it helps you develop your own flexibility as a speaker!*

Summary

Whether or not, as a citizen, you ever choose to assume the responsibility for speaking in public, you will no doubt listen to speeches. You will listen to political candidates vying for your vote in local, state, and national elections. You will listen to commercials seeking your dollar. You will listen to speakers addressing important issues that affect your life and wellbeing. Your effectiveness as a critic and your expertise in rhetorical analysis can provide a basis for responsible citizenship and effective choices.

With these skills to serve as your insulation, you no longer will be a vulnerable target for unethical appeals and false claims. You also have the skills to find pleasure and appreciation for the skills of responsible and ethical speakers, as well as the skills to listen before making judgments regarding a speaker's claims.

Think about the service we give to ourselves and to our democratic system when ethical and responsible speakers and effective listeners interact to exchange information and ideas!

Check Your Knowledge

1. Make three suggestions for effective listening.

2. What are five components of effective criticism?

3. Define four perspectives that can be used as a basis for criticism.

4. What is rhetorical analysis?

5. List four steps to follow in rhetorical analysis.

Check Your Understanding

1. Explain the importance of each of the steps for effective listening.

2. What are the role and responsibility of the critic?

3. Why is it important to identify critical perspectives?

4. What is the advantage of considering multiple criteria in giving criticism?

5. Why is descriptive, rather than evaluative, language important in giving criticism?

6. How can conducting rhetorical analysis help you to become a better speaker?

Check Your Skills

1. Report and discuss your responses to a classroom speech.

2. Analyze a written model of a speech and discuss your observations.

3. Choose a well-known speaker and conduct an in-depth rhetorical analysis of his or her speeches.

Communication in Your Future

*Communication
Essay*

You know that communication is vitally important in your relationships, in your group memberships, and in sharing ideas and information through public speaking. It won't surprise you to hear that your ability to recognize and apply communication skills will be important in your future! In your further studies, your ongoing relationships, and, eventually, in your career, effective communication will make a difference.

How does communication relate to building skyscrapers or studying mathematics? How might communication skills influence the success of a pilot or a professional tennis player? Effective communicators increase their chances for success, whatever they do. Let's review the levels of communication and think about the future.

Effective intrapersonal communication skills will help you understand yourself and others. Imagine how your aware, effective ''self-talk'' might influence your future as a songwriter, a counselor, or a designer.

Interpersonal communication skills provide the foundation for effective relationships. How might effective nonverbal and language skills influence the success of a performer in a play, a police officer, or a factory supervisor? How could skills in listening and responding influence the success of a medical researcher, a reporter, or a kindergarten teacher?

You know that communication skills help all groups to reach their goals. Imagine how group communication skills could serve you as a management consultant, a submarine captain, or chairperson of a service group.

Public communication skills help individuals achieve self-confidence and personal goals. It is also vital that citizens develop and apply skills in evaluating public messages. Think about the public communication situations in which *you* will be a receiver. How will you vote? How much money will you give? How much time will you volunteer?

As you continually use your communication skills, you will have many opportunities to make choices. When it comes time for you to choose a career, remember that *all* of your communication skills will be fundamental to your success.

CHAPTER 21

Mastering Speech Forms

After reading this chapter, you should be able to:

1

Describe the types of informative speeches.

2

List the criteria for evaluating informative speeches, and use them to improve your own informative speaking and evaluate such speeches.

3

Describe the types of persuasive speeches.

4

List the criteria for evaluating persuasive speeches, and use them to improve your own persuasive speaking and evaluate such speeches.

5

Describe the types of ceremonial speeches.

6

List the criteria for evaluating speeches for special occasions, and use them to improve your own speeches and evaluate such speeches.

7

Identify six major speech forms.

Key Terms

Proposition of fact

Proposition of value

Proposition to create concern for a problem

Proposition of policy

Y ou have now worked your way through a ten-step process for developing public speaking skills. You have also studied critical listening and rhetorical analysis. This chapter will focus on mastering more specific skills used in presenting and evaluating particular types of speeches.

We will examine strategies used in informative, persuasive, and ceremonial speeches. Informative speeches are designed to impart knowledge and to create interest in a topic. Information is presented objectively, and the topic should be appropriate to the audience.

Persuasive speeches are designed to change the listeners' perceptions, attitudes, feelings, and actions. In persuasion, the speaker attempts to establish facts; in several forms of persuasive speaking, the speaker also presents an argument based on a value assumption. In this chapter, we will discuss four persuasive speech forms. It will help to review the material on values and priorities in Chapter 5 before preparing a persuasive speech. As a persuasive speaker, you will often defend a value related to the particular position you choose to take.

Ceremonial speeches can be designed to unite an audience or to be entertaining. They are presented on special occasions, so topics must relate to the occasion as well as to the audience.

Each of the six basic speech forms is described in this chapter, and each description is followed by a list of suggested questions to use in evaluating the specific speech form. A particular speech model in the appendix is cited for each speech form. Practice in evaluating the models can help you in preparing speeches of your own.

Mastering the Informative Speech

When you choose to inform your audience about a topic, your two-fold purpose is to share data and create interest in your topic. You want your audience to say "Wow! I didn't know that!" You want to create curiosity, so that your listeners will want to ask questions after your speech. When a listener asks questions, you should be pleased because questions indicate interest. You have then accomplished your purpose.

As a speaker you should concentrate on using the most interesting and appealing supporting and amplifying strategies available to you. Emotional appeal is important in gaining and maintaining audience interest. The result should be that your listeners will be more open, more interested, and more enthusiastic about your topic as well as more knowledgeable. Use of logical, ethical, and pathetic proofs that appeal to your particular audience can assist you in creating interest in your ideas.

Types of Informative Speeches

People, places, events, concepts, problems, policies, things, and processes all hold potential for effective topic development in informative speeches. Chronological, spatial, or topical patterns of organization are the most common patterns used in such speeches.

A well-known type of informative speech is the "process" speech or the "thing" speech, in which a speaker seeks to instruct the audience about how to do something or how to use an object. This type of speech has also been called the demonstration or "how to" speech. The speaker uses a chronological or "step-by-step" pattern of organization. He or she will probably use visual aids to demonstrate how the process is accomplished. In all informative speaking, it is the responsibility of the speaker to present information as fairly and objectively as possible.

A popular type of informative speech involves demonstrating how something works.

Criteria for Evaluation

Informative speeches can usually be evaluated in terms of the information the speaker presents and the interest the speaker creates in his or her topic and ideas. Sample questions for evaluating an informative speech include:

1. Did the speaker choose an important and timely topic?

2. Has the speaker demonstrated good character, good will, and sound qualifications?

3. Was the information presented in a unified and interesting manner?

4. Was the information accurate and up to date?

5. Did the speaker relate the topic to the audience in an interesting and meaningful way?

6. Did the speaker use appropriate and appealing language?

7. Would I like to know more about the topic?

Checkpoint

Using the questions listed, evaluate the model informative speech in the appendix ("David: And a Whole Lot of Other Neat People" by Kathy Weisensel).

How can you use the information in this section to improve your own speeches and to become a better listener?

Mastering the Persuasive Speech

When a speaker chooses to persuade, he or she usually has one of four purposes in mind. The speaker may persuade the audience to accept a proposition of fact; to agree with a proposition of value; to create concern for a problem; or to change a policy. Each of these purposes requires the use of a particular speech form.

Proposition of Fact

The persuasive speech concerning a **proposition of fact** advances a thesis as being true or false. The speaker tries to convince the audience to accept a basic claim (or proposition) as a fact. Such a proposition advances a condition for listener acceptance or rejection. For example, a proposition could be: "Faulty O-rings caused the space shuttle disaster of 1986." The points in the speech could be:

1. Photographs indicate smoke in the area of the O-ring joints.

2. NASA engineers verify problems with O-rings in sub-freezing temperatures.

3. The Presidential fact-finding committee concluded faulty O-rings were responsible for the disaster.

The thesis in this instance proposes a fact for the audience to accept or reject. Each point then states a fact that must be supported by statistics, instances, or testimony. A persuasive speech concerning a proposition of fact must include as many logical proofs as are needed to prove the thesis statement as true or false.

Criteria for Evaluation

Sample questions for evaluating a persuasive speech concerning a proposition of fact include:

1. Has the speaker advanced a clear thesis statement or question asking me to respond with "true" or "false"?

2. Has the speaker demonstrated good character, good will, and sound qualifications?

3. Has the speaker presented an adequate number of logical, factual claims as points to support the basic proposition?

4. Has the speaker used adequate and appropriate logical supports to gain acceptance of each claim (or point) as fact?

5. Do the sources quoted meet the tests for evidence in order to gain my acceptance of the proofs and arguments they support?

6. Has the speaker used clear language?

Checkpoint

Using the questions listed, evaluate the model proposition-of-fact speech in the appendix ("Are They Unteachable?" by Carolyn Kay Geiman).

How can the information in this section help you to improve your own speaking and listening?

Proposition of Value

In a speech concerning a **proposition of value,** the speaker must convince the listener to accept a claim because it is good or bad, beneficial or harmful. For example, the proposition might be: "The study of humanities is beneficial to students."

The value assumption is that the study of humanities is good or beneficial. The assumption is rooted in social values. Because the speaker values people and human relationships as expressed in arts and languages, the listener is asked to share this value and accept the speaker's claim.

In the background part of the speech, the speaker will probably advance a claim that humanities are not emphasized enough, or perhaps will say that a recent study indicates benefits from studying humanities. The speaker's points should then advance claims that the study of humanities is good:

1. The study of humanities encourages appreciation of various cultures.
2. The study of humanities encourages positive human relationships.
3. The study of humanities encourages appreciation of the arts.

The value assumption is that, after considering these three points indicating that the study of humanities is beneficial, the audience will *agree* that the study of humanities is beneficial.

In a speech concerning a proposition of value, the speaker should be prepared to explain and defend a basic value assumption.

For this type of persuasive speech, a variety of proofs would be appropriate. The acceptance of the proposition of value may depend on emotional appeals as well as logical proofs. Motivational devices will help the listener to understand his or her relationship to the topic. Strategies to help listeners visualize and need-satisfaction materials may also influence acceptance of the proposition. The listener must be moved to accept the value assumption, and must be convinced to accept the proposition for logical reasons as well.

Criteria For Evaluation

Sample questions for evaluating a persuasive speech concerning a proposition of value include:

1. Has the speaker clearly advanced a thesis statement or question that asks me to respond with "right" or "wrong," "good" or "bad?"

2. Has the speaker demonstrated good character, good will, and sound qualifications?

3. Has the speaker presented a sufficient number of value statements as points or as supporting claims to gain my support of his or her argument?

4. Are the claims presented consistent in their value appeal?

5. Has the speaker obviously used audience analysis and analysis of the occasion in constructing his or her arguments?

6. Has the speaker considered other biases and presented a fair view of the topic?

7. Has the speaker offered sufficient logical proofs from valid sources to gain my agreement?

8. Has the speaker used appropriate ethical proofs and appropriate pathetic proofs and value appeals in constructing his or her arguments?

9. Has the speaker used language choices consistent with the mood and tone of the speech?

It is important to make use of a thorough audience analysis in developing value appeals.

Checkpoint

Using the questions listed, evaluate the model proposition-of-value speech in the appendix ("Five Ways In Which Thinking Is Dangerous" by Stephen Joe Trachtenberg).

How can the information presented in this section assist you in becoming a better speaker and listener?

Proposition To Create Concern For a Problem

In the persuasive speech involving a **proposition to create concern for a problem,** the speaker asks listeners to share a concern. In some cases, the speaker must first convince the audience that a problem exists. The concern the speaker wishes to create is based on a value assumption of what is good and bad. The speaker must also show how the problem relates to the listener. We can, in this case, define a *problem* as a particular circumstance that presents a threat or barrier to the speaker. In this speech form, the speaker must show how this is also a problem for the audience.

Let's assume the speaker wants us to be concerned about a condition he or she perceives as threatening—the neglect of the study of humanities in our educational system. The speaker will state the problem as a proposition for us to accept: "The neglect of the study of humanities in public schools is damaging to our society."

The speaker will probably describe the value (such as a social value concerning education) that underlies his or her concern. The speaker will then support this value assumption with testimony from qualified sources (perhaps educators and psychologists). The speaker may make the following claims:

1. The study of humanities is neglected (fact).

2. This neglect has negative results in light of the value described.

3. These results affect you (the listener) in a negative manner.

You could use this model to win the concern of your audience for a problem you feel is significant, or you could adapt the model to suit your specific purpose. However, you must always clearly describe the value assumptions, prove that a problem does indeed exist, prove the resulting negative effects, and relate the harmful effects to the audience in a specific manner.

In this type of speech, you do not always have to prove that something is harmful. You could win positive support by showing that an existing condition is beneficial, and by demonstrating how listeners profit from the benefits. For instance, you can show that your school has an excellent humanities program. You can then persuade listeners to support continuation of the program.

Criteria For Evaluation

Sample questions for evaluating a persuasive speech to create concern for a problem include:

1. Has the speaker advanced a thesis statement or question that asks me to respond with "significant" or "insignificant"?

2. Has the speaker described a clear value assumption from which his or her concern stems?

3. Has the speaker presented claims and supports that indicate facts exist to verify that negative results exist for the listener?

4. Has the speaker demonstrated that the problem has scope and significance?

5. Has the speaker related his or her arguments to the specific audience?

6. Has the speaker demonstrated good character, good will, and sound qualifications?

7. Has the speaker advanced valid and appropriate pathetic and ethical appeals?

8. Has the speaker used language strategies consistent with the mood and tone of the speech?

Checkpoint

Using the questions listed, evaluate the model persuasive speech that create concern for a problem ("The Crown of Life?" by Lisa Golub).

How can the information in this section assist you in becoming a better speaker and listener?

Proposition of policy

The **proposition of policy** speech involves a speaker's claim that a change in policy is necessary. The speaker must convince the audience that a problem or situation exists, and must then persuade listeners to do something specific to improve the situation.

Let's assume the speaker wishes to gain support for a required course in humanities. The speaker should give special attention in the introduction to establishing acceptance for his or her value assumption. The proposition would be: "All students should take a course in humanities."

In the background section of the speech, the speaker will probably establish as fact that humanities courses are not required under the present policy. He or she will probably use a problem-solution pattern of organization. The points could be:

1. Present requirements keep many students from taking humanities courses (cause).

2. Our society, as well as students, is harmed by this practice (effects).

3. We should require all students to take a course in humanities (new policy).

4. Benefits will result (advantages related to the specific audience).

It is important to note that, in proposition of policy speeches, the speaker must show that the solution will be beneficial. Not only must the speaker identify the problem; the speaker must also persuade the audience that the proposed new policy solves the problem and is *better* than the current policy.

Criteria For Evaluation

Sample questions for evaluating a persuasive speech concerning a proposition of policy include:

1. Has the speaker clearly presented a thesis or claim calling for action that asks you to respond with "wise" or "unwise"?

2. Has the speaker clearly described the value assumption from which his or her argument stems?

3. Has the speaker advanced logical, relevant factual claims and supports as a basis for his or her argument?

4. Has the speaker demonstrated the significance of the problem for which the policy is designed?

5. Has the speaker presented a clear plan or policy?

6. Has the speaker demonstrated that the policy will have desirable impact on the problem?

7. Has the speaker shown himself or herself to be of good character, good will, and sound qualifications for speaking on this topic?

8. Has the speaker used sound emotional and value appeals to gain acceptance from his audience?

9. Has the speaker related his or her argument to the specific audience?

10. Has the speaker used compelling language to gain acceptance of his or her ideas?

Checkpoint

Using the questions listed, evaluate the proposition of policy speech in the appendix ("The Battle Against Drugs" by Nancy Reagan).

How can the information in this section help you to become a better speaker and listener?

Mastering Ceremonial Speeches

Ceremonial speeches represent a special area of public address. Many of the speeches that are referred to in history, government, or literature books fall into one of the various categories of ceremonial address:

Inaugural Addresses

Acceptance Speeches

Keynote Addresses

Sermons

Eulogies

Commemorative Addresses

Tributes

Welcoming Speeches

Graduation Speeches

Dedication Speeches

After-dinner speeches and speeches to entertain can also be called speeches for special occasions.

Characteristics of Ceremonial Speeches

Ceremonial speeches are given on special occasions, and a speaker's appearance should always be appropriate to the occasion.

One characteristic that sets ceremonial speeches apart is that they are presented when a speaker and audience come together to celebrate or commemorate an event. Some common interest has brought the speaker and audience together at a special time and place for a special purpose.

The speaker's task is often to unite listeners in a common concern, cause, or spirit. Such speeches are referred to as speeches to promote social cohesion.

The speaker wisely takes the cue in choosing a topic and purpose from the values that motivated the occasion. The speaker must also consider the specific situation and the expectations of the audience. The speaker can usually assume that listeners are knowledgeable and interested in the topic because of their attendance. Consequently, the speaker may touch lightly on facts and factual information. The speaker may, however, relate the topic to historical events or to very recent events that have impact on the audience. Consider Martin Luther King's ''I Have A Dream'' as an example of such a speech.

In ceremonial speeches, the speaker is likely to address values and experiences that he or she shares with the audience. Since the speaker's purpose is to unify listeners, the tone can range from anger to inspiration. The speaker will probably use pathetic proofs and literary devices to accomplish his or her purpose. Speeches to promote unity are frequently eloquent in style and literate in form, as speakers strive to meet the demands of the occasion and the expectations of the audience.

One kind of ceremonial speech familiar to students is the graduation speech. The graduation speaker usually looks back with humor or nostalgia at the years of experiences shared by ''relatives, classmates, teachers, and friends.'' The speaker touches on a value or theme common to classmates. He or she looks forward, with optimism and inspiration, to the future.

The challenge of writing a graduation speech comes down to the question, ''What is left to be said?'' Thousands of graduation speakers have approached thousands of podiums, addressed thousands of audiences, and have sent millions of eager graduates on their way. What can be said that is new and different?

Fortunately, like most ceremonies, graduation is very traditional. A fresh approach to an old topic is the course most speakers take—and it is one that works very well.

Criteria for Evaluation

Sample questions for evaluating a speech for a special occasion could include:

1. Has the speaker presented a thesis claim or question that reflects a common value or goal of the audience?

2. Has the speaker demonstrated sound qualifications, good will, and good intent?

3. Has the speaker related the topic and thesis to the specific audience and to the specific occasion?

4. Has the speaker used sufficient logical proofs to demonstrate that he or she is informed in the topic?

5. Has the speaker used appropriate emotional and value appeals for the audience and occasion?

6. Has the speaker used language effectively and appropriately for the purpose, audience, and occasion?

Checkpoint

Using the questions listed, evaluate the model ceremonial speech ("Will and Vision" by Gerry Sikorski).

How can the information in this section assist you in becoming a better speaker and listener?

Summary

There are three primary speech forms—informative, persuasive, and ceremonial. Persuasive speeches can be divided into four forms: 1) proposition of fact; 2) proposition of value; 3) proposition to create concern for a problem; and 4) proposition of policy.

As you master speech forms, you fine-tune your public communication skills. Important elements of each speech form include speaker ethos and the analysis of audience and occasion. It is also important to understand the impact of the appropriate use of emotional and value appeals in developing interesting messages.

Mastering speech forms reinforces the idea that the criteria for speaking also apply as criteria for listening. This completes the circular process of communication.

Check Your Knowledge

1. Describe the six basic speech forms identified in this chapter.
2. List some guidelines for designing each type of speech.
3. List some questions to be asked in evaluating each type of speech.

Check Your Understanding

1. Why must the informative speaker use ideas and information in a manner that creates interest in the topic?
2. Why must a persuasive speaker present basic facts prior to developing his or her arguments?
3. Explain the role of the basic value assumption in propositions of value, problem, and policy.

Check Your Skills

1. Plan and present an informative speech.
2. Plan and present a speech designed to lead an audience to accept a proposition of fact.
3. Plan and present a speech designed to lead an audience to accept a proposition of value.
4. Plan and present a speech designed to lead an audience to accept a proposition to create concern for a problem.
5. Plan and present a speech designed to lead an audience to accept a proposition of policy.
6. Plan and present a speech designed for a special occasion and for a special audience.

Model Speeches

The seven model speeches in this appendix provide examples of informative, persuasive, and ceremonial speech forms. The first two speeches are annotated to reflect the organization and development skills covered in Chapters 16 and 17 of the text.

"David: And a Whole Lot of Other Neat People" is an example of an informative speech. The speech is fully annotated to illustrate overall organization, the arrangement of points, and the use of supporting and amplifying devices.

"Color Me Dumb" is an example of a persuasive speech involving a proposition of policy. It uses a problem-solution order and is lightly annotated to illustrate the organization of points. Following the speech is a full outline, listing the types of supporting and amplifying devices used in the presentation. Using this outline, you may wish to reread the speech to practice identifying the various types of devices. "Color Me Dumb" is followed by a brief set of questions intended to provide you with a foundation for evaluating the speech.

Speech A

David: And a Whole Lot of Other Neat People

Kathy Weisensel

Kathy Weisensel from Sun Prairie, Wisconsin, delivered this speech in the summer of 1976.

I. Introduction
Startling statement

There is a problem which is shared by millions of people in the United States. It knows no barrier to age, sex, or social class. Yet, it is a problem that for years was hidden in society's darkest closet. Only recently has the closet door begun to open. That problem is mental retardation.

Current statistics (note that current statistics in introduction replace background)

One out of thirty-three persons is born mentally retarded. It is the most widespread, permanent handicap among children. It is among the least understood handicaps of adults. In Wisconsin alone, there are 120,000 retarded people.

Ethical proof

My involvement with mental retardation has been lifelong and deeply personal. For you see, David, my older brother, is mentally retarded.

II. First Transition
Thesis statement (subject statement)

As our family adjusted to David's problem, we became aware of a number of misconceptions which cloud the public's vision.

Preview

Among these misconceptions are: that mentally retarded people are mentally ill and therefore dangerous; that mentally retarded people are ineducable; and that mentally retarded people are incapable of leading happy and productive lives.

Thesis restatement
Purpose statement

Since these misconceptions are socially harmful and painful to the retarded and their families, it is important that they be corrected.

III. Body
Point A (rhetorical question)

How do you correct the notion that retarded people are somewhat crazy and therefore not really to be trusted?

States subpoint 1

It may be helpful to start with a definition.

Logical support, testimony

According to Dr. E. Milo Pritchett, "Mental retardation is a condition of impaired, incomplete, or inadequate mental development. . . . Mental retardation is NOT mental illness.

Restates subpoint 1

Mental illness is a breakdown of mental functions which were once normal. Specialized care and treatment may restore the person to normalcy. Retardation is a condition for which there is no cure.''

States subpoint 2,
provides link,
internal summary

But let's extend that definition with a series of contrasts.

Support, examples

Mental retardation is always permanent; mental illness is usually temporary. Mental retardation is subnormal intelligence; mental illness is distorted intelligence. Mental retardation involves deficient cognitive abilities; mental illness involves emotional impairment of cognitive abilities. Mental retardation is manifested early; mental illness may occur anytime in life. The mentally retarded person is behaviorally stable; it is the mentally ill person who is given to erratic behavior. The extremely mentally retarded person is submissive and mute; the extremely mentally ill person may be violent and criminally dangerous.

Restates Point A

Thus retarded people are retarded, and no more. We need no longer place them in pens with the criminally insane, as was the custom in medieval societies.

Point B (restates first
point, providing link;
states Point B)

OK, the skeptic says, so what if they aren't mentally ill— they're still ineducable.

Logical support,
testimony

Those who favor this misconception have, in the words of Dorly D. Wang, formerly of Woods School in Pennsylvania, ''one-dimensional views of the retarded.'' They fail to ''distinguish degrees of retardation'' and tend to perceive ''all the retarded with one image''—and that image is of the intellectual vegetable, more appropriately planted in a cell or ward than in the school classroom.

Previews subpoints

But retarded people are not all alike. Most psychologists identify three subgroups of mentally retarded people: the educable, the trainable, and the custodial.

States subpoint 1;
amplifying device,
examples

The educable mentally retarded have IQ's ranging from 75 to 50. In the nation's schools, they are placed in a curriculum with a special classroom base, but are encouraged to enter the curricular mainstream whenever it is possible. Most of these students share with normal students instruction in home economics, physical education, shop, and music.

The trainable mentally retarded's I.Q. is usually 50 to 30. In the schools, these students are not found in any normal classes. Rather, they work exclusively in special classrooms under the direction of teachers who understand their needs. In these classes they learn self-care, and they train for social and economic usefulness.

Three percent of the present school population is made up of the educable and trainable mentally retarded.

The custodial mentally retarded have IQ's below 30. They are usually confined to institutions such as Central Colony; just across Lake Mendota from this University. These people experience little mental development. Few exceed the intellectual acuity of a normal three year old.

Thus, the mentally retarded are not a faceless, hopeless mass. While not all of them may profit from schooling, many will. Careful and loving teachers will eventually be rewarded by what one teacher of the retarded has called "the smile of recognition."

But to say that the mentally retarded person is not mentally ill and is not ineducable is not enough. It does not destroy the myth that one must be of average mentality to be socially productive and happy.

In a society characterized by speed, change, competition, and progress, it is difficult for us so-called "normals" to understand that retarded people can live happily and productively in a life pattern alien to our own.

Bernard Posner, Deputy Executive Secretary of the President's Committee on Employment of the Handicapped, has captured society's dilemma in coming to grips with the mentally handicapped. He commented:

> . . . ours are norms in which change is a way of life. In the United States, we change jobs every five years and homes every seven years. We say that to stand still is to regress. Where do the retarded fit in, those without the capacity for constant change?
> . . . ours are norms of competition. We compete in school, at play, at love, at work. Where do the retarded fit in, those

who can go to school, can play, can love, can work, but who cannot always come out on top in competition?

. . . ours are norms of discontent. Life becomes a series of stepping-stones leading who knows where? Each of life's situations is not to be enjoyed for itself, but is to be tolerated because it leads elsewhere. Where do the retarded fit in, those who can be happy with a stay-put existence?

Restates Point C; internal summary

But retarded people do fit in and do lead useful and rewarding lives.

Logical support, instance (note pathetic appeal)

A few years ago, I worked with a girl who is educably mentally retarded. Mary went to my high school and attended two normal classes—home economics and physical education. She had a driving desire to become a waitress. Her determination was evident as I tutored her in addition, subtraction, making change, and figuring sales tax. She is working today in a small restaurant—happy and self-supporting.

Logical support, instance (note pathetic appeal)

My brother David is another example. Under Wisconsin law he was entitled to school until age twenty-one, and he spent all those years in a separate special class. There he learned the basic skills of reading, writing, and mathematics. After graduation he was employed by the Madison Opportunity Center, a sheltered workshop for the retarded. He leaves home each morning on a special bus and returns each evening after eight hours of simple assembly-line work.

Restates Point C; relates to title ("nea person")

While he is by no means self-supporting and independent, he loves his work, and he is a happy man and a neat person with whom to share a family.

Logical support, instance (note pathetic appeal)

As a final example, I give you Jeff, age 14. He is custodially mentally retarded at Central Colony. In the three years that I have worked with him, I have found him to be incredibly happy and content in his "permanent childhood." He enjoys toys, writing letters of the alphabet, and watching Sesame Street. This last summer he was especially proud to be selected as a jumper in the Special Olympics. To tell you the truth, he was chosen because he was one of the few kids in the ward who could get both feet off the floor at the same time. But Jeff doesn't know that the competition wasn't keen, and he's proud and happy.

IV. Second Transition
Second thesis statement, summary

While misconceptions are slow to pass away, they must surely die. Our nation's retarded are not mentally ill, totally ineducable, or incapable of happy and productive lives. I know, in a deeply personal way, the pain that these misconceptions inspire.

V. Conclusion; *logical support, testimony*

But I also know that the world is changing. I have a deep faith that you and others of our generation will reject the senseless and destructive stereotypes of the past. As Bernard Posner has said:

> . . . the young people of the world seem to be forging a new set of values. It appears to be a value system of recognizing the intrinsic worth of all humans, retarded or not . . . a value system of acceptance: of accepting life as it is, and people as they are.

Acknowledgement (optional)

Thank you for your acceptance.

Speech B
Color Me Dumb

Karen Cochran was a high-school sophomore in an Introduction to Speech Communication class when "Color Me Dumb" was written. The speech was written in response to an assignment that could be prepared any time during the semester, whenever the student felt ready.

You will find that Karen chose the rhetorical question as an organizational device and that her research is evident. Her use of ethical proofs compensates, to some extent, for the fact that Karen chose not to use extensive source citation. The speech follows the problem-solution pattern of organization. Karen polished the speech to use in competition in original oration.

I. Introduction

What do Thomas Edison, General George Patton, President Woodrow Wilson, Hans Christian Anderson, and I have in common? The common factor is a "learning disability" called *Dyslexia*.

II. First Transition

Many of you may be unfamiliar with this term, but one out of seven Americans are handicapped by dyslexia.

A. Thesis Statement	What is dyslexia?
B. Definition	According to *Black's Medical Dictionary,* dyslexia is "difficulty in reading or learning to read. It is accompanied by difficulty in writing and spelling correctly."
C. Background *1. Historical*	Even though dyslexia was identified in the 19th century by British and German opthalmologists, it can probably be traced through the ages since man first sought to express himself with symbols.
2. Current/personal information	Almost everyone can remember that first grade classmate who made his "N's" and "Z's" backwards. He failed to read on the same level as the rest of the class. You may have laughed at him at recess, and your teacher may have labeled him a "slow learner." That classmate may have had dyslexia.
D. Preview	Although dyslexia is unrelated to basic intellectual capacity, the affliction causes a mysterious difficulty in handling words and symbols. There are literally dozens of unproven theories about dyslexia. What do we know about the causes and effects of this mysterious condition?
III. Body *A. Causes*	Some early experts thought brain damage was responsible for the condition, since it became known that patients with head injuries lost their reading and writing skills, but brain wave tests have ruled this out. The theory that dyslexia is caused by outward scars and neurological damage was soon discarded. The theory that dyslexia is inherited is the closest guess doctors have. But what does it *mean* to have dyslexia?
B_1. *Effects (personal)*	It means not being able to learn to tell time. When I was six, the attempt made by my sisters to teach me to tell time turned into disaster. They became angry with me, because, when I read the clock backward, my sisters thought I was not trying to learn. For Woodrow Wilson, it meant not learning the alphabet until the age of nine and not learning to read until he was eleven. It meant only fair grades in Princeton University. For General George Patton it meant not being able to read until he was twelve and five hard years in West Point memorizing text books *word for word.* For Kathy Rice, a student at Columbia University, it means memorizing her books from tapes. One math book, consisting of 15 tapes and 60 hours of listening.

For me, it meant being called "slow" and often having the stifling feeling that I could not do, and dare not try, what others in my class did with ease. I sat in the reading circle dreading the time for my name to be called to read aloud—because everyone knew I was the slowest reader in the class.

Even though most dyslexics learn to cope with, or compensate for, their handicap, they cannot escape the lasting scars of the condition.

B₂. Effects (general)

But what are the effects of dyslexia? The most harmful effect of all is the loss of self esteem or self confidence. Once a teacher asked me to draw a picture of my family. I did as asked. My family, father, mother, and three sisters dominated the page in vivid color. But in the corner I drew myself very small and in black and white. A perfect description of how I saw myself—just color me dumb.

But what about the resentment and lack of interest in school? Frustrated teachers, agonized parents, and humiliated victims forces the interest in school to decline to disastrous levels.

Kathy Rice was labeled a failure at age 13.

The stereotype of dyslexia as a "learning disability" affects the dyslexic because it is just that—a label. Dummy, Failure, Slow!

The fact that the term dyslexia is generally accepted to mean a learning disability results in labels that a child will never be able to escape.

C. Solution

However, hope for the dyslexic is now available. Most schools recognize the problem and provide qualified professionals to work with the troubled student. Pediatricians and psychologists are familiar with the symptoms. Learning aids are available. All adding up to significant strides in the diagnosis and treatment of dyslexia.

But what can you—one of the fortunate ones who do not know what it is to look at the printed page and see a backward image, like holding a page to a mirror—do to help those of us who struggle daily with the problems of dyslexia?

We only ask you to understand—perhaps knowing what our problem is and being a little patient with our slowness in deciphering symbols is the single most significant thing you can do.

Parents have no need to rationalize or be ashamed of their child's problem.

Classmates have no reason to ridicule because in a reading circle we may appear a little different.

Teachers could apply a little understanding when interpreting the seemingly low scores of dyslexics on standardized tests.

Doctors and educators can continue research into the diagnosis and treatment of dyslexia.

If you are dyslexic you can take a _new look_ at yourself.

Recently, one of my teachers asked my speech coach, "What is Karen doing in competitive speech when according to her latest test score she ranks in the lowest percentile in her class?"

The answer obviously is I have realized that there is little relationship between my inability to read symbols and my ability to learn and to perform.

IV. Second Transition
A. Summary

I am one of the fortunate ones along with Thomas Edison, General George Patton, President Woodrow Wilson, Hans Christian Anderson, and Kathy Rice who has learned to cope and to compensate for the problems of dyslexia.

B. Second Thesis

Dyslexia is a perceptual problem, but not necessarily a disability.

V. Conclusion

Today, I have a healthy self-concept and a renewed interest in school because I have learned to face the problem of dyslexia.

Recently on the cover of an education magazine I read the caption, "In the soul of every child blooms a flower."

Today if a teacher asked me to draw a picture of myself—I just might draw myself as a flower—and NOT COLOR ME DUMB.

Outline for "Color Me Dumb"

I. Introductory Device
   Rhetorical question

II. A. Thesis Statement
   Rhetorical question

II. B. Definition
   Logical proof (Citation from medical dictionary)

II. C. 1. Historical approach
   Logical proof (source not cited)
   2. Description
   Example

II. D. Preview
   Rhetorical Question

III. A. Causes
   Logical proof (source not cited)

III. B$_1$. Effects (personal)
   Ethical proof
   Instance
   Instance

Instance
(source not cited)
(relates to introduction)
III. B₂. Effects (general)
Ethical proof
Instance (relates to introduction)
III. C. Solution
Examples
Ethical proof

IV. Second Transition
A. Summary (pulls introduction and instances through)
B. Second Thesis (answers questions posed in first thesis)

V. Conclusion
Literary device

Questions:

1. Would Karen's speech have been stronger if she had used more logical proofs?
2. Would her speech have been more believable if she had cited her sources?
3. Do you think you could have followed Karen's speech more effectively if she had stated her points in declarative sentences rather than using rhetorical questions?
4. Did Karen's use of rhetorical questions and ethical proofs add interest to the speech?
5. Can you think of other devices she might have tried?
6. Can you think of a topic upon which you are uniquely qualified to speak?

Speech C

Are They Really "Unteachable"?

Carolyn Kay Geiman

Carolyn Kay Geiman delivered this speech to fulfill an assignment in a speech class during the 1964 spring semester.

In Charles Schulz's popular cartoon depiction of happiness, one of his definitions has special significance for the American school system. The drawing shows Linus, with his eyes closed in a state of supreme bliss, a broad smile across two-thirds of his face and holding a report card upon which is a big bold "A." The caption reads: "Happiness is finding out you're not so dumb after all." For once, happiness is not defined as a function of material possessions, yet even this happiness is practically unattainable for the "unteachables" of the city slums. Are these children intellectually inferior? Are they unable to learn? Are they not worth the time and the effort to teach? Unfortunately, too many people have answered "yes" to these questions and promptly dismissed the issue.

If we base our answers on the results of IQ tests, "yes" answers may seem justified. In the largest American metropolitan areas, the students in the top school of the wealthiest suburbs have an average IQ of 120; those in the bottom school of the worst slums have an average IQ of 85. Valid factual proof, right?

In a city-wide group testing program in the New York City schools, IQ scores showed a lower and slower rate of increase with grade advancement in the large, low socio-economic districts than in the median for the city as a whole. In the third grade, there was a ten-point difference in IQ's; in the sixth grade, a seventeen-point difference; and in the eighth grade, a twenty-point difference. Valid factual proof again, right?

No, wrong! The fallacy of these "facts" lies in the IQ test itself. The very fact that IQ test results vary over a given span of time indicates, as many educators today are realizing, that these are in truth tests of cultural experience and not of native ability. These children of the slums are underdeveloped culturally, but are not innately unintelligent, and this deficiency can and should be corrected.

Horace Mann Bond, Dean of the School of Education at Atlanta University, in his lecture entitled "The Search for Talent," points out that the almost universal reliance upon the results of standardized testing is allowing an enormous leakage of human resources in our society. The results of such tests, he argues, tend to follow the lines of social class and cultural opportunity and thus tend to mask the real intellectual ability of children in slum areas. There are two specific problems which limit the educational development of these children. The first is that many of them arrive at school-age possessing very little skill in communication as a result of the stifling environment of the slum. Secondly, children in slum areas, and often their parents as well, show little interest in education.

Let's take a look at the culturally deprived child and his environment. First of all, what he calls home may be one poorly-lit room on the sixth floor of a large apartment building—a room which he shares with eleven other people. On either side loom identical buildings. The noise and filth are inescapable. Look around. There are no pencils, no paper, no books, maybe a few scattered toys. To gain even a semblance of privacy in the midst of the clatter, he must train himself to shut out the noise so that he hears only what he wants to hear. He has learned to communicate by pulling or pointing, by grunts or groans. In the "living unit," which can hardly be called a home, a question such as, "How are we going to eat?" is valid, but there is no time for questions like "Where do the stars come from?" or "What causes rain?" When the child talks baby talk, his parents are either too harassed or not articulate enough themselves to correct him. This child may not even know that things have names, that he himself is a somebody with a name. He may seem to have trouble looking at things, but the fault lies not in his eyes, but in his experiences. He can't see differences in size, shape, color, and texture because he hasn't been taught to look for them. So what happens when he starts to school? He is branded as "unteachable" by teachers who cannot or will not understand this background or its effect on the child.

Dr. Martin Deutsch, the Director of the Institution for Developmental Studies of New York Medical College's Department of Psychiatry, became interested in the plight of the culturally deprived child in the public schools and studied the problem for five years. Following his theory that "intelligence is not inherited, but a dynamic process that can be stunted or stimulated by experience," he inaugurated the first scientific and concerted attempt by any public school system to confront the problem of the education of the poor pre-school age child. Ninety-six four year olds in New York City were given the advantage of this progressive program. Let's see what methods were used.

First, each child was taught that he had a name of his own, that he was somebody special, a unique person. Every work of art was signed. Parents were urged to make a fuss over the child's work, even if it was poorly done. "If a child doesn't feel pride, he can't learn."

Secondly, each child was urged to express his thoughts and wishes in words. Teachers were instructed not to respond to tuggings at their skirts or mumbled noises. The formation of a thought into a complete sentence, with subject, verb, and predicate was lauded as a major accomplishment.

Rhoda was one of the subjects of this experiment. In the classroom she stands, "clutching her favorite toys—a Negro doll and a toy baby bottle. The only game she knows is caring for the baby—bathing it, feeding it, rocking it. Fatherless Rhoda lives with her mother, who bore her at fifteen, her thirty-eight year old grandmother, two younger sisters, and eight uncles and aunts ranging in age from two months to ten years. After eleven weeks in school, Rhoda still hasn't spoken or smiled. Scowling fiercely now, she reaches out for some wax grapes and puts them in a frying pan on the stove." Hearing a noise behind her, the teacher turned around to discover Rhoda struggling with a pan. She heared Rhoda speak her first whole sentence: "Dem goddam peaches is burnin'." It's poor English, it's profane, but it is a complete thought, and this is a major achievement. Rhoda was rewarded with a big hug from her teacher, not scolded for her profanity.

Projects such as this one indicate that with care, understanding, and attention children in slum areas can be helped in mastering the basic skill of communication so vital to their educational process. What then of the indifference so prevalent in slum areas? Frank Reissman, a noted educator who has spent much of the last twenty years dealing with problems in the education of underprivileged children, is quick to point out that a distinction must be made in talking about indifference to education. Children and parents in slum areas, he says, are apathetic, and even antagonistic, not toward education, but rather toward the school system which writes them off as hopeless. Parents see the teacher as a middle-class citizen uninterested in their or their children's problems. The children, who sense their rejection strongly, begin to simply tune the teacher out. The results of this neglect are that the streets that used to be their playgrounds become their hangouts. They roam the streets. They join the ranks of the unemployed. Instead of becoming constructive citizens of the community, they become anti-social and rebellious. But this need not be. Dr. Reissman points out that time and time again projects in our major cities have established that interest in the schools can be achieved simply by demonstrating the school's interest in the underprivileged child. Parents called in for conferences, not because Johnny played hookey, but because the teacher wanted to discuss his progress have responded gratefully. Children treated with respect and interest have blossomed.

When we understand that these two major stumbling blocks to the educational progress of the underprivileged child can be eliminated—that they can be encouraged to communicate and that apathy and antagonism can be conquered—we realize that we need not write these children off as a lost cause. We need not lose these valuable human resources. We can help the "unteachables" to discover the magic of learning and achieving. We can help them to understand Schulz's definition: "Happiness is finding out you're not so dumb after all."

Speech D

Five Ways in Which Thinking is Dangerous

Rebellion, Risks and Outrageous Behavior

Stephen Joel Trachtenberg

Dr. Stephen Joel Trachtenberg, President of the University of Hartford, delivered his speech, "Five Ways in Which Thinking is Dangerous (Rebellion, Risks, and Outrageous Behavior)" at Newington High School Scholars' Breakfast, Newington, Connecticut, on June 3, 1986.

It's an honor and a pleasure for me to be here today, and to have this opportunity to address this year's Newington High School Scholars' Breakfast.

I've been giving a lot of thought in recent weeks to what I ought to be saying to you this morning. The obvious thing would be to praise you for your hard work and your accomplishments, and encourage you to continue achieving at this very high level.

But the more I thought about it, the less inclined I felt to do that. And when I asked myself why, a little voice inside my head replied as follows:

"Look, Steve, these kids are *teenagers*. And one thing we know about teenagers is that they are given to questioning the values handed them by adults. Sometimes they rebel in *not*-so-obvious ways. But if you go in there and praise them outright for their accomplishments, maybe one or two of them will reason that anything an adult tells them is good is probably bad."

Let me tell you, that voice inside my head really gave me pause. Basically it seemed to be suggesting that I use some reverse psychology. Instead of doing the obvious, I should do the *opposite* of the obvious.

In turn, that seemed to leave me only one course of action. I could come here today and *criticize* you for working so hard and accomplishing so much. I could urge you to relax a little, to lower your standards, and to try out the pleasures of poorer grades and a generally lower academic status. Then

I imagined what the local newspapers would make of my remarks, and what the chances were that I would ever again be invited to address a group of students in any high school in Connecticut.

So I found myself back at Square One. Now I *really* had to get back to basics inside my head, and, drawing on all of the studying I did at Columbia, Yale and Harvard, I reasoned as follows:

Those of us who have studied Western history of the 19th and 20th centuries know that the Romantic movement left us with a permanent bias in favor of rebellion, risk, and generally outrageous behavior. In other words, if you can pin an *"Establishment"* label on any particular set of behaviors . . . if you can make it sound as if everybody behaving in that particular way has a potbelly that is also bright yellow . . . then most folks in our culture will shy away from it, in favor of someone or something that is closer to Burt Reynolds or Humphrey Bogart.

Now I asked myself: Why is it that no one has considered the hypothesis that academic high achievement is actually as romantic, risky and generally outrageous as being a pirate, or flying experimental jets, or doing any of the other things that most people are *afraid* to do? Maybe those who get high honors in a place like Newington High School are not just *smarter* than most of their contemporaries but braver too?

The more I considered this hypothesis the better I liked it, and I decided to entitle my talk today "The Five Major Risks of

Academic High Achievement.'' An alternative and slightly broader title might be: ''Five Ways in Which Thinking is Dangerous.''

Way Number One, it seems to me, is that thinking—analysis—the habit of probing deeply into things—can lead to depression.

Remember that people who are regarded as not being clever aren't necessarily lacking in brain-power. They just don't make use of the brain-power that they have available. And one of the reasons for that may be that when you inquire carefully into a lot of things that go on in our world, you find that many of them fall short of perfection. In fact, quite a few of them are positively lousy.

So you can't altogether blame folks who, rather than get upsetting answers, simply don't ask questions! They stay reasonably happy by not doing too much reasoning!

A second risk of academic high achievement is that there are those who will actually hold it against you—in other words, that it can sometimes lead to a lack of popularity where particular individuals are concerned. They're the ones who will label you a—quote—''brain,'' and imagine that this is a deadly blow, sort of like calling you a rat or a fink.

Though I imagine that some of you have had experiences like that, I wonder if you've considered the possibility that people like that are motivated by a good deal of fear and anxiety? Once you've established your reputation as having a lot of analytic capacity, *they* become nervous that you might turn that capacity in *their* direction. In other words, the person who fears your brain-power is probably a person with something to hide.

The third risk of academic high achievement lies, believe it or not, in your relationship to the adult world. I hope it won't come as a tremendous surprise when I tell you that many adults feel quite ambivalent where talented and high-achieving teenagers are concerned. On the one hand, they can't help but admire the energy and initiative

teenagers like that are showing. At the same time, they can't altogether avoid the awareness that the young people they are admiring are also the—quote—''next generation'' that is going to—quote—''take over the world.''

In other words, a typical fear that adults have is that they are on the way to becoming obsolete. That's why dedicated teachers don't necessarily leap to their feet with enthusiasm when one of their students proves beyond a shadow of a doubt that they just made a mistake. *First* they wince. *Then* they manage to eke out a small smile. And *then,* having thought the whole thing over—then and *only* then—they leap enthusiastically to their feet!

A fourth risk of academic high achievement, in my opinion, is despair. Once you've set a high standard for yourself, there *have* to come moments when you ask yourself: ''Can I keep this up?'' At the age of 13 or 14 or 15, you ask whether you can keep going at this pace until you're *really old*— until you're 25, say, or 32. Then, when you've been doing it for 30 or 40 years, you wonder whether you can keep going at this pace until retirement. And after retirement, you look at the other vigorous senior citizens—every one of them playing championship golf or giving guest lectures at a nearby college—and you wonder whether you'll *ever* be able to take it easy!

It's no accident that it was eating from the Tree of Knowledge that got Adam and Eve expelled from the easy life. Though they did with their jaws rather than their neurons, they were academic high achievers of a certain kind—and—as the Bible tells us—had to work hard and have sweat on their brows for the rest of their time on earth.

Finally, there is another risk of academic high achievement that bears some thinking about, which is that it often leads people to transform the world in which they are living, which in turn can cause a good deal of personal upset.

Let's say that you are in your teens or early twenties and you work really hard to develop a brand new concept and a brand new range of intellectual or scientific possibilities. Now the world begins to change because _you_ dreamt up the microchip . . . or genetic engineering . . . or some altogether new way of looking at the human past. Well, by the time the revolution is peaking, you'll probably be 35 or 40 years of age—ready to settle down and be a little comfortable and complacent. At that point everything around you will get shaken up, and you'll find that your teenage son or daughter is criticizing you for being so completely out of it!

Now let me tote up the risks that I've set before you in the last few minutes:

Risk number one: You may find that you sometimes get depressed.

Risk number two: Some people won't like you.

Risk number three: Grown-ups may get a little nervous when they're near you.

Risk number four: You may feel an occasional twinge of despair over "keeping up the pace."

Risk number five: You may begin to have an impact on the world around you —and you will have to live with the changes you've helped to bring about.

Looking over those five risks of academic high achievement, I realize that they look very much like the risks of maturity. When you criticize someone for being too much of a kid, you usually mean that he

or she is giggly even when that's not appropriate, that he or she tries to be universally popular, that he or she wants grown-ups to be godlike in their complete fairness, that he or she expects life to be a nonstop party, and that he or she can't imagine things being different from the way they are right now.

What that suggests to me is that academic high achievement—the kind represented here at Newington High School today—may also be a synonym for maturity. It carries some risks—which is _always_ true of maturity. It means that life gets a little more complicated—which is what true adults take for granted as they try to get through an average day. It means that life is only _sometimes_ a party, and that it is full of the unexpected.

Yes, there are some risks . . . but they are risks well taken. The benefits are worth the dangers. The eagle flying high always risks being shot at by some hare-brained human with a rifle. But eagles—and young eagles like _you_—still prefer the view from that risky height to what is available flying with the turkeys far, far below.

Personally, I admire eagles. That's because I am an unreconstructed romantic. And I admire _you_ for what you've accomplished. Keep up the good work! My congratulations to you all!

Speech E

The Crown of Life?

Lisa L. Golub   Lisa L. Golub delivered this speech in a public speaking course during the 1980 fall semester.

Old age is creeping up on you with every second that passes. Someday you too will be elderly. "So what?" you may be thinking, "That just means being a grandma or

grandpa, being respected by the young folks, and retiring to the 'good life.' "

Chances are it won't mean that at all. You might be a shut-in, confined to a wheelchair. But if you're blessed with good health and able to make your way out in society, you may be met by disrespect and ridicule. And your dream of the good life may be so ravaged by inflation that you are forced to add cat food to your diet because the social security check hasn't come yet, and there just . . . isn't . . . enough . . . money.

Does that seem hard to believe? Sadly it's not unrealistic at all. Our elderly are often forgotten, stereotyped, and disrespected. Our aged are often impoverished and ill-housed. And yes, our elderly are often physically abused by those they must depend on for care. It's no wonder gerontophobia, the fear of old age, is very common. Neglect of our elderly is a serious problem in American society.

The first sign of neglect is isolation. Consider family isolation. There is a woman at a nursing home I visit frequently who is a case in point. Gloria is 95 years old. She has been a resident of the Madison Convalescent Home for 13 years. Though she is confined to a wheelchair and cannot speak well due to a stroke, she is a bright and interesting woman. Each day she can be found fully dressed, make-up, and jewelry, her chair near the lobby door—waiting for a friend . . . who never comes. Where is her family?? Though she has outlived most, her remaining family lives in Florida. *Florida!* Tell me why have they left a 95 year old woman alone to die, over a thousand miles away from them? "Forgotten." Do you know that there is actually a service in California that you can call if you are near death and for $7.00 an hour they will have someone sit beside you while you die?! If you have no one. If they have forgotten.

Consider media induced isolation. Our aged are mocked in movies and on television where they are depicted as dirty old men, saucy rich nags, or delirious no-minds. According to Public Affairs Researcher, Irving Dickman, "true senility, or chronic organic brain syndrome, probably affects as few as 3% of all elderly."

Cicero once called old age ". . . the crown of life, our play's last act." Today old age is considered more a sickness than a joyous finale. This change in perception has led us to a paradox which the Catholic Bishops have expressed in this way:

(America) "is an aging nation which worships the culture, values, and appearance of youth. Instead of viewing old age as an achievement and a natural stage of life with its own merits, wisdom, and beauty, American society all too often ignores, rejects, and isolates the elderly."

Before we laugh at and accept media stereotypes of our aged, let us not forget that we are *all* going to be elderly someday—the only prerequisite is to live.

Consider isolation from the world of work. Older people have also faced disrespect in their jobs, or should I say the lack of their jobs due to mandatory retirement. In *Ageism—Discrimination Against Older People,* one forced retiree states it this way:

"I don't want to fill in the time before I die. I want to use the time. I need to work . . . I want my old job back. I was good at it. To be considered unfit for the very job for which I was trained, in which I have many years of experience, is the cruelest kind of rejection. Then I am truly unfit, no good at anything."

Are we so narrow in our view of growing older that we have made true the saying, "King of the hill one day—over the hill the next."? Herman Loether, a professor at California State College, pictures job isolation in this way:

"The man who has spent 40 years or more in the labor force, devoting a major portion of his life to his job, is suddenly handed a gold watch in recognition of his faithful service and told to go home and relax."

Maybe he doesn't want to relax! But the choice has been taken away from him. The respect for his goals, his opinion is gone.

Isolation—from family, by media; from work—is a major dimension of the problem. But as if loneliness were not enough, many of America's elderly live in abject poverty. Consider these facts from Public Affairs Pamphlet #575 published in 1979: Of the twenty-two million people over 65, one in every five had an income below the official poverty level. Old people, who are only 10% of the population, are 66.6% of the poor. And poverty, not poor health, has been cited as the chief source of unhappiness and worry among our aged. In that same pamphlet, pollster Louis Harris provided a summary of the economic plight of the aged when he said:

". . . two out of every three people with incomes below the poverty line are older citizens . . . victimized by inflation . . . desperate . . . hungry, ill-clad, in debt, and ill-housed."

According to Senator Charles H. Percy in _Growing Old in the Country of the Young,_ one out of three of our elderly live in substandard housing, and three out of four of our elderly blacks live in such housing. In addition, the quality of life decreases with each increase in inflation. In Percy's book, one aged person offers this testimony:

"I am 74 years old and living in a building 70 years old. I moved here 9 years ago and paid $90 a month for rent. Then the building was sold. The first two years, my rent was raised $4 each year. Then I got a $10 increase. Now, $20 more. I get $141 social security. Rent is $130. Plus gas, plus utilities, plus telephone. How can I eat?"

While Social Security was not designed to provide sole or adequate support, it now struggles to provide at least 90% of the total income for more than four million of our older people. The battle is being lost. The Social Security system is experiencing great stress as it tries to increase benefits and meet the needs of a rapidly graying America. And to what end? Today the average Social Security benefit still falls below the federal government's poverty line.

But perhaps worse than all of the aforementioned put together is the physical abuse that our elderly endure. According to Richard Douglass, a researcher at the University of Michigan Institute of Gerontology, physical abuse of the elderly is pervasive and serious, involving "beating, burnings, cutting or battering with fists or objects," and resulting in physical injuries ranging from "superficial wounds" (to) dislocations (to) bone fractures and many resulting fatalities." And who inflicts this abuse on our elderly? Often their own children. The adult children expect them to be "strong", and when the aged are not, they are "punished."

This abuse is also prevalent in our institutions. In _Growing Old in the Country of the Young,_ Percy tells of a recent event in Miami where ". . . two elderly men—critically ill, homeless, penniless—were put into wheelchairs to sit in a jammed aisle of a hospital until nursing home space could be found for them. Both men died in those chairs and it was hours before anyone even noticed they were dead. One man had been sitting in his chair for three days and the other man for two. As the hospital told of the deaths of these men, ten more just like them were still sitting in that aisle."

Nursing homes themselves are at fault for abusing our senior citizens. Have you ever been to a nursing home where the air did not smell rancid, where the TV worked well, where the food looked _and tasted_ appetizing? They are few and far between. I have personally read about and seen instances where patients have been hit or slapped. In a recent case at Hillhaven Convalescent Home in Milwaukee a patient was forced to eat his own excrement. It's sick!

This directly affects your life. Because you are getting older today. Right now.

Psalm 71 says "Cast me not off in the time of old age, forsake me not when my strength faileth."

A recent article in the *Milwaukee Journal* on aging closed with a view of a woman who visited her mother in a nursing home:

"Around the room a few more chant. 'I want to go home. I want to go home.' An ancient figure strapped in his wheelchair covers his ears with trembling, skeletal fingers and begins to sob.

My mama, as though roused from a deep sleep, begins to look around—her eyes suddenly comprehending.

'What is it, Mama? Tell me what it is.'

She looks terrified, but her voice is without emotion.

"All of my nightmares came true.' She says."

Our elderly have been greatly neglected, and I tell you, NOW is the time to care.

Speech F

The Battle Against Drugs
What Can You Do?

Nancy Reagan　　　"The Battle Against Drugs, What Can You Do?" was delivered by First Lady Nancy Reagan at the World Affairs Council, Los Angeles, California, on June 24, 1986.

Thank you. And before I go any further let me tell you that the great communicator sends his regards. I can't tell you how honored I feel to be speaking before the World Affairs Council. I know of the great leaders and intellects who have appeared in the place where I'm standing today—and it's a little overwhelming.

I certainly don't put myself on their plane, but I believe what I want to discuss with you is just as important as anything previous speakers have discussed.

I want to talk about the battle against drugs.

Now before any of you can think to yourself, "Well, drug abuse really doesn't concern me," let me say it does concern you. It concerns you if you have a family, because drugs can unexpectedly tear a family to pieces—even the most loving families.

It concerns you as an employer, because drugs cost billions in illness, accidents, lost productivity and corruption.

It concerns you as a citizen, because there's a direct and undeniable link between crime and drugs. Law enforcement officers are being murdered in their efforts to protect our society from those who would destroy it with drugs.

And furthermore, it concerns you as an individual of conscience, because the tragedy and pain drugs cause are staggering.

Ladies and gentlemen, there's a drug and alcohol epidemic in this country and no one is safe from its consequences—not you, not me, and certainly not our children. Drugs are a very powerful force in America, and we cannot ignore them.

Let me begin by taking you back, if I may, and telling you of my personal journey of awareness and commitment in regard to drug abuse . . . because in many ways my journey reflects that of the nation as a whole.

I first became aware of the problem in the 60's in Sacramento when my husband was Governor. To be honest, I really didn't understand the scope or the intensity of the problem then. Few of us did. But I knew something was happening to our children, something very tragic—even deadly.

I began getting calls from friends—calls of hurt and embarrassment and self-consciousness that their child could be on drugs—calls of confusion and ignorance about what was happening to their family, and on occasion calls of great pain at the loss of a son or daughter.

We were all so naive then.

Trying to raise children in the 60's was a terrifying experience. It seemed everything was against you—mainly your children. It was often hard—and still is—to tell the signs of drug abuse from normal adolescent rebellion. Parents didn't know where to turn, didn't know what to do.

In the movie, "The Dark at the Top of the Stairs," a woman says of her children, "I always wanted to give them life like a present, all wrapped up with every promise of happiness." This is what every parent wants for a child, but it was becoming painfully obvious, this wasn't the way it was to be.

As time went on, I got more calls. I began reading a little more about it in the papers. The age of the children involved seemed to be getting younger and younger. Clearly, we had the makings of a tremendous problem.

Then when we moved to Washington I learned something. I learned I had a chance to make a difference. I had a platform I would never have again and I should take advantage of it. Before I even got started though, March 30th and the attempted assassination happened—obviously my world stopped. But during the recuperation period, I met with doctors, teachers, and experts in the field of drug and alcohol abuse. For the first time, I began to understand the full frightening extent of the problem.

Yet all the statistics, all the clinical studies, all the expert briefings in the world can't match the reality of one deeply suffering young person. When people learned I was interested in drug abuse, I began getting letters that would simply pierce your heart, letters of pain and loneliness and confusion—thousands of them.

In the beginning, I got a letter from a 16 year-old girl I'll call Joni. I want to read it to you. Part of it's rather raw, but this letter tells you what drugs can do and tells it better than all the facts and figures I could present.

"Dear Mrs. Reagan, it has taken me many months to finally write you. At the age of 13 I was a regular user of anything and everything—pot, LSD, heroin, even nail polish remover, and if I was really desperate, liquid paper. I really don't know why I became a drug user, I guess because I never really liked myself, and now I hate myself even more.

"I destroyed my parents' hearts. Out of three boys, they thought their one and only little girl would follow their footsteps and be a good girl. I failed them . . . I hurt them. Because of what I've done, drugs have now affected my social and family life—I'm a loner, and it's all because of drugs.

"It got to the point where I was high all the time . . . for me, drugs were the escape from reality . . . to top it off, I was adopted as a baby, and when I found out I was different, I never wanted to be in the real world.

"Drugs are terrible, and it was a horrible, vicious cycle I lived in—drugs took me over. I can remember one time when I was high I needed a fix so bad, I had sex with a man around 55 years or older. For five hundred dollars worth of drugs, it was worth it at the time. I was once pregnant, but because of the drugs, I had the baby when it was five months into my pregnancy—the baby's arm was at its leg and its ear was at its cheek—the baby died.

"Drugs ruined my life, and I regret it so much. I long for the day when anyone will say to me, 'Joni, I love you—because of who you are, not who you were.' ... Mrs. Reagan—please reach kids my age and younger—don't let what's happened to me and which destroyed my life happen to them."

How could anyone resist such a plea? But I realized our children's pleas weren't getting through to us. In fact, the whole problem of drug abuse was being denied. For too long our nation denied that a problem even existed. We denied that drug abuse had health and social consequences. We denied that anything could be done to counter widespread drug use.

There was almost a stigma in trying to take on drugs. It was unfashionable. It was illiberal and narrow-minded in our live-and-let-live society. Movies and television portrayed drugs as glamorous and cool. We heard a lot about the recreational use of drugs as if drugs were as harmless as Trivial Pursuit. Even law enforcement was weakened by the moral confusion surrounding drug abuse. It was as if all the people who sought to fight drugs had to justify their actions. As a matter of fact, no one was especially thrilled at the idea that this was what I wanted to do. And we had a lot of conversations about it.

Yet for five years now I've been trooping around this country and the world—over 100,000 miles, 53 cities in 28 states, 6 foreign countries, and countless interviews and television appearances. My main purpose when we started, was to raise the level of awareness in the country and to stress the importance of becoming knowledgeable about the danger of drug abuse.

I think we've succeeded in that. I certainly see more about drug abuse in the papers and on television. More well-known people are coming forward and talking about

their addiction. Slowly, the wall of denial seems to be crumbling.

We now have 9,000 parent groups, which sprang up independently and are doing marvelous work in closing down headshops, becoming involved in school drug programs, and forming support groups for one another.

I always thought if we could just get the young people involved it would be a giant step forward. And now that's happening with the "Just Say No" clubs. Young people are forming their own positive peer groups to counter the pressures to use drugs. It's sometimes hard to believe how complex our children's lives are today—in my day peer pressure meant your saddle shoes had to be dirty.

Internationally, we're also making progress. I've twice invited the First Ladies of other countries here to discuss the drug abuse problem and to let them hear from experts and young people who are former addicts. The numbers of these concerned First Ladies is rapidly growing and their influence is being felt around the world. The first time we had 17 acceptances, the second time we had 30 acceptances. I was very gratified to learn that as a result of those meetings there are now parents groups in Germany, Portugal, Malaysia, Ireland, and Thailand. Hopefully, these will grow even more.

I feel very good that we've succeeded in raising the level of awareness. We are more aware of drug abuse than ever before—but now it's time for the next step.

It's time to let people know they have a moral responsibility to do more than simply recognize the problem. They have an obligation to take a personal stand against drugs.

You know, one young girl wrote to me about her brother, who had helped raise her. She still loved him despite the fact he'd become so possessed by drugs he's even threatened to kill them both. She wrote, "One day he was so drugged up that he couldn't walk, he sat on a step and gave me a look of 'help me' straight in the eyes. I started to cry. Later than night we found out he overdosed on heroin. . . . He hurt me so bad, but never bad enough that I hated him. I love him more than anyone knows. . . .'' At the bottom of her letter in large plaintive letters she wrote, ''Help!''

Ladies and gentlemen, each of you has a moral obligation to provide that help. I don't mean you have to work in a drug rehabilitation center or join a parents group. But you do have the responsibility to put your conscience and principles on the line. You have the responsibility to be intolerant of drug use anywhere-anytime by anybody. You have the responsibility of forcing the issue to the point of making others uncomfortable and yourself unpopular.

Recently, I was interviewed by a magazine reporter who told me of a dinner she'd attended where cocaine was passed around. She felt uncomfortable, but she didn't do anything. Well, she should have. She should have gotten up from the table, told the people what she thought, and left. By staying she gave tacit approval.

A sports broadcaster told me he was having dinner with a group of people at a well-known restaurant and the same thing happened—out came a bowl of cocaine. What should he have done? He should have pulled together the courage—and it would take courage—and spoken against what was going on and then left.

In all likelihood, this will cost you some friends. But if a friendship is based on nothing more than condoning drugs, it's not much of a friendship anyway. This is a moral issue and you have to make a decision. By accepting drug use you are accepting a practice that is destroying lives. You cannot separate polite drug use at a chic L.A. party from drug use in some back alley somewhere. They are morally equal.

Those who believe that people who use drugs aren't hurting anyone but themselves are wrong. Drugs hurt society. The money spent on drugs goes into the hands of one of the most ruthless, despicable lots ever

to breathe—the drug producers. They are often murderers. They are sometimes terrorists. They are always criminals. They represent man at his most debased. They are the people who are financing the death and destruction of our young people.

And by doing nothing when you know of drug use, you're conspiring with them as they line their pockets with even more blood money.

I have a message for the drug dealers and producers and pushers, and the message is this: The parents throughout the world are going to drive you out of business. We're the ones who are going to be the pushers from now on. We're going to push *you* out. Push you out of our schools, out of our neighborhoods, out of our communities, and out of existence!

There's nothing remarkable about how we'll do it. We'll do it through education and commitment. We'll do it through individual responsibility. We're going to dry up the dealers' markets. We're going to make the poison they push as worthless as they are. We're going to take the customer away from the product.

Schools, too, have to face up to their responsibility. They owe our children a drug-free environment in which to grow and learn. I think there are schools who haven't made this commitment because they believe drug abuse is society's problem. Yet schools can be made clean with a no-nonsense approach that simply says drugs will not be tolerated. Such tough measures have proven successful time and again.

Schools need to set up uncompromising no-drug, no-alcohol policies, like Northside High School in Atlanta. Each school needs to find and develop its own tough policies.

Corporations have to take greater responsibility, too. Employees have a right to a drug-free workplace. Workers on drugs are a danger to fellow employees and to the public. Too many companies don't know how to deal with drugs, so like certain parents and schools they pretend it's not a problem. Well, all the research tells us it is a problem, and corporations need to set up their own tough no-drug policies. Roger Smith, Chairman of General Motors, has said that drug and alcohol abuse was costing the corporation a billion dollars a year.

Ladies and gentlemen, you are fortunate. You're not as vulnerable as the 12 or 13 year-old, who has some drinks, which lowers his inhibitions, so he takes a pill or a snort to be accepted by his peers. And then he takes more drugs, more frequently.

You are accomplished people. You strive. You achieve. You enjoy. You grow. You look forward. You're open to life and to its hopes.

Can you imagine being young and yet without the spark and enthusiasm of youth? Can you imagine being young and yet an empty shell of vacant stares, vacant emotions, and vacant hopes? Can you imagine not caring about anything in this entire world except the chemical you're going to force into your body? That is what it means to be young and possessed by drugs.

You have a moral duty to prevent this loss. You have the responsibility to be intolerant of drugs and to be forceful in your intolerance. You have the obligation to remember the words of Whittier, who unwittingly explained the essential tragedy of drug abuse among our young:

"For of all the sad words of tongue or pen, the saddest are these: It might have been."

I've often been asked, well, don't you get discouraged? Doesn't it seem like the problem is so big that it can't possibly be overcome? And I refuse to say yes to that. I don't believe that's true. I believe when you say that, it becomes a self-fulfilling prophesy, for one thing. And every time I'm reminded of those wonderful words of Winston Churchill's when he said, "never give in, never give up, never, never, never."

Thank you for inviting me and thank you for your hospitality.

Speech G

Will and Vision
The Tools You Need

Gerry Sikorski

Gerry Sikorski, United States Congressman from Minnesota, delivered the following commencement address, "Will and Vision, (The Tools You Need)" to the graduating class of Breckenridge High School, Breckenridge, Minnesota, on June 1, 1986.

Graduates, parents and friends: I'm proud to be from Breckenridge and happy to be back today. And I'm really happy to see Ms. Linneman from my old days at Breckenridge High School. Did you know that she can predict the future? Time and again during my high school career, in library and study hall, Ms. Linneman would stop me in the halls and say, "SIKORSKI—I'VE BEEN WATCHING YOU. AND IF YOU DON'T CHANGE YOUR WAYS, YOU'RE GOING TO BE HERE 20 YEARS FROM NOW!" And Ms. Linneman was right. Here I am.

Writing a graduation speech is a real challenge. No graduation speaker I know has ever delivered a speech that any graduate has ever remembered 10 minutes after it ended. That's probably why so many

Congressmen feel qualified to deliver them. I mentioned that to one of my colleagues in Washington last week, and she said, "Why go all the way back to Minnesota not to be listened to? Why don't you just write a letter to the President?"

Frankly, I don't remember who spoke at my graduation here 20 years ago. I don't remember a thing that he or she said. I do remember that it was hot as heck. The auditorium was packed and un-air-conditioned. And I remember thinking to myself: "HERE I AM SITTING INSIDE ON A 98 DEGREE DAY WITH A WOOL SUIT ON AND A GOWN OVER THAT. I SPENT HALF AN HOUR COMBING MY HAIR SO I COULD MESS IT UP WITH A HAT THAT LOOKS LIKE A GEOMETRY PROBLEM. AND I'M DOING ALL THIS BECAUSE TODAY'S THE DAY I'M SHOWING THE WORLD HOW SMART I AM."

Let's see. What else do I remember? I guess just that I was wearing a carnation that my Great Aunt Alice had crushed to death when she hugged me. And I remember that the kid sitting in front of me was wearing enough English Leather cologne to risk being shut down by the EPA. One of my classmates clipped his fingernails during the commencement address. Click. Click. Click.

But as I said, I don't remember the speaker. I suppose we were told that today was the first day of the rest of our lives. And I suppose we were told that we were about to enter "the golden door of opportunity." In 1966, the only door many young people were entering was the door to the draft board office—and the sign above it might just as well have said THIS WAY TO VIETNAM. It was a door from which too many did not return to finish the rest of their lives.

But you are a new generation and you don't need embroidered cliches any more than we did. I don't have to tell you that the world has changed in astounding ways during your lives. But it's amazing to think that when I went to B.H.S. we were reading

the book "1984" as science fiction—while you read it as history.

The year 2000 was used as a science fiction writer's shorthand for some far-distant era. Today, the college class of 2000 is already in grade school. We are now as close to the 21st Century as we are to Vietnam and Watergate . . . and, I was going to say, to Richard Nixon. But I've just seen his smiling face on the cover of Newsweek. And I was reminded of the little girl in the TV ad for the new horror movie POLTERGEIST TWO, saying HEEE'S BAAAAAACK!

The re-emergence of Nixon got me to thinking that rather than spending these few minutes talking about changes—as exciting as they are—I want to talk with you about some things that stay the same. Countries change, technologies change, leaders change, but human nature and human challenge don't really change.

So to give you something to remember 10 minutes after graduation today, I did a little research. One of the best things about being a Congressman is that I meet a lot of exciting, successful people—religious, political, business and scientific leaders. So a few months ago, I started carrying a note pad around with me and asking those folks a question that went something like this:

"TELL ME THE MOST IMPORTANT THING YOU'VE LEARNED ABOUT LIFE AND YOURSELF AND PEOPLE SINCE YOU GRADUATED FROM HIGH SCHOOL?"

I want to pass along some of the best ones. Some you may agree with. Some you may think are crazy. But I can almost guarantee you've heard every one of them from your parents. ("HEY NO GROANING THERE IN THE BACK ROWS!)

Number one is—BE ABSOLUTELY DETERMINED TO _ENJOY_ WHAT YOU DO.

I've never met anybody who succeeded at something he or she hates. A news reporter interviewed Kenny O'Donnell, John Kennedy's friend and White House Chief of Staff some years ago. The interview was recorded shortly before O'Donnell's death, and you can tell by his voice that he wasn't well. But when the reporter asked him about the best part of his job with Kennedy, you could hear the energy coming back. He said:

"THE BEST PART WAS EVERY MINUTE OF EVERY DAY. I MEAN IT. I LOVED TO GO TO WORK EVERY DAY. BECAUSE I WAS DOING EXACTLY WHAT I WANTED TO DO . . . WHERE I WANTED TO BE . . . WORKING WITH WHO I WANTED TO BE WITH." Same with Kennedy.

Point number two—and almost everybody told me this in one way or another: DON'T BE AFRAID TO FAIL.

Lou Brock holds two baseball records: most stolen bases—and most times being thrown out trying to steal bases.

Babe Ruth holds two short season records: Most home runs—and most strike outs.

Columbus left Spain to find India. He failed. But he found America.

Lee Iacocca was fired by Ford Motor. Then he went to work and saved Chrysler. (Iacocca understood another great truth: Don't get mad. Get even.)

I'm not advising you to go out and fail. But when you fail at something—and you probably will—learn from it. An old saying goes: "The gifts are burdens. The burdens are gifts."

In 1972, I managed a congressional race and we lost. The next time, my candidate won.

In 1978, I ran for Congress and I lost. The next time I won.

Abe Lincoln lost five elections before he won the Presidency.

That brings me to another piece of good advice. NEVER GIVE UP ON ANYBODY. After all, Mark Twain pointed out 100 years ago that the only true and unredeemable criminal class in America is Congress.

"Never give up on anybody" was one of the favorite sayings of Minnesota's Hubert Humphrey. One of the last calls he made from his bed before he died was to Richard Nixon. They didn't agree on very much, but they shared a determination never to accept any defeat as final.

When you come back here for your 20th reunion, the success stories from this class of 1986 will amaze you. Don't be surprised if the fat kids with pimples come back looking more like Don Johnson or Christie Brinkley. Don't be surprised if the kid who got the "D" in speech class comes back earning a quarter of a million dollars as a network newscaster. And don't be surprised if you come back happily married to the girl or guy you couldn't even stand to dance with at the prom.

And I hope you come back home often, because I can tell you from personal experience that when you face the toughest times in life, you have to be able to GET BACK TO YOUR ROOTS AND REMEMBER YOUR FUNDAMENTALS. That's the fourth point and those roots begin right here with your family and your community.

I'm proud to have my parents here in the audience today. Because when I talk about successful people, people who know a lot, they're on the list. My dad was a railroad worker. And for over 40 years, he worked on the bridges and buildings of Great Northern in the blistering heat of July and the terrible cold of January.

My mom took in laundry and gutted turkeys at the Swift plant. They had 8th grade educations. And now as they approach their 50th wedding anniversary, they don't have a lot of bucks. They're not written up in Who's Who. And Dan Rather doesn't interview them on the CBS Evening News. But that doesn't diminish the importance of their lives. They raised five kids and they raised us well. They overcame their problems. And they love each other. They taught us to work hard and care deeply. To suspect people on the make and still respect people who just can't make it. In the words of the song from the country-western band "Alabama:" "THEY DIDN'T KNOW NOTHING ABOUT A SILVER SPOON. BUT THEY KNEW A LOT ABOUT THE GOLDEN RULE." Thanks, mom and dad, for everything.

Speaking of getting back to fundamentals, I remember a Sunday twenty years ago when Coach Vince Lombardi watched his Green Bay Packers—the best team in football in the 60's—get absolutely slaughtered by the Chicago Bears—the worst team in football. (In those days, William "The Refrigerator" Perry was just a bouncing 100 pound baby boy).

Anyway, after that disastrous game, Lombardi got on the team bus. He was angry—really angry. And he shouted: "THIS TEAM IS GOING BACK TO FUNDAMENTALS. AND I MEAN REAL FUNDAMENTALS. AND WE'RE GOING TO START RIGHT NOW. THIS," he said holding up the ball, "IS A FOOTBALL." And from the back of the bus, player Max McGee shouted back: "HEY COACH . . . COULD YOU GO A LITTLE SLOWER? SOME OF THE GUYS AREN'T GETTING THIS ALL DOWN!"

Fifth, TRUST YOUR INSTINCTS. Your instincts come from the fundamentals. So develop good ones and depend on them.

In one of his last songs, John Lennon wrote that "life is what happens to you while you're busy making other plans." And sometimes, your instincts are all you've got to tell you you're moving in the right direction when everyone else is telling you you're going crazy.

Sometimes your instincts will tell you to break the rules. A couple of years ago, a small New York City advertising firm landed the account for NIKE shoes and sportswear. And they developed an ad campaign that everybody in the advertising industry predicted would be a disaster. Because they broke all the rules. They produced a series of billboard and magazine ads with people wearing Nike products. But the people didn't look like the glamorous and sophisticated sorts who lounge around. They were runners—dirty, sweaty, exhausted—finishing a race and looking like they were about to throw up. And the word NIKE appeared on the ad—not in huge letters at the top—but in tiny, almost unreadable letters at the bottom. The ad campaign failed miserably—right? Wrong! It boosted Nike sales by 25 percent and helped

make the firm one of the fastest growing, most successful advertising agencies in the world. That happened because those people trusted their instincts. But there's more to it: _Trust your instincts and never give up on yourself._ That's the sixth point.

Just a few years ago, a young writer named John Kennedy O'Toole won a Pulitzer Prize for his book "A Confederacy of Dunces." [sic] It was not a history of Congress or an analysis of this Administration's farm policy. Rather, it is hailed as one of the great humorous works of the 20th Century. But O'Toole never knew he'd won the Pulitzer Prize, because after having his manuscript rejected by 17 publishers, he took his own life.

His mother found the hand-typed manuscript when she was going through his things and she took it to publishers. The rest is history and the lesson is clear. Never, never give up on yourself—and never ever underestimate the power of others who love you and will never give up on you either.

When you make the commitment never to give up on yourself, you come to understand the last bit of advice I want to leave you with today. And it's simply that in your own life, and in the life of your country—ONE PERSON—YOU—CAN MAKE A PROFOUND AND LASTING DIFFERENCE.

It's easy to diminish our own importance. The mathematicians tell us that in terms of size, our significance is infinitesimal. A map of the universe that we know of would be 80 miles long. On that map, our galaxy would take up one 8 1/2 by 11 sheet. Our solar system would be a molecule on that sheet. And Earth would be a speck on the molecule. The astronauts tell us that as they observe Earth from outer space, they don't think about Star Wars defense systems. Instead they see Earth as one vulnerable ship Gallactica, riding through a cold and dangerous universe as the lone outpost of humanity.

We are the stewards of human progress on this planet. Human progress is a chain, and every generation forges a little piece of it. You've heard the old expression that a chain is only as strong as its weakest link. My challenge to you today is to do what you can in your own lives to strengthen your link and thereby hand down a stronger chain to the next generation.

That's what President Kennedy had in mind when he told us that from now on, every generation will have the capacity to make theirs the best in the history of the world—or the last. For from those to whom much is given, much is expected. Now, the great unfinished tasks are being passed into your hands. And your obligation is to carry on for those who have gone before and after you. Truly: "If it is to be . . . It is up to you."

IF JUSTICE IS FINALLY TO BE GAINED FOR THE OPPRESSED, it will be because your generation gives us people like Martin Luther King—who faced guns and police dogs because he believed that injustice *anywhere* is a threat to justice *everywhere*.

It will be because your generation gives us people like Lech Walesa—who stood before God and the world and insisted on basic human rights for Polish workers and farmers; Jacabo Timmerman—who had just toured the Argentinian jail cell where he was tortured—but this time as a free man; Cory Aquino, who with a yellow dress, tenacity and right, brought down a mighty and corrupt regime in the Philippines.

IF THE HUNGRY ARE TO BE FED, it will be because your generation gives the world people as committed as Harry Chapin, who gave the last years of his short life, not to the riches he could gain for himself as a singer, but instead to raising millions of dollars to help feed the hungry. Harry died on the way to one of those concerts. But just a few days ago, millions joined "Hands Across America" to help finish what he began.

IF OUR CHILDREN ARE TO HAVE CLEAN AIR, GREEN TREES AND CLEAN WATER, it will be because your generation gives the world more people like Lois Gibson—who risked her life to expose what the chemical companies had done at Love Canal.

AND IF WE ARE TO GET WASTEFUL SPENDING CHECKED, it will be because your generation gives us more people with the courage of Ernie Fitzgerald. He sacrificed a career at the Pentagon by telling what he knew about a $3 billion cost overrun for the C58 Transport Plane almost 20 years ago. Since then, he's been harassed, threatened and demoted. But he's still talking. And he's giving others the courage to talk about $5000 toilet seats and generals and admirals spending tax dollars like drunken ensigns and privates.

In short, WHEN OUR TWO TRILLION DOLLAR NATIONAL DEBT IS FINALLY PAID, WHEN RURAL AMERICA IS FINALLY SAVED, WHEN THE ARMS RACE IS ENDED BEFORE THE HUMAN RACE IS ENDED, it will be because your generation and those who come after you take to heart what Robert Kennedy told students just your age in South Africa 20 years ago. He said:

"EACH TIME A HUMAN BEING STANDS UP FOR AN IDEA . . . OR ACTS TO IMPROVE THE LOT OF OTHERS . . . OR STRIKES OUT AGAINST INJUSTICE . . . HE OR SHE SENDS OUT A TINY RIPPLE OF HOPE. IN CROSSING EACH OTHER FROM A MILLION DIFFERENT CENTERS OF ENERGY AND DARING, THOSE RIPPLES BUILD A MIGHTY CURRENT WHICH CAN SWEEP DOWN THE MOST TERRIBLE WALLS OF OPPRESSION AND INJUSTICE."

I submit that you do not represent America's last generation—but America's best generation. You will not find all the answers. The poet Carl Sandburg once wrote that as a nation, America is more the seeker than finder—ever seeking its way through storms and dreams.

And as you seek your way for yourself and America, you will have the tools you need. All the tools Americans have needed to overcome world wars, great depressions, and terrible natural disasters:

—The values of a just society.

—The strength of a revolutionary democracy.

—The power of a free economy.

—The muscle of a skilled workforce.

—The talents of an educated people.

But that's not enough. As the Book of Proverbs tell us, "where there is no vision, the people perish." We need the vision of a restless people.

Our vision for ourselves and our country should be as John Steinbeck described it:

"I SEE US . . . NOT IN THE SETTING SUN OF A DARK NIGHT OF DESPAIR AHEAD. I SEE US IN THE CRIMSON LIGHT OF A RISING SUN, FRESH FROM THE BURNING, CREATIVE HAND OF GOD. I SEE GREAT DAYS AHEAD. GREAT DAYS MADE POSSIBLE BY MEN AND WOMEN OF WILL AND VISION."

You are those men and women of will and vision. So go to work and carry on.

Thank you very much.

Appendix B

Applications

Contents

This appendix is divided into two major sections. The first section is a general guide to competitive speaking events. It includes brief descriptions of forensics contest activities in public speaking, oral interpretation, and debate. These competitive events are then tied to the skill areas you have been studying. The numbers in parentheses are references to the Chapters of this text that relate to skills involved in each event.

The second section of this appendix addresses the important topic of being interviewed. You will surely be interviewed for a job or as part of a school-application procedure, and your speech communication skills will serve you well in those situations. This section includes tips on preparing for and participating in an interview. Chapter references are given in parentheses after most items, so that you can practice developing your professional, interpersonal communication skills.

Your teacher can provide you with information about local and state tournaments and other public speaking opportunities. He or she may also be able to direct you to primary and secondary sources that will help you prepare for future interviews. In both cases, you will find that putting your communication skills in action can be an enjoyable and rewarding experience!

A Guide to Competitive Speaking Events

As you study speech communication, you will hear about debaters, people who perform "extemp," or dramatic interpretation. Your school or school district probably has a program for students who wish to apply their speech communication skills in competition. If you are interested in finding out about the competitive opportunities that are available to you, you may begin by reviewing this guide.

Competitive speaking "events" (sometimes called *forensics*) vary from school to school and state to state. Generally, however, they fall into the three broad categories of public speaking, oral interpretation, and debate. Public speaking activities usually include original oratory, extemporaneous speaking, and impromptu speaking. They may also include informative (or expository) speaking, and ceremonial (or special-occasion) speaking. Radio speaking is also an event in some states.

Interpretation events usually include the serious interpretation of prose and poetry, humorous interpretation of prose, and dramatic interpretation. Events may also include duet or choral reading and readers' theater. Interpretation is rarely mixed with "acting" or actual theater in competition.

In addition to the classic team format, debate has several other forms. One is Lincoln-Douglas debate, which take place between two people. Another form involves cross-examination by teams of students.

Individual students usually concentrate on one event or category of events. Some states may permit or encourage students to participate in combination events within certain categories. Your teacher can tell you about the activities available and direct you to new sources.

Public Speaking

Public speaking activities are usually defined by the types of preparation and delivery. There are, for example, contests in extemporaneous speaking, original oratory (memorized delivery), and impromptu speaking.

All of the events involve various preparation requirements and speaking time limits. Rules and guidelines are established by state associations or the schools involved in the competition.

Original Oratory

Oratory is a persuasive speaking event. The student must present a prepared, memorized speech. A copy of the speech manuscript is usually provided to the competition judges.

In oratory, you should choose a topic of interest and relevance, and choose your specific purpose to conform to the rules of the competition and the needs of the listeners. It is important that you take a position on an issue, use credible, appropriate evidence to support your claims, and provide alternative solutions to the issue or problem. You will be judged on your organized, convincing delivery. Every skill you apply—from topic limitation, through research, to language and rehearsal skills—will be evaluated by the judges.

Orators are given six to ten minutes to deliver their speeches. Consult the rules of your competition for further suggestions.

Extemporaneous Speaking

Extemporaneous speaking, or "extemp" as it is often called, involves preparing a speech *at* the competition. A student chooses one of several topics provided by the judges, and is given thirty minutes to one hour to prepare a speech that will be delivered from notes.

Extemp topics are usually related to current events in some way. Different contests may have categories of strictly informative or strictly persuasive topics. Topics may also be divided by national or international events and people.

Students participating in extemp base their speech preparation on their own ongoing, careful, current research. Extemp speakers read widely in periodicals and keep articles organized in files for easy reference. Students are expected to take a position or stand on the topic, follow a standard speech outline using careful organization, and offer alternative solutions.

Students are evaluated on their command of information, their approach to the topic, and on the quality of their sources and the evidence they choose to support their points. Students are usually given from five to ten minutes to present their speeches. Consult specific contest guidelines for further information.

Impromptu Speaking

Impromptu speaking involves a minimum of preparation. Topics are assigned to students *at* the competition and are changed from round to round of the competition. Topics are generally serious, but do *not* require extensive research or background knowledge in current events.

In some contests, students are given several minutes to prepare the speech, and another time limit for speaking (usually, from five to eight minutes). In other contests, students are given a total amount of time (for example, eight minutes) that they can choose to use however they wish (for example, no preparation, or four minutes of preparation and four minutes of speaking).

It is clear that impromptu speakers must be able to quickly organize their thoughts and plan supports and amplifying devices. Notes may or may not be allowed. Speakers are judged on their ability to devise an approach to the topic, organize their thoughts, and give a smooth presentation.

Important Skills

In choosing to participate in public speaking competition, students should understand the common features as well as the differences of the various contest events. Students should also understand how the competition is judged. The following aspects of preparation and delivery are usually evaluated in all competitive speaking events.

- **Analysis,** or the speaker's approach to the topic. Analysis may also reflect the speaker's research and knowledge of the topic. In impromptu, analysis is reflected in the speaker's stance concerning the topic. (5, 14, 21)

- **Research,** especially the credibility and relevance of the sources and evidence used in the speech. This aspect of preparation is particularly critical in oratory and extemp. (15, 17)

- **Organization,** following standard speech form and logical thought. Organization may be the primary consideration of judges in oratory and extemp. The organization should be appropriate to the speaker's chosen purpose. In all three types of competition, the speech should have a clear introduction, body, conclusion, and transitions. (16, 17, 21)

- **Using Proofs and Amplifying Devices** appropriately and effectively. In oratory and extemp, proofs must be chosen from existing research and should meet the standard tests for evidence. Sources should be credible. In impromptu speaking, proofs may not leap readily to mind. If they are used, they should be simple and highly appropriate. (15, 17, 21)

- **Using Language** in an articulate, precise, and pleasing manner. In oratory, language skills and choices will be refined during rehearsal. In extemp and impromptu speaking, no rehearsal is possible, so a speaker should be comfortable with standard usage, and should use language that is appropriate to the topic and the audience. (7, 18)

- **Memory and Concentration Skills,** which give a general impression of poise, confi-

dence, and command of the situation. Demonstrating a command of knowledge and information is often referred to as "the ability to think on your feet." (14, 18, 19)

- **Delivery** is crucial. The final vocal and physical presentation will determine the level of success. Presentations include good posture, eye contact, and the production of clear, resonant sounds. In oratory, rehearsal and practice are essential. The speaker's confidence in his or her ability to deliver the speech smoothly will help any presentation. (6, 19)

As a final step, you will want to consult your teacher or school forensics coach, and look over contest manuals and guidelines provided by the organization sponsoring the activity or contest.

Oral Interpretation

Oral interpretation is the act of sharing a literary work with an audience in a way that brings to life the literature's meaning, feeling, beauty, and significance. There are several competitive events that are basically contests in oral interpretation. The most common are defined by _genre_ (or kinds of literature), such as poetry, prose, and drama.

Other events are identified by their purposes. One is humorous interpretation, designed to entertain; another is the compiled script, designed to make a statement or to develop a theme. Serious dramatic interpretation may be included here. In some competitions, group reading or "readers' theater" may be listed as events.

No matter what the event, there are definite criteria to meet in selecting literature, and some important steps to follow in preparing it for performance. Performances have assigned time limits. Some competitions may require interpreting a combination of prose and poetry or a group of short selections. If you are interested in participating in oral interpretation events, talk with your teacher and consult local or state guidelines for competition.

The skills involved in interpretation can be divided into three broad areas:

1. Selection and analysis of the literature

2. Adaptation of the literature for performance

3. Performance of the literature

The interpreter's ethical responsibility is to preserve the integrity of the author and of the literature in all aspects of preparation and performance. Distortion of the text should be avoided.

Selecting and Analyzing Literature

Selection
Selecting literature for performance involves criteria similar to those used in selecting topics for speeches. (14)

- The literature should be appropriate to the reader.

- The literature should be appropriate to the audience.

- The literature should be appropriate to the occasion (contest guidelines must be considered).

- The literature should meet the requirements of 1) a universal human experience or theme, 2) originality, and 3) suggestion. *Suggestion* refers to the imagery evoked by the selection. The best performance material has strong imagery, and is written in an oral style with the tone of human speech. It must also have whatever spe-

cial literary characteristics the competition dictates.

Analysis
Once you have selected the piece or pieces you will interpret, read them in their entirety. Then follow the steps below. (7, 18, 20)

- Analyze the selection paragraph by paragraph or verse by verse for general meaning.

- Analyze the selection sentence by sentence or line by line for specific meaning.

- Analyze the selection phrase by phrase for figures of speech and imagery.

- Analyze the selection word by word for tone, texture, connotation, denotation, and synthesis of sense and sound.

- Describe the writer's style as a guide to performance style.

- Trace the emotional events in the piece.

- Analyze the *persona* (the character of the author or speaker in the literature).

- Analyze the *locus* (the place) and the time.

- Analyze the shifts in *personae* and *loci*.

- Analyze the attitude of the author *and* the narrator toward the situation, action, and characters.

- Determine performance choices, based on analysis (how you will use manuscript, body, and voice).

Some literature requires additional analysis. Poetry needs to be generally defined as lyric, narrative, or dramatic in mode and performed accordingly. It requires special attention to emotion, imagery, line lengths, meter (rhythm or beat), and sound. Dramatic literature needs analysis of the element of conflict, and as in prose fiction, the performer should understand the purpose of each character in the selection.

Humorous literature must be analyzed and rehearsed with great attention to timing and pacing. Not all humorous writing was meant to be read aloud! In preparing a compiled script, there must be a clear thesis, a developmental sequence, and transitions that create a smooth flow of content.

Conducting Research

Once a selection is analyzed, it is important to investigate the context in which it was written and elements within the piece that deserve further explanation. Research provides both the performer and the audience with a basis for understanding and appreciating the selection. (7, 15, 20)

- Investigate the author for insights into the literature.

- Investigate literary criticism that is focused on the particular selection or on the writer's general works, to open doors to understanding and provide depth in the performance.

- Investigate the author's *allusions* (indirect references) to history, social issues or conditions, geographical regions or customs, or other literature (especially to mythology, Shakespeare, or scripture). This will provide knowledge and a depth of understanding that will be helpful in interpretation.

- Look up the meaning, pronunciation, connotation, and denotation of unfamiliar or questionable words or terms.

Adapting Literature for Performance

Transforming a written text into an oral performance often requires making a major adaptation. Frequently, interpreters lift scenes or make cuttings from text to accommodate time restrictions. Interpreters may also combine selections into a "program" (or a compiled script) to make a comment or develop a theme.

Making Cuttings

Prose selections must frequently be cut to a performance length. Great care must be taken to preserve the integrity of the literature. It is, in fact, often preferable to select a scene of appropriate length and to preserve the scene in its entirety. In either instance, continuity is important. It is difficult to attempt to tell an *entire* story, unless the selection is short and requires only minor adaptation.

Poetry cannot be cut in the sense of deleting lines or words, because of the condensation of ideas and the form of poetry in general. Sections of poems that are already divided may be performed as segments, however.

Programming

Interpreters may wish to combine pieces of literature into a *program* to focus on a theme or make a statement about an author. Programs are similar in form to speeches. Skills in selecting and limiting topics, selecting a purpose, and organizing a speech can be useful in preparing programs for performance. Care should be taken in selecting literature to provide variety among lengthy selections, or perhaps to vary the mood or tone of the program. (14, 16)

Developing Introductions

As in public speaking, the purpose of the introduction is to prepare the listener for the experience (intellectual, emotional, and sensory) and to establish communication with the audience. Introductions should be presented in a personal and conversational manner.

The introduction should focus the attention of the listener on the particular elements of the literature that the interpreter feels are crucial for understanding and appreciating the work. For example, the interpreter may talk about plot, character, setting, theme, and/or the writer's style. (16)

The introduction must include the name of the author and the title of the selection. Interpreters may use quotations or excerpts from their investigation of the author and his or her works, when appropriate. One word of caution: The introduction should arouse curiosity and make the listener want to hear the selection. Therefore, it is best to avoid revealing the complete plot or including more information than the audience needs to appreciate and enjoy the presentation. (15, 17)

Rehearsal

When you know the guidelines of the competition in which you will participate, and have selected and adapted the pieces you will interpret, you must rehearse your delivery. It is best to rehearse before an audience—friends, family, or classmates—as often as possible. You will find that you will make final cuts and adjustments to the selections based on your rehearsal experience.

It is important to rehearse with an audience so that you may see if their reactions coincide with your intentions. If you are interpreting humorous material, you must learn when to leave time for laughter in your delivery. Of course, you will also rehearse by yourself, and you may find that taping your presentation is useful. Strive for an effective reading, but avoid being melodramatic. Practice your nonverbal cues, so that they seem natural and "in character."

If your selection includes dialogue, you will want to establish a vocal representation for each character. You may eliminate phrases such as "he says" or "she answered" if you have established convincing tones. Experiment with pacing, rhythm, and accent. Refine your performance through repeated rehearsals. (19)

Performing the Selection

Performance styles vary. However, interpretation is an act of sharing a literary text with an audience. Your performance choices should be based on your research and analysis of the selection. Also, the more you perform and hear others perform, the more familiar you will become with the styles that best suit your chosen genre or collection of materials.

The primary criterion for evaluating the interpreter's performance lies in the question, "Did the interpreter share the essence of the literature with the audience in an appropriate manner?" Performance techniques should never be obvious or detract the listeners' attention from the literature. Instead, the interpreter should seem to be speaking in the voice of the writer or character. A performance works best when it seems to the audience to be a natural reading and interpretation of the literature.

Debate

Debate is the organized, formal presentation of issues in support of and in opposition to a stated resolution or proposition, the relative strength of which is judged by a third party.

This definition reflects debate's relationship to the communication skills you have studied. We usually communicate to reach mutual understanding and consensus of opinion. You have seen that we can use group process as one means of exploring issues and reaching agreement. Sometimes, however, group process does not result in agreement. When this occurs, we turn to persuasive speaking as a means of securing agreement for the position we support. If our efforts at persuasive speaking do not succeed, the next logical step is debate. In debate, we:

1. Identify an issue and take a position of either affirmative or negative.

2. Generate reasons for our position.

3. Support our viewpoint with specific facts and examples.

4. Anticipate the arguments of the opposition and refute them.

Points to Consider

I. **Resolution:** A declarative statement of the debate topic, calling for a change from the current situation (or _status quo_) and worded so that there are valid arguments for both sides. A typical resolution might be:

Resolved: that Americans arrested abroad as mercenaries should forfeit their rights of citizenship.

II. **Sides:**

A. **Affirmative:** Those who debate on the affirmative side will _support_ the resolution. They will present reasons for the indicated action and will support those reasons with evidence, both factual and emotional.

B. **Negative:** Those who debate on the negative side will _oppose_ the resolution. They will present reasons against the indicated action and will support those reasons with evidence, both factual and emotional.

III. **Formats:**

A. **Team** — two individuals take the affirmative position and two take the negative position.

B. **Individual** — (often called "Lincoln-Douglas debate") one person takes the affirmative position and one takes the negative.

IV. **Time and Order:** Because debate is argumentation, not arguing, it is formalized and regulated by rules. These rules ensure fairness. They also ensure that the judge's decision is based on which side has the best logic and proof, rather than on who has the loudest voice or the most intimidating manner.

One rule is that the affirmative side that is asking for a change gets to speak first and last. The affirmative position in debate is much like the prosecutor in a court; the affirmative is saying that the way we are doing something is "guilty of" needing improvement or change.

The negative side, which is essentially defending things as they are, gets a lengthy period of time in the middle of the debate to speak without interruption. In team debate, this is called the _negative block._

Another rule to ensure fairness is the time rule. Each side will have exactly the same amount of total time to speak, although the time may be divided differently for the two sides. (2)

Case Construction

Each side must construct the strongest possible case for the position it has taken. Research is essential to debate. In addition, the organization of arguments will be vital in debate. (15, 16, 21)

Not only does a debater have to think of the arguments in _favor_ of the chosen position, a good debater anticipates what the other side will offer as arguments. A good debater builds the evidence and logic to defeat those arguments. This is called *refutation.* An effective debater also determines what arguments the opposition might offer in refutation of his or her *own* case, and plans ways to counter them. This is called *rebuttal.* (4, 8, 9)

There are special speaking times designated for building your own case. These are called the *constructive speeches,* and are the first ones given. The special speeches for refutation and rebuttal are called *rebuttal speeches* and are given last.

Judging

The presence of a judge or panel of judges is one of the unique parts of debate as a communication activity. Judges will usually have a ballot, and will be given specific criteria on which to judge the debate. Evaluation may be made on a combination of elements: organization, support, refutation, strength of arguments, and delivery of materials.

Debate is a specialized, formalized communication activity. The ability to debate effectively has been the trademark of lawyers, ministers, and theoreticians for centuries. Debate is a skill in itself, which can give important dividends if its component skills are acquired and used responsibly.

A Guide to Being Interviewed

Communication skills are extremely important in the business world. Before you are hired for part-time or full-time work, you must communicate with a prospective employer in a job interview. Colleges, universities, and training schools often interview applicants as well. In all cases, a decision may be greatly influenced by the impressions you make at the first meeting. Being prepared and aware of the interviewing process will increase your chances for success!

Preparation

Preparation is essential to your success in an interview.

- Begin to prepare early. Learn as much as possible about the company or school to which you are applying. How big is it? How long has it been operating? Does it have a good reputation? Is it financially sound? If you are planning for a job interview, find out if the company's employees are unionized. Are they happy? On a school interview, try to learn about the student body. (15)

- Salary or scholarship money is not the only consideration. You should seek to join a firm or attend a school whose philosophies and policies are compatible with your own system of ethics. (5)

- Find out who will interview you and learn about his or her title and role in the organization. Be sure you can pronounce the interviewer's name correctly. (9)

- Next, give serious thought to the responses you can make to questions that are often asked in interviews, such as why you are interested in the position, the company, or the school. You will also be asked to describe your work or educational history and how your past experience qualifies you for the position or school. (5, 9)

- If you have prepared a resume or an application, make sure the interviewer has a copy of it before you meet, and plan answers to questions that may be based on the information you have provided. (8)

- Be prepared to discuss the kind of work or subjects you like best, your long-term career goals, how you expect to achieve your goals, and how this position or school fits into your plans. (3, 5)

- In a job interview, be ready to explain why you left your previous positions. Some interviewers ask applicants to describe their attitudes about work, supervision, and employers. They will definitely want to know about your formal training and any special skills you have. They may want to know how many days you have missed work or school during the past six months or a year. (5)

- In a job interview, also be prepared to ask some questions of your own about the specific responsibilities of the position, the potential for advancement, and who your supervisor would be. What training programs are there? Are there fringe benefits or incentives? If you ask questions of this kind and listen carefully to the answers, the interviewer will understand that you have serious interest in the position and the company. (15)

- Remember that while the interviewer is deciding whether you will fit into the organization or school, you must decide whether you really want to work for the company or attend the school. The match between employee and employer or student and school should be positive for both. (4, 5)

- Plan what you will wear. You should dress appropriately. It may not be necessary to look fashionable, but it is important to look businesslike. Above all, you will want to look clean and neat. Dark, solid colors or subdued patterns are the best fabric choices. (6)

- On the day of the interview, you should make a special effort to be rested and look your best. (3)

- Know the exact location of the interview site and plan your transportation there.

Plan your time carefully, and arrive for the interview a few minutes early.

Participating in the Interview

Remember that an interview is an interpersonal communication situation. Using your skills in perception, nonverbal communication, and the use of language will contribute to effective interaction and success.

- Greet the interviewer pleasantly by name. Smile, and give her or him a firm handshake. Remember that your posture, direct eye contact, and movement can make a positive first impression. (6, 9)

- Be aware of your nonverbal messages. Look confident, but avoid overconfidence. Sit comfortably erect and face the interviewer. Avoid slouching or fidgeting. (6)

- A good interviewer will begin and end the interview with a bit of informal conversation to let you relax and adjust to the setting. _Use_ that time to relax and focus your attention on the interview and your goal. (3, 8)

- Look at the interviewer and show interest. Keep your voice pleasant and interested. Speak up so you can be heard, but avoid talking or laughing loudly. (6)

- Be open and honest, and look for the same honesty from the interviewer.

- Never misrepresent your qualifications.

- Be sure you understand the expectations the company or school will have of you.

- If you do not understand a question, be sure to clarify it before replying. Do not be afraid to take time to think before answering a question, or to ask questions about anything that is unclear. (4, 8, 9)

The questions you are asked in an employment interview must be concerned with real occupational qualifications. It is unlawful to be asked questions relating to gender, age, race, religion, or marital status. If you are asked such questions, or questions that seem flirtatious, avoid making rude replies, but do not feel pressured to answer. Instead, with good humor ask, "Is that information essential?" or "How might that relate to the responsibilities of the position?" If the question has been asked thoughtlessly, the interviewer will quickly revise the line of questioning. If not, you may want to reconsider your interest in the organization. (4, 5)

- Remember that refusing to answer an interview question will make a negative impression. It is wise to be aware of this in considering a response to a poor question. Try to think of pleasant ways to respond to such questions by focusing clearly on the job being discussed. (8)

- Before leaving, ask if there is any further information you can supply, and when a decision will be reached.

- Thank the interviewer as you leave.

Following Up

The interviewing process is not complete until you have followed through by acknowledging the interview and assessing your perfomance.

- Immediately following an interview, you should write a brief note, thanking the interviewer for his or her consideration (or for a pleasant interview), and stating that you will look forward to seeing him or her again.

- The note should be mailed the same day as the interview, if possible. A courteous follow-up note indicates that you understand etiquette and that you are a thoughtful person. (9)

- Whether or not you get the job or are accepted into the school, you should mentally review the steps you followed in the interview process, the questions asked, and the answers you gave. Think of better ways to carry out every step and to answer every question. If there were surprise questions, think about appropriate ways to answer them in case they are asked in another interview. You can become a better interviewee with every interview. (2)

Glossary

The numbers that follow the entries indicate the chapter in which the glossary word is introduced.

accommodation   in communication, a strategy for resolving conflict that involves giving in to the wishes of another person. (9)

act   a behavior that begins and ends within a specific time frame. Compare to *process*. (1)

agenda   in problem-solving and parliamentary groups, the outline for discussion during a meeting, based on the order of business and including the specific topics to be discussed. (12,13)

alliteration   the repetition of initial consonant sounds. (18)

amplifying device   information that adds depth to a point in a speech by enlarging, extending, or clarifying an idea. (17)

antithesis   a rhetorical strategy that involves placing two contrasting ideas into a similar structure. (18)

appropriateness   in communication, the basic principle of making choices that reflect good judgment and represent ethical and artistic standards expected in a particular instance. (2)

articulation   1. the formation of speech sounds. 2. the clarity and distinctness of consonant sounds. (6, 19)

artistic judgment   a critical perspective that involves making a judgment based on style and the application of skills. (20)

attitude   a belief, opinion, or feeling resulting from a series of experiences. (5)

autocratic style   a kind of organizational leadership in which the leader keeps firm control and retains all decision-making power (also called *authoritative style*). (11)

avoidance   in communication, a strategy for resolving conflicts that involves denial that a problem exists, refusal to discuss a problem, or discussion of superficial issues. (9)

background   in the first transition section of a speech, material designed to convey the history of the topic, the current status of the topic, or the speaker's stance or value position. (16)

barrier   an obstruction to communication that can exist within any variable in the process. (1)

beauty   an element of style involving the image and emotional response evoked by language through the meaning and sound of words. (18)

body   the section of a speech in which points are stated, supported and amplified, restated, and related to one another. (16)

body image   an aspect of physical self-concept; the picture an individual has of his or her own physical appearance. (3)

brainstorming   in group communication, a process by which a small group generates creative ideas, usually relating to problem solving. (12)

brief   a rough manuscript for a speech, combining the basic outline with supporting and amplifying devices. (17)

burnout   a state of hopelessness that results from unrelieved stress. (9)

buzz group   in group problem solving, a small discussion group that studies and reports on a portion of the topic to the entire group. (12)

bylaws written rules used in formal groups. (12,13)

c _____

card catalogue an index of books referenced by title, author, and subject, used in a library or media center. (15)

casual group a group that is unstructured and whose activities are generally unplanned; a group that develops spontaneously and exists only as long as it is beneficial or convenient to members. (10)

cause-effect order a form of problem-solution order. (16)

ceremonial speech a speech for a special occasion or a special purpose, which inspires, unites, or entertains. (14, 21)

channel in the communication process, the means for interaction, or the space through which messages pass from one person to another. See also *medium. (1)*

choice in communication, the basic principle of making decisions relating to communication skills and strategies. (2)

chronological order the arrangement of points in a speech according to a time sequence. (16)

citation an exact, complete record of the source of a quotation or idea. (15)

clarity an element of style involving the precise use of language. (18)

classification in the speech preparation process, the assigning of a topic to a category (such as person, concept, event) according to the speaker's approach. (14)

climax a rhetorical strategy involving a series of statements that lead to an emotional peak or turning point. (18)

coercion in communication, a strategy for resolving conflicts that involves forcing someone to bow to the will of another. (9)

collaboration in communication, a strategy for resolving conflict that involves mutual, creative thinking about and discussion of alternatives; often combined with confrontation. (9)

colloquial usage the employment of language appropriate to a particular area or region. (7)

commitment the investment of time and energy in a relationship. (9)

committee in group communication, a subdivision of the total group that addresses a particular task or responsibility. (10)

communication the process of exchanging messages; interaction and negotiation. (1, 2)

communication apprehension anxiety experienced prior to communicating or speaking before an audience; "stage fright"; fear of initiating an interaction. (2, 19)

communication attraction an immediate sense of wanting to communicate with another individual. (9)

communication competence what an individual knows about communication process and theory. (2)

comparison an amplifying device that involves pointing out similarities between listeners' experiences and the topic or point being presented. (17)

competitiveness a barrier to effective communication that reflects diminished trust, may result in unethical behavior, and limits equality and positiveness in an interaction. (2)

conclusion the final section of a speech, which rounds out the topic and often includes strong emotional appeals.(16)

conflict a struggle between two forces. (9)

confrontation in communication, a strategy for resolving conflict that involves open, honest discussion of issues; often combined with collaboration. (9)

connotation the implied or suggested meaning of a word. See also *denotation. (7)*

consensual perception an impression shared by group members, or an agreement that an impression is shared. (4)

consensual reality the result of compared perceptions that encourages group members to affirm, as reality, the perceptions they share. (4)

consensus in group process, a total agreement among group members. (11)

context in the communication process, the environment in which interaction occurs; the situational component of the communication process. (1)

contrast an amplifying device that involves sharpening listeners' perception of a point by saying what it is *not*. (17)

critic an individual who observes, analyzes, and sometimes expresses a judgment about a performance or a work of art. (20)

critical listening a level of listening for the purpose of evaluating ideas and making decisions, requiring high energy and focused attention. (8)

critical perspective in evaluating speeches, a set of criteria for judging the style and content of a performance. (20)

d —————————————————————

decoding in communication, the filtering process used to interpret meaning, which personalizes the message being sent or received. (1)

defensiveness a barrier to effective communication that may lead to unethical behavior involving self-protection and secrecy, and which limits positiveness in the interaction. (2)

definition 1. in limiting a topic, the process of deciding what a topic means to the individual speaker. 2. in the first transition of a speech, a clarification and limitation of the topic for the audience. (14, 16)

delivery in public speaking, the skill cluster that includes all verbal and nonverbal aspects of presentation. (14)

democratic style a kind of organizational leadership in which the leader encourages all members to participate in the responsibility for group decisions. (11)

denotation the literal meaning of a word. See also *connotation*. (7)

description an amplifying device that helps listeners to experience a topic as the speaker does. (17)

dialect the oral language of a particular region, culture, or group; the unique characteristics of a group or their oral language. (7)

diction 1. the overall clarity of speech. 2. the shaping of sounds and syllables into intelligible speech. 3. the structuring of words into phrases and sentences. (7, 18, 19)

dilemma a situation, often involving ethical choices, in which there is no "right" or "wrong" answer, or in which an individual cannot find a desirable solution. (9)

duration in communication, the length, in time, of a unit of sound. (7)

e —————————————————————

effective communication an interaction in which the message in the mind of the sender/receiver is accurately recreated in the mind of the receiver/sender. (2)

emotional component in relation to *message,* the portion of the message that is usually transmitted nonverbally and has to do with feelings. Also called *relationship component.* (1)

emotional self the aspect of self-concept that involves an awareness and expression of feelings. (3)

empathic listening a level of listening for the purpose of interpersonal understanding, requiring energy to tune out noise, recall messages, and tune in to the emotional component of messages. (8)

empathy an aspect of effective communication involving "feeling with" another person; putting oneself in another's place; trying to see another's point of view. (2, 8)

encoding in communication, the process of assigning meaning by placing concepts into a code, which involves classifying, organizing, and naming the concepts. (1)

enunciation the clarity and distinctness of vowel sounds. (19)

equality in effective communication, the concept that individuals have equal rights, and should be given equal respect and equal opportunity to participate in interactions. (2)

ethical proof   a form of evidence made up of personal experiences or insghts. (15, 17)

ethics   in communication, an individual code or system of choices and behaviors through which a person interacts with others; standards of conduct and moral judgment. (5)

ethos   speakers image; characteristic attitudes and habits; in speaking, elements of ethos include sound qualifications, good character, and good intent. (14)

example   an amplifying device that involves providing listeners with real, hypothetical, or literary instances or demonstrations of a point. (17)

experience   a root of attitudes, values, and priorities; a stimulus plus a response. (5)

extemporaneous delivery   a speech presentation involving the use of a few well-planned notes, allowing the speaker freedom to adapt the speech during presentation. (19)

eye contact   an aspect of nonverbal communication. (6, 19)

f _____

facial communication   eye contact and facial animation; an important aspect of nonverbal communication that reflects and enhances the verbal message. (6, 19)

facilitator   a leader who makes the work of the group easier. (11)

feedback   a verbal or nonverbal response to a message; the response of the receiver/sender as it is seen, heard, or perceived by the sender/receiver. (1, 8)

figures of speech   devices that make language artistic, visual, and memorable. (18)

first transition   a link or bridge between the introduction and the body of a speech, designed to prepare the audience for understanding the points developed in the speech. (16)

force   1. the energy or intensity of the voice, which can balance volume. 2. an element of style involving the energy or intensity of the message. (6, 18)

formal group   a group that is carefully structured and whose activities are carefully organized (often with parliamentary rules); a group with a name, a statement of purpose, and bylaws. (10)

formal usage   the employment of language that is appropriate for special tasks and for occasions that require a definite format. (7)

frustration   the feeling that results from an inability to make choices or resolve problems. (9)

g _____

gesture   a movement of the body that supports, reinforces, or indicates meaning; movement used to enhance a point in a speech. (6, 19)

grammar   a component of language relating to rules of structure. (7)

group   in communication, a collection of more than two individuals who communicate face to face, work together toward a common goal, think of the group as a unit, and recognize group norms. (10)

group communication   the sending and receiving of messages through direct interaction among a number of individuals. (2)

h _____

hearing   the physical process of receiving sound from the environment. (8)

heirarchy of needs   Abraham Maslow's ranking of human needs, from basic survival needs, through security, social, and esteem needs, to self-actualization needs. (5)

i _____

imaging   in speech preparation and rehearsal, a process of visualizing the actual performance to determine desired behavior and results. (19)

impromptu delivery   a speech presentation made without time for formal preparation. (19)

incidental motion   in parliamentary groups, a statement used to appeal a decision of the chair, suspend rules, raise a point of order, withdraw a motion, or divide the question under consideration. (13)

individual value   a belief or principle concerning the worth and dignity of individuals. (5)

inflection   the rising or falling of a voice on a musical scale. See also *pitch*. (6)

informal usage   the employment of language that is appropriate for casual conversations and in close relationships. (7)

informational listing   a level of listening for the purpose of acquiring ideas or facts to be remembered, requiring energy to tune out noise and recall the message. (8)

informative speech   a speech that imparts knowledge and creates interest in a topic. (14, 21)

intellectual component   in relation to *message,* the portion of the message that is usually transmitted verbally and has to do with ideas. (1)

intellectual self   the aspect of self-concept that involves an awareness and assessment of one's mental ability, one's mental ability compared to that of others, one's capability of thinking clearly and productively, one's expectations for mental accomplishment, and one's willingness to attempt mental tasks. (3)

intention   in communication, the purpose a communicator feels or assigns to an expression or interaction, which guides choices related to the means of expression. (8)

interaction diagram   a picture of the communication pattern that is developing in a group. (11)

interaction pattern   the network of communication among all members of a group. (11)

internal preview   a means of providing "memory hooks" for listeners as points are developed, by warning or clueing them into items to be discussed. (16)

internal summary   a means of providing "memory hooks" for listeners as points are developed, by wrapping up information or reminding listeners of what they have already heard. (16)

interpersonal communication   the sending and receiving of messages through direct interaction between two or several individuals. (1)

interpretation   In perception, the process of assigning meaning to selected, organized stimuli, which can involve imagining, making assumptions, and making decisions. (4)

intrapersonal communication   the sending and receiving of messages within an individual; "self-talk"; internal dialogue. (1)

introduction   the section of a speech in which the speaker gets the audience's attention, creates interest in the topic, demonstrates ethos, and sets the tone of the speech. (16)

invention   See *selection*.

j _____

jargon   a type of slang involving a specialized vocabulary shared by people within a group or profession. (7)

judgment by ethical standards   a critical perspective that involves making a judgment in terms of a personal response to what is "good" or "bad"; such a judgment does not involve critical thinking. (20)

judgment by results   a critical perspective that involves making a judgment based on a competitive outcome. (20)

l _____

laissez-faire style   a kind of organizational leadership in which the leader does not interfere in the activities of group members. (11)

language   a code for exchanging messages; a system of symbols (words or gestures, for example) used to exchange messages. (7)

listening the mental process of focusing attention, interpreting, and understanding what is heard. (8)

logical proof a form of evidence made up of statistics, specific instances, and testimony. (15, 17)

m _____

main motion in parliamentary groups, a statement used to propose business about which the group should decide. (13)

maintenance roles group member roles that center on making the group's work pleasant and comfortable. (11)

majority decision in parliamentary groups, a decision reached by voting, in which the larger number of voters carries the motion; the minority (or smaller block of voters) agrees to abide by the outcome of the vote. (13)

manuscript delivery a speech presentation read from written manuscript, often used on special occasions or in formal addresses. (19)

marginal member in a group, someone who has limited power and receives limited acceptance and consideration. (10)

mass communication the sending and receiving of messages through electronic or printed channels (media), usually involving large numbers of people. (1)

medium in the communication process, the channel for interaction; the vehicle by which a message passes from one person to another. See also *channel.* (1)

memorized delivery a speech presentation made from memory, often used in contest competition. (19)

memory in public speaking, the skill cluster related to recalling ideas and information. (14)

message an idea, concept, or feeling that is assigned meaning and transmitted by a sender/receiver and is acquired and assigned meaning by a receiver/sender. (1)

metaphor a figure of speech; a stated or implied comparison that does not involve the use of *like* or *as.* (18)

moderator the organizational leader in public discussion. (12)

moral value a belief or principle concerning what is "right" and "wrong." (5)

motion in parliamentary groups, a formal proposal for group action. (13)

motivation device in the first transition of a speech, a language strategy used to create interest in a topic toward which an audience may feel neutral or negative. (16)

movement a change in the position of the body from one space to another; in public speaking, a motivated shift in body position. (6, 19)

n _____

needs inborn human drives or urges. (5)

negative roles group member roles that work against group goals and activities, and which may create conflict. (11)

negotiation in communication, a strategy for resolving conflict that involves bargaining, with each party trading to get something he or she values. (9)

noise any temporary condition that interferes with the communication process. (1)

nonverbal communication all communication behavior *other than* speech, including both silent language and sound language. (6)

nonverbal message a message transmitted by actions and/or vocalizations. (1)

norms the rules of a group; standards of conduct or ways of doing things that are accepted without discussion. (10)

nuclear member in a group, someone who is part of the central core of decision makers and has power. (10)

o _____

obscenity temporal language involving the use of body-related terms or phrases with negative connotations. (7)

openness a characteristic of effective communication that reflects a willingness to share, to listen, and to be involved in new experiences. (2)

order of business in parliamentary groups, a master plan for conducting a meeting that lists the sequence in which each division of work will be handled at every meeting. (13)

organization 1. In perception, the process of making sense of selected stimuli, which may involve sorting, stereotyping, categorizing, enlarging, and creating closure. 2. in public speaking, the skill cluster related to arranging the elements of a speech into a particular form. (4, 14)

organizational leader in a group, the individual who presides over group activities, applies problem-solving techniques, gives all members a fair hearing, and keeps members from manipulating one another. (11)

P _____

panel discussion a form of public discussion designed to inform or persuade an audience, involving a small group of participants and an organizational leader. (12)

pause silence that is used for vocal punctuation. (7)

paralinguistic cues vocal adaptations including the qualities of voice that convey direct, subtle, or implied meanings and feelings along with the language message. (7)

parallelism a rhetorical strategy that involves using similar words, phrases, or sentences to introduce ideas. (18)

parliamentary rules a system of group process designed to protect rights of freedom of speech, freedom to hold meetings, and freedom to form organizaitons based on common goals; used in legislative and deliberative groups. (13)

pathetic proof a form of evidence used for emotional appeal. (15, 17)

perception the process of noticing the developing mental impressions of persons or things; perception occurs in three states— selecting, organizing, and interpreting. (4)

perception check in communication, an intentional pause used to clarify the meanings

the participants have assigned to messages, in order to ensure that perceptions match. (4)

perceptual readiness in perception, a condition of expecting to find or being "ready" to notice some stimuli. (4)

periodicals magazines or newspapers that are printed on a regular basis. (15)

personification a figure of speech that involves assigning human qualities or behaviors to objects or concepts. (18)

persuasion a communication designed to change a listener's perceptions, attitudes, beliefs, or values. (8)

persuasive speech a speech designed to change an audience's perception of facts, to change an audience's attitudes or feelings, to encourage audience concern for a problem, or to encourage an audience to take action. (14, 21)

phonation the formation of sound resulting from the passage of air over the vocal folds. (6)

physical self the aspect of self-concept that involves an awareness and assessment of the space one's body needs and of one's appearance, health and well being, coordination and agility, and sensory perception. (3)

pitch the highness or lowness of a sound on a musical scale. See also *inflection*. (6)

positiveness a characteristic of effective communication that reflects an amount and quality of energy invested in an interaction, which serves to move an interaction or relationship forward. (2)

posture 1. the position of the body. 2. an aspect of nonverbal communication that reflects a level of confidence. (6, 19)

practical value a belief or principle relating to what is useful or efficient in everyday activity. (5)

precedence in parliamentary groups, the priority of motions. (13)

prejudice a barrier to effective communication that involves making a judgment based on previous (vs. current) experience, or making a judgment that is not based on personal knowledge. (2)

presiding officer   the elected organizational leader of a formal, task-oriented group. (12)

preview   in the first transition, a plan presented to the audience to help them identify the points of the speech. (16)

primary (predetermined) group   a group in which membership usually begins at birth and that usually includes a lifelong commitment; a principle source of physical and emotional support. (10)

primary research   gathering information from personal sources or other people. (15)

priorities   in communication, the degree of importance assigned to particular values. (5)

privileged motion   in parliamentary groups, a statement related to emergency situations, including motions to adjourn or recess and questions of privilege. (13)

problem-solution order   an arrangement of points in a speech from facts, to problems, to solution, or from cause, to effect, to solution. (16)

process   an ongoing, cyclical series of events and interactions. Compare to *act.* (1)

profanity   temporal language involving the use of god-related terms or phrases with negative connotations. (7)

projection   in speech communication, a vocal activity combining force and volume to make sure that all listeners will hear the message. (19)

pronunciation   the general sounding of a word as described in a dictionary. (7)

proposition of fact   a type of persuasive speech designed to convince listeners that something is true or false. (21)

proposition of policy   a type of persuasive speech designed to convince listeners that something should be done to solve a problem or to prevent a problem from occuring. (21)

proposition of value   a type of persuasive speech designed to convince listeners that something is good or bad. (21)

proposition to create concern for a problem   a type of persuasive speech designed to convince listeners that a significant problem exists. (21)

public communication   The sending of messages by a single speaker to an audience of receivers in a public-speaking context. (1)

q _____

quality   in communication, unique characteristics of an individual voice. (6)

r _____

rate   the speed of speech. (7)

reasoning errors   misleading or confusing patterns of logic used by a speaker, which can be detected through critical listening. (8)

receiver/sender   in the communication process, an individual who acquires a message and transmits feedback. (1)

recreational listing   a level of listening for the purpose of enjoyment, requiring attention to the extent that interfering noise must be tuned out. (8)

reference group   a group that is significant to an individual, against whose expectations the individual evaluates and adapts his or her behavior. (10)

relationship   a bonding between two or more individuals, which is a result of interaction between the individuals. (9)

relationship component   See *emotional component.*

repertoire   a collection of pieces used for performance. (18)

repression   the denial of feelings. (3)

resonation   enrichment and amplification of sound in the head and chest. (6)

resonance   vocal variations reinforced or amplified by resonation. (6, 19)

respiration   breathing. (6)

response the receiver/sender's voluntary or involuntary, physical or mental reaction to a stimulus or a message, which is largely a product of individual perception. (1, 8)

responsibility in communication, the basic principle of holding oneself answerable or accountable for one's choices and behaviors. (2)

rhetorical analysis. a process of evaluating speech manuscripts, recordings, or videotapes. (20)

rhetorical question a question intended to provoke thought or interest instead of an answer. (16, 18)

rhetorical strategy in speaking, a device used to create a special effect in a particular instance. (18)

s ———————————————

sample in research, the group responding to a survey. (15)

second in parliamentary groups, a statement made to open a motion to discussion. (13)

secondary research information gathered from print or electronic media. (15)

second thesis statement in the second transition, the final expression of the topic and purpose of the speech. (16)

second transition a link or bridge between the body and the conclusion of a speech, designed to put points into final focus or perspective. (16)

selection 1. in perception, the process of choosing to notice or focus on particular stimuli, which is influenced by conditions within the perceiver, the situation, or the object perceived. 2. in public speaking, the skill cluster related to choosing a topic and ideas to support the topic; also called *invention.* (4, 14)

self-acceptance positive self-concept; the quality of valuing one's self while acknowledging both personal strengths and weaknesses. (3)

self-concept one's total attitude toward and definition of oneself, which develops out of communication with others throughout one's life. (3)

semantics the meaning components of language; language-related processes of organizing and assigning meaning. (7)

sender/receiver in the communication process, an individual who transmits a message and acquires feedback. (1)

sensory perception a physical process by which senses (seeing, hearing, smelling, tasting, and touching) relay images to the brain. (1)

signposts in public speaking, labels given to points that indicate their position in the body of the speech, such as "first," "next," and "finally." (17)

silent cues stimuli perceived through the senses of seeing, touching, smelling, and tasting. (6)

silent language all behaviors or messages transmitted without sound and acquired through sight, touch, smell, taste, or subconscious processes. (6)

simile a figure of speech; a comparison using *like* or *as.* (18)

slang a temporal or temporary language related to cultural influences; colloquial language outside of standard usage. (7)

social group a group whose primary purpose is companionship for members; may be casual or formal. (10)

social value a belief or principle related to people, interactions, and interpersonal relationships. (5)

sound cues stimuli perceived through the sense of hearing. (6)

sound language all messages or behaviors transmitted by sound and acquired by hearing. (6)

spatial order the arrangement of points in a speech according to how they occupy space (for example, where they are). (16)

specific instances   verifiable accounts of actual events that are used to support points. (15, 17)

speech communication   a process in which individuals send and receive vocal, verbal messages in order to reach common understanding. (1)

speech forms   the classical, standard principles of organizing a speech presentation. (16, 21)

standard tests for evidence   questions for evaluating the sources of information used in a speech, relating to the sources' qualifications, credibility, and competence. (15)

standard usage   the employment of language appropriate in most situations among articulate, educated people. (7)

statistics   numerical results from studies and records that are used to support points. (15, 17)

stereotyping   a barrier to effective communication that involves assigning characteristics of a group to an individual, or judging an individual based on characteristics of a group to which he or she belongs. (2)

stimuli   data received by sensory perception; actions or agents that cause or change an activity. (1)

stress   strain or pressure that results from unrelived frustration. (9)

style   1. in communication, a system of clear, consistent, and appropriate language choices. 2. in public speaking, the skill cluster related to making and applying language choices. (14, 18)

stylistic devices   language strategies that increase appeal, including rhyme, rhythm, and alliteration. (18)

subsidiary motion   in parliamentary groups, a statement used to change a motion that has been proposed, or to change the way a motion is being dealt with. (13)

summary   in the second transition section, a restatement of points or an eloquent description of the central idea or value in the speech. (16)

supporting device   information that provides factual evidence for a point in a speech. (17)

supportiveness   a characteristic of effective communication reflecting the participants' recognition of and respect for the worth and dignity of others. (2)

symposium   a form of public discussion in which each of a group of participants gives a short speech on an aspect of a topic, in order to inform an audience. (12)

syntax   the linear, structural component of language. (7)

t _____

task-oriented group   a group that exists to do work, to fill a specific need, or to perform a particular function; such a group usually has an internal communication focus and goals of making decisions or choosing policies. (10, 12)

task roles   group member roles that focus on helping the group reach its goals or get its work done. (11)

temporal language   the aspect of usage that changes with time. (7)

testimony   quotations from recognized, respected sources that are used to support points. (15, 17)

theory   a way of explaining how something operates, which can be tested and refined. (2)

thesis statement   a single, concise sentence that states the speaker's primary message, encompassing the topic and the purpose of the speech. (14)

tempo   the "beat" or rhythm of a voice, including accent and stress. (7)

tone   the quality of a sound (as mellow, flat, thin, resonant, or metallic). (7)

topical order   the arrangement of points in a speech according to parts or aspects of the general topic. (16)

transient message   in public speaking, a message that will be transmitted to a live audience and cannot be repeated. (14)

transmitting   in the communication process, the act of sending a message. (1)

trust   confidence in the words and actions of another person. (9)

u _____

urgent message   in public speaking, a message that is timely, designed to be of immediate interest to the particular audience, and to meet the needs of the speaker, the audience, and the occasion. (14)

v _____

value   a personal evaluation of various beliefs according to their importance or worth. (5)

variable   an element of component within a process that has the potential to change (or vary) during the process. (1)

verbal message   a message transmitted by speech. (1)

visual aids   amplifying devices that help listeners to visualize a point. (17)

vocal message   a message transmitted by the sound of the voice, including sound cues and paralinguistic cues. (6)

volume   the loudness of softness of a sound. (19)

Literary Credits

51, adaptation of Dean Barnlund's "six faces," _Dyadic Communication,_ second edition, W. W. Wilmot, Reading, Mass.: Addison-Wesley Publishing Co., Inc., 1979, p. 47 • **76,** adaptation of "Hierarchy of Needs," _Motivation and Personality,_ 2d ed., Abraham Maslow. New York: Harper & Row, Publishers, Inc. Reprinted by permission of Harper & Row, Publishers, Inc. • **209,** adaptation of "Communication Patterns," "Communication Patterns and Task-Oriented Groups," _Group Dynamics Research & Theory,_ 3d ed., by Dorwin Cartwright, Alvin Zander, eds. New York: Harper & Row, Publishers, Inc., p. 503. Reprinted by permission of Harper & Row, Publishers, Inc. • **219,** adaptation of "Problem Solving Steps," _Small Group Communication: A Functional Appearance,_ 4th ed., by Michael Burgoon, Judee K. Heston (Burgoon), James C. McCroskey. New York: Holt, Rinehart & Winston. Copyright 1974. Reprinted by permission of Holt, Rinehart & Winston. • **237,** adaptation of "Order of Business," _Sturgis' Standard Code of Parliamentary Procedure,_ 2d ed., by Alice Sturgis. New York: McGraw-Hill Book Co., copyright 1966 by Alice Sturgis. • **242,** adaptation of "Order of Precedence," _Sturgis' Standard Code of Parliamentary Procedure,_ 2d ed., by Alice Sturgis. New York: McGraw-Hill Book Co., copyright 1966 by Alice Sturgis. • **244,** adaptation of "Table of Parliamentary Motions," _The Principles and Methods of Discussion_ by James H. McBurney, Kenneth G. Hance. Copyright 1939, by Harper & Row, Publishers, Inc. Reprinted by permission of Harper & Row, Publishers, Inc. • **279,** excerpt from _Readers' Guide to Periodical Literature,_ copyright © 1986 by The H. W. Wilson Co. Material reproduced by permission of the publisher. • **331,** excerpt of George McGovern's Acceptance Speech (1972), _Vital Speeches of the Day._ Mount Pleasant, S.C.: City News Publishing Co. • **332,** excerpt of Martin Luther King, Jr.'s speech, "I Have a Dream." Reprinted by permission of Joan Daves. Copyright 1963 by Martin Luther King, Jr. • **333,** excerpt of Carl Sandburg's speech (1959), _Vital Speeches of the Day._ Mount Pleasant, S.C.: City News Publishing Co. • **334,** excerpt of Ronald Reagan's State of the Union Address (1986), _Vital Speeches of the Day._ Mount Pleasant, S.C.: City News Publishing Co. • **395,** "David and a Whole Lot of Other Neat People," by Kathy Weisensel from _Contemporary American Speeches: A Source Book of Speech Forms and Principles,_ 3d ed., by Will A. Linkugel, R. R. Allan, Richard L. Johannesen, eds. Belmont, Calif.: Wadsworth Publishing Co., 1972. • **399,** "Color Me Dumb" by Karen Cochran. • **403,** "Are They Unteachable?" by Carolyn Geiman from _Contemporary American Speeches: A Source Book of Speech Forms and Principles,_ 2d ed., by Will A. Linkugel, R. R. Allan, Richard L. Johannesen, eds. Belmont Calif.: Wadsworth Publishing Co. • **406,** "Five Ways in Which Thinking is Dangerous," by Stephen Joel Trachtenberg, Ph.D., from _Vital Speeches of the Day._ Mount Pleasant, S.C.: City News Publishing Co. • **408,** "The Crown of Life," by Lisa Golub from _Contemporary American Speeches: A Source Book of Speech Forms and Principles,_ 5th ed., by Will A. Linkugel, R. R. Allan, Richard L. Johannesen, eds. Belmont, Calif.: Wadsworth Publishing Co. • **411,** "The Battle Against Drugs," by Nancy Reagan (1986) from _Vital Speeches of the Day,_ Mount Pleasant, S.C.: City News Publishing Co. • **415,** "Will and Vision," by Gerry Sikorski (1986) from _Vital Speeches of the Day._ Mount Pleasant, S.C.: City News Publishing Co.

Art/Visual Credits

Part 1/Chapter 1 Eric Futron, p. xi; ©Paul Conklin, p. 4; ©The Shaffer Group, p. 5; Imagesmythe, Inc. pp. 6, 8, 9, 11 (both), 12; ©Bob Coyle, p. 10 **Chapter 2** ©The Shaffer Group, pp. 16, 19, 22, 25, 28 (all); Imagesmythe, Inc., p. 30 **Part 2/Chapter 3** ©The Shaffer Group, pp. 34, 39, 41, 42, 45, 46, 50; Fred Womack, p. 49; Imagesmythe, Inc., p. 51 **Chapter 4** ©The Shaffer Group, pp. 55, 63, 66, 71; Fred Womack, pp. 57, 59, 60; "Sky and Water II, copyright ©M. C. Escher Heirs, c/o Cordon Art—Baarn, Holland, p. 58; Kirk Barron, p. 68; R. L. Gregory, _Eye and Brain: The Psychology of Seeing,_ New York: World University Library/McGraw-Hill, 1966 (pp. 136–37), p. 65 **Chapter 5** Imagesmythe, Inc., p. 76; ©The Shaffer Group, pp. 80, 82, 83, 85, 88; Eric Futron, p. 78 **Part 3/Chapter 6** ©The Shaffer Group, pp. 94, 97, 101, 102, 103 (top left, top center, center left, center right, bottom left, bottom center), 104, 113; Kirk Barron, p. 100, 106; ©Bob Coyle, p. 103 (top right, center center); ©Jean-Claude Lejeune, p. 103 (bottom right); AP/Wide World Photos, p. 108 **Chapter 7** ©The Shaffer Group, pp. 117, 119, 123, 124, 126 (both); Fred Womack, p. 128; ©TexaStock, Photo by Michael D. Sullivan, p. 130; ©KOLVOORD/ TexaStock, p. 132 **Chapter 8** ©Jean-Claude Lejeune, pp. 138, 151; ©The Shaffer Group, pp. 140, 142, 144, 152 (top), 154; Eric Futron, pp. 147, 152 (bottom); Imagesmythe, Inc., pp. 149, 150 **Chapter 9** ©David A. Corona, p. 161; ©The Shaffer Group, pp. 162, 164, 166, 170, 173; Art Shay, p. 164 **Part 4/Chapter 10** Eric Futron, p. 178; ©The Shaffer Group, pp. 183, 184, 186, 188, 192 **Chapter 11** ©The Shaffer Group, pp. 198, 200, 201, 204, 212; Imagesmythe, Inc., pp. 200, 207, 209, 210; ©Milt and Joan Mann, p. 203; ©Cameramann, Intl., Ltd., p. 205 **Chapter 12** ©The Shaffer Group, pp. 219, 223, 225, 226; Imagesmythe, Inc., p. 220 **Chapter 13** ©The Shaffer Group, pp. 234, 236, 241; Imagesmythe, Inc., pp. 237, 242, 244; Eric Futron, p. 238 **Part 5/Chapter 14** ©The Shaffer Group, pp. 248, 252, 253, 256, 263 (all); Fred Womack, pp. 257, 259, 261 **Chapter 15** ©The Shaffer Group, pp. 269, 271, 273 (bottom), 274, 275, 280, 283; Fred Womack, pp. 272, 285; Imagesmythe, Inc., pp. 273 (top), 284; Courtesy, Hempstead High School, p. 278; _Reader's Guide to Periodical Literature,_ copyright ©1986 by the H. W. Wilson Company. Reproduced by permission of the publisher, p. 279 **Chapter 16** Imagesmythe, Inc., pp. 290, 292, 298, 299, 300 (both), 301, 302, 304; ©The Shaffer Group, p. 294; Fred Womack, pp. 295, 297 **Chapter 17** ©The Shaffer Group, pp. 311, 312, 315; Carlisle Graphics, p. 310; Fred Womack, p. 313; Imagesmythe, Inc., pp. 317, 319 **Chapter 18** AP/Wide World Photos, pp. 323 (both), 325 (top), 332 (both), 335; ©The Shaffer Group, pp. 324, 333; ©Bob Coyle, p. 325, 326 (bottom) **Chapter 19** ©The Shaffer Group, pp. 339, 341, 342, 343, 346, 352, 353, 354, 359; Fred Womack, pp. 347, 350, 355, 356; Imagesmythe, Inc., p. 345 **Chapter 20** ©The Shaffer Group, pp. 365, 366, 369, 373, 374; Imagesmythe, Inc., p. 375 **Chapter 21** Eric Futron, p. 382; ©TexaStock, Photo by Michael D. Sullivan, p. 385; ©The Shaffer Group, pp. 386, 391

Book and Cover Design: David A. Corona
Cover Photo: James L. Shaffer

Index